THE JESUITS AN

THIRTY YEARS

From 1618 to 1648 Christian princes waged the first pan-European war. Brought about in part by the entrenched passions of the Reformation and Counter Reformation, the Thirty Years War inevitably drew in the Society of Jesus, or Jesuits, who stood at the vanguard of Catholic reform. This book investigates for the first time the Jesuits' role during the war at the four Catholic courts of Vienna, Munich, Paris, and Madrid and the challenge to the Jesuit superior general in Rome to lead a truly international organization through a period of rising national conflict.

War goals varied and changed at the courts as the conflict progressed. Advocates of "holy war" contended with moderates, or *politiques*. This book brings to light the extent to which the Thirty Years War was a religious war, and it shows how ideas about the proper relationship between religion and politics shifted under the pressure of events.

Robert Bireley, S.J., is Professor of History at Loyola University Chicago. He is the author of four previous books, including *The Counter-Reformation Prince: Antimachiavellianism or Catholic Statecraft in Early Modern Europe* and *Religion and Politics in the Age of the Counterreformation: Emperor Ferdinand II, William Lamormaini, S.J., and the Formation of Imperial Policy*.

THE JESUITS AND THE THIRTY YEARS WAR

KINGS, COURTS, AND CONFESSORS

ROBERT BIRELEY
Loyola University Chicago

CAMBRIDGE
UNIVERSITY PRESS

CAMBRIDGE UNIVERSITY PRESS
Cambridge, New York, Melbourne, Madrid, Cape Town, Singapore, São Paulo, Delhi

Cambridge University Press
The Edinburgh Building, Cambridge CB2 8RU, UK

Published in the United States of America by Cambridge University Press, New York

www.cambridge.org
Information on this title: www.cambridge.org/9780521820172

First published 2003
This digitally printed version 2008

A catalogue record for this publication is available from the British Library

Library of Congress Cataloguing in Publication data

Bireley, Robert.
The Jesuits and the Thirty Years War : kings, courts, and confessors / Robert Bireley.
p. cm.
Includes bibliographical references and index.
ISBN 0-521-82017-0
1. Jesuits – Europe – History – 17th century. 2. Thirty Years' War, 1618–1648.
3. Europe – History – 17th century. 4. Europe – Church history – 17th century.
I. Title.
BX3715 .B57 2003
271'.53'09032–dc21 2002073686

ISBN 978-0-521-82017-2 hardback
ISBN 978-0-521-09932-5 paperback

Contents

A map of the Holy Roman Empire appears on page 8 and a series of illustrations appears on pages 129–38.

Abbreviations

AHSJ	*Archivum Historicum Societatis Jesu*
APW	*Acta Pacis Westphalicae*
ARSJ	Archivum Romanum Societatis Jesu, Rome
Aust.	Austriae Provincia
Boh.	Bohemiae Provincia
Cong.	Congregationes
Epist. Ext.	Epistolae Externorum
Epist. Gen.	Epistolae Generalium
Francia	Franciae Provincia
Gallia	Galliae Assistentia
Germ.	Germaniae Assistentia
Germ. Sup.	Germaniae Superioris Provincia
Hisp.	Hispaniae Assistentia
Rheni Inf.	Rheni Inferioris Provincia
Rheni Sup.	Rheni Superioris Provincia
Tol.	Toletana Provincia
ASV	Archivio Segreto Vaticano, Rome
BA	*Brief und Akten zur Geschichte des Dreissigjährigen Krieges*
BL	Barberini Latini, Biblioteca Apostolica Vaticana, Rome
BN	Bibliothèque National, Manuscrits Français, Paris
HHStA	Haus-, Hof- und Staatsarchiv, Vienna
HStA	Bayerisches Hauptstaatsarchiv, Munich
Kriegsakten	Akten zur Geschichte des Dreissigjährigen Krieges
KSchw	Kasten Schwarz

Preface

FROM 1618 to 1648 Christian princes waged the first pan-European war, and the devastating Thirty Years War has since generated an enormous literature. The Society of Jesus, or Jesuits, has regularly attracted the attention of historians and writers, not to mention polemicists. In the early seventeenth century it stood in the vanguard of Catholic Reform and Counter Reformation. Yet very little has appeared recently about the role of the Jesuits in the war and especially about the part played by Jesuit confessors of rulers during the protracted conflict. To be sure, my earlier studies investigated the activities of two of the most prominent Jesuit court confessors in Germany during the central period of the war, from 1624 to 1635, Adam Contzen in Munich and William Lamormaini in Vienna. This present book, however, steps back to look at the Jesuit confessors at the four courts of Vienna, Munich, Paris, and Madrid during the whole course of the war, and it does so from the vantage point of the Jesuit superior general in Rome. It attempts a synthesis that views the long conflict from a peculiarly Roman perspective, often similar to but by no means identical to the papacy's. Indeed, as one of its topics the book investigates the relationship between the superior general and the papacy.

The varying conceptions of the war and of war goals at the courts and among the Jesuits and especially the changes that these conceptions underwent as the conflict progressed are brought to light and analyzed in the narrative. Advocates of "holy war" contended with moderates, or *politiques*, in princely councils. We see here the mutual interaction of religion and concrete policy, and we come to understand better the extent to which the war was a religious conflict. In addition, multiple conceptions of what the relationship between religion and politics ought to be were at work, and we watch as these, too, shifted under the pressure of events.

Three basic, interrelated questions emerge to govern the narrative. First, what influence on policy in the war did the Jesuits have at the four courts? Second, was there a "Jesuit" policy toward the war and a Jesuit position on the desirable relationship between religion and politics? Third, what principles and policies characterized the superior general as he guided the Society through a conflict that found Jesuits at courts that were often at odds with one another? It was an age of nascent "national spirit," a term that frequently turned up in official Jesuit correspondence. As I attempt to answer these questions, I compare the situations at the various courts and the different attitude of the superior general toward each of them.

Watching the Jesuit superior general can prove to be fascinating as he attempted to administer a truly international organization of about 16,000 men in the face of pressures from rival courts and from Jesuits who closely identified with the interests of the courts and who often wrote in their support. Muzio Vitelleschi filled the office of superior general of the Jesuits from 1615 to 1645. He stemmed from an old Roman family and was the first superior general who was not a subject of the King of Spain. There exists virtually no scholarship on Vitelleschi despite his position and his massive correspondence, which can be found in the Roman Archives of the Society of Jesus. In a report dated April 8, 1626, the French ambassador at the papal court referred to him as "un homme advisé et le plus sage politique qui j'aye jamais traité." Vincenzo Carafa, of the famous Neapolitan family that produced one pope and a number of cardinals, succeeded Vitelleschi. Carafa governed the Society for only three years, from 1646 until his death in 1649. But these were the critical years of the Congress of Westphalia, and they saw a bitter struggle within the Society in Germany between those who favored the concessions made to the Protestants and those who rejected them.

This book is based largely on primary sources, published and unpublished, above all in the Roman Archives of the Society of Jesus, but also in other archives and libraries in Rome, Munich, Vienna, Paris, and Madrid where I have worked over the years. The material in the Roman Archives of the Society consists chiefly of the outgoing correspondence of the superior general with Jesuits and other figures secular and ecclesiastical at the various courts. The letters for this period have generally survived and have been reasonably well preserved. The same is not true of the incoming mail, which, to a large extent, has been lost. Yet one can often glean the content of an incoming letter from the summary found in the response to it or from other documentation.

A few remarks about procedure and usage are in order. All translations are my own unless otherwise noted. In citing documents and especially letters, I have not indicated whether a document is an original, a register copy (as which the final draft usually served), or another copy, unless this seemed significant. Often it is evident from the text. Nor have I indicated the place of origin of letters unless this was particularly noteworthy and not clear from the text. With regard to the names of persons and places, my chief concern has been to employ the form that seemed most natural in the context. Usually this meant the anglicized form for rulers and major figures of the narrative, for example, *William* not *Wilhelm* or *Guillaume* Lamormaini, but *Heinrich* rather than *Henry* Philippi. Ranks, titles, and place names are given in the English form.

Many folks have assisted and encouraged me in the writing of this book. I am grateful to all of them, but, unfortunately, I cannot mention them all. The National Endowment for the Humanities generously supported my fellowship at the National Humanities Center (NHC) in North Carolina for the academic year 1998–99, when I wrote the first draft of the manuscript. At the NHC amid the pines of North Carolina, the director, W. Robert Connor, and his deputy director, Kent Mullikin, provided an idyllic atmosphere for study and writing. It was a year that I will long fondly remember, also for the stimulating conversation with my "classmates" for the year, especially, if I may single out three of many, Melissa Bullard, Edward Friedman, and Michael Lienisch. A further privilege that year was participation in the Center's Colloquium on Religion and Humanities, which was sponsored by the Lilly Endowment.

A paid leave from Loyola University enabled me to spend the spring and summer of 1995 on the book, and the Istituto Storico della Compagnia di Gesú in Rome provided me with a three-month fellowship that spring so that I might fill in gaps in my research in the Roman Archives of the Society of Jesus. Laszló Szilas, S.J., facilitated this arrangement. A Loyola University research grant then made possible a research trip in the summer of 2000 to Paris and Munich, where I checked further materials in a number of archives and libraries, not least of all the wonderful new Bibliothèque National in Paris.

Eliza Robertson, Alan Tuttle, and Jean Houston of the library staff at the NHC showed great efficiency and patience in assisting me as did Linda Morgan with her computer skills. At Loyola University, Interlibrary Loan Librarian Ursula Scholz and her staff deserve special mention for their constant prompt and efficient service.

John Patrick Donnelly, S.J., and John Headley both read the whole manuscript. I am grateful to them and to the three anonymous readers of Cambridge University Press for their encouragement and helpful suggestions. Their comments led to revisions that have made this a better book. The late Michael Grace, S.J., and Simone Zurawski kindly assisted me with the selection of illustrations. Lewis Bateman of Cambridge University Press has encouraged me from the start, and Alia Winters and Jennifer Carey have guided me with skill and patience in preparing the manuscript for publication.

Finally, I am grateful to my fellow Jesuits at Ignatius House and the Gonzaga House of Loyola University Chicago for their constant support.

CHAPTER 1

Setting the Scene

AT about nine o'clock on the morning of May 23, 1618, members of a Protestant assembly meeting in Prague burst through the door of the Hradschin Castle and forced their way up the narrow staircase into the council room. There they confronted four of the ten regents appointed by the Habsburg Emperor Matthias to govern the Kingdom of Bohemia. Two regents were the object of their assault, Vilém Slawata and Jaroslav Martinitz, reputed to be advocates of an imperial policy to recatholicize Bohemia and establish an absolute royal government. A spokesman for the intruders accused the two of attempting to subvert the Letter of Majesty of 1609, which guaranteed widespread religious freedom in the kingdom. So they deserved to be treated as enemies of the common welfare. Five assailants seized Martinitz and, despite his plea for the chance to go to confession, pitched him out the window and certainly, they thought, to his death. Slawata received the same treatment, though he managed to cling to the edge of the sill until a blow with a knife handle forced him to let go. A secretary was then hurled out the window in their wake. Thus occurred what came to be called the Defenestration of Prague. It set off the first Europeanwide war that was to continue for thirty years and to ravage Germany, carrying off between one-third and one-fourth of the population.[1]

The event seemed to flow spontaneously from an outraged Protestant assembly, and it was meant to seem so. But it had been carefully planned and was the result of a long-simmering conflict. Bohemian Protestants, who composed more than two-thirds of the population, had pressured Emperor Rudolph II in 1609 to grant them the Letter of Majesty. But the document left openings for differing interpretations. One issue on which interpretations collided was whether Protestants could construct

[1] Ronald G. Asch, *The Thirty Years War: The Holy Roman Empire and Europe* (New York, 1997), 185.

churches on ecclesiastical lands. These lands were, Protestants argued, ultimately royal lands and thus accessible to the construction of Protestant churches. But the government responded vigorously to attempts to build churches there, imprisoning citizens of Braunau and razing a structure constructed in Klostergrab. It was to protest these actions that the assembly gathered in Prague. Heinrich Count Thurn, a Protestant leader long hostile to Habsburg rule, along with a few associates prepared the seemingly spontaneous march to the Hradschin. Their intent from the beginning was to murder the regents and so create an incident that would provoke a clear break between the assembly and the Habsburg ruler and so end the drawn-out, indecisive contest between the two parties. Initially, some favored stabbing the regents, but the group then opted for defenestration. There was a precedent for it in Bohemia dating from the Hussite wars. But all three victims landed on a compost heap. Two walked away nearly unharmed, while Slawata suffered minor injuries to his head. Surely, Catholics were to assert, God had worked a miracle.[2]

The very next day the Protestant assembly constituted itself as the Bohemian estates, or representative body, and established a government of thirty "directors." After the Defenestration, it was a foregone conclusion that the expulsion of the Jesuits would follow, and in an apology for their actions issued on May 25, the estates blamed the Jesuits for the unrest in Bohemia. Yet Count Thurn himself intervened on May 28 to prevent a hostile mob from sacking the Jesuit college in Prague, apparently aware of the dire political repercussions that such violence against the Society might provoke. Five days later notification reached the Jesuits that they would have to leave Bohemia within six days. Jesuit efforts to secure the revocation of the decision proved unavailing.

The actual decree of expulsion, dated June 9, accused the Jesuits of both undermining the Letter of Majesty and twisting its meaning to suit their purposes and, it added interestingly, of so weakening imperial government. The "hypocritical sect" of Jesuits used their influence to have Protestants excluded from governmental offices, regularly vilified Protestants as heretics in their writings and preaching, and so they continually incited unrest in the kingdom.[3] Within a few days the Jesuits departed Prague – two remained incognito to aid the frightened Catholic populace – and then they gradually took their leave from the other towns

[2] Hans Sturmberger, *Aufstand in Böhmen: Der Beginn des Dreissigjährigen Krieges* (Munich, 1959), 7–14.

[3] "Praescriptio Patrum Societatis Jesu ex Regno Bohemiae," June 9, 1618, in Francesco Gui, *I Gesuiti e la rivoluzione boema: Alle origini della guerra dei trent'anni* (Milan, 1989), Allegato 1: 414–16.

of Bohemia. Severe penalties threatened those who harbored Jesuits. An intense pamphlet war followed the expulsion in which the Jesuits responded in detail to the accusations of their Bohemian adversaries.[4]

The decree expelling the Jesuits from Bohemia repeated other charges against the Society that circulated especially in Protestant Europe. These accusations help us to understand the enmity that the Society aroused in some quarters. The Jesuits meddled in politics. They allegedly used the sacrament of confession to penetrate the designs of princes and to manipulate consciences to their own purposes. Two charges in particular drew impetus from recent history. First, the decree accused the Society of promoting sedition and even encouraging political assassinations. On December 27, 1594, a crazed former student at the Jesuit College of Clermont in Paris attempted to murder King Henry IV of France. As a result of the ensuing uproar, the Society suffered banishment from most of France for eight years, from 1595 to 1603.[5] The Spanish Jesuit Juan de Mariana provided further grist for the mill of the Society's enemies with the publication of his *The King and the Education of the King* in 1599.[6] In it he defended tyrannicide under certain extreme circumstances. Then, in late 1604, a small band of English Catholics, disillusioned that James I did not moderate the penal laws against Catholics as they understood him to have intimated that he would, engineered the Gunpowder Plot. They planned to blow up Parliament as the king addressed the Commons and the Lords jointly and thus overthrow the government of England. Only at the last hour was the plot foiled, according to the government's account. Jesuits were accused of knowledge of the plot's existence if not participation in it, a charge that they denied vehemently.[7] Five years later, in 1610, enemies of the Society pounced upon the assassination of Henry IV as another opportunity to attack the Jesuits and Mariana's teaching on tyrannicide.

The second charge, that the Jesuits aimed to undermine the legitimate sovereignty of kings and to submit them to papal authority, though not completely new, gathered renewed prominence from two conflicts. These erupted in 1605, over the Venetian Interdict and the Oath of Allegiance that James I demanded from Catholics after the Gunpowder

4 Alois Kroess, *Geschichte der böhmischen Provinz der Gesellschaft Jesu* 1 (Vienna, 1910): 919–43; Gui, 36, 226–45. Gui analyzes the polemics in detail.

5 Roland Mousnier, *The Assassination of Henry IV: The Tyrannicide Problem and the Consolidation of the French Absolute Monarchy in the Seventeenth Century,* trans. from the French (New York, 1973), 217–24.

6 *De Rege et Regis Institutione.*

7 Antonia Fraser, *Faith and Treason: The Story of the Gunpowder Plot* (New York, 1996), gives a judicious account of events.

Plot. Paul V imposed an interdict, that is, the prohibition of most church sacraments and rites, on Venice when it refused to turn over to the ecclesiastical courts two clerics accused of crimes and to rescind limitations on the acquisition and use of church property. The dispute threatened to end in war until mediation, especially by Henry IV of France, effected a compromise.[8] For their support of the papal position, the Jesuits were then expelled from Venice also, to return only in 1656.

The Oath of Allegiance that was prescribed for Catholics in England did not require that they renounce the spiritual authority of the pope nor even that they deny his power to excommunicate a king. It did insist that Catholics forswear any right of the pope to depose or take any political action against a sovereign ruler. But according to the oath, the power of the pope to depose rulers was "damnable" and "impious and heretical."[9] Pope Paul V rejected this. First James's theologians and then James himself took up the pen on his behalf, as did the Scottish Catholic theologian William Barclay.[10] Prominent Jesuits took the lead in defending the papal position in the ensuing "battle of books."[11] In the most important of his several contributions to the exchange, Cardinal Robert Bellarmine, now a major figure in the Roman curia, responded to Barclay in 1610 with his *Treatise on the Power of the Roman Pontiff in Temporal Affairs*.[12] Four years later the Spanish Jesuit Francisco Suarez published his *Defense of the Faith* against James.[13]

Both books elaborated variations on the theory of the indirect power of the pope in temporal affairs. It had originated with Thomas Aquinas in the thirteenth century, had been developed further by the Dominican Francisco Vitoria in the first part of the sixteenth, and was in fact held by many contemporary Catholic theologians, but with the growth of the sovereign state in the sixteenth century, it was outliving its usefulness in the seventeenth. According to this theory, the pope might by virtue of his spiritual authority, or indirectly, intervene in the temporal order, when a prince stood in the way of his subjects' attainment of their ultimate, spiritual goal, eternal life. This intervention could take the form of a warning, a correction, and finally, of deposition should such a drastic measure be called for. To implement such a measure, of course, the pope

[8] W.B. Patterson, *James VI and I and the Reunion of Christendom* (Cambridge, 1997), 115–17.
[9] Ibid., 79–81, citation of the oath on 81.
[10] *De potestate papae: An et quatenus in reges et principes seculares ius et imperium habet*, ed. John Barclay (London, 1609).
[11] Patterson, 100, citing James Brodrick, *Robert Bellarmine, 1542–1621* 2 (London, 1950): 224.
[12] *Tractatus de potestate summi pontificis in rebus temporalibus.*
[13] *Defensio fidei.*

would have to call for the assistance of other princes.[14] "The controversy over the Oath of Allegiance showed the highly wrought intellectual and emotional state of Europe" as the year 1618 approached.[15]

Tensions similar to those in Bohemia had long been rising between Catholics and Protestants in Germany, or the Holy Roman Empire of the German nation. Martin Luther had launched the Reformation with his *Ninety-Five Theses* in 1517, so that Protestants were celebrating the centennial of the Reformation on the eve of the outbreak of the Thirty Years War. Luther's movement spread rapidly out from Wittenberg. After the disastrous Peasants War of 1524/25, some German princes and imperial cities began formally to establish Reformation churches, and their number steadily increased in the following two decades. Attempts at reconciliation failed, either through a council or at the Diets of Augsburg in 1530 or Regensburg in 1541. Eventually, with papal backing, Emperor Charles V (1519–55) took up arms against the Protestants. He won a decisive triumph over the Protestant League of Schmalkeld at Mühlberg on the Elbe River in 1547, but with assistance from the French King Henry II, the Protestants subsequently overturned this result so that the emperor was forced to grant the Protestants formal legal status at the Diet of Augsburg in 1555. Rather than take responsibility for this, Charles resigned in favor of his younger brother, Ferdinand I (1558–64). He divided his patrimony between Ferdinand and his son Philip II, thus creating the two branches of the House of Habsburg, the Austrian and the Spanish.

The diet (or Reichstag) constituted the representative body in the cumbersome political structure of the Holy Roman Empire, which comprised around 1,000 separate, semiautonomous political units. Many of them were very small, especially in the south and west. Three councils made up the diet. The council of electors took its name from its privilege to elect the emperor; and in the course of the late sixteenth and early seventeenth centuries, its status grew at the expense of the other two. Since the fourteenth century it included three ecclesiastical princes, the archbishops of Mainz, Trier, and Cologne, and four secular ones, the count palatine of the Rhine, the duke of Saxony, the margrave of Brandenburg, and the king of Bohemia. The remaining princes, both ecclesiastical and secular, were represented in the council of princes and the imperial cities in the council of cities. As was customary in representative bodies of the

[14] F.X. Arnold, *Die Staatslehre des Kardinals Bellarmin: Ein Beitrag zur Rechts- und Staatsphilosophie des konfessionellen Zeitalters* (Munich, 1934), 324–60, esp. 347–60.
[15] Patterson, 120.

early modern period, each council as a body possessed one vote. Above the diet stood the emperor, who was an elective rather than a hereditary ruler as in the monarchies of France and Spain. Efforts in the late fifteenth and early sixteenth centuries to strengthen the central authority of the empire, either the diet or the emperor, met with little success, and the Reformation further weakened it. Elected emperors through nearly all the early modern period were members of the Habsburg family, who governed as their own the principalities of the various Austrian lands in the south of the empire. Emperor Ferdinand I combined these with the kingdoms of Bohemia and Hungary, which he had acquired through marriage in 1526, to form what would become the Habsburg Monarchy. So he was both ruler of the monarchy and Holy Roman Emperor.

The Peace of Augsburg of 1555 provided Germany with relative peace into the early seventeenth century at a time when conflict was convulsing France during its religious wars from 1562 to 1598 and the Dutch were fighting for their independence from Spain starting in 1568. Each prince in the empire was granted the right to determine whether Lutheranism or Catholicism was to be the established religion in his territory according to the principle later enunciated by the jurists, "whose the region, his the religion." Complicated provisions were worked out for the possession of church property according to the general principle that Catholics would surrender permanently the property confiscated by the Protestants up to that time with the understanding that they would seize no more. But like the Letter of Majesty in Bohemia, the peace was open to varying interpretations. The fate of the ecclesiastical principalities that had fallen into Protestant hands, for example, was left unclear.

Meanwhile, reform had taken hold within the Catholic Church and the Council of Trent, which convened for three periods between 1545 and 1563, gave it further impetus. As a new generation replaced the war-weary one that had concluded the Peace of Augsburg, militance revived, and conflicts about interpretation of the peace spilled over from the legal into the political and military spheres. The Protestant states of the empire divided into two parties increasingly hostile to each other. The Palatinate, which had first gone over to Calvinism in 1563, led the more activist party. A more moderate Lutheran party usually took its direction from the elector of Saxony. In the War of Cologne of 1583 Bavarian forces with Spanish and papal assistance prevented the archbishop, who had taken a wife, from secularizing this critical ecclesiastical state along the Rhine. Had he been successful, the Catholics would have lost their four-to-three majority in the council of electors and the way would have been open to the election of a Protestant emperor. The victory of the Catholic forces revealed their growing power in the empire. The two dynasties of Wittelsbach in Bavaria and Habsburg in Austria served as pillars of strength for the Catholics, though the Habsburgs wavered for a time in the second half of the sixteenth century and were weakened by strife within the family early in the seventeenth.

In 1607 Duke Maximilian of Bavaria, with imperial sanction, intervened in the south German free city of Donauwörth to guarantee the Catholic minority its right to freedom of worship, but then in an action of questionable legality, he incorporated the city into Bavaria as compensation for his costs and soon prohibited the exercise of Protestantism. The upshot was a Catholic–Protestant stalemate at the Diet of Regensburg in 1608 – the Imperial Supreme Court had already been paralyzed by the confessional conflict – and the formation of the Protestant Union, comprising six states led by the Palatinate, to defend Protestant interests. In response the following year Duke Maximilian organized the Catholic League, including Bavaria and a number of ecclesiastical states. Confessional alliances were forming.

Founded at Rome in 1540 by the Spaniard Ignatius Loyola and a small group of companions when they received papal approval as a new religious order, the Jesuits had risen to prominence in Germany in the second half of the sixteenth century. They had greatly contributed to the Catholic revival there. From their foundations at Cologne in 1544, Vienna in 1552, and Ingolstadt in 1556, they expanded into three Jesuit provinces. The Rhine Province with its headquarters at Cologne counted close to 600 Jesuits in 1614, and in 1626 it was to be divided into two provinces, the Lower Rhine Province, with 406 members, ten colleges, and a number of smaller houses, and the Upper Rhine Province centered in Mainz, which comprised 434 members and twelve colleges or academies plus other houses. To the south the Upper German Province, which included large communities in Munich and Ingolstadt, numbered 465 Jesuits in 1611, with twelve colleges and other houses, and by 1630, when Bavaria had not yet experienced the war directly, grew to 800 members with twenty colleges. The Austrian Province to the east, with Vienna at its center, possessed a multiethnic character unlike the others, where not only German but Czech, Hungarian, Slovenian, Croatian, and Italian were spoken. Superiors indeed complained that it was difficult to transfer men from Bohemia, where beer was the preferred drink, to other areas where wine was usually on the table. Five hundred thirty members were attached to the province with its twenty-three colleges and other houses when in 1622 it was divided into Austrian and Bohemian provinces, the former counting 850 members

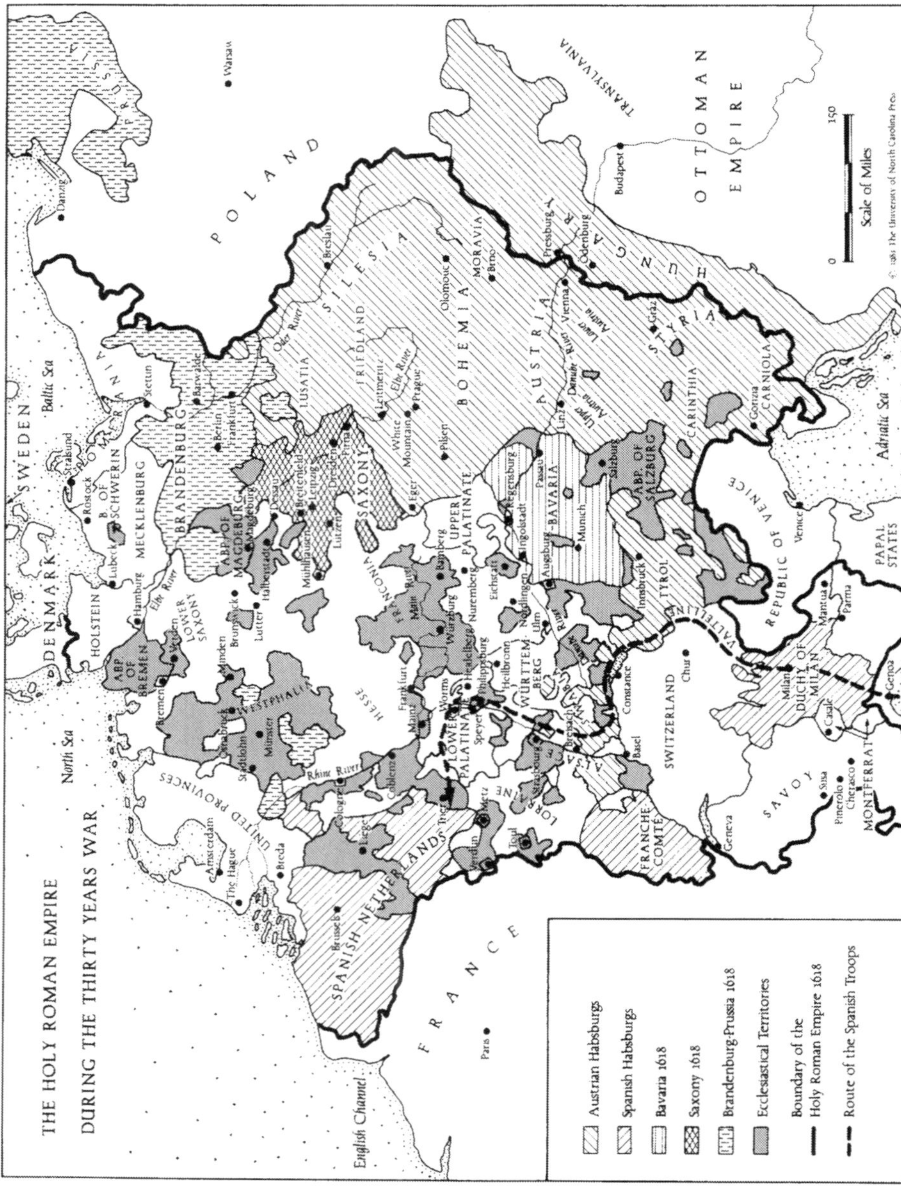
THE HOLY ROMAN EMPIRE
DURING THE THIRTY YEARS WAR
Austrian Habsburgs
Spanish Habsburgs
Bavaria 1618
Saxony 1618
Brandenburg-Prussia 1618
Ecclesiastical Territories
Boundary of the Holy Roman Empire 1618
Route of the Spanish Troops
Scale of Miles
0
150
© 1983 The University of North Carolina Press
North Sea
Baltic Sea
English Channel
Adriatic Sea
SWEDEN
DENMARK
POLAND
FRANCE
OTTOMAN EMPIRE
TRANSYLVANIA
HUNGARY
SWITZERLAND
SAVOY
REPUBLIC OF VENICE
PAPAL STATES
DUCHY OF MILAN
MONTFERRAT
SPANISH NETHERLANDS
UNITED PROVINCES
FRANCHE COMTÉ
LORRAINE
ALSACE
LOWER PALATINATE
UPPER PALATINATE
WÜRTTEMBERG
BAVARIA
TYROL
ABP. OF SALZBURG
CARINTHIA
CARNIOLA
STYRIA
AUSTRIA
BOHEMIA
MORAVIA
SILESIA
LUSATIA
FRIEDLAND
SAXONY
BRANDENBURG
POMERANIA
MECKLENBURG
B. OF SCHWERIN
HOLSTEIN
LOWER SAXONY
ABP. OF BREMEN
ABP. OF MAGDEBURG
WESTPHALIA
HESSE
FRANCONIA
VALTELLINA
Paris
Brussels
The Hague
Amsterdam
Breda
Liège
Cologne
Coblenz
Trier
Metz
Toul
Verdun
Strasbourg
Breisach
Basel
Constance
Geneva
Susa
Pinerolo
Cherasco
Casale
Genoa
Milan
Mantua
Parma
Venice
Chur
Innsbruck
Munich
Augsburg
Ulm
Nördlingen
Ingolstadt
Regensburg
Passau
Salzburg
Linz
Vienna
Pressburg
Odenburg
Budapest
Graz
Gorizia
Brno
Olomouc
Prague
Pilsen
Eger
White Mountain
Leitmeritz
Breslau
Warsaw
Danzig
Stettin
Stralsund
Rostock
Lübeck
Hamburg
Bremen
Verden
Minden
Osnabrück
Münster
Stadtlohn
Brunswick
Lutter
Halberstadt
Magdeburg
Dessau
Breitenfeld
Leipzig
Dresden
Pirna
Lützen
Mühlhausen
Berlin
Frankfurt
Barwalde
Bamberg
Würzburg
Nuremberg
Eichstätt
Heilbronn
Heidelberg
Philippsburg
Speyer
Worms
Mainz
Frankfurt
Rhine River
Elbe River
Oder River
Main River
Danube River
Upper Austria
Lower Austria

in 1634, the latter over 600.[16] The later years of the war saw all these numbers decline substantially.

Two German princes closely associated with the Jesuits were the Wittelsbach Duke Maximilian of Bavaria, who ruled from 1598 until 1651, and his Habsburg cousin, Archduke Ferdinand, who governed Inner Austria from his residence at Graz from 1595 to 1619, when he began his reign as Holy Roman Emperor Ferdinand II, which lasted until his death in 1637. They were the two leading princes of the Counter Reformation in Germany. Both studied with the Jesuits at the University of Ingolstadt. Maximilian's grandfather, Albert V, had first brought the Jesuits to Munich in 1559. His father, William V, laid the cornerstone for the magnificent complex of the Jesuit college in Munich in 1583, and he saw the completion of St. Michael's Church, the greatest Renaissance church north of the Alps, in 1597. The construction costs of the buildings nearly bankrupted the principality, and the disastrous state of finances prompted William's abdication in 1597 in favor of his twenty-five-year-old son. By the start of the war Maximilian turned Bavaria into the best-administered and most financially stable German territory.[17] He was a man of genuine piety, perhaps tinged with scrupulosity, and a highly self-conscious prince with a grasp of the worldly realities of power. Besides advancing Bavaria's welfare, Maximilian was intent on maintaining the character of the Holy Roman Empire, especially its Catholic character. This was one reason why he assumed the leadership of the Catholic League when dynastic quarrels known as the *Brüderzwist* distracted the Habsburgs in the early decades of the seventeenth century.

A number of Jesuits were closely associated with Maximilian. The well-known Spanish Scholastic Gregory of Valencia taught him at Ingolstadt. Among the others were Jakob Keller and Jeremias Drexel. Keller served for an unusually long period as rector of the college in Munich, from 1607 to 1623 and again from 1626 to his death in 1631, and he frequently wrote on controversial topics for Maximilian. Drexel preached at court from 1615 to 1638, and his ascetical works circulated in the major European languages. From 1595 until his death in 1623 the Luxembourger Johann Buslidius accompanied Maximilian as his confessor as well as his wife's. In 1615 Maximilian would not allow Buslidius to follow the summons of the new Jesuit superior general, Muzio Vitelleschi, to Rome to serve as a councillor, on the grounds that

16 Bernard Duhr, *Geschichte der Jesuiten in den Ländern deutscher Zunge* 2, 1 (Freiburg, 1913): 15–17, 143, 315–16.

17 Dieter Albrecht, *Die auswärtige Politik Maximilians von Bayern, 1615–1635* (Göttingen, 1962), 2.

the prince and his spouse could not dispense with his presence.[18] Shortly after the outbreak of the Bohemian rebellion, when Emperor Matthias and Archduke Ferdinand asked him to mediate with the rebels, the duke sought the opinion of Buslidius and Keller, who encouraged him to do so.[19] But events quickly moved beyond this stage.

Ferdinand was the grandson of Emperor Ferdinand I and son of Archduke Carl, founder of the Styrian Habsburg line that governed Inner Austria from Graz from 1564 to 1619. Carl looked to the Jesuits as allies in his struggle to improve the precarious position of Catholics in Inner Austria. Five years before Ferdinand's birth in 1578 the archduke brought in the Jesuits to open a college in Graz, and when the college was raised to the status of a university in 1586, Ferdinand, though only eight years old was the first student to have his name inscribed in the book of matriculation. In 1596, a year after his return from study in Ingolstadt, Ferdinand assumed the responsibility for government in Inner Austria. As his confessor he chose the Belgian Jesuit Bartholomew Viller, who had served as provincial of the Austrian Province from 1583 to 1590. Viller remained in this office until Ferdinand's coronation as Holy Roman Emperor in 1619, when he resigned because of age. While returning in 1616 from the Jesuit General Congregation in Rome that elected Muzio Vitelleschi, Viller was arrested and imprisoned for nearly two years by the Venetians, who were then at war with Ferdinand.[20]

Ferdinand's years in Graz saw him carry through a vigorous program of Counter Reformation in Inner Austria. This campaign won for him the reputation of a Catholic militant. A codicil to his testament of 1621 made explicit the principle on which he acted from the start of his reign, that his first responsibility as ruler was for the preservation of his people in the Catholic faith. The same document contained an eloquent recommendation of the Society of Jesus to his heir.

In the first place, with special concern we earnestly commend to you the well-deserving Society of Jesus and its priests. Through their skill, their instruction of our dear youth, and their exemplary manner of life, they do much good in the Christian Catholic Churches and more than others loyally work and exert themselves to maintain and propagate the Catholic religion not only in our Inner Austrian lands but in all our kingdoms and territories and throughout Christendom. In this ungrateful and perverse world they encounter more hatred

[18] Duhr 2, 2 (Freiburg, 1913): 246.

[19] See their two common position papers, HStA, Kschw 8613, ff. 1–2; these are undated but stem from late 1618 or early 1619. A third Jesuit, Casper Torrentinus, who was the confessor of Maximilian's father, Duke William, also signed the papers.

[20] Duhr, ibid., 214.

and persecution than others and so are more in need of protection, help, and assistance.[21]

From 1605 on, the contest between the two Habsburg brothers – Emperor Rudolf II, whose fitness for government was now in question, and Archduke Matthias – weakened Habsburg rule in the territories of the monarchy. The Protestants exploited the situation to secure new guarantees from the competing rulers. One result was the Letter of Majesty itself, which the Bohemian Protestants extorted from Rudolf. Matthias finally succeeded Rudolf as emperor in 1612. But he was childless, so the question of his successor quickly arose. A Habsburg family conference decided upon Ferdinand as their candidate for the imperial throne. Accordingly, he was reluctantly recognized as king of Bohemia by the estates in 1617, while Matthias was still living, and he was in the process of being recognized as king of Hungary by the Hungarian estates when the Bohemian rebellion broke out. After the death of Matthias in early 1619, Ferdinand was elected Holy Roman Emperor in August of that year.

The lot of the Jesuits in France consistently wavered precariously, because of the hostility not only of the Huguenots but of the parlements, especially the Parlement of Paris, and of the universities, especially the University of Paris. Deeply seated Gallican sentiments imbued these institutions and made them wary of the Jesuit attachment to Rome. More than any other Catholic country, France had advanced toward the formation of a state. The protonational feeling accompanying Gallicanism raised particular difficulties for the Jesuits in France. University professors often saw unwanted rivals in the Society's educational institutions. In addition, as the seventeenth century progressed, an increasingly self-conscious hierarchy and diocesan clergy, especially in Paris, resented the privileges that the religious orders, in particular the Jesuits, received from Rome. The Jesuits came to look to the king for protection; hence, the crucial importance to them of the post of royal confessor.

Ignatius Loyola and his early companions had studied at the University of Paris, but Ignatius did not achieve his goal of a college there before his death in 1556. Only in 1562 did the Society obtain formal legal recognition in France, though several colleges were already in operation by then. In 1564 the College of Clermont opened its doors in Paris, and it enrolled more than 1,000 students by 1570. Ten years later the

21 Gustav Turba, *Die Grundlagen der Pragmatischen Sanktion* 2: *Die Hausgesetze* (Vienna, 1913): 351–2.

Jesuits counted fifteen colleges concentrated in south and central France. During the Wars of Religion that wreaked havoc in the country through the second half of the sixteenth century, Jesuits were divided in their sentiments between the Valois and the extremist Catholic League. The superior general in Rome, Claudio Acquaviva, urged them to stay out of politics.[22] After the assassination of the last Valois king, Henry III, at the end of 1589, the Huguenot Henry of Navarre, a Bourbon, stood next in line for the throne. His conversion to Catholicism and coronation in 1593–4 and the support he increasingly gathered from French Catholics, including the theologians of the University of Paris, put the Jesuits in a difficult position. Acquaviva directed the French Jesuits not to take an oath of allegiance to Henry until his excommunication for heresy was formally lifted by Pope Clement VIII. Yet, with the approval of the papal legate, they did so, an action that brought them a stern rebuke from Acquaviva. Then the attempt of their former student Jean Chastel on the life of Henry IV energized the opponents of the Society, and in early January the Parlement of Paris expelled the Jesuits from much of France and the College of Clermont was forced to close.[23]

In 1595 Pope Clement VIII formally lifted the excommunication of Henry. One condition for this was that he work for the return of the Jesuits to all France. The religious wars came to an uneasy conclusion in 1598 when Henry issued the Edict of Nantes granting limited toleration to the Huguenots along with the right to fortify a number of towns as a guarantee of their security. But the king remained suspicious of the Jesuits.

At this point there entered the scene the Jesuit Pierre Coton, who was to play a significant role in France for the next quarter century. Born at Néronde in the Forez in 1564 to a family of the nobility of the robe, he entered the Jesuits in 1583 and did most of his studies in Italy, where Robert Bellarmine was among his instructors. His personal charm, deep spirituality, and preaching style impressed his superiors, and his early missionary work in southern France brought many back to Catholicism. In 1599 Pope Clement VIII dispatched a special legate to Paris to encourage Henry to readmit the Jesuits to the kingdom. A member of the legation introduced Coton to the king. His conversation immediately impressed Henry, who requested that he preach for him. Coton's sermon captivated the king and won him over completely. Gradually the terms were negotiated on which the Society could return to all of France.

22 See A. Lynn Martin, *Henry III and the Jesuit Politicians* (Geneva, 1973), esp. pp. 123–4, 125, 127–8, 140, 160, 195, 203–4, 214, 217–18.

23 William Bangert, *A History of the Society of Jesus* (St. Louis, 1972), 64–71, 119–22.

The Jesuits had to swear an oath of allegiance to the crown, and they were not allowed to reopen the College of Clermont in Paris, their flagship school. On September 1, 1603, the edict permitting their return was issued, and within five months there were applications from thirty-two towns for colleges. Coton became a genuinely close friend of the king and began to function as his confessor in 1602, even though he was not formally appointed to the post until 1608.[24]

France rebounded gradually from the upheaval of the Wars of Religion during the first decade of the seventeenth century as Henry took measures to restore political stability, promote commerce, and raise living standards. In 1600 he married the Florentine princess Marie de Medici, and she bore him a son, the future Louis XIII, in 1601. The king encouraged Catholic reform in France while at the same time he carefully protected the privileges granted the Huguenots by the Edict of Nantes. As the decade progressed and the situation of France improved, Henry's thoughts turned increasingly to a reassertion of France's role in Europe and a challenge to the Habsburg rulers, Emperor Rudolf II and Philip III of Spain. A dispute in 1609 over the succession to the duchy of Jülich-Cleves just over the border in the empire seemed to offer the opportunity for this. The duchy's location between the Dutch United Provinces and their allies in Germany made it strategically of great importance. Imperial troops occupied it provisionally.[25]

By 1610 the French Jesuits too were flourishing, roughly 1,300 of them residing in forty-five communities organized in four provinces.[26] But that year proved to be a fateful one for them as well as for France. On May 14, as he was preparing to invade Jülich-Cleves, King Henry fell victim to the assassin Ravaillac. Immediately their enemies blamed the doctrine on tyrannicide found in Mariana's *The King and the Education of the King*. His tract had raised no eyebrows in Spain, but already in the year of its publication the Jesuit provincial superior in Paris complained about Mariana's book to Acquaviva because of the problems it could cause the Society in France. When French Jesuits once again complained to him in 1606, Acquaviva ordered that the book be reissued in a corrected edition.[27] In the wake of the murder of Henry, then, he promulgated a decree dated July 6, 1610 prohibiting any Jesuit from writing or speaking

24 Bangert, 120–5; Georges Minois, *Le confesseur du roi: Les directeurs de conscience sous la monarchie française* (Paris, 1988), 339–45.
25 David Buisseret, *Henry IV* (London, 1984), 173–5.
26 Bangert, 123–4.
27 Robert Keating O'Neill, "Politics and the New Orders in France, 1584–1629," Dissertation (U. of Chicago, 1975), 108, 114.

in defense of tyrannicide under pain of excommunication.[28] Meanwhile, by order of the Parlement of Paris, Mariana's treatise had been publicly burned on June 8.

But more was yet to come. Bellarmine's *Treatise on the Power of the Supreme Pontiff in Temporal Affairs* appeared in 1610, and traditional as his doctrine was at the time, it touched a sensitive nerve in Gallican France and further embroiled the Jesuits with parlement and the university. Parlement condemned the treatise on November 26, 1610. The Jesuits, then, inopportunely, petitioned the reopening of the College of Clermont, a measure that Henry IV despite his affection for the Society had for political reasons refused to allow. His widow, the regent Marie de Medici, gave her approval, but again the Jesuits became entangled with parlement. The upshot was that they did not obtain permission to resume teaching at the college. Perhaps more significantly, under great pressure several leading Jesuits, including the provincial of Paris, declared that they upheld the teaching of the university that denied the pope any role in temporal affairs and that they would teach accordingly. For this compromise of papal authority, they garnered a severe reprimand from Acquaviva in Rome.[29]

But the issues of the indirect power of the pope and tyrannicide refused to go away. *The Anglican Controversy over the Power of King and Pope*[30] published by the German Jesuit theologian Martin Becan in 1612 was condemned by the university and criticized by Rome for its overstatement of papal power.[31] But the publication of Suarez's *Defense of the Faith* in 1614 caused a greater stir. It not only defended the indirect power of the pope in temporal matters but also allowed for tyrannicide in extreme cases. Both Philip III of Spain and Pope Paul V praised the work, but it was bound to embarrass the Jesuits in France, and parlement condemned it. Suarez had indeed secured permission for the publication of his volume, and Acquaviva now apologized to the French Jesuits that his prohibition of writings on tyrannicide had not been adequately communicated to the whole Society.[32] In 1614 the Jesuits of the

[28] ARSJ, Francia 32, f. 431; an English translation of this is found in Guenter Lewy, *Constitutionalism and Statecraft during the Golden Age of Spain: A Study of the Political Philosoophy of Juan de Mariana, S.J.* (Geneva, 1960), 167. This decree seems to have been sent only to the French provinces. A later decree of August 14, 1610, forbidding any Jesuit to take up the defense of Mariana was sent to all the provinces; see Lewy, 143 and 167, where it is printed in English translation.

[29] Pierre Blet, "Jésuites et libertés gallicanes en 1611," AHSJ 24 (1955): 165–7; id., "Jésuites gallicanes au xviie siècle?," ibid., 29 (1960): 61–2; Bangert, 126–9; Henri Fouqueray, *Histoire de la Compagnie de Jésus en France* 3 (Paris, 1922): 253–67, 268–94.

[30] *Controversia anglicana de potestate regis et pontificis.*

[31] Fouqueray 3: 302–5; Gui, 64–5.

[32] Fouqueray 3: 301–13.

Paris Province again urged the superior general to prohibit the publication of books that dealt with tyrannicide or the temporal power of the pope, and he responded with decrees to this effect on August 1 and 2, 1614.[33]

Two years before his assassination, Henry IV had entrusted his son Louis to Coton for instruction in the faith. Shortly after Henry's death, his widow Marie asked the Jesuit to remain at court as confessor of the nine-year-old king, who was crowned at Rheims on October 17, 1610.[34] So Louis began to acquire an affection for the Jesuits that lasted until his dying day and that greatly benefitted the Society in France. He did more than any other prince to secure the canonization of Ignatius Loyola in 1622.[35] As confessor, Coton stood out as an early exponent of a double marriage alliance between France and Spain that would unite the two crowns against the Protestant threat emerging in Germany. So he was in agreement with a fundamental element of papal policy that aimed at a common Habsburg-Bourbon front against the Protestants. According to the contract concluded in 1612, Louis would marry the Spanish Infanta Anne, and his sister Elizabeth would marry the future Philip IV. After the marriages were celebrated in 1615, the Spanish chief minister, the Duke of Lerma, wrote Coton thanking him for his role in bringing them about.[36] Coton was also involved in negotiations for the marriage of Louis's sister Christine, who wed the heir in Savoy in 1612 after the breakdown of discussions with England, and he enjoyed contacts at the courts of Munich and Mainz.[37]

In 1614 the French Estates-General met for the only time between the start of the reign of Henry IV and the French Revolution. The event signaled the weakness of the crown during the regency of Marie de Medici following the death of Henry. Allied with *parlementaires*, the third estate once again raised the issue of the Jesuit position on papal power and tyrannicide, and on January 2, 1615, the Parlement of Paris renewed its decrees against the Jesuits and their teaching. But the king and his council along with the clergy and the nobility opposed

[33] ARSJ, Cong. 54, ff. 196–7, 204; the decrees are published in English translation in Lewy, 167–8. The Provinces of Paris and Lyons proposed that these matters be taken up at the Seventh General Congregation in 1615–16, but it issued no decree on them; see Cong. 54, ff. 204, 222, and Ignace Armand (provincial) to the provincials of Italy and Spain, Paris, June 29, 1614, in Jean-Marie Prat, *Recherches historiques et critiques sur la Compagnie de Jésus en France du temps du P. Coton, 1564–1626* 5 (Lyons, 1878): 336–9.

[34] Fouqueray 3: 230, 322–3.

[35] Ibid., 324, 477–8; Eugène Griselle, *Profils des Jésuites du xviie siècle* (Lille/Paris, 1911), 2–3, 32–3.

[36] Fouqueray 3: 331–2, 357; O'Neill, 105, 134.

[37] Prat, *Recherches historiques* 3 (Lyons, 1876): 471, 486, 488–91; 5: 310–14.

the third estate and parlement in what was a victory for Rome, the Jesuits, and especially the young king. But by no means did the issues disappear.[38]

After attaining his majority in 1614 and taking a wife, Louis began to chafe under the tutelage of his possessive mother, and, of course, there were figures at court waiting to exploit any differences between the two. Their divisions spilled over into factional conflict and eventually open war. Several Jesuits, including Coton, helped facilitate the periodic reconciliations of mother and son. In the summer of 1616 there were six Jesuits in the service of the court. When Coton wrote asking the superior general Vitelleschi whether these Jesuits should accompany the court on its journeys, the response was that this depended upon the desire of the king and the queen-mother, which the Jesuits were to obey.[39] Vitelleschi deferred to the royal wishes.

As was usually the case at the time of weak royal government, leading nobles raised their heads in rebellion, this time including the king's cousin, Henri de Bourbon, the prince of Condé. Marie's Italian favorite, the corrupt, arrogant Concino Concini, awakened widespread resentment among the French and offered the restive nobles a convenient target. Increasingly, Charles Albert de Luynes, who began in Louis's entourage as falconer, grew in the king's affection and became his favorite. Luynes urged Louis to assert himself as king. Finally, on April 24, 1617, in what amounted to a coup, Concini was assassinated – whether this was intended by Louis or not is unclear – and Marie was imprisoned briefly and then exiled to Blois and her entourage turned out.[40]

Now a duke and "minister-favorite," Luynes stood out as the most influential figure with the king.[41] He steered Louis away from Coton, whom Luynes considered too sympathetic to Marie de Medici. The new papal nuncio in 1617, Guido Bentivoglio, attributed Coton's departure in May to his urging the position of the queen-mother with the king.[42] Coton also, Bentivoglio himself thought, was involved in too many matters at court and tended to favor a Spanish view. The year before Coton had complained to Vitelleschi about the "national spirit" increasingly

[38] Fouqueray 3: 343–53; Pierre Blet, *Le clergé du Grand Siècle en ses Assemblées, 1615–1715* (Paris, 1995), 23–9.
[39] Vitelleschi to Coton, Sept. 4, 1616, ARSJ, Francia 3, f. 205.
[40] A. Lloyd Moote, *Louis XIII, the Just* (Berkeley, 1989), 80–102, esp. 94. Most historians would allow that Louis ordered the killing.
[41] Ibid., 102.
[42] Bentiviglio to Scipione Borghese (cardinal-nephew), May 9, 1617, Guido Bentivoglio, *La nunziatura di Francia del Cardinale Guido Bentivoglio: Lettere a Scipione Borghese* 1 (Florence, 1863): no. 220: 218–19; Fouqueray 3: 418–21; Prat 3: 735.

evident among his Jesuit brothers,[43] which perhaps was an indication that they did not share his enthusiasm for the marriage alliance with Spain. Bentivoglio recommended that the cardinal-nephew speak to Vitelleschi, "a padre of great prudence," about removing Coton from court.[44] So Coton departed for Lyons, eased out by Luynes but also desirous himself to leave the court. His departure cannot be considered a fall from favor with the king, who testified in a warm letter to Coton's long and faithful service. Coton journeyed to Italy, where he fulfilled vows on Louis's behalf in Milan, Loretto, and Rome.[45] The storm that broke over the Jesuits in 1625 would bring him back to Paris as provincial superior.

Coton's successor was a well-known Paris Jesuit, whom Bentivoglio called a "grand preacher," Jean Arnoux.[46] He was already confessor of the favorite Luynes, so that he and the king made their confession to the same priest, as Louis wanted and undoubtedly Luynes did too. Vitelleschi welcomed the appointment, and he thanked Louis for his benevolence toward the Society in again choosing a Jesuit as confessor. Louis would continue, Vitelleschi was confident, to protect the Jesuits as his father had.[47] Luynes, in turn, helped the Jesuits secure a goal they had long pursued, the reopening of the College of Clermont, for which Vitelleschi expressed his gratitude.[48] The Jesuits had invested heavily in France; by 1623 they conducted fifty-eight colleges, which in 1627 enrolled more than 13,000 students.[49]

Spain remained the most powerful state in Christendom on the eve of the Thirty Years War, though cracks had long since shown up in its armor. In addition to its holdings in America with the appendage of the Philippines, the Monarchy of Spain had assumed control of Portugal and its colonies in 1580 and dominated Italy through its rule in Milan, Naples, and Sicily. The Dutch had compelled Spain to recognize their de facto independence in the Twelve Years Truce of 1609, but Spain still remained the ultimate authority in the Spanish Netherlands. There in 1598 just before his death Philip II had turned over control to the

43 Vitelleschi to Coton, Aug. 4, 1616, ARSJ, Francia 3, f. 196'.
44 Bentivoglio to Scipione Borghese, June 20, 1617, Bentivoglio, 1: no. 359: 301–2.
45 Louis XIII to Coton, Fontainebleau, June 7, 1617, in Prat, *Recherches historiques* 5: 381; Griselle, *Profils des Jésuites*, 20–5.
46 Bentivoglio to Scipione Borghese, May 9, 1617, Bentivoglio 1: no. 220: 218–19.
47 Vitelleschi to Arnoux, June 27, 1617, ARSJ, Francia 3, f. 233; Vitelleschi to Louis XIII, July 16, 1617, ARSJ, Gallia, 46I, f. 43'; see also Vitelleschi to Louis, May 27, 1617, ibid., f. 42.
48 Vitelleschi to Luynes, Apr. 10, 1618, ARSJ, Gallia 46I, ff. 49–49'.
49 Fouqueray 3: 531; Bangert, 215.

"archdukes," Albert, brother of Emperor Rudolf II, and Isabella, his wife and Philip's daughter. The hope was that from this union would sprout a new branch of the dynasty, but the pair had no children, and so after the death of Albert in 1621 and Isabella in 1633, the Spanish Netherlands reverted to direct Spanish control.

Spanish predominance in the second half of the sixteenth century owed much to the weakness of France resulting from its religious wars. Another of its periodic bankruptcies hit Spain in 1598, a sign of its straitened economic and financial status. That year Philip II withdrew from his war with France in the Peace of Vervins. The new government of Philip III, under the direction of the favorite, the duke of Lerma, adopted a policy of retrenchment, making peace with England in 1604 and then concluding the truce with the Dutch. Lerma turned his attention to the Mediterranean, and in 1609 the Moriscos were expelled because they jeopardized Spanish security. The assassination of Henry IV in 1610 ended the revival of France that had reached the point of challenging Spanish hegemony. The Franco-Spanish double marriage of 1615 brought the two rival powers closer together in what many Catholics, including the pope, hoped would lead to an alliance against the heretics of Europe.

In 1617 Baltasar de Zúñiga returned to Madrid from his post as ambassador to the Habsburg Court of Vienna. Around him coalesced a party hostile to Lerma that was determined to reassert the Spanish position throughout Europe. Lerma, whose power had long been eroding, fell from favor the next year, and Zúñiga became the most influential of the king's ministers. When the Bohemian rebellion erupted, he urged Spanish assistance to Vienna, on grounds of loyalty to its Habsburg cousin but also because he foresaw that the collapse of the German Habsburgs would adversely affect the Spanish position in Italy and in The Netherlands. Spanish support for the German Habsburgs in 1619 anticipated the resumption of the war with the Dutch in 1621.

The Jesuits never enjoyed the influence in Spain that they did in Germany or even in France, even though they counted more than 2,000 there in 1616 distributed among four provinces and eighty-seven communities.[50] One reason for this was that the older religious orders like the Dominicans and Franciscans had been decimated by the Reformation in Germany and much weakened in France, and the Jesuits then arrived in the vanguard of a revived Catholicism. But the older orders remained vigorous in Spain as they did in Italy. In addition, Philip II and the Spanish Inquisition remained wary of the Jesuits and

[50] Bangert, 193.

particularly suspicious of their attachment to Rome. The King of Spain traditionally chose his confessor from among the Dominicans. Fray Luis de Aliaga, who became Philip III's confessor in 1608, was deeply involved in the factional politics of the court, assumed a post as councillor of state in 1611, and was quickly banished from Madrid after the king's death.[51]

Jerónimo de Florencia, preacher to the king, stood out as the most prominent Jesuit at the court in 1618. Florencia had been popular with Queen Margaret, Philip's Austrian wife who died in 1611, and like her, he criticized Lerma's policies and his enrichment of himself and his family. Florencia's influence was considerable. One of his sermons, the king himself asserted, convinced him to dismiss Lerma in 1618; yet the duke subsequently, even though aware of the Jesuit's opposition to him, asked Florencia to intercede for him with the king. Florencia assisted Philip III on his deathbed, and he preached a funeral sermon for the king as he had for Queen Margaret.[52] Earlier another Jesuit, Richard Haller, a native of Nuremberg and former rector of the Jesuit university in Graz, played a significant part in Madrid. He accompanied as confessor the fifteen-year-old Margaret, sister of Archduke Ferdinand of Inner Austria, when she journeyed to Madrid in 1599 to marry Philip III. By tradition, the confessor of the Spanish queen was a Franciscan, but Margaret insisted on bringing along a Jesuit because of the Society's support of her family in Germany.[53] The queen along with her mother, Empress Maria, the widow of Emperor Maximilian II, and her sister, the nun Margaret of the Cross, the Austrian ambassador Franz Christoph von Khevenhiller, and Haller constituted a party at court that encouraged Spanish support for the Austrian Habsburgs. They ultimately shared Zúñiga's triumph with the Spanish intervention in 1619 to help suppress the Bohemian rebellion, even though the queen, the empress, and Haller were dead by then.[54]

Florencia did not lose his position after Philip IV assumed the throne in 1621. His sermon in praise of the new government indirectly lauded

51 Magdalena S. Sánchez, *The Empress, the Queen, and Power at the Court of Philip III of Spain* (Baltimore, 1998), 18, 19, 56, 181; Antonio Feros, *Kingship and Favoritism in the Spain of Philip III, 1598–1621* (Cambridge, 2000), 210–11, 220–1, 228, 241, 256.

52 Sánchez, 23, 143; Feros, 246, 264; *Copia y declaration de la platica que tuvo su Majestad con el Padre Florencia, y sus hijos, y otras personas de su corte, a la hora de su muerte*, Biblioteca Nacional, Madrid, ms. no. 2352, f. 400a ff., dated Apr. 13, 1621.

53 Later in 1631 the Infanta Maria Anna brought her Capuchin confessor with her when she traveled to Vienna to marry the future Ferdinand III despite Austrian Habsburg pressure that she take a Jesuit confessor; see Robert Bireley, *Religion and Politics in the Age of the Counterreformation* (Chapel Hill, NC, 1981), 161.

54 Sánchez, 21–2, 58, 183.

the count-duke of Olivares, who the same day acquired the title of grandee. Soon afterwards Florencia became confessor to the two Infantes, the brothers of Philip IV.[55] Once Olivares maneuvered into the post of favorite, his confessors emerged as Jesuit figures at court, first Hernando de Salazar and then, after 1631, Francisco Aguado. The two could not have been more different, Salazar, financial consultant and candidate for a bishopric, and Aguado, master of the interior life and ascetical writer. Vitelleschi himself maintained formal contact with the Spanish court but showed little knowledge of its workings. Shortly after he took office, he warmly if routinely offered the Society's services to Philip III, and he requested direction in Spanish affairs from the Dominican confessor Aliaga.[56] He congratulated the duke of Lerma on being created a cardinal in 1618 shortly before his fall from power. Later he sidestepped Lerma's request for the services of a Jesuit to help in the business affairs of the two young dukes of Medina Sidonia. The Jesuit rule prohibited this type of involvement in secular matters, he wrote to the duke.[57]

The Seventh General Congregation of the Jesuits elected Muzio Vitelleschi superior general on November 15, 1615. He would serve for thirty years, until his death on February 9, 1645. At his election the Society had grown to roughly 13,100 members since 1540, when Ignatius Loyola and his companions received papal approval for their new foundation. By the death of Ignatius in 1556 the Jesuits numbered approximately one thousand. Under Vitelleschi's predecessor, Claudio Acquaviva, who governed the Society from 1581 to 1615, the Society more than doubled in numbers. Most members were active in Europe, but a not insignificant number labored in America as well as in areas of Asia and Africa. Jesuits were distributed over thirty-two provinces or administrative units, each with a provincial superior, or simply provincial, whom the superior general appointed after receiving recommendations from the province.

At its inception Ignatius and his companions had placed the Society at the special disposition of the Holy See. They looked upon the pope as the vicar of Christ on earth, and they considered him to have from his vantage point in Rome the clearest view and broadest perspective on the needs of the universal church. Fully professed Jesuits took a special

[55] Ibid., 23; John H. Elliott, *The Count-Duke of Olivares: The Statesman in an Age of Decline* (New Haven, CT, 1986), 45, 105.

[56] Vitelleschi to Philip IV, Mar. 5, 1616, ARSJ, Tol. 7I, f. 222; Vitelleschi to Aliaga, Jan. 5, 1616, ibid., f. 217.

[57] Vitelleschi to Lerma, Mar. 26 and Dec. 23, 1618, ARSJ, Hisp. 70, f. 107'; Tol. 7I, f. 354.

vow promising to undertake any mission to which the pope might call them. The allegiance of the Jesuits bolstered the authority of the popes during the early modern period, and the Jesuits certainly benefited from papal support, not least of all from the many privileges granted them. But the relationship between pope and Society could become rocky.[58]

The general congregation constituted the highest authority within the Society and was its legislative body. It did not meet on a regular basis. One of its principal functions was to elect the superior general, who then served for life, so that it had to be convoked on the death of a superior general. Otherwise, there was a complicated process for the calling of a general congregation. Every three years a provincial congregation was held in each province, to which the senior professed fathers of the province were summoned. These congregations had two tasks. First, they were to vote on whether there was need for a general congregation. Second, they were to elect a delegate, or procurator, who would carry this vote to Rome and also report on the state of the province, raising, in particular, issues and questions of concern to the province. The Acts of many of these provincial congregations survive in Rome and constitute a valuable source. The delegates then met in Rome in a congregation of procurators. There they voted on whether a general congregation should be summoned and also served as a conduit of information from around the Jesuit world, which enabled the superior general better to assess the state of the Society. It was at its provincial congregation of 1614, for example, that the Paris Province listed the reasons why the superior general should prohibit writings on the pope's temporal power.[59] A superior general could also on his own initiative convene a general congregation to take up issues that he judged needed attention.

Should a general congregation be convened, the senior professed fathers were first summoned to congregations in the respective provinces. There the first order of business was to elect two delegates from the province who would accompany the provincial superior to Rome to participate in the general congregation. Second, they drew up a list of issues and questions that they wanted the general congregation to consider. Two general congregations were held during the long generalate of Acquaviva, one in 1593 and another in 1605. No general congregations were convoked during the lengthy tenure of Vitelleschi.

58 On the Jesuits' relationship to the papacy, see John W. O'Malley, *The First Jesuits* (Cambridge, 1993), 32, 35, 285–6, 296–310.

59 ARSJ, Cong. 54, 198–8'.

This was partly due to the upheavals caused by the war, which also interrupted the regular congregations of procurators, but the failure to summon a general congregation became a matter of concern in the last years of Vitelleschi's generalate.

Vitelleschi, the first non-Spanish subject to be elected superior general of the Jesuits, was born in Rome on December 2, 1563. His father Alessandro stemmed from a prominent Roman noble family, and his mother, Gismonda de'Rustici, also was of noble lineage.[60] His most famous forebear was the fifteenth-century Cardinal Giovanni Vitelleschi, who has been called a true precursor of Cesare Borgia. Essentially a military captain, among other exploits Cardinal Giovanni pacified the city of Rome for Pope Eugene IV in 1434 with great cruelty. Later he was named archbishop of Florence and patriarch of Alexandria. A monument was planned for him on the Campidoglio until he was accused of attempting to seize control of the Papal States and perhaps the papacy itself, was imprisoned in the Castel Sant'Angelo, and fell victim there to a rival's poison.[61] Most of his property was seized, but the family continued to enjoy papal favor and to move in high Roman social circles. Muzio's father seems to have squandered a significant portion of the family's wealth in order to maintain his standard of life. Yet the English traveler John Evelyn writing in November 1644 identified one member of the family, Hippolito, as a leading collector of classical antiquities in Rome.[62]

Muzio was the third of three brothers. Marc Antonio married and had a family of six daughters and one son. Marcello was ordained a priest and later became a canon of St. Mary Major. Both the older brothers, and to a degree Muzio himself, frequented the circle of Philip Neri, and Marcello became a close friend of "the Apostle of Rome" in the saint's last years.[63] Comfortable circumstances were the rule for Muzio as he grew up in the family palazzo. His father kept a *maestro* in the house to oversee the boys' education. An ecclesiastical career was foreseen for him; the servants even took to calling the boy "Cardinal Muzio."

[60] My remarks on Vitelleschi's early life are drawn from a manuscript found in the ARSJ in three copies, "Vocatione d. Mutio Vitelleschi della Comp[a] di Giesu, scritta da Virgilio Cepari, 1588," Vitae 127, ff. 1–21, 23–38, and 62: 1–15.

[61] Ferdinando Gregorovius, *Storia della Città di Roma nel medio aevo*, vol. 3 (Rome, 1901): 702–48, esp. 713–18, 726–9.

[62] Irene Fosi, *All'ombra dei Barberini: Fedeltà e servizio nella Roma Barocca* (Rome, 1997), 44, 156; John Evelyn, *The Diary of John Evelyn*, ed. E.S. de Beer, 2 (Oxford, 1955): 283. From my next paragraph it is clear that Hippolito cannot have been a brother of Muzio as de Beer writes.

[63] Louis Ponnelle and Louis Bordet, *Saint Philip Neri et la Societé romaine de son temps (1515–1595)*, 3rd ed. (Paris, 1929), 454–5 and n. 9.

Muzio first felt drawn to the Jesuits when his *maestro* began taking him to the Jesuit Church of the Gesù on feast days. At age twelve or thirteen, then, he started to attend the Jesuit college in Rome; later he would for a brief time study at the English College. Alessandro opposed the budding vocation of his son, and he took up the matter with Acquaviva himself, who agreed that the young man should not enter without his father's consent. Muzio himself then approached Acquaviva, who encouraged him to speak further with his father. Eventually, in 1582, when Muzio was nineteen, the provincial of the Roman Province accepted him into the novitiate without Acquaviva's knowledge. Furious, Alessandro appealed to Pope Gregory XIII, who compelled Acquaviva to send Muzio home. Now Muzio sought out the great Cardinal Alessandro Farnese, a friend of his father, who interceded with the pope on his behalf. Cardinal Ubaldini also put in a word for him. Nothing resulted. Acquaviva raised the matter again with Pope Gregory, who now gave him permission to receive Muzio into the Society and assured him that he would handle Alessandro. So Muzio entered the Society a second time in 1583, despite the continued if moderated opposition of his father. The whole episode reveals Vitelleschi's determination, but perhaps even more the Roman social circles in which his family moved and the importance he later attached to personal contacts. Vitelleschi's dealings with people and especially his connections with personalities of high status owed much to his background in the Roman nobility.

Little detail is known of Vitelleschi's early life in the Society. After the completion of his studies, he taught philosophy and theology at the Roman College from 1588 to 1591 and from 1599 to 1602. From this activity there remain only two philosophical treatises in manuscript.[64] His appointment as rector of the English College in Rome in 1592 pointed toward a future in administration and helps explain his particular concern for English Catholics. He was named provincial superior of the Neapolitan Province in 1602 and then of the Roman Province in 1606, and in 1608 he was called to the Jesuit curia in Rome as assistant to Acquaviva for the Italian provinces. Along the way he acquired a reputation as a fine preacher as the French bishop Jean-Pierre Camus reported from Rome after Vitelleschi's election as superior general.[65]

64 "Lectiones in octo libros physicorum et quattuor de caelo" and "In libros meterologicorum," both dating from 1589–90; Carlos Sommervogel, S.J., *Bibliothèque de la Compagnie de Jésus* 8 (Brussels/Paris, 1898): 851.

65 Prat, *Recherches historiques* 4 (Lyons, 1876): 187–8; M. Fois, "Generales: 6, Vitelleschi," in *Diccionario Histórico de la Compañía de Jesús*, eds., Charles E. O'Neill, S.J. and Joaquín M. Domínguez, S.J. (Rome/Madrid, 2001), 2: 1621–7.

There was considerable opposition to Vitelleschi's election. It came from Jesuits within Rome itself, and it does not seem to have been dictated by international politics or national sentiment.[66] Among those who machinated against him were the provincial of Rome and the former provincial of Naples, the rectors of the Roman and German Colleges, and the secretary of the Society. They claimed that "all his life he had pursued friendships with the powerful, and he exploited the number of people who came to seek favors from him to demonstrate his influence."[67] Such charges might have emerged from an interpretation of a style of governing that originated in his roots in Roman society. His later direction of the Society offered some grounds for such a view. An undated note from Cardinal Bellarmine calling all the congregations's members to vote out of a pure intention and not out of ambition suggests that the opposition to Vitelleschi had been brought to his attention.[68] Vitelleschi's opponents took their case to both the French and the Spanish ambassadors, but neither was inclined to attempt to influence the election.[69] Pope Paul V also rebuffed requests that he intervene.[70] Afterward, Vitelleschi refused to follow those like the assistant for Spain who insisted that the schemers be punished, and he sought reconciliation with them. Only the secretary of the Society, Bernard ab Angelis, was sent away from Rome. Vitelleschi was not a man of harsh measures.

As superior general, Vitelleschi resided in the Jesuit curia in Rome next to the Church of the Gesù, where a secretary and five assistants helped him carry out his responsibilities. The secretary, according to the Jesuit Constitutions, "should be his memory and hands for everything which he must write and handle."[71] The assistants as a group served as a body of councillors to the general, and each assisted him in his management of affairs with one of the five assistancies, or groups of provinces, the Italian, the German, the French, the Spanish, and the Portuguese. They

[66] There is considerable material on this election in the ARSJ, much of it nearly illegible. See "De creatione 6ti Praep. Gen. Commentarius," by an unknown author, Vitae 127, 56–103, and Cong. 20a, 451–2, a statement made in 1657 by Fr. Lindanus Columellus, who was a seminarian in Rome at the time.

[67] Giulio Cesare Cordara, *Historiae Societatis Jesu Pars Sexta complectens res gestas sub Mutio Vitellescho* 1: *1616–1625* (Rome, 1750): 13–14, "qui potentiorum amicitias in omni vita captasset, qui frequentia clientularum abuteretur ad potentiae ostentationem." Cordara had access to materials which have since been lost; his second volume, which dealt with the period from 1625 to 1633, was only published in 1859, also at Rome.

[68] ARSJ, Vitae 127, f. 138.

[69] Cordara, 3–4.

[70] Ibid.; ARSJ, Vitae 127, ff. 101′, 158–9′.

[71] Saint Ignatius of Loyola, *The Constitutions of the Society of Jesus*, trans. and with an Introduction and Commentary by George E. Ganss, S.J. (St. Louis, 1970), no. 800: 327.

were not canonical superiors like the provincials, and they were chosen by the general congregation not the superior general.[72]

For Ignatius Loyola himself regular correspondence among Jesuits was meant to serve as a means of preserving union among them as well as providing the information necessary for effective administration. He wrote into the Constitutions provisions for this correspondence. Provincials were to write at least once a month to the general, more frequently if they were close by, and the general in turn should send a letter to each provincial at least once a month. Many rectors and local superiors were also to write monthly to Rome.[73] In addition, any individual Jesuit could address a letter to the general. This generated an enormous correspondence in and out of Rome dealing with all manner of business. Correspondence with Germany and France was carried on in Latin, but for Spain Spanish was employed. For the period 1624 to 1635 Vitelleschi addressed 125 letters to Adam Contzen, confessor of Maximilian of Bavaria, and just under 1,000 to William Lamormaini, confessor to Emperor Ferdinand II. Seventy-seven letters were dispatched to Jean Arnoux between 1617 and 1621, when he was confessor to Louis XIII.

For Vitelleschi's generalate only a relatively small number of incoming letters survive, but the registers of the outgoing mail remain and constitute a rich source, especially because Vitelleschi or his secretary frequently summarized incoming letters in their responses. Early in Vitelleschi's tenure Coton indicated that he had written more extensively about a matter to the assistant, who would then fill Vitelleschi in on it. Vitelleschi answered that it would be more efficient if Coton wrote directly to him, and he would then pass on what he thought suitable to the assistant. He himself opened all the mail addressed to him, he assured Coton.[74] A significant number of letters in the registers have been altered or thoroughly revised before their dispatch. Sometimes these changes point to differing views or second thoughts within the curia.

Vitelleschi's contacts with the papal curia are difficult to document directly, because they were usually carried on viva voce. At the time of Vitelleschi's election the Borghese Pope Paul V had governed the church for eleven years; his pontificate had opened with the disputes with Venice and James I. Vitelleschi's background points to his familiarity with leading members of the court of Rome even apart from his position

[72] John W. Padberg, S.J., Martin D. O'Keefe, S.J., and John L. McCarthy, S.J., *For Matters of Greater Moment: The First Thirty Jesuit General Congregations: A Brief History and a Translation of the Decrees* (St. Louis, 1994), 250.

[73] *Constitutions*, ed. Ganss, nos. 673–5: 292–3.

[74] Vitelleschi to Coton, Aug. 4, 1616, ARSJ, Francia 3, f. 196'; see also Vitelleschi to the Provinces of France, Feb. 8, 1621, ibid., 38, ff. 4'–5.

as superior general of the Jesuits. Frequently in his correspondence he referred to a conversation with an influential cardinal or with the pope himself. A letter to Coton of November 8, 1616 reported an enigmatic remark about the Jesuits that Scipione Borghese, cardinal-nephew under Paul V, had made in a conversation with Vitelleschi.[75] Over a year later Vitelleschi wrote Arnoux that he had frequently related to the pope the confessor's achievements in dealing with the Most Christian King.[76] Vitelleschi appears to have met frequently with the pro-Jesuit, Ludovisi pope, Gregory XV (1621–3). But personal meetings with the Barberini pope, Urban VIII (1623–44), seem to have been rare. Instead, Vitelleschi spoke regularly with the cardinal-nephew, Francesco Barberini.

In his first circular letter to all Jesuits, dated January 2, 1617, Vitelleschi declared that he found the Society to be essentially in sound health, its spirit "robust." There was no need for major changes nor for new laws or regulations. Rather, he wrote, Jesuits were called to eliminate remaining defects and to carry out more effectively existing programs. One fear that he had also shared with the general congregation that elected him was that Jesuits had become excessively involved in family affairs, promoting the advancement of their own or other families.[77] This led to their being caught up in family disputes and controversies. He urged superiors to take a strong line in this regard and not to allow their subjects to yield to the pleas and importunities of friends and relatives. Vitelleschi himself, as will become apparent, faced difficulties in this respect. One complaint frequently heard about the Society, he noted in his letter, was that Jesuits were "more prudent men, politicians (politicos) rather than solidly spiritual."[78] Not mentioned in the letter directly was Jesuit involvement in politics. But the Sixth General Congregation of 1608 had promulgated a decree on the confessors of princes,[79] and the seventh attempted to clarify the issue further. Vitelleschi would certainly have to deal with it too.

The first Jesuit to serve as confessor to a prince took up his task at the command of Ignatius himself. King John III of Portugal requested in 1552 that either the provincial of Portugal, Diego Mirón, or his associate, Luis Gonçalves da Câmara, become his regular confessor. After taking counsel, Mirón turned down the king's request, on the grounds that this involved occupying a position at court unsuitable for a member of the Society, committed as it was to a simple life and service of the

[75] ARSJ, Francia 3, ff. 210–11.
[76] Dec. 8, 1617, ibid., f. 245′.
[77] *Institutum Societatis Jesu* 2 (Florence, 1892): 310.
[78] *Epistolae Quattuor Adm. R.P. Mutui Vitelleschi, S.J.* (n.p., n.d.), 1–24.
[79] Padberg et al., 226, 267.

poor. He then reported his decision to Rome, in the expectation that it would be summarily ratified there. But Ignatius, much to his surprise, ordered that one of the two assume the post. He gave two reasons. First, the Society ought to administer the sacraments to those of high as well as low station, and especially in this case, because King John was an unusually generous benefactor of the Society. Second, and more significant, the greater good and service of God called for acceptance of the position. "All members of the body participate in the welfare of the head, and all subjects in the welfare of the prince, and so we ought to esteem the spiritual assistance that we give to these [princes] more highly than the assistance that we provide others." Nor should Jesuits be scared off from such positions because of the concomitant dangers, in this case the allurements of life at court. God would protect them in the face of temptations, provided they sincerely sought his service, and those at court would recognize that they did not pursue offices or honors for themselves. So Gonçalves da Câmara became the first Jesuit court confessor.[80]

Subsequently, Ignatius wrote into the Constitutions of the Society a provision that it endeavor "to retain the benevolence of the Apostolic See, which the Society should especially serve; and then that of the temporal rulers and noble and powerful persons whose favor or disfavor does much toward opening or closing the gate to the service of God and the good of souls."[81] One normally needed a prince's approval even to undertake an activity in his lands. Yet the Constitutions also summoned Jesuits "to abstain as far as possible from all secular employments," so that they might devote themselves more fully to the spiritual pursuits of their vocation. What was to happen when princes, benefactors, or family members pressed Jesuits to engage in "secular" and especially political matters? According to the Constitutions, they were to resist such importunities, as Vitelleschi impressed upon them in his letter of 1617.[82] But the matter was not so simple.

Problems arose as more Jesuits became court confessors, especially in Germany. The Second General Congregation in 1565 responded to a request for direction from the Upper German Province, where the prince-bishop of Augsburg had asked for a Jesuit to accompany him as confessor. No Jesuit was to travel with the court as confessor or in any other function of either a secular or ecclesiastical prince, except for a

80 Ignatius Loyola to Diego Mirón, Feb. 1, 1553, *Obras Completas de San Ignacio de Loyola*, ed. Ignacio Iparraguirre, 2nd ed. (Madrid, 1963), 803–6; Bernhard Duhr, *Die Jesuiten an den deutschen Fürstenhöfen des 16. Jahrhunderts* (Freiburg, 1901), 2–3.

81 *Constitutions*, ed. Ganss, nos. 823–4: 337.

82 Ibid., no. 591: 263. The Constitutions did allow for exceptions in no. 592.

brief period, which it determined to be two months.[83] Ten years later the Upper German Province requested that the Third General Congregation declare that only the superior general could grant permission to serve as a court confessor and that he grant it rarely. But the congregation did not act on the request. The same province asked at the Fourth General Congregation, which elected Acquaviva in 1581, that the superior general issue an instruction on court confessors.

The Fifth General Congregation of 1593–4 then issued a more general decree on Jesuit involvement in politics. By now some Jesuits had figured in the French Religious Wars and in the mounting of the Spanish Armada.[84] No Jesuit, the decree read, "was for any reason to dare or presume to become involved in the public and secular affairs of princes which have to do with, as they say, reason of state." Nor were they to deal with political matters, no matter who might urge them to do so. The canonical penalties were deprivation of the right to vote within the Society, ineligibility to hold office, and if an office was held, removal.[85] Not everyone was happy with this decree. Antonio Possevino, who had undertaken a number of diplomatic missions for the pope, challenged Acquaviva on the issue. He drew up a paper listing more than twenty examples that, he argued, showed that the decree was not in harmony with the Society's practice.[86]

Under continued pressure Acquaviva in 1602 published an Instruction for Confessors of Princes. This was then ratified by the Sixth General Congregation in 1608 and so became the official position of the Society.[87] The general goal of the instruction was to secure the advantages that went with the post of court confessor while avoiding the disadvantages. The Society did not want to offend princes, especially those who were generous benefactors, by turning down requests for a confessor.

83 Padberg et al., 122.

84 See, for example, Martin, *Henry III and the Jesuit Politicians*, and John Bossy, "The Heart of Robert Persons," in *The Reckoned Expense: Edmund Campion and the Early English Jesuits*, ed. Thomas M. McCoog (Woodbridge, NJ, 1996), 141–58.

85 "ne, scilicet, quispiam publicis et saecularibus Principum negotiis, quae ad rationem status, ut vocant, pertinent, ulla ratione se immiscere, nec etiam quantumvis per quoscumque requisitus aut regatus, ejusmodi politicas res tractandi curam suscipere audeat vel praesumat," Decree 79, *Institutum Societatis Jesu* 2: 288; the corresponding canon 12 repeated virtually the same words, 547; Duhr, ibid., 4–5. See Padberg et al., 201, 214.

86 "Dubii proposti dal P. Possevino l'anno 1594 circa il decreto del non trattar cose di stato," ARSJ, Cong. 20b, ff. 342–4'. I am grateful to Father László Szilas, S.J., of the Jesuit Historical Institute in Rome, who called my attention to this document and provided me with a transcription of it.

For one of Possevino's diplomatic missions, see John Patrick Donnelly, S.J., "Antonio Possevino, S.J., as Papal Mediator between Emperor Rudolf II and King Stephan Báthory," AHSJ 69 (2000): 3–56.

87 "De Confessariis Principum," *Institutum* 2: 281–4, 297; see Padberg et al., 226.

Nor did it want to pass up the opportunity that the position offered to influence events for the good of the church and the Society. To lay out these goals on paper was difficult enough, to achieve them in practice considerably more so. The Instruction first stipulated norms about the confessor's personal conduct. He was normally to live in a Jesuit community according to its style of life. He ought not to frequent the court regularly but to wait until he was summoned. The key passage of the Instruction was ambiguous. The confessor, it read, "should be careful lest he become involved in external and political matters, mindful of what the Fifth General Congregation had severely prohibited in canons 12 and 13; he should deal only with those affairs which pertain to the conscience of the prince or are related to it, or to certain pious works."[88] But how could one remove from the domain of conscience all "external and political matters?"

Furthermore, the confessor was to avoid even the appearance of exercising political power. Such a perception severely damaged the Society. He ought not seek favors for others, nor should he allow himself to serve as a channel for the ruler's directives much less his reprimands. To be avoided at all costs was association with unpopular measures of the prince as well as entanglement in conflicts between princes or among factions at court. These brought the Society untold harm. Before a Jesuit assumed the office of confessor, the prince had to agree that he would hear the confessor out whenever he saw fit to call to the prince's attention abuses in government or other princely shortcomings. In difficult cases the confessor was expected to consult with his Jesuit superiors, presumably with the consent of the prince. Should the prince not be satisfied with the confessor's opinion on a matter, he was encouraged to seek the advice of two or three theologians. In this event the confessor was expected to support their view. In addition, the confessor should recognize that the prince was always free to change his confessor or consult others. Prior to acceptance of a post as confessor of a prince, the Jesuit was to show the prince the instruction and be assured that the prince agreed with its terms.

This Instruction of Acquaviva was to serve as the principal official document issued by the Society as a directive for the confessors of princes. Its ongoing interpretation is intertwined with the history of the court confessors. The Seventh General Congregation of 1615, which elected Vitelleschi, tried to clarify what was meant by "external and

88 "caveat, ne se implicet externis negotiis ac politicis, memor eorum quae a quinta Congregatione generali severissime praescribuntur canone 12 et 13; sed in ea solum incumbat, quae ad Principis conscientiam pertinent, vel ad illam referentur, aut in alia certa pia opera."

political matters." "Examples can be: what bears upon treaties of princes among themselves, or rights and successions to thrones, or foreign or civil wars." What was prohibited to the Jesuit was to be "involved in public consultations or negotiations about these or similar issues,"[89] where "public" had the sense of "official." This last provision seemed to allow for advice that was given to the prince in confession itself or in a private forum and that came under the heading of spiritual counsel. Vitelleschi himself soon was called upon to interpret Acquaviva's instruction.

The court confessor was a member of the court but not of the government, a distinction that was blurred in the seventeenth century. Apart from regularly hearing the prince's confession, the function of the confessor was not clearly defined. What was said under the seal of confession is obviously closed to us, but it is unlikely that the counsel given the prince in confession differed from that provided in other ways. In any event, the confessor enjoyed regular access to the center of power. His influence depended upon his own personality and even more so on that of the prince as well as on other circumstances. Emperor Ferdinand III differed greatly in this regard from his father, Ferdinand II. Cardinal Richelieu watched carefully the activity of Louis XIII's confessors and several times secured their dismissal. All the confessors of German princes that we will meet, however, served until either they or the prince died or retired because of old age. So it is difficult to generalize about the confessors' influence. One must look to individual cases.

Vitelleschi's overall policy as general was to advance the many apostolic works of the Society in service of the church. Necessary for this was the maintenance of harmony within the Society at a time of intensifying national rivalries. The task of preserving union among Jesuits during the protracted war would challenge him. Vitelleschi shared the general papal goal of reconciling the differences among the Catholic powers and especially of stilling the enduring rivalry between Bourbon France and the Habsburgs, especially the Spanish branch of the dynasty, so that they might effectively combat the heretical powers. Coton warned Vitelleschi early of the "national spirit, as it was called," that was appearing among Jesuits. In his response Vitelleschi characterized it as "most vicious" and alien to the spirit of the Society. In a follow-up letter he urged the provincial of Paris to take measures to uproot it.[90] His first circular letter took

89 Decree 46, canon 13, Institutum 2: 332, 553; Padberg et al., 267. These examples were taken from Responses of Acquaviva to queries from Jesuits in the field.

90 Vitelleschi to Coton, Aug. 4, 1616, ARSJ, Francia 3, f. 196'; Vitelleschi to Étienne Charlet (provincial), Aug. 5, 1616, ibid., f. 198. There were five Jesuit provinces in France by this time; the province of France included only the area around Paris and the Ile de France. To avoid confusion, in the text I refer to this as the Province of Paris.

up the matter but only briefly, encouraging Jesuits to a universal charity and setting aside attachments to provinces and nations.[91]

Vitelleschi believed firmly in the necessity of securing the goodwill of princes and rulers if the Society's labors for the glory of God and the salvation of souls were to be successful. This was a leading characteristic of his government. "Without their support our labor can accomplish very little or even nothing in many places," he wrote in 1625 to William Lamormaini, then the confessor of Emperor Ferdinand II.[92] To secure this support it was also necessary to cultivate those who were close to the prince. Some Jesuits, Vitelleschi complained, did not appreciate this adequately. The specific case Vitelleschi had in mind was the need to take measures to ensure that Archduke Ferdinand, eldest son and heir of Ferdinand II, would be well disposed to the Society. A minister or friend of the prince disaffected toward the Society could with one word undo many of its works, the general noted.

Vitelleschi justified his concern for the benevolence of princes with an appeal to the aforementioned passage of the Constitutions that emphasized the need to secure the favor of rulers. Ignatius made the same point when he ordered one of the two Portuguese Jesuits to accept the post of confessor to King John III. Influence upon the ruler or leaders would have an impact upon the whole body of a society. Vitelleschi's language was more emphatic than Ignatius's, but the idea was the same: Win over the ruler and the elite, and gradually the rest will follow. This method was fundamental to Jesuit activity in the foreign missions, especially in China or Japan, where an initial goal was to gain the support of the emperor, and then in China among the Mandarin class, in Japan among the *daimyos*, or local princes. This strategy helps to explain Vitelleschi's deference to princes and to nobility, which may strike us as excessive.

Acquaviva's Instruction prohibited confessors from using their position at court to obtain favors for individuals. But Vitelleschi's desire to retain the goodwill of benefactors and certainly his own background led him to burden the confessors with requests for favors, usually for Italian noblemen, and in Vienna usually for posts in the imperial military. Already in 1617 he let Bartholomew Viller, Archduke Ferdinand's confessor, know that he was to treat these requests with prudence and within the limits set by the Society's law.[93] Later he advised Lamormaini not to take his letters of recommendation too seriously. He simply

91 *Epistolae Quattuor*, 14–15.
92 Vitelleschi to Lamormaini, Aug. 2, 1625, ARSJ, Aust. 3II, ff. 641–2.
93 Vitelleschi to Viller, Dec. 2, 1617, ARSJ, Aust. 2, ff. 856–6'.

could not refuse benefactors. Lamormaini ought to use his own judgment whether or not a petition should be presented to the emperor.[94] Leading Spanish Jesuits had to spend considerable time in the waiting rooms of grandees for the sake of Italian petitioners recommended by Vitelleschi.[95] As general, Vitelleschi was also liberal in allowing Jesuits to provide services to powerful men. In 1618, for example, he permitted the confessor of Johann Schweikard von Kronberg, archbishop-elector of Mainz, to accompany the elector's nephew first on a journey to France and Spain and then to Rome, because Schweikard "had so merited of our Society . . . that nothing ought to be denied of the services which we are able to provide him."[96]

During Vitelleschi's generalate, confessors of princes were in practice chosen by the princes and their choice ratified by Jesuit authorities. Upon learning that Jean Arnoux had been summoned to serve as confessor to the young Louis XIII, Vitelleschi wrote the Jesuit on June 27, 1617, that he was to respond to the "commands and wishes of the prince" and so accept the charge. His guide was to be the Instruction of Acquaviva.[97] To Arnoux's request for instructions about his participation in secular affairs, which crossed Vitelleschi's letter in the mail, the superior general once again pointed him toward Acquaviva's Instruction.[98] But that would not be adequate.

94 Vitelleschi to Lamormaini, June 30, 1629, ibid. 4I, ff. 125–6.
95 Antonio Astrain, *Historia de la Compañia de Jesús en la Asistencia de España* 5 (Madrid, 1916): 260.
96 Vitelleschi to Reinhard Ziegler, June 30, 1618, ARSJ, Rheni Inf. 5, f. 597'.
97 ARSJ, Francia 3, f. 233.
98 Vitelleschi to Arnoux, Aug. 7, 1617, ARSJ, Francia 41I, 40–40'. Arnoux had written on July 4.

CHAPTER 2

The Bohemian Rebellion and Its Aftermath, 1618–1624

BLEAK was the outlook for the Austrian Habsburgs in the months following the Defenestration of Prague. The estates of Silesia joined the Bohemian cause in October 1618; Moravia hesitated but then, too, threw in its lot with the Bohemians the following April. Charles Emmanuel of Savoy, a rival of the Spanish Habsburgs in North Italy, helped finance the German mercenary Count Ernst of Mansfeld, who brought a small army to the aid of the rebels. At first the Austrian Habsburg camp was divided over the approach to take toward the rebellion. The elderly Emperor Matthias, who was strongly influenced by his chief minister, Cardinal Melchior Klesl, favored the way of negotiation and limited concessions. Archduke Ferdinand, who had by now won election as king of Bohemia and Hungary and was the Habsburg candidate for the imperial succession, favored a hard line, as did Archduke Maximilian, who from Innsbruck ruled the Tyrol, Vorarlberg, and the Austrian lands along the Upper Rhine. Together Ferdinand and Maximilian, without the knowledge of Matthias, engineered the arrest of Klesl, cardinal-archbishop that he was, and his sequestration in the Tyrol until he was allowed to move to Rome in 1623. Deprived of his principal political supporter and increasingly isolated, Matthias died on March 20, 1619. His death left Ferdinand effectively in charge in Vienna and made an imperial election necessary.

Fighting broke out in Bohemia and spilled over into Austria. Bohemian troops under Thurn laid siege to Vienna in early June 1619. Here Ferdinand was only saved at the last minute by Thurn's withdrawal, which was compelled by a threat to his rear; later a legend evolved surrounding the event about a "miraculous" rescue of Ferdinand that was to have an impact in the future. In August Ferdinand was able to depart for the imperial election in Frankfurt. But that month the Upper Austrian estates in Linz and the Lower Austrian estates in Vienna went over to the Bohemians. These, in turn, deposed Ferdinand as king of Bohemia on August 19 and in his place elected the youthful Calvinist Elector Frederick of the Palatinate. After initial hesitation Frederick accepted and entered Prague on October 31, 1619, as the new king of Bohemia. Meanwhile, to the east, Bethlen Gabor, prince of Transylvania, a perennial Habsburg rival for control of the portion of Hungary not occupied by the Turks, came to the aid of the rebels. This resulted in a second siege of Vienna in November. But the appearance of an old enemy behind his lines supported by a Cossack force compelled Bethlen to withdraw.

Ferdinand had not been inactive. He secured the international support that eluded Frederick. Bavaria and the Catholic League, Spain, and the papacy all came to his assistance, whereas the Protestant Union, the Dutch, and England effectively turned their backs on Frederick and the Bohemians. But the assistance Ferdinand received would make him politically dependent on both Maximilian and Spain, whose interests frequently clashed.

Despite Ferdinand's troubles, the seven imperial electors assembled in Frankfurt chose him on August 28, 1619, to succeed Matthias as Holy Roman Emperor. On his way home he concluded the Treaty of Munich with Maximilian of Bavaria. This committed Maximilian and the League to raise an army of 24,000 in his support. It also required that Ferdinand pay the League's expenses; as guarantee until payment, Maximilian was to retain Habsburg lands that he reconquered for Ferdinand. The new emperor also verbally promised to place Frederick under imperial ban and then to transfer his electoral title to Maximilian. This promise responded to a long-standing and persistently pursued goal of the Munich Wittelsbachs, and it was to have far-reaching political consequences. The Spanish ambassador in Vienna, Count Oñate, had on his own initiative promised Spanish support in the wake of the Bohemian rebellion. Philip III approved this only after heated discussions in Madrid, and Spanish troops in The Netherlands then prepared to march south into Frederick's Palatinate. King Sigismund III of Poland, Ferdinand's brother-in-law, dispatched 4,000 Cossacks, and Paul V sent regular if generally modest subsidies. Lutheran John George of Saxony also came to Ferdinand's support in March 1620, motivated by distaste for the Calvinist Palatinate, loyalty to the emperor, and promise of Upper and Lower Lusatia as a reward. Later that year, after they had received guarantees of their religious practice, the greater portion of the Lower Austrian estates accepted Ferdinand as their ruler, as opposed to the estates of Upper Austria.[1]

[1] Hans Sturmberger, *Aufstand in Böhmen: Der Beginn des Dreissigjährigen Krieges* (Munich, 1959); Dieter Albrecht, *Die auswärtige Politik Maximilians von Bayern, 1618–1635*

What about France? Both the Elector Palatine and Emperor Ferdinand II dispatched envoys to Paris at the end of 1619 to secure Louis XIII's support. There the decision was to send an embassy into the empire to attempt to mediate the dispute while assisting the Catholics without unduly strengthening the traditional Habsburg rival.[2] The French diplomats arranged the Treaty of Ulm of July 6, 1620, between the Catholic League and the Protestant Union, which committed both to desist from recourse to arms in the west of the empire but left them free to fight in the Habsburg lands. The French party then proceeded to Vienna, where their intent was to mediate between Ferdinand and Frederick. But here they received a cold shoulder, so that the unintended upshot of their efforts was to allow Maximilian and the League to proceed with their offensive in the Habsburg lands without concern about an attack from the Union in the west. Archduke Albert in The Netherlands, who was not a party to the treaty, sent Spanish troops south to seize and occupy the Palatinate lands on the left bank of the Rhine.[3] By the summer of 1620 the forces of the Catholic League and the emperor began the campaign that ended with the great victory at the White Mountain outside Prague on November 9, 1620. Meanwhile, campaigns against the Huguenots first in Béarn in late 1620 and then in the Midi in 1621 kept Louis XIII occupied.

Vitelleschi's first response to news of the Defenestration and the Jesuits' expulsion from Bohemia was to console the rector of the college in Prague, Valentino Coronio, whose exact whereabouts he did not know, for the sufferings of his dispersed community. In the "wonderful" (*mirabilem*) preservation from harm of the three government officials who had been heaved out the window, he found a sign of God's favor for the Catholic cause.[4] So there appeared what would become a recurring theme in his correspondence: God's providence looked after the Catholics and, in a special manner, Ferdinand, soon to be emperor. A letter to Viller, his confessor, referred to God's "singular" providence for Ferdinand. Vitelleschi was "deeply confident that the Divine Majesty, having begun to gladden the *respublica christiana* with the propitious guidance of events it had shown to the Serene King, would continue its initial favor," even in the present upheaval.[5] Ferdinand himself

(Göttingen, 1962), 29–44; Geoffrey Parker, ed., The *Thirty Years War*, 2nd ed. (London, 1997), 42–55.

2 Gabriel Hanotaux, "La crise européenne de 1621," *Revue des deux mondes* v, 7 (1902): 21–7.

3 Albrecht, 44–9.

4 Vitelleschi to Coronio, June 23, 1618, ARSJ, Aust. 2, f. 930.

5 Vitelleschi to Viller, Aug. 4, 1618, ibid., ff. 937–8.

possessed a profound sense of a mission to which God had called him and for which God promised his assistance.

This theme came powerfully to the fore at the time of the first siege of Vienna in June 1619. As the rebel troops under Thurn besieged the city, so Viller reported, the confessor found Ferdinand in his room praying before the crucifix. Upon being surprised by Viller, Ferdinand told him, "I have weighed the dangers that approach from all sides, and since I know of no further human aid, I asked the Lord for his help. But if it should be the will of God that I go under in this struggle, so be it." Thurn, as we have seen, withdrew at the last minute because of a Catholic victory in southern Bohemia. This sudden reversal of fortune was interpreted as another example of God's special care for Ferdinand. Later, a legend developed that Christ had spoken to Ferdinand from the crucifix, "Ferdinand, I will not desert you." Whether Viller reported these words of Christ from the cross to Vitelleschi or not, we do not know. But Vitelleschi as well as many others saw God at work in the rescue of Ferdinand from the hands of his enemies.[6]

Ferdinand desperately needed military and financial aid as he attempted to suppress the rebellion threatening to engulf him. In May 1619 Vitelleschi offered even to put up for sale the gold and silver liturgical vessels in the Society's possession, comparing his offer to that of fourth-century Ambrose of Milan, who sold off church treasures to raise money for the poor and for the redemption of captives. "Would that the Society could transform its blood into gold so that it could more generously support the Serene King in his defense of the Catholic religion." That this was not merely a rhetorical flourish was evident from a follow-up letter three months later inquiring about his offer.[7] So Vitelleschi identified Ferdinand's cause with the Jesuits. On a perhaps more realistic level, he agreed to intercede with those who were able to send greater financial help in this moment of crisis. No persons or names were mentioned, but this must have applied to the pope and cardinals.[8] So the superior general aligned himself with the efforts to secure subsidies from Rome.

Early in 1620 rumors circulated that the Turks at the behest of Frederick of the Palatinate stood on the verge of aiding the Bohemian and Hungarian rebels. Vitelleschi appealed to Arnoux in Paris to urge

[6] Vitelleschi to Viller, June 23, 1619, ibid., f. 1042. Lamormaini reported this event in his *Ferdinand II Romanorum Imperatoris Virtutes* (Vienna, 1638), 9–11, without confirming or denying the apparition. One can find a print illustrating it in Franz Christoph von Khevenhiller, *Annales Ferdinandei* 11 (Leipzig, 1726); see p. 132.

[7] Vitelleschi to Viller, June 8 and Sept. 14, 1619, ibid., ff. 1029, 1057.

[8] Vitelleschi to Viller, June 22, ibid., f. 1036.

Louis to take advantage of the French diplomatic position in Constantinople to convince the Turks to desist.[9] Shortly before this the cardinal secretary of state and papal nephew, Scipione Borghese, had instructed the nuncio in Paris, Bentivoglio, to intervene similarly with leading ministers in Paris; Vitelleschi probably worked in concert with Borghese.[10] The French initiative was successful, according to the nuncio; at any event, the Turks caused no trouble. They remained faithful to the treaty of Zsitvatorok, which they had concluded in 1606 with Archduke Matthias ending their thirteen-year war with the empire and subsequently confirmed in 1615 and 1618.[11]

Martin Becan replaced the aging Viller as Ferdinand's confessor in January 1620. Shortly afterward he found himself at odds with the Holy See over toleration of Protestants. Born in The Netherlands at Hilvarenbeek in 1563, he had taught philosophy and theology in Cologne, Würzburg, and Mainz before being called to a chair of theology in Vienna in 1614. He had published a number of significant theological works besides *The Anglican Controversy* of 1612 including *A Compendium of Scholastic Theology* that appeared in several volumes at Mainz starting in 1612. Later he dedicated to Emperor Ferdinand his popular *Handbook of the Controversies of Our Time*, which was first published at Würzburg in 1623.[12] Bad health led to his return to Mainz in August 1619. But shortly after Ferdinand's coronation as emperor that same August, Viller resigned as his confessor. A replacement was needed. The suggestion of Becan appears to have originated with Vitelleschi in response to a request from Ferdinand for a new confessor. Becan was to proceed to Vienna as soon as the emperor's summons arrived, the superior general wrote him, "since all Jesuits should be prepared to offer not only health and studies but also life to the service of the emperor."[13] Ferdinand himself twice wrote Becan, on December 18 and January 1, 1620, calling him to court as soon as possible. He arrived in early 1620.[14]

9 Vitelleschi to Arnoux, Jan. 12, 1620, ARSJ, Gallia 41I, f. 58.

10 Borghese to Bentivoglio, Nov. 28, 1619, Guido Bentivoglio, *La nunziatura de Francia del Cardinale Guido Bentivoglio: Lettere a Scipione Borghese* 3 (Florence, 1867): no. 1984: 626–7.

11 Bentivoglio to Borghese, June 3, 1620, ibid., 4 (1870): no. 2268: 255; see Johann Rainer, "Kardinal Melchior Klesl (1562–1630). Vom 'Generalreformator' zum Ausgleichspolitiker," *Römische Quartalschrift* 49 (1964): 22–7.

12 *Summa theologiae scholasticae* and *Manuale controversiarum hujus temporis*; for the publication history of both, see Carlos Sommervogel, *Bibliothèque de la Compagnie de Jésus* 1 (Brussels, 1891; rpt., Louvain, 1960): 1091–111, esp. 1100–1, 1107–11.

13 Vitelleschi to Becan, Nov. 16, 1619, cited in Bernhard Duhr, *Geschichte der Jesuiten in den Ländern deutscher Zunge* 2, 2 (Freiburg, 1913): 218.

14 Beda Dudik, "Korrespondenz Kaiser Ferdinands II und seiner erlauchten Familie mit P. Martinus Becanus und P. Wilhelm Lamormaini, kaiserl. Beichtväter S.J.," *Archiv für österreichische Geschichte* 54 (1876): 258–9.

Vitelleschi provided Becan with no instructions. In response to Becan's complaints about the many grievances and petitions that were brought to him, the superior general advised him to set aside matters that did not pertain to his office and to consult with the superior and other prudent men when the matter allowed.[15] Eventually, Vitelleschi came to consider Becan an ideal court confessor. He lauded him in July 1622 for excusing himself from negotiating on behalf of courtiers and from serving as a channel for recommendations. Would that other confessors of princes did the same.[16] Vitelleschi returned to the point later in October, when he wrote that the extraordinary nuncio Fabrizio Verospi had no reason to take offense because Becan refused to recommend his candidates for office.[17] For Vitelleschi, intervention in personal ecclesiastical or court politics was prohibited for Jesuits, but not the promotion of high policy when this concerned religion or was advocated by the papacy.

Upon Becan's return to Vienna Ferdinand began difficult negotiations with the largely Protestant estates of Lower Austria. Previously, after the outbreak of the rebellion in 1618, Rome had feared that Becan sympathized with Klesl's inclination to make concessions to the Bohemian rebels.[18] The Lower Austrian estates now refused to render Ferdinand homage as their new ruler unless he confirmed for them the concession of limited religious liberty made by his predecessors Maximilian II and Matthias. If Ferdinand granted their request, they would recognize him and withdraw from their alliance with the Bohemian, Upper Austrian, and other rebellious estates.

The emperor then dispatched his minister Maximilian von Trautmannsdorf to Rome in October 1619 to inquire about the possibility of making the concession to the Lower Austrian estates, in addition to seeking funds from Paul V. The pope told Trautmannsdorf that as supreme head of the church he could not approve such a concession, indicating at the same time in their conversation that he would act prudently.[19] Ferdinand then turned for their views to Becan and to William Lamormaini, rector of the Jesuit university in Graz, a longtime friend, and Becan's eventual successor. Johann Ulrich von Eggenberg, Ferdinand's chief minister, was dispatched to Graz to gather the opinion of Lamormaini and the Graz theologians. Lamormaini permitted the concession on two conditions: one, that there existed "an insuperable

[15] Vitelleschi to Becan, Apr. 4, 1620, ARSJ, Aust. 3I, f. 43.
[16] Vitelleschi to Becan, July 30, 1622, ibid., f. 288.
[17] Vitelleschi to Becan, Oct. 15, 1622, ibid., f. 307.
[18] Francesco Gui, *I Gesuiti e la rivoluzione boema* (Milan, 1989), 244.
[19] Ludwig von Pastor, *The History of the Popes* 26: *Leo XI and Paul V, 1605–1621*, trans. from the German (London, 1937): 361–2.

necessity and a clear future danger that should it not be made and promised, the Catholic religion would either perish or suffer much greater evils," and two, that the concession would last only as long as a state of necessity persisted.[20] But Lamormaini set the requirements for a state of necessity so high – with divine intervention possible, could one ever admit a state of necessity? – that it was nearly impossible to admit that one was at hand. On the basis of Becan's less rigid position, Ferdinand conceded toleration to the Lower Austrian Protestant nobility. A significant minority accepted and joined their Catholic counterparts in swearing fidelity to Ferdinand on July 13, 1620.[21]

Neither Ferdinand's action nor Becan's argument found favorable reception in Rome. Vitelleschi sharply criticized the concessions approved by Becan. Paul V in a personal meeting with the superior general now expressed his extreme displeasure, adding that such concessions only served to elicit further demands from the Protestants. In the future, if the situation at all allowed, the pope wanted Jesuits who were consulted on such important matters to seek the opinion of Rome before they stated their own positions. Vitelleschi seconded the pope's desire, which he considered fair and reasonable, and he hoped that divine providence would speak through his vicar. But Becan was not to reveal to anyone in Vienna, not even to Ferdinand himself, that he sought guidance from Rome.[22]

Six weeks later the superior general reported to Becan that complaints about him continued to reach Rome. He too easily accepted the exaggerations of the imperial councillors about the dangers threatening the emperor and overlooked the assistance soon to be provided by Maximilian of Bavaria. So he compromised the status of Catholicism in Lower Austria for the future. The matter was causing pain for the Society in Rome.[23]

Meanwhile, Becan sent off to Rome a paper justifying his position. He had defended similar principles earlier in his *On Keeping Faith with Heretics* of 1608. There in his support he cited the Flemish theologian Joannes Molanus (Jan Vermeulen), who in 1584 had defended the concession of toleration to the Calvinists by the Estates-General of The Netherlands in the Pacification of Ghent of 1579.[24] Becan argued that

[20] Dated April 20, 1620, ARSJ, Boh. 94, ff. 65–6′.
[21] Grete Mecenseffy, *Geschichte des Protestantismus in Österreich* (Graz, 1956), 156–7.
[22] Vitelleschi to Becan, June 20, 1620, ARSJ, Aust. 3I, ff. 67–8.
[23] Vitelleschi to Becan, Aug. 1, 1620, ibid., f. 79.
[24] *De fide haereticis servanda*; see Joseph Lecler, *Toleration and the Reformation, trans. from the French* (London, 1960), 1: 299–303. See also Becan's later *Manuale controversiarum* (Würzburg, 1623), no. 16: 479–80.

in this desperate situation Ferdinand could without sin concede toleration. In the first place, the emperor simply did not have the resources to impose any other religious settlement on the Protestants. Second, to grant toleration was to choose the lesser of two evils, a position for which he cited Thomas Aquinas. The greater evil was the continued alliance of the Lower Austrian estates with the rebels plus the exercise of their religion, which the emperor could not prevent anyway; the lesser was mere toleration. Furthermore, toleration of the Protestants helped secure the support of Lutheran John George of Saxony for the suppression of the rebellion in Bohemia; but if Ferdinand refused to agree to toleration for the Lower Austrian estates, John George would balk. Chances that Lutherans would convert to Catholicism were also better if they lived under Ferdinand's rule. Becan made a rhetorical point when he contended that Ferdinand had much greater reason for tolerating the heretics in Austria than the pope did for allowing the Jews in Rome the practice of their religion.[25]

The pope as well as cardinals, including Cardinal Bellarmine, rejected Becan's arguments, to Vitelleschi's chagrin. The general was aware of the pressures under which Becan stood.[26] Becan threatened to resign. He also sent a further explanation of his position to Vitelleschi in response to the Roman objections, especially Bellarmine's. It restricted Ferdinand's concession of toleration. The emperor did not promise the Protestant estates in Lower Austria indefinite toleration, he wrote. Indeed, if the Protestants followed their normal pattern of action, as Ferdinand himself had remarked to him, they would not hold fully to the agreement and so would provide him with a justification for withdrawing his concession. Furthermore, according to the teaching of many theologians, substantially altered circumstances liberated one from promises. In his present straitened situation, Ferdinand could grant toleration. But should he overcome his enemies and consolidate his rule, then it would be sinful for him in this new situation to continue his policy of toleration, and so he would be bound to revoke it.[27]

Vitelleschi quickly declared himself fully satisfied with Becan's explanation, and he indicated that he would make efforts to convince others of its validity. His hope was that before long Ferdinand's rule would be solidified so that he would not have to conciliate his subjects with indulgence of heresy.[28] The confessor should set aside any thought of

[25] A copy of Becan's position paper is in ARSJ, Boh. 94, ff. 80–9a'; see Alois Kroess, "Gutachten der Jesuiten am Beginn der Katholischen Generalreformation in Böhmen," *Historisches Jahrbuch* 34 (1913): 9–10.

[26] Vitelleschi to Becan, Aug. 22, 1619, ARSJ, Aust. 3I, f. 84.

[27] Undated, ARSJ, Boh. 94, ff. 69–73, printed in part in Kroess, ibid., 13, n. 1.

[28] Vitelleschi to Becan, Oct. 3, 1620, ARSJ, Aust. 3I, f. 88.

giving up the post to which he had been called by the emperor and by obedience, and to continue "to bear up in a courageous spirit, certain that whatever is done after suitable reflection and prudent counsel, would be approved by God if not by all men."[29] In fact, Ferdinand did honor his promise to the Lower Austrian estates till the end of his reign, while interpreting it narrowly.[30] No one challenged similar concessions that he made to the Silesian and Hungarian estates in 1621.[31]

On June 21, 1620, Maximilian, his veteran general Count Tilly, and 30,000 troops started off on the campaign that led them through Upper Austria, where they joined with the imperial army under Count Bucquoy, and then into Bohemia, ending with the victory at the White Mountain on November 9. One member of this multinational force was the young Frenchman René Descartes. Four Capuchins and eleven Jesuits accompanied the soldiers, among them Buslidius, Maximilian's confessor, and Drexel, his court preacher. But the predominant ecclesiastic was the charismatic Carmelite superior general Domenico à Jesu Maria. Maximilian had asked Pope Paul to send him to accompany the troops and to aid with his prayer and counsel, because only with God's help could one hope for victory over the heretics. Domenico's presence accentuated the religious and holy nature of the campaign; he saw to it that Maximilian's standard bore the image of the Blessed Mother, he distributed scapulars to the soldiers, and he preached to them.[32]

Buslidius and Drexel both kept diaries of the campaign, with entries for nearly every day.[33] Maximilian, who against his normal practice led his troops throughout the campaign, kept the two near him. Buslidius stood only one step from the young Count Fugger, and only ten from Maximilian, when a cannonball mortally wounded the count.[34] Yet the duke does not seem to have involved them in either political or military

29 Vitelleschi to Becan, Oct. 10, 1620, ibid., f. 92.

30 Robert Bireley, *Religion and Politics in the Age of the Counterreformation* (Chapel Hill, NC, 1981), 30, 45.

31 Ludwig Petry, "Politische Geschichte unter den Habsburgern," *Geschichte Schlesiens*, ed. Ludwig Petry and J. Joachim Menzel, 2: *Die Habsburgerzeit, 1526–1740* (Darmstadt, 1973): 60, 74–7. For Hungary, see Mecenseffy, 150–60. That Ferdinand consulted with Becan on Hungary is evident from his note to the confessor of Feb. 25, 1621, Dudik, ibid., 259–60, that he would make no decision until he spoke with him.

32 Dieter Albrecht, *Maximilian I. von Bayern (1573–1651)* (Munich, 1998), 523, 528; for an extensive study of the role of Domenico à Jesu Maria in the campaign and subsequent Battle of the White Mountain, see Olivier Chaline, *La bataille de la Montagne Blanche: un mystique chez les guerriers* (Paris, 1999).

33 These were published by Sigmund Riezler, ed., "Kriegstagebücher aus dem ligistischen Hauptquartier 1620," *Abhandlungen der Phil.-Hist. Klasse der Bayerischen Akademie der Wissenschaften München* 23, 1 (Munich, 1906): 77–210.

34 Buslidius, Oct. 31, Riezler, 131–2.

decision making. They provided him with regular Mass and also ministered to the troops and camp followers. Their diaries communicate the horror, brutality, and often the religious fanaticism of the war. The imperial troops outdid Maximilian's in terms of cruelty. On September 27 they seized the town of Brahatz, proceeding to slaughter up to two thousand men and women, sparing only forty.[35] Soldiers regularly set fire to peasants' farms and dwellings, often in retaliation for peasants' attacks on soldiers. At one point Maximilian ordered that sixteen soldiers be hanged for torching villages.[36] But most devastating of all during this campaign was the plague, or as it was called, "the Hungarian fever." Ten to twelve thousand of the thirty thousand soldiers fell victim to it. Buslidius reported already on July 6 that five hundred soldiers lay sick in barns near Petersworth.[37] The diaries' descriptions remind us that neither Grimmelshausen in *Simplicissimus* nor Callot in his "Miseries of War" series of drawings exaggerated. Drexel lamented the horrors of war. "War is the attractive face put on all hardship and suffering," he wrote, but he showed no sympathy for the suffering of the heretical enemy.[38]

The decisive battle of the White Mountain was fought on November 9, 1620, just outside Prague. With his call for confidence in God, Domenico à Jesu Maria confirmed the decision to attack made by Maximilian and the generals, and he blessed the League standards.[39] The Catholic forces won a major victory, retook Prague, and soon Ferdinand began to consolidate his hold on Bohemia. Maximilian ruled provisionally in Upper Austria, holding the territory as surety for Ferdinand's payment of his military costs, according to the Munich Treaty. Frederick fled westward and eventually took refuge in the Dutch Republic. Vitelleschi congratulated Maximilian effusively on his victory for the "universal Christian commonwealth." Prayers to the "Lord of Hosts" had not been in vain.[40] Later he recognized with enthusiastic gratitude how the Society was now to share in the victory. "That divine Spirit who moved Your Highness to war, strengthened you for battle, and made you superior on the field of battle, at the same time taught and moved you to desire this fruit of military victory." The fruit was the canonization of Ignatius Loyola. As a reward for his victory, Maximilian had determined to ask of the

35 Drexel, Sept. 27, ibid., 168.
36 Ibid., 93.
37 Ibid., 84, 109.
38 Ibid., Sept. 10, 161. "Bellum pulcherrima est facies calamitatum et aerumnarum omnium." The sense seems to be that a romanticized view of war covers over its terrible misery and suffering.
39 Chaline, 231–50.
40 Vitelleschi to Maximilian, Dec. 12, 1620, ARSJ, Germ. Sup. 4, ff. 339–9'.

new Pope Gregory XV the raising of Ignatius into the ranks of the saints. The Jesuits had long aimed at this goal, which the previous pope, Paul V, had hesitated to grant. Now the Society, "already bound to Maximilian and Bavaria by so many titles, would consider itself elevated to a more noble and holy life, by him from whom it received its parent as a saint."[41]

But soon a problem threatened to cloud Vitelleschi's relationship with Munich. A jubilant reception greeted the duke upon his return to his residential city; it featured a panegyric delivered by Jacob Keller that quickly appeared in print. But soon a pseudonymous account of the Bohemian campaign, *On the Battle of Prague and the City's Surrender*, was published.[42] Without containing any criticism of Maximilian, it attributed the victory chiefly to the imperial general Bucquoy. Shortly afterward it came out that the author was none other than Henry Fitzsimons, an Irish Jesuit who served as confessor to Bucquoy and who accompanied him throughout the campaign. Maximilian considered himself insulted. Letters flew from Jesuits in Munich to Rome. Vitelleschi investigated, and he determined that Fitzsimons had published his account without observing the normal procedure for Jesuit internal censorship. Fitzsimons received a public penance for his conduct.

But this outcome did not satisfy Maximilian, or at least the Jesuits at court. Keller, who often resorted to gross and offensive language, responded to Fitzsimons anonymously.[43] He claimed for Maximilian the principal credit for the success of the campaign and the victory at the White Mountain, and he viciously attacked the author of *On the Battle of Prague* without mentioning his name. Now the Austrian provincial in his turn complained in Rome. The provincial in Munich then admitted that Keller had authored the offensive tract. Vitelleschi responded that he had never seen one Jesuit attack another in print so harshly as Keller had Fitzsimons. The superior general imposed a penance on Keller and then quietly removed him from his position as rector of the college in Munich, a post to which he returned in 1626.[44] Maximilian was not to find out about the penance.[45] In the future Vitelleschi would frequently

41 Vitelleschi to Maximilian, Feb. 5, 1621, Germ. 113I, ff. 7–8.

42 *De Praelio Pragensi Pragaeque Ditione*. The pseudonym was Candido Eblano (Eblana is Dublin). A second, expanded edition appeared in Vienna in 1621, under a different title, with the author given as Constantius Peregrinus. See Duhr 2, 2: 406–7. Large extracts from this short book have been published under the title "Diary of the Bohemian War of 1620," in Henry Fitzsimons, *Words of Comfort to Persecuted Catholics, With a Sketch of His Life*, ed. Edmund Hogan, S.J. (Dublin, 1881).

43 *Constantius Peregrinus castigatus*. The place of publication was given as Bruges.

44 Duhr 2, 2: 408–10.

45 Vitelleschi to Christoph Grenzinus (provincial), Mar. 11, 1622, ARSJ, Germ. Sup. 5, f. 242'.

have to deal with political pieces written by Jesuits pseudonymously or anonymously.

In France, as we have seen, Jean Arnoux assumed the office of confessor to the sixteen-year-old Louis XIII in May 1617, replacing Coton, who had been increasingly considered too favorable to Marie de Medici and to Spain. A genuine piety characterized the young Louis. He attended Mass and prayed daily, made a regular confession, and maintained a high standard of personal morality. The nuncio Bentivoglio reported that according to Luynes, the favorite, Louis had chosen the Jesuit Arnoux over non-Jesuit candidates for the post of confessor to show that his alleged dissatisfaction with Coton did not carry over to the whole Society.[46] Vitelleschi congratulated Luynes on his position with the king, about which Arnoux had informed him, and requested that he favor the work of the Society. Luynes had already begun to do so by supporting the restoration of the College of Clermont.[47] Vitelleschi diligently cultivated contact with Jesuit supporters at court in France. A year later the superior general congratulated both Cardinal de La Rochefoucauld on his appointment as royal almoner and to a place on the king's council[48] and Cardinal de Retz, bishop of Paris, on his appointment as president of the council. The second measure the nuncio attributed in part to Arnoux, and, he reported, it left the Huguenots gnashing their teeth.[49]

Two matters especially claimed Arnoux's concern as confessor. First, he pursued a satisfactory rapprochement between Louis and his mother. The relationship between king and queen-mother complicated French politics until her death in 1642, and a number of Jesuits were involved in the many attempts to resolve the differences between the two. Second, he advocated a campaign against the Huguenots, not to compel them to convert but to reduce their power within France, where as Richelieu later put it, they constituted "a state within a state." But other matters also received his attention. After the Bohemian rebellion Arnoux made an effort to drum up support for the emperor in France, where, the Venetian ambassador reported in late August 1618, the court generally favored Ferdinand.[50] Then there was the consummation of the marriage

[46] Bentivoglio to Borghese, May 16, 1617, Bentivoglio 1: no. 245: 238–9.
[47] Vitelleschi to Luynes, Nov. 1617, ARSJ, Gallia 46I, ff. 46–6'.
[48] Vitelleschi to La Rochefoucauld, Oct. 8, 1618, ibid., f. 54.
[49] Vitelleschi to Retz, Nov. 12, 1618, ibid., ff. 54'–5; Bentivoglio to Borghese, Sept. 25, 1618, Bentivoglio 3: no. 1574: 27.
[50] Dispatch of Angelo Contarini, Aug. 30, 1618, *Relazioni di ambasciatori Veneti al Senato*, ed. Luigi Firpo, 6: *Francia, 1600–1656* (Turin, 1978): 688.

between the young Louis and Anne. This took on political importance because until consummation took place dissolution of the marriage remained a possibility with profound implications for the relationship with Spain. So we find Arnoux regularly informing the nuncio and the Spanish ambassador of the marital situation, until consummation was accomplished in early 1619.[51]

In July 1617, shortly after he assumed office, Arnoux preached a sermon at Fontainebleau at the king's request. He analyzed and criticized the Huguenot profession of faith. Soon published as *The Confession of Faith of the Ministers Convicted of Nullity by Their Own Bible*,[52] the sermon provoked the Huguenot response *Flights and Evasions of Mister Arnoux the Jesuit* of 1618, which under the later title *Shield of the Faith, or Defense of the Confession of Faith of the Reformed Churches of France, against the Objections of Mister Arnoux the Jesuit*, greatly expanded and signed by the four ministers of Charenton, became a standard Huguenot controversial work.[53] On All Saints Day, November 1, 1617, Arnoux preached a "truly apostolic" sermon, according to Bentivoglio, and then he revealed in confidence to the nuncio that the king considered the Huguenots his greatest enemy. The nuncio suggested that Borghese, while remaining in generalities, speak the praises of Arnoux, "a man of great discretion and prudence," to Vitelleschi and to the pope.[54] Subsequently a papal benediction and a letter from Vitelleschi greatly consoled the confessor.[55]

Yet the Jesuits wanted to avoid rabble-rousing sermons against the Huguenots. A Jesuit preacher in Chalons provoked Huguenot complaints to parlement with a vicious attack on them as "wolves in sheep's clothing." Reports of his sermon upset the Paris Jesuits and prompted Bentivoglio to suggest to Borghese that he alert Vitelleschi about the matter. Conduct of this type only stirred up the Jesuits' enemies in France, where the Society's "venial sins were counted as mortal."[56] Vitelleschi then took up a task that was to be a frequent one for him, instructing Jesuits to moderate their polemical language. Twice he wrote, at the

51 See, for example, Bentivolgio to Borghese, Apr. 25, 1618, Bentivoglio 2: no. 1080: 341; on consummation, Bentiviglio to Borghese, Jan. 30, 1619, ibid., no. 1545: 169.

52 *La confession de foys des ministres convainçu de nullité par leur propre bible.*

53 *Fuites et évasions du sieur Arnoux Jésuite; Bouclier de la foy, ou, défense de la confession de foi des Eglises Réformées du Royaume de France: contre les objections du Sr. Arnoux, Jésuite;* Bentivoglio to Borghese, July 19, 1617, Bentivoglio 1: no. 416: 361–3; Henri Fouqueray, *Histoire de la Compagnie de Jésus en France* 3 (Paris, 1922): 435.

54 Bentivoglio to Borghese, Nov. 8, 1617, ibid., 2: no. 727: 64–5.

55 Bentivoglio to Borghese, Jan. 17, 1618, ibid., 2: no. 888: 186.

56 Bentivoglio to Borghese, Aug. 2, 1617, ibid., 1: no. 471: 405.

behest of Borghese, to the French provincial superiors that they see to it that their subjects avoid inflammatory language. It only stirred unrest and disorder and angered the Society's enemies.[57]

Arnoux along with his fellow Jesuits Gaspar de Séguiran and the confessor of Marie de Medici, Jean Suffren – both of whom would in turn succeed Arnoux – Armand du Plessis de Richelieu, then Bishop of Luçon and a confidant of Marie, and Pierre de Bérulle, superior of the French Oratory, all participated in the efforts at an understanding between Louis and Marie, who resented those around her son and especially Luynes. In mid-September 1618 Arnoux journeyed to Blois and successfully brokered a settlement.[58] But it did not last. Arnoux himself strongly opposed a resort to arms in order to bring the queen-mother and her supporters to heel, and he angered Luynes by supporting her desire to return to the royal court. Bentivoglio reported that Arnoux showed "such a great passion in matters of the queen."[59] At one point Arnoux preached before the king that it would be a terrible scandal for Louis to make war on his mother.[60] Luynes and Arnoux were starting to fall out. This time Richelieu was called in to mediate, and he negotiated the Treaty of Angoulême on April 30, 1619, between the two factions. But this agreement did not endure either, and gradually the two parties drifted toward civil war as more of the *grands* of the realm went over to Marie's camp. Finally it did come to a test of arms. At the short battle of Ponts-de-Cé, a bridge over the Loire, on August 7, 1620, the forces of Louis roundly defeated those of his mother. The upshot was the renewed acceptance of the terms of Angoulême by both sides and peace between the two factions. The victory also consolidated the position of Luynes as the power within the government.[61]

While the queen-mother and the queen returned to Paris, the king and Arnoux marched to the southwest to restore the Catholic Church and assert royal authority in Béarn in the southwest corner of France, the homeland of the Bourbons and a Huguenot stronghold. Henry IV at the time of his absolution had promised to reestablish Catholic worship there and to restore to the church the lands seized by the Huguenots, but he hesitated to take effective action. Louis now fulfilled his father's promise, though he also compensated from the royal treasury the Huguenot holders of

[57] Borghese to Bentivoglio, Aug. 25 and Sept. 3, 1617, ibid., no. 609: 515–16, and no. 632: 570. I have not been able to find either of the letters of Vitelleschi to which Borghese refers.

[58] Bentivoglio to Borghese, Sept. 25, 1618, ibid., 3: no. 1578: 30–1.

[59] Bentivoglio to Borghese, Mar. 6, and Sept. 22, 1619, Tours, ibid. no. 1605: 234–5 and no. 1908: 535–6.

[60] A. Lloyd Moote, *Louis XIII, the Just* (Berkeley, 1989), 110.

[61] Hanotaux, 5.

the lands, and he fully incorporated Béarn into the kingdom of France. He was back in Paris by November 7.[62] Vitelleschi expressed his delight at the results of the expedition to Béarn.[63] Bentivoglio reported Luynes's zeal against the Huguenots. The minister, two cardinals informed him, had taken a vow before Arnoux "to bring it about through all possible ways that this spring the king undertake some grand enterprise of importance against the heretics."[64]

While the struggle between Louis and his mother and the campaign against the Huguenots occupied France, the conflict in Bohemia expanded. Frederick of the Palatinate and Ferdinand both looked to Paris for support. Frederick received short shrift, even though he appealed to a French tradition of aid to dissident German Protestant princes. France refused to recognize him as king of Bohemia.[65] From mid-November 1619 until early the next January an imperial emissary, Count Wratislaw von Fürstenberger, argued the case for French aid to Ferdinand in a series of audiences with the king himself. He emphasized Catholic solidarity with France as well as the threat to monarchy posed by the rebels. Arnoux, he reported home on November 22, supported his case.[66] The confessor followed this up with a vigorous sermon on Christmas Eve stressing Louis's duty to aid the persecuted Bohemian Catholics. By then a decision probably had been made.[67] Louis did in fact promise military aid to the emperor, and a small army actually assembled.[68] Bentivoglio reported the king's commitment, but he noted the gap between promising and acting. If the French sent help to the emperor, he wrote, it would be "a manifest miracle of the providence of God."[69] No troops ever crossed the border. There was opposition at court to assistance to the emperor. What the French really wanted, Bentivoglio thought correctly, was to arbitrate the dispute and so enhance their own prestige. Furthermore, so long as the conflict between the king and queen-mother carried on, the French government could not act effectively.[70] As we have seen, Bentivoglio and Arnoux did secure French diplomatic intervention in Constantinople.

62 Ibid., 496–8.
63 Vitelleschi to Arnoux, Dec. 7, 1620, ARSJ, Francia 4, f. 47'.
64 Bentivoglio to Borghese, Nov. 18, 1620, Bentivoglio 4: no. 2557: 477–8.
65 Hanotaux, 20, 23–4, 29.
66 BA 1, 1: 490.
67 Victor-Louis Tapié, *La politique étrangère de la France et la début de la Guerre de trente ans (1616–1621)* (Paris, 1934), 430.
68 Albrecht, *Auswärtige Politik*, 45.
69 Bentivoglio to Borghese, Jan. 29, 1620, Bentivoglio 4: no. 2095: 110–11.
70 Bentivoglio to Borghese, Jan. 2, Feb. 26, July 1, 1620, ibid., no. 2042: 66–7, no. 2153: 146–7, and no. 2558: 301–3.

The French eventually undertook the dispatch of the embassy to Germany already mentioned with the purpose of mediating the dispute in such a way that Catholicism did not suffer, the emperor's position was not notably strengthened, and the prestige of the King of France increased. The resultant Treaty of Ulm contributed to Ferdinand's victory at White Mountain and to an imperial recovery beyond French desires or foresight.

Shortly after the king's return from the successful expedition to Béarn, unrest percolated again among the Huguenots in the southwest. A Huguenot assembly met at La Rochelle on December 25, 1620, and it became increasingly threatening despite rifts within its ranks. The Duke de Rohan assumed its leadership. Hostilities broke out in late February.

Luynes now determined to quell the rebellion through a campaign headed by the king. He received encouragement from the new, more militant Ludovisi pope, Gregory XV, who had emerged from the conclave on February 9. A papal brief of March 13, 1621, was addressed to Arnoux, beseeching him to persuade and to counsel the king to "make war on the heretics for the glory of God and the greater peace of his kingdom; because we have such great confidence in the divine mercy that he [the king] will carry off the victory, which we promise to him, for we believe firmly that with regard to merit before the Divine Majesty and in the church, he will equal the great kings, his ancestors." Louis was called to respond "to the inspiration that God had sent him and ardently to embrace the enterprise."[71] Briefs of Gregory to Louis himself in March and again in July used similar words. "Follow God who fights with you," the pope wrote, "so that you who are now seen as the bolt of war and the shield of peace may soon be held to be the praise of Israel and the glory of the whole earth."[72] The language conjured up not only a religious but a holy war, that is, one fought at God's behest and with promise of his support. Vitelleschi informed Louis that he had requested all the provinces of the Society to support the king's efforts against the heretics, especially with prayers to the "Lord of Hosts."[73]

71 Gregory XV to Arnoux, Mar. 13, 1621, cited in J.M. Prat, *Recherches historiques et critiques sur la Compagnie de Jésus en France du temps du P. Coton, 1564–1626* 4: 299, n. 1; see also Klaus Jaitner, ed., *Die Hauptinstruktionen Gregors XV* (Tübingen, 1997) 2: 550, n. 30.

72 Citation from Gregory XV to Louis XIII, July 12, 1621, BN, Collection Dupuy 92, f. 192 (published in French translation in the *Mercure français* for 1621 [Paris, 1622], 704–8, but misdated Sept. 14); see also Jaitner 2: 549, n. 28.

For the brief of Mar. 13 to Louis XIII, see Jaitner 2: 550, n. 30; and the Instruction for the new nuncio to France, Ottavio Corsini, Apr. 4, 1621, ibid., no. 4: 535–74, who was encouraged to work with Arnoux, p. 545.

73 Vitelleschi to Louis XIII, July 17, 1621, BN, Manuscrit français 18016, ff. 348–9; Vitelleschi to all Jesuit provincials, July 17, 1621, Prat 5: 423–4.

But Louis did not share the vision of a holy war. Distasteful as the Reformed religion was to him and as desirous of the peaceful conversion of the Huguenots as he was, Louis respected the rights granted them by the Edict of Nantes. His goal on the expedition was to quell rebellion and to force the Huguenots to recognize Catholic rights in areas they controlled.[74] Huguenot strongholds fell to the sieges of the royal army. Vitelleschi, reflecting the sentiments of Arnoux's letter of August 6, wrote that the surrender of the rebel stronghold of Clérac compelled even those who rejected the role of providence in the campaign to recognize the "Finger of God" at work.[75] Louis provided an inspiring example, he added, for other Christian princes, "that they with a similar zeal and effort propagate the Catholic religion and do their part for the extinction of heresy."[76] But then Louis began, against the advice of his veteran captains, the siege of Montauban, a fortified Huguenot city of about 20,000. The city held out obstinately. Louis scaled the effort back from a siege to a blockade and departed with his entourage for Toulouse, where he arrived on November 15. There he laid the cornerstone for the new Jesuit church on November 23, 1621.[77] The next day Arnoux was dismissed from office.

The confessor himself has left an account of events. On the morning of November 24 Arnoux had assisted at Mass with the king, who spoke with him in a friendly fashion. The confessor was then asked to meet with Luynes within an hour. There the chief minister instructed him that he was not to follow the court to Grenades but to remain in Toulouse. Nor should he make any effort to bid adieu to the king because this would cause the monarch pain. Arnoux responded, according to his account, that he had not sought the position of confessor and that he was ready to give it up, as God willed. But he asked Luynes for some explanation. To this Luynes responded "that you do not love me and that you have some design against me, about which you have treated with the king to my prejudice, and that you are resolved to carry on." Luynes recounted that he had told the king of his decision no longer to confess to Arnoux, and Louis seeing that he was fixed in his purpose and desiring to have the same confessor as his minister, determined that he would seek another confessor too. The king then asked Luynes to notify Arnoux of the decision and to make it clear to him that Louis was in no way dissatisfied with his service. Arnoux's

74 Moote, 120–2, 124.
75 Vitelleschi to Arnoux, Sept. 7, 1621, ARSJ, Francia 4, f. 76′.
76 Vitelleschi to Arnoux, Sept. 4, 1621, ibid., f. 76.
77 Fouqueray 3: 465–9.

request for a farewell interview with the king was not granted.[78] In a letter to Luynes shortly afterward, Arnoux maintained that he only sinned through an excess of affection for the favorite and that his concern for the favorite's true interest would eventually be borne out. But he harbored no intention now of making a further case for himself, because he obviously could no longer be spiritually useful to Luynes, and an attempt to justify his actions in detail would be unworthy of one who sought only God.[79]

Why did Luynes, and the king, dismiss Arnoux as confessor? When he undertook the office, Arnoux had entered a tangled political situation, especially in light of the conflict between Louis and his mother. Coton's sympathy for Marie and his inclination toward Spain had cost him his position. We have seen Luynes's unhappiness with Arnoux's more sympathetic stance toward Marie during the tense period from 1618 to 1620. Arnoux seems then to have pushed the religious issue too hard; that caused his downfall.

Arnoux was a vigorous personality and forthright. At his behest Luynes had reportedly vowed to promote the expedition against the Huguenots. Aid to the emperor and the Catholic cause in Germany had been part of Arnoux's agenda, and shortly after his coronation Gregory XV urged Louis in this direction with a brief of March 6, 1621, when Ferdinand had already emerged from his difficulties much strengthened.[80] The militant tone of Gregory XV's briefs struck a new note with their call to a holy war; Arnoux took it up, and Vitelleschi echoed it. Furthermore, that spring Arnoux asked Louis to intervene in the negotiations between the Spanish and the Dutch as the Twelve Years Truce came to an end, to ensure that the Dutch Catholics obtained liberty to practice their faith.[81] Later Vitelleschi pressed Arnoux to intercede on behalf of the Catholics in the Valtelline. This strategically crucial valley in the Swiss Alps along "the Spanish Road" helped connect Milan with the German Habsburg lands across the mountains and then with The Netherlands. Venice, Savoy, and the Protestant Swiss Grey Leagues all hoped for French assistance to dislodge the Spaniards.[82] From the start of his pontificate Gregory XV even contemplated an attack on Geneva itself, the Calvinist stronghold. For this project he would have liked active

[78] Printed in Prat 4: 302–5 and cited in Fouqueray 3: 469–71. According to Prat, a copy of this account is in the Bibliothèque de Carpentras, among the papers of the savant Nicole de Peiresc, vol. 30, p. 88ff. The account is in the third person.

[79] Arnoux to Luynes, late Nov. 1621, Eugène Griselle, *Louis XIII et Richelieu: Lettres et pièces diplomatiques* (Paris, 1911; rpt. Geneva, 1974), 16–17.

[80] Jaitner 2: 551; see also the Instruction for Corsini, Apr. 4, 1621, ibid., 551–2.

[81] Vitelleschi to Arnoux, Feb. 15, 1621, ARSJ, Francia 4, f. 54.

[82] Vitelleschi to Arnoux, June 29, 1621, ibid., f. 69.

French support, but he only asked that Louis overlook the French commitment to the defense of Geneva and not interfere with the attack that Charles Emmanuel, the duke of Savoy, was planning with the pope. Sent as an extraordinary nuncio to gain support at the French court for the enterprise, which the pope compared to the Crusades of old, the Barnabite Father Tobia Corona was instructed to look to Arnoux for assistance. He remained with the court from September 14 to December 15, so he was there arguing his case at the time of Arnoux's dismissal. Luynes, while in favor of the recatholization of Geneva, refused to acquiesce in any project that would increase the power of the duke of Savoy.[83]

Thus increasing demands were put to the king for a policy dictated by religious issues and often submitted as requirements of conscience to wage a holy war. Eventually, this became too much for Luynes, even though he generally sympathized with a policy that fostered church interests. According to the Venetian ambassador, an accommodation had been worked out with the city of Montauban, which would have made some concessions to the Huguenots – for example, that the king would agree to pay their soldiers, but Arnoux convinced Louis not to accept it.[84] The siege then failed. Luynes now advocated a more moderate religious policy. Louis told his friend Marshall François de Bassompierre that he had discussed complaints and doubts that he had about Luynes's policy with Arnoux. Bassompierre then informed Luynes of Louis's conversations about him with the confessor.[85] This would explain Luynes's words to Arnoux that the confessor did not love him and was designing against him. Luynes then confronted the king, who had to choose between his minister or his confessor. He chose Luynes, and so Arnoux had to go. His successor, Gaspar de Séguiran, a Jesuit of a different mind than Arnoux, fit this scenario.

Vitelleschi had sent mixed signals, or at least subtle ones, to Arnoux as confessor. He urged or supported initiatives on behalf of politico-religious issues, that is, those related to action against Protestants. But in interpreting Acquaviva's Instruction for Arnoux, he tended to be simply unclear. Following Arnoux's appointment, he reminded the confessor that in a recent letter to the French provincials he had prohibited involvement in the affairs of states or princes.[86] Arnoux's activities quickly

[83] Instruction for P. Tobia Corona, extraordinary nuncio to Savoy and France, July 16, 1621, Jaitner 2: no. 14: 741–60, esp. 759; Gregory XV to Louis XIII, July 16, 1621, ibid., 758, n. 22; ibid., 1: 269; Vitelleschi to Arnoux, Oct. 15, 1621, ARSJ, Francia 4, f. 80.

[84] Fouqueray 3: 473; see also François de Bassompierre, *Journal de ma vie: Mémoires du Maréchal de Bassompierre* 2 (Paris, 1873): 336–7.

[85] Bassompierre, 383–8.

[86] Vitelleschi to Arnoux, Oct. 3, 1617, ARSJ, Francia 3, f. 240′. I have not been able to find the letter to the French provincials.

became a matter of concern to Étienne Binet, superior of the Jesuit residence in Paris where, the confessor lived. In response to Binet's query about what constituted "reason of state" and so was closed to the confessor's activity, Vitelleschi conceded that in practice there was nothing "that did not seem to be able to be referred to a matter of conscience" and so could be taken up by the confessor. Here prudence came into play. Because an action was permitted, one did not have to perform it. Referring to the pertinent canon of the Seventh General Congregation, Vitelleschi then distinguished between the general and the particular. To the confessor was permitted the general – for example, to respond to a ruler's query about the justice or injustice of a war – but not the particular, to argue for or against a war or to deal with the time, place, or method of the war.[87] In other words, it seems, the confessor should deal with the properly moral issue of a war, whether it was just or not, but not with its politics. But in reality the two often overlapped.

The following fall of 1618, at the time of Arnoux's mission to the queen mother, Vitelleschi clearly stated for Binet that neither it nor the parallel mission of Séguiran was foreign to the Jesuit Constitutions.[88] But Arnoux should not take the title of a "councillor" of the king, for which, apparently, he had asked Binet.[89] Before this, on October 8, 1618, Vitelleschi had advised Arnoux to attend only to matters in accord with the Society's spirit and Institute and to avoid mingling in dangerous affairs.[90] In February 1620, when the emperor pressed his case for assistance from France, there was talk of a Jesuit coming to Paris on his behalf. The mission had been canceled, according to Vitelleschi, but not because such a venture was forbidden to a Jesuit. "In protecting religion against the common enemies of piety, the labor of no one could be censured."[91] This seemed to open the doors wide to nearly any political activity on behalf of religion. It was then that Vitelleschi urged Arnoux to intervene with the king of France on behalf of the Dutch Catholics and the Catholics in the Valtelline, though in the latter case he realized that he was approaching issues of state.[92]

In the course of 1621, as Louis launched his campaign against the Huguenots with the pope's and the superior general's enthusiastic encouragement, Vitelleschi tightened the reins on Arnoux. He gently

87 Vitelleschi to Binet, Apr. 20, 1618, ibid., f. 262.
88 Vitelleschi to Binet, Oct. 29, 1618, ibid., f. 276.
89 Vitelleschi to Binet, Jan. 20, 1620, ibid., f. 286'.
90 Vitelleschi to Arnoux, Oct. 8, 1618, ibid., f. 275.
91 Vitelleschi to Arnoux, Feb. 7, 1620, ibid., Francia 4, f. 20.
92 Vitelleschi to Arnoux, Feb. 25 and June 29, 1621, ibid., ff. 54, 69.

refused his request to reside at court – allegedly this would benefit his health and his work – because it would only provide fodder for those who accused him of meddling in matters of state,[93] and they apparently were not few even within the Society. Arnoux's request for a dispensation, either public or secret, to deal with political matters, was denied, because this would fly directly in the face of the Society's policy, would implicate it in many quarrels, and in the long run do harm to the Society and to the common good.[94] Arnoux pressed the issue. On June 8, 1621, Vitelleschi agreed once again that many matters of state were also affairs of conscience and thus pertained to the confessor's direction of a soul. These were not prohibited. But Vitelleschi cautioned, perhaps sensing what would come, that "given this opening, zeal sometimes is carried too far." He warned Arnoux to be careful amidst the multiplicity of the affairs in which he took part lest he give any handle to those who were hostile. He did trust Arnoux's prudence, but he closed with another warning to avoid any activity prohibited by the Society.[95]

Vitelleschi generally showed more restraint in requesting favors in Paris than in Vienna for friends and benefactors of the Society, usually Italians, but he asked Arnoux at different times to put in a good word with the king for his two nephews, Alessandro and Francesco, who traveled to Paris on undetermined business.[96]

The dismissal of Arnoux came as a surprise to Vitelleschi, but not apparently to Bentivoglio, now a cardinal in Rome. He expressed agreement with his correspondent, the French secretary of state for foreign affairs, the marquis of Puysieux, that "it would be much better for the Society and for the Fathers themselves who are confessors, that they do not exceed the limits of their vocation."[97] Yet Gregory XV had urged Arnoux on. The superior general consoled Arnoux, encouraging him to see his removal from court in the eyes of eternity and to indicate to the king that he remained ready to serve him.[98]

The new confessor chosen by Louis was Gaspar de Séguiran, a well-known preacher who had helped mediate differences between Louis and his mother. Already on November 27 Luynes notified him of the king's choice and requested that he make haste to join the court. It was

93 Vitelleschi to Arnoux, Mar. 22, 1621, ibid., f. 60.
94 Vitelleschi to Arnoux, May 1, 1621, Francia 41I, f. 64.
95 Vitelleschi to Arnoux, June 8, 1621, Francia 4, f. 65.
96 Vitelleschi to Arnoux, May 21, 1619, and May 4, 1621, ibid., 3, f. 309, and 4, 63'.
97 Cardinal Bentivoglio to Pierre Brülart de Puysieux, Rome, Jan. 14, 1622, Prat 5: 439–40.
98 Vitelleschi to Arnoux, Dec. 30, 1621, ARSJ, Francia 4, f. 88.

a toilsome burden to which God called him, the favorite added, but one that bore spiritual fruit. He realized that the change in confessors came as a surprise to many, but it was the king's will. Both the king and he himself saw the dismissal of Arnoux as an individual matter that did not reflect on the Society for which he and the king felt great affection.[99] Vitelleschi congratulated Séguiran on his appointment and expressed his satisfaction to Louis that the king once again chose his confessor from the Society. He recognized the delicacy of the task that Séguiran took on, and he hoped that he and the new confessor would communicate regularly with mutual openness and frankness.[100] Séguiran was in camp with Louis by Christmas. By that time death had removed Luynes from the scene; he died on December 15. The Peace of Montpelier of October 20, 1622, ended Huguenot rebellion for the time being and once again regulated their status.

Shortly after Séguiran took office, the provincial superior of Paris, Ignatius Armand, communicated to him several guidelines for the conduct of his office that allegedly originated with the king himself.[101] We do not have these guidelines, but presumably they were incorporated into the norms for the French royal confessor that were drawn up by the provincial congregation of 1622, were modified in Rome, and then, with Vitelleschi's approval, were given to Séguiran. The norms explicitly modified the Instruction for Confessors of Princes for the case of the French king. Of the six norms, three dealt with the confessor's manner of life – for example, that because of his journeys with the court he was allowed to administer his own funds. The other three appeared to represent a mild setback for those at the congregation who, like Arnoux, favored a more active role for the confessor in politics. Whenever matters of conscience and affairs of state seemed to be so conjoined that they did not admit of separation, the first stipulated, the confessor could continue to function in office as the Seventh General Congregation allowed, but he was to be wary of overstepping the bounds set by the Society. Should the king himself press the confessor to handle political matters, he should do the best he could to excuse himself in the hope that the king would recognize that the Society prohibited such activity and that the confessor's noninvolvement best served the long-term interest of the Society and the king. Strangely, the final norm prescribed that the Instruction for Confessors of Princes was not to be shown to the French

99 Luynes to Séguiran, Nerac, Nov. 27, 1621, Griselle, 18–19.
100 Vitelleschi to Séguiran, Jan. 28, 1622, ARSJ, Francia 4, f. 90'; Vitelleschi to Louis XIII, Feb. 9, 1622, ARSJ, Epist. Gen. 2, f. 221'.
101 Vitelleschi to Ignatius Armand (provincial), Feb. 8, 1622, ARSJ, Francia 4, f. 91.

king as it was to other princes.[102] Perhaps the reason for this was its insistence on the confessor's access to remonstrate with the king about abuses in government or shortcomings in policy. We can only surmise that the guidelines attributed to the king were also somehow behind this provision.

But the last word had not yet been heard about Arnoux's dismissal. Letters were coming to Rome, Vitelleschi wrote Séguiran, asserting that the king's displeasure with Arnoux not the initiative of Luynes forced the removal of the confessor and that many Jesuits, including the superior general, were relieved to see him go. Séguiran was frequently mentioned as the source of these rumors. Vitelleschi disputed them. He cited in substance Arnoux's own account of his dismissal, which "many" important Jesuits had sent to Rome. Obviously, the Paris Jesuits were divided over Arnoux. Other accusations about him reached Rome, especially that he meddled in affairs of state. Vitelleschi defended Arnoux. He and Father Armand had investigated these charges, and there was no substance to them. Experience will teach you, he advised Séguiran, "how many affairs of state are intertwined with the king's conscience, so that the confessor cannot remain silent, and that the preeminent charge leveled against princely confessors by those who dissented from their counsel, was that they involved themselves in affairs of state." Vitelleschi asked Séguiran to clear Arnoux as best he could, especially with the king.[103]

Still this was not the end. Arnoux wanted to return to Paris to preach in the city. But according to the former confessor, Séguiran stood in the way of this. For his part, Séguiran asserted that he only passed on the king's will. Vitelleschi asked the provincial Armand to try to clear up the dissension between the two men, which was turning into a public scandal, and if possible to secure an audience with the king himself to determine his desire in the matter. Vitelleschi even drew up a letter for the king, which he asked Armand to deliver at his audience.[104] But the superior general subsequently acquiesced to the Paris Jesuits, who thought it best not to pass on the letter. Eventually, the king let it be known that he did not want Arnoux back in Paris.[105] But after a visit with Vitelleschi in Rome in 1624, Arnoux did return to the city, where he flourished once again as a preacher. But he was forced to depart again in 1631 for Toulouse, under pressure from Richelieu, who suspected that

102 ARSJ, Cong. 57, f. 131.
103 Vitelleschi to Séguiran, Mar. 21, 1622, ARSJ, Francia 4, f. 99; see also Vitelleschi to Armand (provincial), Mar. 21, 1622, ibid., f. 99′.
104 Vitelleschi to Armand (provincial), Sept. 15, 1623, ibid., ff. 140′–1.
105 Vitelleschi to Armand (provincial), Dec. 11 and Dec. 26, 1623, ibid., ff. 145′, 146′.

he supported Marie de Medici at the time of the Day of Dupes. He died in Toulouse in 1636.[106]

Jubilant fanfare accompanied the celebration in Rome of the victory at the White Mountain.[107] The leading issue for Vitelleschi, and for the papacy, now became the transfer of the electoral title from Frederick to Maximilian, in accord with the promise made by Ferdinand at the time of the Treaty of Munich. But other issues came to the fore as well. Ferdinand's first wife, Maria Anna of Bavaria, Maximilian's sister, had died in 1617. Upon learning that Ferdinand was considering another marriage, Vitelleschi, though realizing that this was not usually Jesuits' business "yet consider[ing] nothing foreign [to us] which pertains to His Majesty," tactfully suggested an Illyrian princess as Ferdinand's spouse. She was a twenty-one-year-old woman of singular prudence and outstanding piety, he wrote, and endowed with many gifts of spirit and of body. Should dispensations be necessary, Vitelleschi offered to help secure them.[108] Nothing seems to have resulted from this, and the following year Ferdinand took Eleanora of Mantua as his wife.

Another concern of Vitelleschi and Becan was tension between Ferdinand and his two brothers, Archduke Carl, who soon became bishop of Breslau, and especially the rambunctious Archduke Leopold, who had been bishop of Passau and Strasbourg, though never ordained, until he resigned these offices in order to marry. Important for the development of the Austrian Habsburg territories was their consolidation under one line of the family. Ferdinand pursued this goal, and for the most part he achieved it. But he yielded to Leopold's rule of the Tyrol and two-thirds of Anterior Austria, so making him founder of a Tyrolean Habsburg dynasty that lasted until 1665. The necessity of maintaining harmony among the brothers ran through Vitelleschi's correspondence with Becan and then with Lamormaini as a subordinate theme.[109] As he noted, rivalry among brothers was not uncommon.

Most important, however, was that harmony reign between Ferdinand and Maximilian, and this meant agreement on the transfer of the electoral title. Associated with this was the compensation to be granted Maximilian for his war costs; after the Bohemian campaign he occupied Upper Austria in Ferdinand's name and held it as a pledge of payment. Ferdinand hesitated to take action on the electoral title, at

[106] Fouqueray 4: 56–61; 5: 259–60.

[107] Pastor 26: 370–2.

[108] Vitelleschi to Becan, Aug. 28 and Oct. 25, 1621, ARSJ, Germania 111, f. 64. For Lamormaini's fear that Ferdinand marry a Protestant princess, see Robert Bireley, *Religion and Politics in the Age of the Counterreformation* (Chapel Hill, NC, 1981), 9.

[109] Vitelleschi to Becan, Aug. 7, 1621, and Apr. 2, 1622, ARSJ, Aust. 3I, ff. 140, 246.

first perhaps for legal reasons, but these were soon dissipated. He worried that if Frederick were deprived of the electoral title in addition to losing Bohemia, he would never be reconciled and would always find allies who would be glad to use his restoration as a pretext for intervention in the empire. So it would be difficult to arrive at any permanent peace, and in any event, this was the case. Spain also hesitated about the electorate, which feared that its transfer to Maximilian would generate continued unrest in the empire and so prevent Ferdinand from coming to its assistance in The Netherlands and perhaps in Italy. For a time as well, Spain was negotiating for marriage between the prince of Wales and a Spanish princess. For this reason Spain was interested in conciliating James I of England, Frederick's father-in-law. One way to do this was to help restore Frederick in the Palatinate. On the other hand, Spain gained a major strategic advantage through its occupation of the left bank of the Palatinate and did not want to surrender this as it would have to do should Frederick be reinstated. So there was uncertainty in Spain over policy.[110]

In addition, neither the archbishop-elector of Mainz, Johann Schweikard, nor, in his wake, the archbishop-elector of Trier viewed the transfer of the electoral title with enthusiasm. They also thought that in the long run at least a partial restoration of Frederick would be more beneficial for peace and for the Catholic cause. Schweikard in particular was sensitive to the need to conciliate Elector John George of Saxony. Strictly speaking, to Ferdinand's mind, he did not need the agreement of the electors to act in the matter. But as it was, of the seven electors only Maximilian and his brother Ferdinand, archbishop-elector of Cologne, clearly favored the transfer.[111]

The new pope, Gregory XV, showed much more interest in the German war as a religious contest and aggressively championed Maximilian's claim to the electoral title. For him by giving the Catholics a clear five-to-two majority in the electoral college, the title would stabilize the Catholic position in the empire and render much less likely the election of a Protestant emperor. Gregory also envisioned a Catholic prince as ruler of the Palatinate. That spring of 1621, at the same time that he was urging Louis XIII on against the Huguenots, he dispatched a flurry of briefs endorsing Maximilian for the electorate, and a primary task of the new nuncio to Vienna, Carlo Carafa, was to support the cause. He was instructed to consult with Becan.[112] Shortly after Carafa, there arrived in Vienna from Rome in late July 1621 the Capuchin Hyacinth da

110 Albrecht, *Auswärtige Politik*, 50–65; Bireley, 4–5.
111 Albrecht, ibid., 82–4.
112 Instruction for Carafa, Apr. 12, 1621, Jaitner 2: no. 6: 602–42, esp. 639; Albrecht, ibid., 62–5.

Casale, whose assignment was to convince Ferdinand to proceed with the transfer. He also sought out Becan.[113]

The Bavarian chancellor Joachim von Donnersberg visited Becan when he was in Vienna at the end of June 1621 to promote Maximilian's cause, and the confessor promised to advance the matter with Ferdinand.[114] In mid-August another Bavarian official reported from Vienna that Becan had delivered a written opinion to Ferdinand recommending the immediate transfer of the electoral title to Maximilian. At the time in the imperial privy council only the chief minister, Hans Ulrich von Eggenberg, favored the transfer. The other four, including Trautmannsdorf, according to Maximilian's envoy, all opposed it.[115] Yet on September 22, 1621, in Vienna, Ferdinand secretly invested Maximilian, and his whole line, with the electoral title.[116] The next step was the public transfer. This would require more than a year.

Only at this point did Vitelleschi enter the fray, expressing his pleasure as well as the pope's with the paper that Becan had prepared in support of the transfer of the electoral title to Maximilian, a copy of which he had sent to Rome.[117] But after the first of the year perplexity seemed to overtake the superior general. Others opposed to the transfer had gotten to him, most likely the Spaniards. No matter which side he took, he complained to Becan, he would offend the other, and both were generous benefactors.[118] On January 22, he wrote to Becan that an extraordinary papal nuncio, Fabricio Verospi, was on his way to Vienna and that Becan should do all in his power to support his mission on behalf of the Catholic cause. A copy of the same letter was sent to Reinhard Ziegler, the confessor of the elector of Mainz. Yet Vitelleschi's communication sounded more like a call to obedience to the pope than enthusiastic support of the transfer.[119] Verospi, in turn, was instructed to turn to Becan in Vienna and to Ziegler in Mainz for assistance with his mission to advance the transfer of the electoral title, at the cost of continued war if necessary.[120]

By June the new king of Spain, Philip IV, convinced by the largely religious arguments of Hyacinth da Casale, who had journeyed to Madrid,

113 Jaitner 2: 245; Albrecht, ibid., 67–8.
114 Donnersberg to Maximilian, June 30, 1621, BA 1, 2: 281, n. 2.
115 Johann von Zollern to Maximilian, Aug. 18, 1621, ibid., 325, n. 2.
116 Albrecht, *Maximilian I*, 552–3.
117 Vitelleschi to Becan, Oct. 9, 1621, ARSJ, Aust. 3I, f. 193.
118 Vitelleschi to Becan, Jan. 15, 1622, ibid., f. 224.
119 Vitelleschi to Becan, Jan. 22, 1622, ibid., f. 225 (with indication of a copy to Ziegler).
120 Instruction for Verospi, extraordinary nuncio to the imperial court, Rome, Jan. 13, 1622, Jaitner 2: no. 220: 826–47, esp. 844, 846.

approved the transfer, though Spanish policy would be reversed shortly after the death of Zúñiga and the rise to power of Olivares, as the Capuchin himself expected it might.[121] Those in Rome could not understand the continued delay once the King of Spain had approved. But Maximilian himself now seemed to be hesitating about the public declaration of the transfer without a still more firm commitment from Spain.[122] Vitelleschi suggested to Becan that "he consider whether he could, without any danger of offense, take the matter up with His Imperial Majesty" and encouraged him in turn to urge Maximilian to consent to the public investiture.[123] He wrote in a similar vein to Maximilian's confessor Buslidius, exhorting him to seek a suitable occasion to convince the duke that this was not so much a matter of augmenting his own status – Vitelleschi seemed to attribute Maximilian's temporary reluctance to humility – as it was of restoring the Catholic religion in Germany. "The Lord of Hosts" would protect him.[124]

Indeed, God did appear to be with the Catholic forces. During the spring and summer of 1622, League forces advanced to the west in pursuit of Mansfeld's army, first into the Upper and then the Lower Palatinate. They won great victories at Wimpfen on May 5 and at Höchst on June 17 and by September 22 were to occupy Heidelberg. Rumors of negotiations at Brussels over an armistice in the midst of these victories now stirred the militant spirit of Vitelleschi, who echoed the feeling at the papal court. Becan should take the opportunity "to encourage and strengthen His Majesty lest when the Lord for his part has thus far shown by so many victories that he stands with the Catholics and has their efforts at heart, [the emperor] allow the equally glorious and successful expedition, upon which the restoration of the true religion in Germany depends, to be delayed or hindered by an ignominious and dangerous agreement to the suspension of arms." It was obvious that the enemy exploited this only to regroup his forces.[125] For the conflict in Germany as well as in France Vitelleschi now employed terms of a holy war.

121 Hyacinth da Casale, Madrid, to Becan, May 9, 1622, BA 1, 2: no. 193: 519; Albrecht, *Auswärtige Politik*, 76–8. Hyacinth himself seems to anticipate that this approval would be reversed.

122 Albrecht, ibid., 74; Jaitner 1: 329–30.

123 Vitelleschi to Becan, July 2 (sent July 9), 1622, ARSJ, Aust. 3I, f. 280.

124 Vitelleschi to Buslidius, July 2, 1622, ARSJ, Germ. Sup. 5, f. 256'. Nuncio Verospi also called in Munich to encourage Maximilian.

125 Vitelleschi to Becan, July 23, 1622, ARSJ, Aust. 3I, f. 285; see also Vitelleschi to Joannes Argenti (visitor of the province), Aug. 20, 1622, where he suggests that Argenti caution those who were inclined to peace with the heretics. A visitor was a Jesuit official commissioned to look into and to report on the state of a province.

By late July Ferdinand summoned a Convention of Deputies (*Deputationstag*) for Regensburg in December.[126] In August he announced that there he would publicly invest Maximilian with the electoral title.[127] Yet opposition remained, especially from Spain and from Mainz. In a long letter to Becan at Regensburg, whither he had accompanied Ferdinand, Vitelleschi urged that the decisions taken not be made on the basis only of "human and political" considerations, but also of "divine and eternal" ones; it was not a normal political negotiation involving the transfer of a piece of territory, but it dealt with religion. One needed to consider also the "disposition of divine providence, which up to this point had brought the cause forward not by human counsels and strength but by miracles and prodigies." This was a clear reference to the often unexpected victories of the Catholic armies. Trust in divine providence was called for, not a hesitant timidity based on, again, merely human and political considerations.[128] Vitelleschi had discussed the matter with Pope Gregory, who would soon dispatch briefs to Regensburg on behalf of Maximilian. Becan's was dated December 22.[129]

The Convention of Regensburg turned out to be, for the most part, a success for Maximilian. Becan had a part in this. On February 25, 1623, Ferdinand solemnly invested Maximilian with the electoral dignity, but the opposition of Spain expressed by Oñate, Brandenburg, and Saxony succeeded in limiting the public investiture to Maximilian's person only and not to his successors. The previous day, however, Ferdinand had given the Bavarian duke a secret guarantee that he would extend the investiture to Maximilian's heirs and dynasty.[130] In the weeks leading up to the ceremony Becan worked to convince the elector of Mainz to support the transfer of the title. Only at the last minute, according to one account, did he succeed. In a dramatic gesture, he approached Schweikard, knelt before him, "and by everything that was holy, beseeched him that he no longer continue to delay what the pope, the emperor, and all good men earnestly desired, and what would be of great advantage to the Catholic religion." So Schweikard yielded and signed the imperial decree transferring the electorate to Maximilian.[131] Needless to say, Vitelleschi congratulated Maximilian on the new dignity to

[126] A *Deputationstag* brought together a committee of the imperial diet to conduct business that could not be handled at a meeting of the full diet.
[127] Albrecht, *Auswärtige Politik*, 76–7.
[128] Vitelleschi to Becan, Nov. 15, 1622, ARSJ, Aust. 3I, ff. 321–2.
[129] Vitelleschi to Becan, Dec. 10, 1622, ibid., f. 330; Duhr 2, 2: 224.
[130] Albrecht, *Maximilian I*, 569–71.
[131] Giulio Cesare Cordara, *Historiae Societatis Jesu Pars Sexta, 1616–1633*, 1 (Rome, 1750): 487.

which providence had called him, to the benefit of the Christian commonwealth and to the joy of the whole Society of Jesus.[132]

So the first phase of the war came to an end with the controversial transfer of the electoral title to Maximilian. Several points stand out. Vitelleschi and the Jesuits generally saw the war as a religious conflict; this hardly surprises us. The general identified the Society with the cause of Ferdinand and Maximilian. He joined many Jesuits in a conviction that Ferdinand enjoyed a special divine providence and call from God. Later, after the Battle of the White Mountain, this language began to be applied to Maximilian too. Vitelleschi considered it a principal task of his to preserve harmony between the two cousins who championed Catholicism in Germany.

The language of holy war gradually crept into Vitelleschi's correspondence with Germany and with France. The accession of Gregory XV in February 1621 fostered this. A holy war was more than a religious war. A religious war was fought primarily for the advancement or defense of religious interests. Characteristic of the holy war was the belief in a summons from God to take up the fight and a promise of divine aid that would lead to victory even in the face of great odds. So it was fought at the behest of God and implied some revelation of his will. It was analogous to the Hebrew wars for the conquest of the Promised Land in the Hebrew Scriptures. In addition, a holy war was providentialist. It implied God's singular providence exercised either through his normal guidance of secondary, natural causes or through a direct intervention in the course of events.[133] Christian history has experienced the appearance of this mentality at different times. A striking example contemporary with the Thirty Years War was provided by the Independents in the English Civil War.[134] Events like the last-minute rescue of Ferdinand at the siege of Vienna in 1619 and then the stunning victory of the White Mountain seemed to point to the call of God to Ferdinand and Maximilian. This type of thinking underlay Vitelleschi's words to Becan that divine providence was advancing the Catholic cause "not by human counsels and strength but by miracles and prodigies."[135]

132 Vitelleschi to Maximilian, Mar. 11 and Apr. 22, 1623, ARSJ, Germ. 3I, ff. 112, 116–17.

133 Roland de Vaux, *Ancient Israel* 1 (New York, 1961), 258–61. On holy war, see James Turner Johnson, *The Holy War in Western and Islamic Traditions* (University Park, PA, 1997), esp. pp. 37–42, where he indicates ten features variously attributed to holy war. Johnson does not distinguish between religious and holy war; I follow de Vaux in doing so.

134 Roland Bainton, "Congregationalism: From the Just War to the Crusade in the Puritan Revolution," *The Andover Newton Theological School Bulletin* 35, 3 (1943), esp. 15–20.

135 Vitelleschi to Becan, Nov. 15, 1622, ARSJ, Aust. 3I, ff. 321–2.

Gregory XV, and to a degree Vitelleschi, employed this language in the case of Louis XIII's campaign against the Huguenots, but ideas of holy war never caught on in France. Such militance helped to undo Arnoux. Nor, for that matter, does Becan seem to have been enthusiastic about holy war or providentialism. In response to Becan's pessimistic assessment of the political situation in May 1623, so well after the meeting at Regensburg and undoubtedly provoked by the prospect of continued war, Vitelleschi admitted that there was reason to fear if we looked at the matter from a purely human perspective as Becan seemed to do. But it was necessary to trust in divine providence "which has enabled us up to this point to avoid much greater dangers. I think that we ought to trust in him and hope that he who has begun to put down the enemies of religion will not cease to do so until he has conquered all and subjected his own to Christ."[136]

The situations of Becan and Arnoux differed vastly, as did their personalities. Vitelleschi appreciated this. Arnoux operated in a much more tangled political milieu, and he was more activist than Becan. Paradoxically, the Frenchman Arnoux seemed more open to holy war than the German Becan. Vitelleschi did not feel it necessary to send Becan a copy of Acquaviva's Instruction. They agreed about the role of a court confessor. This was not the case between Vitelleschi and Arnoux where there was unclarity and even disagreement about what types of political activity were permitted Jesuits. Obviously, the confessor should use his position to advance the goals of the church and the Society. Vitelleschi seconded the militant program of Gregory XV in France, but he also warned Arnoux of the danger of excessive zeal. Arnoux overstepped his bounds and lost his position. His successor, Séguiran, followed a different policy. Each, of course, believed that he was doing what was more in the interest of religion.

[136] Vitelleschi to Becan, June 3, 1623, ibid., Aust. 3I, ff. 393–4. Vitelleschi also passed on to Becan that there were those in Rome who thought that the emperor was being too lenient with rebels and this might encourage opposition and uprisings in the future. The confessor might bring this up to the emperor if he thought it opportune. See Vitelleschi to Becan, Oct. 28, 1623, ibid., f. 454.

CHAPTER 3

The Triumph of Militance, 1624–1629

SHORTLY after the transfer of the electoral title to Maximilian, new faces showed up on the European scene and with them shifts in the political constellation. Louis XIII appointed Richelieu, now a cardinal, to the council of state in France in April 1624 and promoted him to chief minister in August. The cardinal continued with greater subtlety the anti-Habsburg policy of his predecessor, the marquis of La Vieuville.[1] In 1623 France had joined the League of Lyons along with Venice and Savoy, and the result was the withdrawal of Spanish troops from the strategically invaluable Valtelline in the Swiss Alps. The next year under Richelieu the French allied with the Swiss Protestant Grey Leagues, who were the overlords of the Catholic Valtelline, and occupied the Valtelline themselves. La Vieuville had agreed to assist the Dutch in their war with Spain in the treaty of Compiègne in June 1624, and he and then Richelieu dispatched envoys to German courts, usually Protestant ones, to enlist support for Frederick of the Palatinate and against the emperor. France also entered negotiations for the marriage of Louis's sister, Henrietta Maria, to the future Charles I of England that were eventually successful – they were married in 1625 – and for English assistance to Frederick of the Palatinate.

But the outbreak of another Huguenot rebellion in 1625 as well as financial difficulties compelled Richelieu temporarily to step back from his anti-Habsburg ventures. French troops withdrew from the Valtelline by the Treaty of Monzon of March 5, 1626, and in March of the following year Richelieu entered a brief alliance of convenience with Spain. It was directed against England, which was supporting the Huguenots. There was even talk, encouraged by the papacy, of a joint Franco-Spanish armada against the Protestant English. But after the reduction of the

[1] Dieter Albrecht, *Die auswärtige Politik Maximilians von Bayern, 1618–1635* (Göttingen, 1962), 124, 128.

Huguenot fortress at La Rochelle in October 1628, following a year-long siege and the outbreak of an ominous dispute with Spain over the succession to the Mantuan inheritance in north Italy, Richelieu reverted to an anti-Habsburg policy.

In Spain the count-duke of Olivares took the helm as favorite and as first minister after the death of Zúñiga in 1622, a post he held until 1643. He intensified the Spanish effort in The Netherlands, where hostilities had resumed in 1621 after last-minute efforts to prolong the Twelve Years Truce failed. But he yielded at first in the Valtelline, because he wanted to avoid war with France at that point. Negotiations for the "Spanish match" between Prince Charles of England and a Spanish princess were broken off in 1623, opening the way for the Anglo-French marriage. The aforementioned Treaty of Monzon then gave Olivares a success in the Valtelline, which was followed by the short-lived alliance with France against England of 1627. Olivares sought then the next year to exploit the conflict over the Mantuan succession in order to install a Spanish client there. This resulted in hostilities with France. Both Spain and France wanted to control the duchy of Mantua, which lay southeast of Spanish Milan and was conjoined as a single inheritance with the marquisate of Montferrat to the southwest of Milan – Spain because it would strengthen the Spanish position in Italy, France because it would give the French a foothold there.

To the east in the empire the League general Tilly decisively defeated the last forces loyal to Frederick at Stadtlohn on August 6, 1623. Then the Danish king, Christian IV, intervened on Frederick's side. With financial assistance from the English and the Dutch – Richelieu withdrew from the agreement – Christian invaded Germany. But the enigmatic imperial general Albrecht von Wallenstein, commander of a newly raised imperial army, defeated Christian's forces at the Dessau Bridge in April 1626, and Tilly did so at Lutter am Baremberg in August of that year. The Catholic armies of Maximilian and Ferdinand now dominated the empire. All the forces in support of Frederick of the Palatinate lay vanquished. This new situation paved the way for the emergence of a militant party in Munich and Vienna that determined to exploit the upper hand of the Catholics to the fullest, especially with the Edict of Restitution. Two Jesuit confessors, William Lamormaini in Vienna and Adam Contzen in Munich, figured prominently in the militant party.

Maffeo Barberini emerged from the conclave as Pope Urban VIII on August 6, 1623, following the two-and-one-half-year pontificate of Gregory XV. Less militant than his predecessor, Urban did not show the same enthusiasm for the Catholic cause in Germany, and he reduced drastically the subsidies to Ferdinand and Maximilian. He considered himself in the papal tradition as a *padre commune* of Christendom who would work for reconciliation of the Catholic states, especially France and Spain. In 1625 he sent his cardinal-nephew Francesco Barberini on a mission to Paris, and then the next year to Madrid, to pursue this goal. But extended stays at both courts produced little in the way of direct results. Yet the Treaty of Monzon was a plus for papal policy in that it defused the threat of war in the Valtelline, as was the Franco-Spanish alliance of 1627.[2] But the conflict over the Mantuan inheritance revealed Urban's tendency to tilt toward France even as he pursued peace among the Catholic powers. This tendency resulted partly from an inclination toward things French that he had developed as nuncio in Paris. More significantly, it grew out of his typical papal fear of Spanish and Habsburg domination, first in Italy and then in Europe. His predominant concerns were the welfare of the Papal States and the enhancement of the Barberini family, which profited immensely from his nepotism. These interests and even the welfare of the church were thought to be better served when France provided a balance to the two Habsburg crowns.[3] Thus, a complex picture came into his vision as Vitelleschi looked out over the European scene from his Roman post.

The situation of the confessor Séguiran in Paris and indeed of the Society in France remained exceedingly delicate. In the years 1625/26 a series of crises came to a head for the French Jesuits as their enemies in parlement and in the universities, especially the University of Paris, pressed them. The universities feared the challenge of the Jesuits in education. Between 1617 and 1623 sixteen new Jesuit colleges were founded; clearly, they were in demand.[4] The Society was persistently criticized for inadequate recognition of royal authority and the rights of France – their schools were under the superior general – and for insufficient subordination to the church hierarchy and respect for the diocesan clergy. Some folks felt that the large number of their colleges, which featured the humanities, slowed the progress of commerce and agriculture.[5] On

2 Ludwig von Pastor, *The History of the Popes* 28: *Gregory XV and Urban VIII, 1621–1644*, trans. from the German (London, 1938): 76–88, 94–7, 103–4. Cardinal Barberini was kept out of the negotiations in Madrid leading to the Treaty of Monzon.

3 Ibid., 125–7; Franz Xaver Seppelt, *Geschichte der Päpste* 5: *Von Paul III: bis zur französischer Revolution*, ed. Georg Schwaiger (Munich, 1959): 275–83. For a penetrating analysis of papal policy from 1626 to 1630, see Georg Lutz, *Kardinal Giovanni Francesco Guidi di Bagno: Religion und Politik im Zeitalter Richelieus und Urbans VIII* (Tübingen, 1971), 469–83; for a more general appraisal, see id., "Roma e il mondo Germanico nel periodo della Guerra dei Trent'Anni," in *La corte di Roma tra cinque e seicento: "Teatro" della politica europea*, ed. Gianvittorio Signorotto e Maria Antonietta Visceglia (Rome, 1998): 425–60.

4 Henri Fouqueray, *Histoire de la Compagnie de Jésus en France* 3 (Paris, 1922): 488–531.

5 *Mercure françois* 10: *1624* (Paris, 1625): 418–32.

September 27, 1624, the royal council rejected the Jesuits' request to raise the College of Tournon to the status of a university.[6] Richelieu himself remained for the most part a supporter and protector of the Society, especially in times of crisis. But as he stated in his Political Testament, he feared lest the Society become too influential, and he shared to a degree in the aforementioned criticisms. Competition between the Jesuits and the universities he considered a boon to the interests of the state.[7]

Factions within the province were forming around Arnoux and Séguiran, and this disturbed Vitelleschi.[8] This development was perhaps due to personality differences but certainly more so to disagreements over the role of confessor and over the direction of French policy. The more activist Arnoux along with Marie de Medici sided with the *dévot* party, which generally advocated a foreign policy of support for the Catholic Habsburgs and at home greater restrictions on the Huguenots. Séguiran was less prominent as confessor, and he was inclined to the *bons français* for whom opposition to the Habsburgs served the best interest of church and state as did a more tolerant policy toward the Huguenots. For a time after he became confessor, rumors circulated that Séguiran also would be dismissed. So in October 1622 Vitelleschi gladly learned from the French ambassador in Rome, who had received the news from the secretary of state Puysieux, that the king was happy with Séguiran.[9] On December 27, 1623, Vitelleschi instructed the provincial to send Arnoux away from Orléans, perhaps to distant Bordeaux to preach Lent, but to do so in such a way that no one realized that the initiative for the move came from Vitelleschi.[10]

From the beginning, Vitelleschi seems to have trusted Richelieu and believed in his goodwill toward the Jesuits and his sincere concern to promote the church's interests. One cannot find a word of criticism of the cardinal in Vitelleschi's correspondence, and the superior general regularly deferred to him. Certainly, this stemmed at least in part from Vitelleschi's awareness of the Society's dependence on Richelieu and the king for support against its enemies. His first letter to Richelieu antedated the cardinal's appointment to the council of state. To Richelieu's request for the services of Father Jean Phelippeau, then a professor at the College of Clermont, who had assisted Cardinal de La Rochefoucauld in

6 Ibid., 447; Fouqueray 4 (Paris, 1925): 44–9.

7 Armand-Jean du Plessis, cardinal de Richelieu, *Testament politique*, ed. Françoise Hildesheimer (Paris, 1995), 137–43.

8 Vitelleschi to Jean Suffren, July 15, 1624, ARSJ, Francia 4, f. 164.

9 Vitelleschi to Séguiran, Oct. 20, 1622, ibid., f. 116'.

10 Vitellechi to Armand (provincial), Dec. 27, 1623, ibid, f. 147.

various ways, Vitelleschi responded that he would instruct the provincial to put him at Richelieu's disposal.[11] Upon Richelieu's taking a seat in the council of state, the general congratulated him effusively, seeing this as a grand opportunity for the cardinal to advance the church's interests as well as the kingdom's. He acknowledged Richelieu's aid to the Society in the past and hoped for his support in the future, "so that protected by such a great authority and [helped] by his counsel and good will it could serve God and the common good in peace."[12] That this was not mere rhetoric intended for Richelieu was shown by the enthusiasm Vitelleschi showed over the cardinal's appointment in a letter to Séguiran.[13]

Richelieu himself expressed to Vitelleschi his goodwill toward Seguiran just as a storm broke over the Society in late 1624,[14] and he helped the Jesuits deal with a compromising situation caused by Arnoux, who continued to be a problem. Having become friendly with a young man named Oudin while confessor at court, after his dismissal he carried on a correspondence with him in which, without betraying any state secrets, he commented imprudently on politics and intrigues at court. Oudin, now sick unto death, in order to pay his medical bills sold Arnoux's letters to the Jesuits' enemies, who attempted to exploit them, but with little success.[15] Vitelleschi gratefully acknowledged Richelieu's assistance in this clumsy matter in letters of February 23 and April 6, 1625, at the same time requesting his continued protection for the increasingly embattled Jesuits.[16]

Jesuit publications themselves, both domestic and foreign, helped incite trouble for the Society in France once again. Vitelleschi faced the issue of excessively zealous or imprudent Jesuit authors. François Garasse, a highly learned and heavy-handed Jesuit writer, took on a number of the Society's enemies – Huguenots, libertines, Gallicans – in a series of pamphlets and books, frequently satirical, written between 1617 and 1625. Most significant was his attack on the multivolume *Investigations in the History of France* of Étienne Pasquier, a long-time *bête noir* of the Society

[11] Vitelleschi to Richelieu, Aug. 2, 1623, ARSJ, Gallia 46I, f. 94'. See Joseph Bergin, *Cardinal de La Rochefoucauld: Leadership and Reform in the French Church* (New Haven, CT, 1987), 274, and J.M. Prat, *Recherches historiques et critiques sur la Compagnie de Jésus en France du temps du P. Coton, 1564–1626*, 4 (Paris, 1876): 462–3, note on Phelippeau. What service he may have performed for Richelieu is not clear.

[12] Vitelleschi to Richelieu, June 3, 1624, ibid., f. 98.

[13] Vitelleschi to Séguiran, June 3, 1624, ibid., Francia 4, f. 157.

[14] Vitelleschi to Suffren, Dec. 2, 1624, ibid., f. 174'.

[15] Fouqueray 4: 56–61; Prat 4: 438–41.

[16] Vitelleschi to Richelieu, Feb. 23 and Apr. 6, 1625, ARSJ, Epist. Gen. 2, ff. 290, 293; see also Vitelleschi to Suffren, Jan. 13, 1625, ibid., Gallia 41I, f. 81.

whose books were being reissued by his son.[17] Even some Jesuits had reservations about the style if not the content of the works of Garasse, who published an attack on the alleged libertine Théophile de Viau without awaiting the verdict of the Jesuit censors.[18] Garasse's *Theological Compendium*[19] appeared in late 1625 and, because of alleged errors and heretical propositions, after a long delay drew upon itself the censure of the Faculty of Theology of the University of Paris on September 1, 1626. The author had failed to make corrections required by the censors.[20]

The first foreign book to raise hackles in Paris was Carlo Scribani's *Christian Politician*, which was published in Antwerp in 1624.[21] Scribani was a prominent member of the Flandro-Belgian or Flemish Province, a prolific author, and a figure close to the archdukes as well as to the Italian general in Spanish service, Ambrogio Spinola.[22] His extensive volume belonged to the Antimachiavellian tradition that aimed to reconcile Christian ethics with political success, and it also proposed a program for more effective Spanish government in The Netherlands.[23] The French objected to the dedication to the young king of Spain, Philip IV. Scribani appeared to exalt Philip above other European rulers. When he wrote "It is for other kings to give themselves to the hunt of animals and birds, but for the Spanish [king] to hunt new worlds for God and glory," the French saw it as a jibe against Louis XIII, whose delight in the hunt was well known. Vitelleschi in early 1625 wrote in response to a complaint from Séguiran that before publication of Scribani's volume he had noted imprudent statements in the dedication and had ordered changes to be made before the book appeared,[24] and they were introduced into subsequent editions.[25] Scribani complained of French sensitivity to Pierre Coton, who in early 1625 came back to Paris as provincial to help the Society navigate through fresh storms.[26]

17 *Recherches sur l'histoire de France*. The first volume appeared in 1560.

18 Fouqueray 3: 563–9.

19 *Somme théologique*.

20 *Mercure françois* 12: *1626–1627* (Paris, 1628): 522–9. William F. Church, *Richelieu and Reason of State* (Princeton, 1972), 154–5.

21 *Politicus christianus*.

22 Scribani was the son of an Italian nobleman, who came north for military service, and the daughter of a prominent patrician of Ghent. He strongly identified with The Netherlands.

23 See Robert Bireley, *The Counter-Reformation Prince: Anti-Machiavellianism or Catholic Statecraft in Early Modern Europe* (Chapel Hill, NC, 1990), 168–87.

24 Vitelleschi to Séguiran, Jan. 27, 1625, ARSJ, Francia 4, 110.

25 Lyons, 1625, and Antwerp, 1626. See L. Brouwers, *Carolus Scribani S.J. 1561–1629: Een groot man van de Contra-Reformatie in de Nederlanden* (Antwerp, 1961), 424, n. 21.

26 Scribani to Coton, undated, Carolus Scribani, *Brieven van Carolus Scribani, S.J. (1561–1629)*, ed. L. Brouwers (Antwerp, 1972), no. 58: 178–82, and Scribani to Séguiran, undated, ibid., no. 59: 183–4.

The few clouds elicited by Scribani's book amounted to little compared to the thunderstorms evoked by two anonymous pamphlets that appeared in 1624/25 and were widely suspected, even by the French Jesuits, to have been authored by a Jesuit. Only recent scholarship has established that the writer was, in fact, Adam Contzen, the new confessor of Maximilian of Bavaria.[27] They were the two most effective of a barrage of pamphets that attacked Richelieu and his foreign policy.[28] Maximilian worried with reason that the shift in policy implied support for the restoration of Frederick in the Palatinate, a worry that was encouraged by reports that French troops leaving the Valtelline were regrouping on the eastern border of France with a view to intervention in Germany. In response to a letter of Contzen, prompted by Maximilian, Vitelleschi asserted that intervention in the Palatinate was not part of the Anglo-French marriage agreement. He gave Séguiran as his source for this information.[29] He then alerted the French confessor to the rumors about which Maximilian was concerned and urged him to work against any French intervention on behalf of Frederick, a move that would clearly work to the detriment of the church in Germany.[30] Maximilian, having learned of Cardinal Barberini's mission to Paris – he arrived in March 1625 – had Contzen write to Rome requesting that the cardinal's efforts to mediate between France and Spain take in the German question, too, for the sake of a comprehensive settlement. Vitelleschi assured Contzen that he would send his letter on to the Roman curia.[31] So Vitelleschi served as a mediator.

Contzen's two pamphlets written at Maximilian's behest attempted to turn French public opinion against Richelieu's support of Protestants in the empire. The first was the *Mysteries of Politics* published at Naples in Latin, which began to circulate in Paris in a French translation at the turn of 1624/25.[32] Written in the form of confidential communications among European political insiders, the *Mysteries* related their consensus that French intervention in the empire on the Protestant side would justify a rebellion of French nobility against the crown. So it raised the specter of a revival of the civil wars of the previous century. The second pamphlet, *A Warning to Louis XIII*, came out in the summer of 1625, first

27 BA 2, 3: no. 2: 3–4; Lutz, *Kardinal Giovanni Francisco Guidi di Bagno*, 49.
28 Church, 121–7.
29 Vitelleschi to Contzen, Feb. 1, 1625, ARSJ, Germ. Sup. 5, f. 361.
30 Vitelleschi to Séguiran, Feb. 10, 1625, ibid., Francia 4, f. 181.
31 Vitelleschi to Contzen, Mar. 22, 1625, ibid., Germ. Sup. 5, f. 371. Cardinal Barberini arrived in Paris on May 21, 1625.
32 *Mysteria politica*, Church, 121, gives Antwerp as the place of publication; the Latin edition in the Bayerische Staatsbibiothek that I have used gives Naples as the place of publication, which may or may not have been an attempt to mislead.

in Latin then in French,[33] written allegedly by a concerned theologian. It was more devastating than the *Mysteries of Politics*. It distinguished between the king and his ministers – first of all, Richelieu – who hid from the ruler the full extent of their support for heretics. But the king could not be absolved of all blame. Dangerous in particular were the questions circulating in France, according to the author: Should a king who allied with heretics be warned by the Estates General? Is this a serious sin; is he excommunicated? Is it legitimate to resist a king who so harms religion and the kingdom itself? In such circumstances, should one appoint a coruler who would provide for the interests of religion? Can the king be compelled by force to desist from aiding heretics?

Richelieu recognized immediately the incendiary nature of these pamphlets, and he unleashed his writers to respond in kind. Among their products were *The Catholic Statesman or a Political Discourse about the Alliance of the Most Christian King against the Calumnies of His Enemies* (Paris, 1625),[34] usually attributed to Jeremie Ferrier, and more directly anti-Jesuit *Political Considerations about the Book Published Several Months Ago under the Title of "A Warning to the King"* (n.p., 1625), which asserted that "never had the Pharisees of Jerusalem achieved such power after the death of Alexander of Judaea as the Jesuits had achieved after the death of Henry IV."[35] Both offending pamphlets were publicly burned in Paris on October 30, 1625, and their publication, reading, and even possession prohibited under pain of death. Barberini, now in Aragon, condemned the *Warning to Louis XIII* to burning.[36] On the first Sunday of Advent 1625 four Jesuits, including Coton and Suffren, preached in different churches of Paris disavowing any connection with the two pamphlets.[37] After the appearance of the first pamphlet and as a result of other recriminations against the Society, the province congregation of the Paris Province, meeting in late April 1625, requested Vitelleschi to reissue the decree on tyrannicide, take more vigorous measures for its

[33] *Admonitio ad Ludovicum XIII*, Church, 123–6; this piece carried no place of publication.

[34] *Le Catholique d'estat ou Discours politique des alliances du Roy très-Chretien contre les calomnies des ennemis de son estat*.

[35] *Considerations d'estat sur le livre publié depuis quelques mois, soubs le tiltre d'Advertissement au Roi*; Church, 126–39; citation from *Considerations d'estat* on p. 198. At this same time there appeared in Paris *Defensus P. Joannis Marianae de grandibus erroribus, qui sunt in forma gubernationis Jesuitarum, ex Hispanico in Gallicum translatus*, which defended a treatise Mariana wrote in criticism of the Society's mode of government. See Sommervogel 5: 563 and Vitelleschi to Coton (provincial), May 26, 1625, ARSJ, Francia 4, f. 192.

[36] Pierre Blet, *Le clergé de France et la monarchie: Étude sur les Assemblées générales du clergé de 1615 à 1666* (Rome, 1959), 1: 336–7.

[37] Prat 4: 593; François Garasse, "Récit au vrai des persécutions soulevées contre les pères de la Compagnie de Jésus dans la ville de Paris l'an 1624, 1625, 1626" in *Documents inédits concernant la Compagnie de Jésus*, ed. Auguste Carayon, 3 (Poitiers, 1864): 69–71.

enforcement, notify the Most Christian King of his actions, and then ask the king to prohibit anyone from attributing to the Jesuits a tolerance of tyrannicide.[38]

Vitelleschi agreed to renew the decree, while wondering why only Jesuits were singled out for a position on tyrannicide that was common to many Catholic authors. Nor did he consider it wise to approach Louis at this time; it would only call his attention to the issue. Some ministers would undoubtedly hesitate to back the statement that the Paris fathers wanted the king to make.[39] The superior general did circulate a letter to all the provincial superiors of the German Assistancy and England instructing them to prevent Jesuits from publishing anonymous or pseudonymous books or pamphlets on political affairs. Nor should other books include anything critical of princes. If any Jesuit were approached by a prince or minister to write on controversial current affairs, he was gently to decline, even if this would offend the prince making the request. Offense to the prince was a lesser ill than the damage done to Jesuits elsewhere by such pieces. Jesuits were to be above suspicion in this regard.[40] But he was not able to discover the author of the two pieces; Contzen's colleague in Munich, Jacob Keller, a frequent writer of polemics for Maximilian, and Scribani both came under suspicion.[41]

Because of the theological nature of the pamphlets' argument, Richelieu wanted them also to be condemned by the decennial Assembly of the French Clergy, which was meeting in Paris in late 1625. This was a touchy matter, because it once again indirectly involved the power of the pope in temporal affairs. Richelieu secured the condemnation, but a document drawn up by the bishop of Chartres and hastily passed by the assembly then proposed total independence of the ruler from the pope in temporal matters as a doctrine of the faith. This was more than Richelieu wanted, and Urban VIII was upset. But now parlement stepped in to support the extreme Gallican position of the condemnation. Significantly, it was the king and the court who supported the Jesuits after Richelieu worked out a formula that completely satisfied neither clergy nor parlement.[42]

But the Jesuits were not yet out of the woods. Early in 1626 there appeared in Paris an anonymous, bitterly anti-Richelieu pamphlet whose

38 ARSJ, Cong. 59, ff. 126, 128, 129.
39 Ibid., f. 133.
40 Vitelleschi to Walter Mundbrot (provincial), Munich, and all provincials of Germany and England, Jan. 31, 1626, ARSJ, Germ. Sup. 5, f. 411.
41 Vitelleschi to Séguiran, Nov. 17, 1625, ibid., Francia 4, f. 204; Vitelleschi to Contzen, Aug. 14, 1627, ibid., Germ. Sup. 6, f. 10.
42 Blet 1: 335–69; Church, 142–8.

title itself referred to the minister as "the Cardinal of La Rochelle."[43] Suspicion fell quickly on Garasse as the author, and he was only able to clear himself through a personal interview with the cardinal and the vigorous intervention with Louis himself of Suffren, who had now become the king's confessor. The aging provincial Coton required Garasse to swear a formal oath that he had nothing to do with the publication of the vitriolic pamphlet.[44]

On February 6, 1626, then, there arrived in Paris the first volume of a compendium of moral theology by the Italian Jesuit Antonio Santarelli.[45] One of its principal topics was, again, the indirect power of the pope in temporal affairs, which the author treated in the traditional fashion of Bellarmine. Browsing in a bookstore in Paris, a Jesuit noticed Santarelli's volume and quickly realized its inflammatory nature. The local Jesuits bought up all but one copy of the shipment to Paris, but the one copy that eluded them sufficed to reinvigorate the storm.[46] Leading French Jesuits were compelled to appear before a committee of parlement, and Richelieu demanded that seven to ten Jesuits sign a condemnation of Santarelli's book that he drew up on behalf of the council of state, under threat of allowing parlement to expel the Society from the kingdom. After intense soul-searching, the Jesuits determined that they could in conscience sign it, and they did so on March 16, 1626, to the great relief of Louis, who anxiously looked for a middle ground and had no desire to ban the Jesuits. Coton died three days later under the enormous strain of events.[47]

Parlement then raised its demands despite Louis's instruction that it drop the matter, and the university produced another condemnation of Santarelli for acceptance by the Jesuits. But when he visited Richelieu the day after Coton's death, the acting Jesuit provincial, Ignatius Armand, found the cardinal much more well-disposed toward the Society; on March 22 he brought Louis a letter from Vitelleschi, and when he informed the king of the new initiative of parlement, Louis promised to protect the Society.[48] Four days later, when Louis came to the Jesuit

43 *Quaestiones quodlibeticae tempori praesenti accommodae ad Illustrissimum S.R.E. Cardinalem di Rochelieu seu de Rupella, Negotiorum Status in Regno Galliarum, Supremem Praefectum . . .* (n.p., 1626); Church, 149–50.

44 Garasse, 126–33; Prat 4: 604–13.

45 *Tractatus de haeresi, schismate, apostasia, et sollicitatione in sacramento penitentiae, et de potestate Romani Pontificis in his delictis puniendis* (Rome, 1625).

46 Prat 4: 716–20.

47 Armand (provincial) to Vitelleschi, Mar. 26, 1626, Prat 5: 475–9; *Mercure françois* 11: *1625–1626* (Paris, 1627): 91–4; Church, 157–9.

48 Armand (provincial) to Vitelleschi, Mar. 26, 1626, Prat 5: 475–9; Prat 4, 789–90. I have not been able find Vitelleschi's letter to Louis.

church of St. Louis in Paris to observe the Jubilee, he assured Armand and Suffren that he would deal with the affair that very day in council, and several weeks later Richelieu's celebration of a pontifical Mass in St. Louis on the occasion of the same Jubilee signaled clearly his support for the Society.[49] The Jesuits themselves prepared a declaration for parlement, with which neither Vitelleschi nor Urban VIII was happy, but which they escaped from having to sign. Once again, the king and Richelieu intervened to take them off the hook. By May the storm had nearly played itself out.[50]

Why did Louis and Richelieu put a stop to the attacks on the Society at this time? Certainly, the death of Coton created a great deal of sympathy for the Jesuits; he was a figure widely revered in France, and the crowds at his wake and funeral demonstrated this. Some Jesuits attributed the shift in royal policy to his intercession in heaven.[51] A second reason may have been the personal appeal of Urban VIII communicated in March through Denis de Marquemont, Archbishop of Lyons and the French cardinal in Rome, and followed up by Marquemont's letter to Richelieu of April 7 advising against forcing the issue further.[52] Most importantly, Richelieu was about to initiate a renewed campaign against the Huguenots; for this to be effective, it would be useful to have unity among the Catholics. The Treaty of Monzon with Spain, which was ratified on May 5, 1626, prepared the way for this by withdrawing France from the conflict in the Valtelline and retreating temporarily from an anti-Habsburg foreign policy.

The concessions that the Jesuits had made in signing the condemnation of Santarelli's book displeased Urban VIII. The day before he died Coton had written Vitelleschi disapprovingly that the fathers in Paris were determined to accept Richelieu's formula, which he himself considered ambiguous.[53] Vitelleschi, for his part, garnered a severe reproach from Urban VIII for allowing Santarelli's volume to slip through the censors and be published. Vitelleschi told the secretary of state, Cardinal Magalotti, in early April that he would inform the fathers in Paris that they should not have signed the decree.[54] But he waited until May 5

[49] Prat 4: 790–2.
[50] Ibid., 792–6.
[51] Ibid., 783–9.
[52] Cardinal Marquemont, Rome, to Louis XIII, Mar. 1626 (day not given), Prat 5: 466–70; idem to Richelieu, Apr. 7, 1626, Paris, Archives Diplomatiques, Rome 38, ff. 217–18; Charles de la Tour, S.J., Paris, to Vitelleschi, May 8, 1626, Vanves, Collection Prat 33, f. 811.
[53] Coton to Vitelleschi, Mar. 18, 1626, Prat 5: 471–3.
[54] Magalotti to Bernardino Spada, nuncio in Paris, early April 1626, Vanves, Collection Prat 35, f. 832; Prat 4: 748.

to do this, issuing three instructions to the acting provincial Armand. Following the orders of the pope, he made it clear that no Jesuit was to publish anything on issues of papal authority. The king would not take it ill of us, he wrote, if out of reverence for the Holy See we imposed an absolute silence on ourselves in this matter. Should authorities there attempt to extort a further opinion from you, "we (and especially you) will all cast ourselves at the feet of the Supreme Pontiff, petitioning all that is good and beseeching him in light of his care for the kingdom [of France]; otherwise we are certainly prepared for anything rather than not to obey the Supreme Pontiff." Second, under no conditions were they to subscribe to the new formula proposed by the university, "even if dangers awaited them and still more severe storms, for the sake of the truth and obedience to the Supreme Pontiff." As we have seen, the formula would soon be removed from the table. Third, they were to follow in all things the advice of the nuncio in Paris as well as that of Cardinal de La Rochefoucauld and the other friends of the Society there.[55]

So Vitelleschi insisted that the Jesuits in Paris hold firm. But prior to this letter, he had taken measures himself that surely helped to defuse the crisis as he attempted to steer between the demands of the French monarchy and attachment to the Holy See. To the French ambassador in Rome, Philippe de Béthune, he expressed his profound regret that the Santarelli book had been published, especially with his permission. The ambassador reported their conversation to Richelieu in a dispatch of April 8. The superior general was, he wrote, "a very wise and prudent man, of whom I am obliged to testify that in all that touches the service and authority of the king, he has always behaved as any one [of us] might desire." Béthune advised against pushing the matter any further and compelling the Jesuits to sign the formula of the university.[56] It was in a communication of the same day to Secretary of State Raymond Phélypeau d'Herbaut that Béthune referred to Vitelleschi as "a prudent man and the wisest politician [*politique*] with whom I have ever dealt." He readily excused Vitelleschi for allowing Santarelli's book to pass the censorship; the general could not possibly personally read all the books published by Jesuits. Vitelleschi now allegedly disavowed the position of Santarelli. "He is with regard to his personal conduct wise and prudent, with the reputation also of a pious and good religious," wrote Béthune, and he went on to use the same terms as in his dispatch to Richelieu to praise the superior general's conduct toward France.

[55] Vitelleschi to Armand (provincial) and the Fathers in Paris, May 5, 1626, Vanves, Collection Prat 33, ff. 791, 793; Prat 4: 799–800.
[56] Béthune to Richelieu, Apr. 8, 1626, Paris, Archives Diplomatiques, Rome 38, ff. 237–8.

The previous ambassador, the duke of Estrées, thought the same of him, Béthune asserted, and he again advised that the government not force the matter with the Jesuits.[57]

Vitelleschi now forwarded to Paris two copies of Santarelli's volume with the controversial chapters excised. But Pope Urban considered this a tacit retraction, and Magalotti instructed the nuncio Spada to keep the volumes in his possession. The general excused himself with Magalotti on the grounds that he had acted in good faith.[58] Urban's vigorous reaction at this point helps explain the firm tone of Vitelleschi's letter to the Paris Jesuits of May 5.

In early October Suffren reported to Vitelleschi that "all had been pacified." The king told him that he had no complaints against the Society for some time and that "he would take up the defense of our Society as often as it was necessary." Richelieu assured Suffren that he had dismissed the calumnies leveled against the Jesuits in the previous months and was convinced that no Jesuit had authored the two pamphlets against the king and himself. He went on to profess his goodwill toward the Society.[59] A royal decree of November 2, 1626, called for the silence of all parties on the issues, and under pressure from Louis, who acted at the behest of the new nuncio, Guidi di Bagno, the university revoked its censure of Santarelli's book on January 2, 1627.[60]

The upshot of the crisis of 1624–26 was on balance a victory for the Jesuits and for the papacy. But it also revealed the dependence of the Society on the king and the cardinal, as well as an increasing tendency toward Gallicanism among the French Jesuits themselves. Vitelleschi seems never to have doubted Richelieu's benevolence.[61] But the constant attacks on the Jesuits in France, which he thought were based on the merest suspicions, exasperated the superior general.[62] On August 13, 1626, he confirmed once again Acquaviva's prohibition of the publication of works dealing with the temporal power of the pope.[63]

Throughout Séguiran's whole period as confessor, Vitelleschi regularly urged him to foster peace in the Valtelline and respect for Catholic

57 Béthune to Phélypeaux d'Herbaut, Rome, Apr. 8, 1626, cited in Prat 4: 745–7.

58 Magalotti to Spada, Apr. 21, 1626, extract, Vanves, Collection Prat 35, f. 869.

59 Suffren to Vitelleschi, Oct. 8, 1626, Prat 5: 461–2; idem to idem, Nov. 3, 1626, ARSJ, Francia 47, f. 71.

60 Fouqueray 4: 140–90; Lutz, *Kardinal Giovanni Francesco Guidi di Bagno*, 58–60; Church, 160–1; Auguste Leman, *Receuil des instructions générales aux nonces ordinaires de France de 1624 à 1634* (Lille, 1920), 117–19.

61 See Vitelleschi to Suffren, Aug. 25, 1625, ARSJ, Francia 4, 199'.

62 Vitelleschi to Séguiran, Nov. 17, 1625, ibid., Francia 4, 204.

63 Guenter Lewy, *Constitutionalism and Statecraft during the Golden Age of Spain: A Study of the Political Philosophy of Juan de Mariana, S.J.* (Geneva, 1960), 169–70.

religious liberty there, without ever taking either the French or the Spanish side in the dispute. Both goals were obtained by the Treaty of Monzon. By this time Jean Suffren had replaced Séguiran.

Séguiran's dismissal as confessor on December 21, 1625, does not appear to have been linked directly either with Jesuit publications or with foreign policy. Ten years later a subsequent Jesuit confessor, Nicholas Caussin, called him an "administro Cardinalis."[64] Different explanations have been proposed for his dismissal. Most likely is that Richelieu forced him out after the cardinal's friend, Bishop Gabriel de l'Aubespine of Orléans, accused Séguiran of undue involvement in the distribution of benefices.[65] Richelieu's subsequent instruction for the new confessor Suffren, which reiterated the prohibition of participation in the assignment of benefices, speaks for this explanation, as does a later letter of Suffren to Richelieu alluding to this prohibition and the fate of his predecessors.[66] There were other grounds also for the bishop's objections to Séguiran, whom he referred to as a "little monk." The Jesuit belonged to an order whose superior general was outside France and "completely Spanish," and he allegedly questioned actions of the Assembly of the Clergy by appealing to the king's conscience. He often took a place of honor next to the king at ecclesiastical functions, ahead of the prelates.[67] Enemies of the Society sought his removal as a means of weakening the Jesuits. They tried to convince Louis that Séguiran was too stiff and inflexible; but the king himself asserted explicitly that he found no fault with Père Séguiran. Louis may simply have wanted a change.[68]

The attempt to take the post of confessor away from the Jesuits failed when Louis accepted the suggestion of Cardinal de La Rochefoucauld that he choose as his new confessor Suffren, who already served Marie de Medici in this capacity. At first Marie balked at the change. She feared that her enemies would charge that this was her scheme to find out what was on the king's conscience. But Louis insisted, moved partly by his mother's claim of the assistance and consolation that Suffren gave her. Suffren himself was reluctant to accept the post, and only did so, according to Garasse, when Séguiran implored him in the presence of Coton, "Mon Père, it is time to sacrifice yourself for the Society; it

64 Caussin to Vitelleschi, Mar. 7, 1638, BN, Manuscrits français 25054, f. 61'.
65 Joseph Bergin, *The Making of the French Episcopate, 1589–1661* (New Haven, CT, 1996), 453.
66 Suffren to Richelieu, undated but probably 1628, Prat 5: 465–6.
67 Eugène Griselle, *Louis XIII et Richelieu: Lettres et pièces diplomatiques* (Paris, 1911; rpt. Geneva, 1974), 20; see also Garasse, 100.
68 Henri Fouqueray, "Le Père Jean Suffren à la cour de Marie de Medicis, d'après les mémoires et des documents inédits." *Revue de questions historiques* 68 (1900): 34. (Also published separately.)

is absolutely necessary to accept this charge, or we will see the Society perish in France."[69] So important was the post of confessor for the Jesuits when they faced such hostility in France. Rumors spread that the king could not sleep the whole night before his first confession to Suffren on Christmas Eve 1625, for fear of the Jesuit's severity. But the contrary was the case. Confession had never brought the king such contentment. The day before, when the king first received Suffren, three times he repeated to him, "I want to save myself."[70]

Born in 1571 in Arles, Jean Suffren entered the Jesuits in 1586 and after ordination to the priesthood acquired a reputation as a preacher, spiritual director, and writer. Francis de Sales encouraged the publication of his two-volume *The Christian Year, or the Holy and Profitable Use of Time in Order to Gain Eternity*, a work of profound religious sentiment that had nothing to say about heresy or heretics.[71] Marie elected him as her confessor in 1615, and he remained in this position until his death. He was a man of reserve, by nature strongly inclined to stay out of political affairs. Already in 1617 the nuncio Bentivoglio criticized him for excessive reluctance to intervene in political matters, specifically for not alerting Marie de Medici to the excesses of Concini about which the whole world was complaining.[72] Richelieu had known him for some years, and they had worked together to resolve issues between the queen mother and the king. In a letter of 1618 to Suffren the cardinal spoke of "the friendship which has existed for a long time between us."[73]

Richelieu now drew up a set of guidelines for the new confessor.[74] In many ways they sounded like a reformulation of Acquaviva's Instruction. Suffren was not to become involved in affairs of state; they were not his charge, and besides, the cardinal added significantly, because Suffren could not foresee their long-term results, he could not judge them with certainty. The confessor was to come to court only when the king summoned him; this would make his visit of greater consequence. In this regard, the king had already told Suffren that he wanted him to visit him once a week; if he needed him further, then he would call for him. There was no need for the confessor to attend the king's

69 Garasse, 116–17.
70 Ibid., 118–19, 121.
71 *L'Année chrestienne ou le sainct et profitable employ due temps pour gaigner l'éternité*, 2 vols., 2nd ed. (Paris, 1641).
72 Prat 3: 735, citing Bentivoglio to Cardinal Borghese (secretary of state), Jan. 27, 1617.
73 Richelieu to Suffren, Dec. 1618, Armand-Jean du Plessis, cardinal de Richelieu, *Lettres, instructions et papiers d'état*, ed. Denis-Louis-Martial Avenel, 1 (Paris, 1853): 557–8.
74 Richelieu to Suffren, late December 1625, Armand-Jean du Plessis, cardinal de Richelieu, *Les papiers: Correspondance et papiers d'état. Section politique intérieur*, ed. Pierre Grillon, 1 (Paris, 1975): no. 81: 238–40.

daily Mass.[75] Acquaviva had instructed confessors to avoid presence at court as much as possible. Richelieu also repeated Acquaviva when he advised the confessor not to serve as a spokesman for those seeking favors at court; should he begin this practice, he would be simply overwhelmed by requests and thus distracted from his life as a religious. As we have seen, Vitelleschi himself offended in this regard, and in a letter to Suffren of March 9, 1626, he recommended a young Venetian patrician, Angelo Baducro.[76] Suffren was also warned not to seek a hand in the disposition of bishoprics and abbacies. But Richelieu did allow that he speak out when his conscience compelled him to do so because of the unsuitableness of a candidate.

Several directives of Richelieu related more directly to the Society of Jesus. The confessor should not be the one to bring the Society's requests for favors or support to the king or court. Already during Arnoux's period as confessor, Vitelleschi had sought to relieve the confessor of this responsibility. Now he drew up an instruction for the Jesuit who was to serve as the Society's procurator at court, to carry on its negotiations there.[77] Richelieu touched upon a recurring source of tension between the Jesuits and secular clergy when he enjoined the confessor to see to it that the Society observed proper obedience toward the hierarchy. Also, he encouraged the confessor to watch that the Society did not pursue the foundation of colleges too aggressively and that it not seek the transfer of benefices from other orders for their support. The cardinal was worried lest the Society become too powerful.

Vitelleschi was happy with the appointment of Suffren, both for the kingdom and for the Society, which confronted such hostility at the time in France. Many had written to him, he advised Suffren, of their satisfaction with the appointment, because of the new confessor's known prudence and deep religious spirit. He himself went quickly to inform Cardinal Barberini, who rejoiced at the news and did not doubt that the pope would too.[78] A secretary of state wrote Béthune in Rome that one could not have made a better choice. Suffren was "one of the best and least interested religious (without wanting to charge, blame or accuse the others) that I know, although [member] of a society which is accused of being ambitious and to have the reputation of wanting to be involved in intrigues and affaires."[79] Suffren remained in office for five years.

[75] Garasse, 119.
[76] Vitelleschi to Suffren, Mar. 9, 1626, ARSJ, Francia 4, f. 215.
[77] Vitelleschi to Coton (provincial), Feb. 7, 1626, ibid., f. 211'.
[78] Vitelleschi to Suffren, Jan. 26, 1626, ibid., 210.
[79] Phélypeaux d'Herbaut cited in Fouqueray "Suffren," 38–9.

On March 7, 1627, amidst great ceremony, Louis XIII laid the cornerstone for the new Jesuit church of St. Louis next to the professed house in Paris. He and Richelieu were to contribute over 78,000 *louis d'or* between them to its construction in the coming years.[80]

Vitelleschi's contacts with the Spanish court or Jesuits at the court were neither as frequent nor as intense as in France or Germany. With Madrid as with Paris, he pursued assistance for the Catholics of the Valtelline. His interest was not directly who controlled the pass but whether the Catholics enjoyed freedom to practice their faith. His thinking in this context about Jesuit participation in politics corresponded to his instructions to Arnoux at the same time. It appeared in a letter of June 29, 1621, to the Jesuit royal preacher, Jerónimo de Florencia: "Although it does not belong to our profession to mix in matters touching reason of state, when these matters are connected with the conservation of the faith, the spiritual good of our neighbor, and the glory of Our Lord, it is necessary that we fulfill our obligations, doing our duty and helping in all we can in a matter of great service of the Divine Majesty, such as that which presents itself in the case of not delivering the Valtelline back to the heretic Grey Leagues."[81] Florencia should work to dissuade the king and his ministers from surrendering the Valtelline Catholics to the oppression of the Grey Leagues. This was a necessary intervention in politics, for a religious goal.

All the while, letters of recommendation from Vitelleschi arrived regularly in Madrid. In 1622 he asked Hernando de Salazar, confessor of the count-duke of Olivares, to put in a word for Señor Rodrigo Bartolini, nephew of the bishop of Fiesole, who sought naturalization in Spain so that he would be eligible for benefices there. But Salazar should do this "without exceeding what our Constitutions and Decrees allow."[82] Later Vitelleschi interceded for the duke of Atri, who was connected with the Acquaviva family, to which the Society was obviously deeply indebted.[83] Cardinal Barberini in 1624 asked Vitelleschi to inform Jesuits at court about a disagreement he had had with a Spanish minister in Rome. The cardinal did not want to write government councillors himself, because this might only draw the matter to their attention. But if word of the disagreement did reach Madrid, then the Jesuits should

80 Louis Blond, "Paris, 2: La maison professe Saint-Louis de la rue Saint-Antoine (1580–1763)," in *Les établissements des Jésuites en France depuis quatre siècles*, ed. Pierre Delattre, S.J., 3 (Enghien, 1955): 1263–5, 1268.
81 Vitelleschi to Florencia, June 29, 1621, ARSJ, Hisp. 70, ff. 131′–2.
82 Vitelleschi to Salazar, Dec. 17, 1622, ibid., f. 146.
83 Vitelleschi to Salazar and Gonzalo de Albornoz, May 7, 1623, ibid., ff. 150–1′.

reassure Olivares and the president of the Council of Italy of the pope's affection for them and of his desire to serve as a "padre" to all.[84]

Yet the superior general took pains to prevent Jesuits in Spain from service in the government. Two significant figures offended in this regard, Pedro Hurtado de Mendoza of a great Spanish noble family and related to the court poet, Antonio Hurtado de Mendoza,[85] and especially Salazar, who was to cause Vitelleschi much grief during the coming years. His participation in government was greater than any other court confessor of the period, but he was at most marginally involved in politico-religious issues and for this reason more subject to the criticism of Vitelleschi. Born at Cuenca in 1576, and so two years older than Olivares, Salazar taught theology in Murcia and Alcalá before coming to the Colegio Imperial in Madrid. What brought him to the attention of Olivares and the king is not clear; it may have been that Salazar came up with the idea to create out of the Colegio Imperial an Estudios Reales or university, a project taken up with enthusiasm by Olivares but that enjoyed only modest success at best and incited the enmity of the old Spanish universities toward the Jesuits.[86] The count-duke turned to him for advice in both public and private matters, and as he wrote to Cardinal Barberini in 1623, Salazar was "the cleric in Spain to whom I owe most and whom I love most, and a man who, in my fallible judgment, is a person of rare and superior parts both in virtue and letters."[87] Salazar was named to the new Grand Commission of Reformation in August 1622, shortly after Olivares came to power, along with the count-duke himself, the presidents of the councils, the Inquisitor General, royal confessor, and others. He was to hold a number of positions on government committees, especially in those dealing with economic and financial matters as Olivares attempted to stimulate Spanish economic development.[88] The activities of Salazar disturbed Vitelleschi, and in 1624 he instructed the provincial, Luis de la Palma, to keep an eye on them.[89]

Two years later a report of de la Palma about the activities of Hurtado de Mendoza and Salazar alarmed Vitelleschi.[90] The former seems to

[84] Vitelleschi to Florencia, Albornoz, and Salazar, Oct. 30, 1624, ff. 70, 160'.

[85] See Gareth A. Davies, *A Poet at Court: Antonio Hurtado de Mendoza (1586–1644)* (Oxford, 1971), on the family where Pedro is not mentioned.

[86] Antonio Astraín, *Historia de la Compañia de Jesús en la Asistencia de España* 5 (Madrid, 1916): 139–70.

[87] Olivares to Barberini, Dec. 18, 1623, cited in J.H. Elliott, *The Count-Duke of Olivares* (New Haven, CT, 1986), 141.

[88] Elliott, 115.

[89] Vitelleschi to de la Palma (provincial), July 1, 1624, cited in Astraín 5: 217–18.

[90] Vitelleschi to de la Palma (provincial), July 20, 1626, ARSJ, Tol. 8II, f. 391'.

have been involved in legal and judicial affairs,[91] the latter in more properly governmental matters. Salazar in a lengthy paper composed with a government advisor recommended a sharp devaluation of the currency, and shortly afterward he undertook a journey to Barcelona to look into reviving the Mediterranean trade that once had flourished there.[92] Salazar was becoming a government official, and this Vitelleschi would not countenance. A sharp letter followed to Salazar himself but not to Hurtado de Mendoza, as well as letters to both Philip IV and Olivares. To the king he wrote that the Jesuits desired to serve him in all the ways that were compatible with their vocation as religious, but not to go beyond those limits, because to do so always proved harmful in the long run. He asked the king to allow superiors to withdraw Hurtado de Mendoza and Salazar from "temporal and political affairs." The same point was made with Olivares, where Vitelleschi emphasized that religious operating outside the sphere of their vocation ceased to serve as the salt that the Gospel expected them to be. Eventually, such activity led to the loss of the religious spirit.[93]

When the provincial attempted to defend Hurtado de Mendoza, Vitelleschi agreed that the two cases were not the same, but he insisted on the removal of the father from the court. Now was the time to take action when it would cause little stir; if we wait until the situation worsens, Vitelleschi wrote, he will not be able to depart from the court without noise and protest.[94] To Olivares he explained that the legal affairs and other temporal matters in which Hurtado de Mendoza was involved were foreign to the Jesuit vocation and were a cause of scandal to others.[95] This seems to have settled the matter for Hurtado de Mendoza. With regard to Salazar, the provincial was instructed to designate four fathers to whom Salazar would describe the nature of the work he was doing and the way he proceeded, and they would then determine whether this violated canon law or the Society's decrees. Exactly how this proceeded, we do not know. But Vitelleschi expressed his satisfaction to the new provincial, Francisco Aguado, who would later become Olivares's confessor, when the count-duke agreed not to employ Salazar in duties inconsistent with a Jesuit. The papal nuncio noticed that he

91 Vitelleschi to Olivares, Oct. 19, 1626, ibid, ff. 409'–10.

92 Elliott, 265, 268–9.

93 Vitelleschi to Salazar, July 20, 1626, cited in Astraín 5: 219–20 (this letter was illegible to me in the archives); Vitelleschi to Olivares, July 20, 1626, cited, ibid., 218; Vitelleschi to Philip IV, July 20, 1626, ibid., 708–9 (appendix).

94 Vitelleschi to de la Palma (provincial), Sept. 21 and Oct. 19, 1626, ARSJ, Tol. 8II, ff. 400'–1, 406.

95 Vitelleschi to Olivares, Oct. 19, 1626, ibid., ff. 409'–10.

seemed to have withdrawn from the scene.[96] But as we shall see, not permanently.

In William Lamormaini and, to a lesser extent, Adam Contzen, Vitelleschi encountered in Germany a new style of court confessor; they had their own programs for the advancement of Catholicism. They were activists, more so than Arnoux had been. Born in Luxembourg in 1570, Lamormaini came to Prague in the entourage of the Spanish ambassador, whom his uncle served as a cook, studied at the Jesuit college there, and entered the Society in 1590. After his studies he was assigned to the university in Graz, where he first taught philosophy, then theology, and from 1613 to 1621 served as rector. During the years in Graz he and Archduke Ferdinand became genuine friends, so that Ferdinand could write many years later, when Lamormaini was under severe fire, "as long as life remains for the two of us, my Father, nothing will separate us from each other."[97] After his term as rector, Lamormaini was summoned to Rome, where he came to know Vitelleschi personally and discussed with members of the papal curia the situation of the church in Germany. While there, the general alerted him to complaints about him as rector, especially that he was too involved politically and not easily available to his Jesuit subjects.[98] Lamormaini returned to Germany in 1622 to become rector of the college in Vienna, where he was reunited with Ferdinand. Complaints about his style of Jesuit government persisted in Vienna, where some considered him high handed,[99] and in February 1625, a year after he took up the office of confessor, he surrendered his post as rector of the college.

Martin Becan died suddenly in February 1624. Vitelleschi was not initially enthusiastic about Lamormaini as his replacement, but it soon became clear that he was the emperor's choice and the logical person for the position. So the general instructed him to set aside his hesitation about assuming the position, which Lamormaini seems genuinely to have felt, and with confidence to accept it for the good of the Christian commonwealth.[100] To Lamormaini's request for guidelines, Vitelleschi

[96] Vitelleschi to Aguado (provincial), Dec. 6, 1627, ibid., f. 477; Astraín 5: 220. Elliott, 319, observes that Salazar seemed to drop from favor for a time in late 1627.

[97] Eustachius Sthaäl, "Vita Lamormaini," ARSJ, Vitae 139, ff. 66, 121. The author of this manuscript life records the quote as approximate. On Lamormaini's early life, see Robert Bireley, *Religion and Politics in the Age of the Counterreformation: Emperor Ferdinand II, William Lamormaini, S.J., and the Formation of Imperial Policy* (Chapel Hill, NC, 1981), 8–11.

[98] Ibid., f. 37.

[99] See, for example, Vitelleschi to Joannes Argenti (provincial), Jan. 23, 1624, ARSJ, Aust. 3I, f. 473.

[100] Vitelleschi to Lamormaini, Mar. 2, 1624, ibid., ff. 489–90; Vitelleschi to Argenti (provincial), Mar. 2, 1624, ibid., f. 489.

sent a copy of Acquaviva's Instruction. It, of course, allowed for the treatment of matters touching conscience but was unclear about their scope. Vitelleschi instructed Lamormaini to take up "affairs" (*negotia*) only when requested by the emperor to do so, and then in the spirit of Acquaviva's directives. When Lamormaini asked how often Vitelleschi expected to hear from him, the general was vague, but he certainly meant to be kept informed, and he especially asked the confessor to let him know how he could assist the emperor.[101] Most of Lamormaini's letters to Rome have been lost, but there remain slightly less than one thousand letters from Vitelleschi to Lamormaini between 1624 and 1635. Later in 1625 Vitelleschi congratulated Lamormaini on his agreement with Ferdinand that, apart from his weekly visit for confession, he would appear at court only when called.[102] Yet neither Lamormaini nor Ferdinand long abided by this agreement.

Lamormaini succeeded in having Vitelleschi bar all other Jesuits from approaching the emperor or the court except through him or the provincial.[103] So Lamormaini was the normal contact for all the Society's business at court, including the foundation of houses and colleges, whereas in France this business was in the hands of a procurator not of the confessor Suffren. Lamormaini undertook a multitude of building projects. Nine colleges in Bohemia and Moravia alone owed their foundation or significant expansion to his efforts.[104] One of his projects of the 1620s, the university church, still dominates Ignaz-Seipel Platz in Vienna today. Creditors of the emperor later claimed that funds that should have been employed to pay them were being used to build new structures for the Jesuits.[105]

A profound sense of his responsibility as imperial confessor marked Lamormaini. He set for himself three goals at the start of his tenure. First, to live his life as completely as possible for the Lord. His performance as confessor depended on the quality of his own religious life. Second, to lead Ferdinand to the highest level of Christian life open to him. Third, to strive "that the Catholic religion with the help and authority of the same emperor be completely restored in the two Austrias, the Kingdom of Bohemia, Hungary, and in the Roman Empire."[106] Ferdinand, for his part, on Lamormaini's assumption of office on March 25, 1624, vowed in the confessor's presence "that he would undertake whatever the circumstances seemed to permit" for the good of religion, "not only gladly

101 Vitelleschi to Lamormaini, Apr. 6, 1624, ibid., f. 499.
102 Vitelleschi to Lamormaini, June 7, 1625, ibid., Aust. 3II, f. 625.
103 Vitelleschi to Lamormaini, July 3, 1625, ibid., f. 632.
104 Sthaäl, f. 55.
105 Vitelleschi to Lamormaini, Mar. 13, 1627, ARSJ, Aust. 3II, f. 812.
106 Sthaäl, ff. 43'–4.

but with great pleasure and joy."[107] In accord with Acquaviva's Instruction, Ferdinand agreed to listen patiently to Lamormaini whenever the Jesuit had something to say that he considered necessary "for the security of both their consciences and the fulfillment of his office." Indeed, Ferdinand requested Lamormaini to alert him to opportunities to advance the faith.[108] It may well have been at the confessor's prompting that just as Richelieu entered the council of state in France the emperor summoned Louis XIII to a common campaign against the heretics.[109] Eventually, Lamormaini himself came to carry on a political correspondence that neither Louis XIII (nor Richelieu) nor Maximilian would have permitted to his confessor.

Both Vitelleschi and Lamormaini aimed to maintain harmony between the emperor and the pope, a task that was not so easy during the pontificate of Urban VIII. The general assured Lamormaini of Urban's goodwill toward Ferdinand in a letter shortly after Lamormaini became confessor, and he promised to bring Lamormaini's recommendations for the church in Germany to the pope the next time that they spoke.[110] Lamormaini himself informed Cardinal Barberini that all Germany might be returned to the Catholic faith if pope and emperor, "the two lights of the world," aggressively pursued this goal.[111]

Ferdinand, and Lamormaini, obviously expected financial subsidies from Rome, but the days of Gregory XV had passed. Vitelleschi reported to Lamormaini that if Urban were less liberal, there were two reasons for this. First, he inherited a treasury nearly empty. Second, rumors suggested that the imperial ministers did not carefully and faithfully administer the wealth that divine providence placed at the emperor's disposal.[112] To be sure, financial management in Vienna was loose, Lamormaini admitted, but he judged it wiser to withhold Vitelleschi's comment from the emperor. Vitelleschi then defended the pope after Lamormaini wrote of the rumors in Vienna about the integrity of papal finances under Urban, who outdid himself in gifts to

107 Lamormaini to Barberini, Aug. 3, 1624, BL 7054, f. 54; see also Vitelleschi to Lamormaini, May 29, 1624, ARSJ, Aust. 3I, ff. 507–8, and William Lamormaini, S.J., *Ferdinandi II Romanorum Imperatoris Virtutes* (Vienna, 1638), 4. I have used Lamormaini's own annotated author's copy of this book, which is found in the Österreichische Nationalbibliothek, Vienna, Handschriftensammlung 7378. References to Lamormaini's annotations will be clearly distinguished from those to the printed text.

108 Sthaäl, f. 41'; Lamormaini, 5 (annotation).

109 Ferdinand II to Louis XIII, Apr. 15, 1624, Armand-Jean du Plessis, cardinal de Richelieu, *Les papiers: Correspondance et papiers d'état. Section politique extérieur, empire Allemand*, ed. A. Wild, 1 (Paris, 1982): no. 37: 63–4.

110 Vitelleschi to Lamormaini, May 29, 1624, ARSJ, Aust. 3I, ff. 507–8.

111 Lamormaini to Barberini, Aug. 3, 1624, BL 7054, f. 54.

112 Vitelleschi to Lamormaini, July 6, 1624, ARSJ, Aust. 3II, ff. 518–20.

his family.[113] Other areas of long-standing tension between Vienna and Rome, which Vitelleschi sought to alleviate, were ecclesiastical jurisdiction in the patriarchate of Aquileia, over which the emperor and the Republic of Venice clashed, and control of the University of Prague, which Ferdinand, Lamormaini, and many Jesuits sought to turn over completely to the Society in the face of opposition from the Congregation for the Propagation of the Faith, other religious orders, and the archbishop of Prague, who generally enjoyed Urban's support.[114] At one point in this conflict Lamormaini urged the emperor to remain firm on this issue, in the face of the "little dogs"(*cuniculos*) in Rome.[115] Vitelleschi admonished Lamormaini in his own fashion that he defend the Holy See in Vienna with the same diligence with which he defended the emperor in Rome, so that "you always, as is right, stand up for the rights and authority of the same See." He asked Lamormaini to provide him with specific examples where he had done this, so that he might relate them to authorities in Rome.[116] The superior general then declared himself satisfied with the virtual book that Lamormaini sent him detailing the allegiance and goodwill of the emperor toward the Holy See.[117]

Vitelleschi generally allowed Lamormaini a long leash and, as in the case of Arnoux, defended him against his critics. They both obviously shared the belief in the need for vigorous princely support for the Society's efforts, a point we adverted to earlier.[118] One of Lamormaini's critics was the Spanish Jesuit Ambrosio Peñalosa, a theologian in Vienna. After hearing from Peñalosa in the summer of 1626, Vitelleschi started to call Lamormaini's attention to concerns of other Jesuits in Vienna, but he then crossed out the pertinent section from his letter. In the deleted passage he had alerted Lamormaini to the fear that the confessor was alienating leading figures in Vienna from the Society, which boded ill for the Jesuits especially when a new ruler succeeded Ferdinand.[119]

In 1630 a formal visitor of the Austrian Province, Florence de Montmorency, required from Lamormaini an accounting of the funds that passed through his hands with his many building projects. The provincial complained that the confessor undertook these projects

113 Vitelleschi to Lamormaini, Aug. 24, 1624, ibid., f. 531.
114 Bireley, ibid., 32–6, 69, 70, 71.
115 Lamormaini to Ferdinand, Jan. 25, 1626, HHStA, Reichskanzlei, Staatenabteilungen, Romana, Varia, 6.
116 Vitelleschi to Lamormaini, Dec. 26, 1626, ARSJ, Aust. 3II, f. 783.
117 Vitelleschi to Lamormaini, Mar. 20, 1627, ibid., f. 812.
118 Vitelleschi developed this idea in a long letter to Lamormaini of Aug. 2, 1625, ibid., ff. 641–2; see p. 31.
119 Vitelleschi to Lamormaini, Aug. 1, 1626, ibid., 731; see Vitelleschi to Peñalosa, July 4, 1626, ibid., 722.

without his permission. In a long letter to Montmorency on the matter, Vitelleschi revealed clearly his method of government. Many times he had admonished Lamormaini about his gruffness, and the confessor had promised to improve. "But his temperament and the multitude of his tasks overcome his will, and so it happens that he again becomes more harsh and more free than is called for towards others and even toward superiors." His virtues and qualities, however, especially his efficacious zeal for the glory of God, were such that "religious wisdom seems to counsel, that superiors admonish him about his shortcomings in such a tactful and mild manner, that the severity of an admonition not divert his spirit from his more important and useful projects for the common good."[120] The general let Montmorency know that he would take the matter of finances up with Lamormaini and that it would not be suitable for the visitor or provincial to do so.[121] But there is no evidence that Vitelleschi ever asked Lamormaini for a financial accounting.

Vitelleschi needed to caution Lamormaini about his tendency to override the claims of other religious orders and to speak derogatorily of them, especially when he pursued their property for the endowment of Jesuit institutions. Even before Lamormaini became confessor, Vitelleschi questioned him about complaints of the Dominicans that he convinced the emperor to take over a part of their school in Vienna for a Jesuit college. He later informed Lamormaini that he and the Dominican superior general in Rome would work the matter out.[122] Rivalry between orders was an element in the dispute over the University of Prague. At one point in a letter to Vitelleschi, Lamormaini noted a remark of Ferdinand that the Society had saved the church in Germany when all the other orders failed her and then another of Prince Eggenberg, Ferdinand's first minister, that without the Jesuits the old orders would revert to their former ways.[123] Such an attitude did not endear Lamormaini to the other orders and embarrassed Vitelleschi. It became a feature of the later monastery controversy.[124]

Adam Contzen was named confessor to Duke Maximilian of Bavaria at almost exactly the same time as Lamormaini was to Emperor Ferdinand. Born in 1571 at Monschau, a village not far from Aachen, he had distinguished himself as a theology professor and writer at the

[120] Vitelleschi to Montmorency (visitor), Oct. 19, 1630, ARSJ, Aust. 4I, ff. 341–2.
[121] Vitelleschi to Montmorency (visitor), Feb. 1, 1631, ibid., ff. 403–5.
[122] Vitelleschi to Lamormaini, Apr. 15, 1623, and Mar. 23, 1624, ARSJ, Aust. 3I, ff. 376, 498.
[123] Lamormaini to Vitelleschi, Oct. 5, 1624, ARSJ, Aust. 23, ff. 28–8'.
[124] Vitelleschi also suggested to Lamormaini a money-raising scheme for the emperor that an Italian nobleman proposed to the superior general. See Vitelleschi to Lamormaini, July 27, 1624, and Aug. 22, 1626, ARSJ, Aust. 3II, ff. 526, 734. But nothing appears to have come of it.

academy in Mainz, where he took Becan's place when he first departed for Vienna. Nearly a book a year came from his pen between 1613 and 1620, many of them directed against Calvinist adversaries in Heidelberg. His most important work, the massive *Ten Books on Politics*, appeared in 1621 in Mainz and exercised a significant impact on seventeenth-century Catholic political thought.[125] Contzen laid out a detailed program for a Catholic state, and his book, Antimachiavellian in character, attempted to show how a prince acting on Christian principles could succeed in the hard world of politics.

The initiative for Contzen's appointment came from Maximilian,[126] certainly on the basis of Contzen's *Ten Books*. The two do not seem to have had any prior personal contact.[127] Contzen's Antimachiavellian approach attracted Maximilian, who as a genuinely religious man as well as a highly self-conscious and ambitious Renaissance prince desired to combine these two features of his personality. We know that Maximilian kept Contzen's *Ten Books* at hand in his private library.[128] Upon receiving Maximilian's request for Contzen, Vitelleschi instructed the Jesuit to set aside his other tasks and proceed to Munich.[129]

Contzen never held the title of councillor in Munich, but Maximilian consulted him on many issues, domestic as well as foreign. The phrase "talk with Father Contzen and report to His Highness" frequently turns up in the private notebook of Bartholomew Richel, the vice-chancellor of the privy council. So Contzen was kept abreast of and had input into the council's deliberations.[130] A number of draft documents in his hand survive in the Munich archives. Contzen along with other Jesuits like Keller also served on governmental committees, such as one created in 1627 to draw up a response to complaints about the expansion of the ruler's hunting rights.[131] We have already seen how Contzen authored anonymously for Maximilian the two pamphlets that weighed heavily on the French Jesuits. Contzen's vigorous personality and outspokenness generated in 1625 an early conflict with Maximilian's veteran crown jurist,

125 *Politicorum libri decem, in quibus de perfectae reipublicae forma, virtutibus et vitiis, institutione civium, legibus, magistratu ecclesiastico, civili, potentia reipublicae itemque seditione et bello, ad usum vitamque communem accomodate tractatur*; a second, slightly expanded edition appeared at Cologne in 1629. See Ernst-Albert Seils, *Die Staatslehre des Jesuiten Adam Contzen, Beichtvater Kurfürst Maximilians von Bayern* (Lübeck, 1968), 191–228.

126 Maximilian to Vitelleschi, Dec. 21, 1623, HStA, Jesuitica 543.

127 Robert Bireley, *Maximilian von Bayern, Adam Contzen, S.J., und die Gegenreformation in Deutschland, 1624–1635* (Göttingen, 1975), 43, and n. 1.

128 Heinz Dollinger, "Kurfürst Maximilian von Bayern und Justus Lipsius," *Archiv für Kulturgeschichte* 46 (1964): 284 and n. 111.

129 Vitelleschi to Contzen, Jan. 20, 1624, ARSJ, Rhen. Inf. 6, f. 108'.

130 For example, for Nov. 20, 1625, HStA, KSchw 5966.

131 Decree, Dec. 6, 1627, HStA, Staatsverwaltung 3, ff. 144–5'.

Wilhelm Jocher, who was willing to entertain the possibility of concessions to Frederick on the Palatinate issue for the sake of peace in the empire. The privy council was divided. Contzen went so far as to assert that Jocher was tainted by heresy and even Machiavellism, a charge the jurist resented profoundly. Written recriminations were exchanged before Maximilian himself had to step in to quell the dispute.[132]

Vitelleschi never mentioned Acquaviva's Instruction for Confessors of Princes in his dealings with Contzen, probably because he wished to avoid a conflict with the deeply Catholic but strong-willed Maximilian over Contzen's role. Contzen and Vitelleschi corresponded regularly, with Vitelleschi occasionally passing on to Cardinal Barberini communications from Contzen that were certainly prepared under Maximilian's eye. In contrast to the 60 letters to Buslidius, Contzen's predecessor, over a 25-year period, from Acquaviva and Vitelleschi, 125 letters survive from Vitelleschi to Contzen over an 11-year period, and many more letters travelled from Contzen in Munich to Vitelleschi than the other way around. But 125 letters of Vitelleschi pale before the nearly 1,000 he dispatched to Lamormaini during roughly the same span.[133]

As with other confessors, Vitelleschi defended Contzen from his critics within the Society. These complained to the general that the popular mind associated the Jesuit confessor with Maximilian's unpopular tax policy and that this hindered the Society's ministry. Acquaviva's Instruction intended to forestall precisely this situation. We know from Richel's notes that Contzen was consulted on tax policy; he also was in favor of the war, which required taxes. Vitelleschi raised the issue, gently, with Contzen, asking him to consider "whether some way might be found whereby the confessor did not deny the prince the service that was owed him without subjecting the name of the Society to so much ill-will and murmuring." Was there not some way that the advice given the prince by Jesuits might be hidden from others? Echoing complaints from Munich, Vitelleschi also suggested that before Contzen make recommendations, especially on tax policy, he consult with other Jesuits.[134] Acquaviva's Instruction prescribed precisely this procedure for difficult cases. But the superior general expressed himself fully satisfied with Contzen's explanation of his procedure, which has not survived.[135] Contzen himself complained to Vitelleschi of his Jesuit critics and suggested that he might resign as confessor. Vitelleschi responded that Contzen should

132 Bireley, ibid., 67–72.
133 Illness in 1634/35 made it difficult for Contzen to function in his last years, and so the correspondence dwindled.
134 Vitelleschi to Contzen, Apr. 7, 1629, ARSJ, Germ. Sup. 6, f. 170.
135 Vitelleschi to Contzen, June 2, 1629, ibid., f. 182.

set aside all thought of resignation. Vitelleschi would also take measures, he indicated, against the excessive liberty of speech in the Munich Jesuit community, which was directed not only against the prince but also, for that matter, against the pope.[136] So Munich Jesuits unhappy with the policy of Maximilian and Contzen found little sympathy with Vitelleschi.

After the Catholic victories at the Dessau Bridge and Lutter am Barenberg in 1626 and Richelieu's temporary withdrawal from intervention in Germany, Catholic forces dominated the empire with the exception of the two Protestant electorates of Saxony and Brandenburg, which remained loyal to the emperor. Two parties now developed at the Catholic courts: the militants, of which Lamormaini and Contzen were leaders, and the moderates. There was a rough analogy between these two groupings and the two factions in France, the *dévots* and the *bons français*. The militants saw the upper hand of the Catholics as a God-given opportunity to restore Catholicism at least to the status it enjoyed at the time of the Peace of Augsburg of 1555. Gradually the war became for them not only a religious but a holy conflict. They also were convinced that eventually Catholic France would enter the fray on their side. The moderates on the other hand warned of overreaching the Catholic hand, provoking Saxony and Brandenburg, and in an expanded war forfeiting what had been won. For them the wise course was to show restraint and consolidate the Catholic gains. They also exhibited greater awareness of the suffering caused by the war and of the need for peace, and they rejected the providentialist theology of the militants. Spain generally favored the moderates because it wanted peace in the empire, which would then enable Ferdinand to assist it in Italy and The Netherlands and against France.

Vitelleschi generally supported the militants during these early years, though not unfailingly. Initiatives in this regard came not from him nor from Rome at all, but from the Catholic courts. The general welcomed the measures taken by Ferdinand in 1627 to restore Catholicism in Bohemia and Lower Austria. One ought not act on the basis of "the human and political" considerations that counseled against them because of the opposition that they might incite but rather trust in the providence of God that was with Ferdinand.[137] As the Catholics secured control over more territory, cases were brought for the restoration of individual ecclesiastical properties. The idea for a general restoration of all

136 Vitelleschi to Contzen, July 21, 1629, ibid., ff. 193–4; see also Vitelleschi to Walter Mundbrot (provincial), July 7 and 21, 1629, ibid., ff. 190–2, 193–4.

137 Vitelleschi to Lamormaini, Oct. 23, 1627, ARSJ, Aust. 3II, ff. 908–9; see also Vitelleschi to Lamormaini, Sept. 18 and Oct. 9, 1627, ibid., ff. 894, 900–1.

ecclesiastical properties confiscated by the Protestants in an allegedly illegal manner since 1555 seems to have originated with Reinhard Ziegler, Jesuit confessor of the elector of Mainz. He first suggested this in 1625, but at the time neither Maximilian nor the emperor showed interest.[138]

Two years later, in the summer of 1627, as preparations began for the Electoral Convention of Mühlhausen, which was meant to stabilize the political situation in the Empire, the time was more propitious.[139] At first it was a question of the restitution of eight monasteries in Württemberg. Contzen's voice decided Maximilian to advocate their restitution when he was consulted by the emperor on this far-reaching measure. God had given the Catholics this opportunity to recover the church property, the confessor asserted, and he would help overcome the resistance the move would engender. Maximilian took over this position in his letter to Mainz of September 7, 1627.[140] At Mühlhausen, the five Catholic electors, with the emperor's encouragement, took a further major step. They proposed to extend the restitution to all the church lands seized illegally by the Protestants since 1555. In Munich Maximilian followed the urging of Contzen to take this step rather than the caution recommended by his moderate councillors.[141] Vitelleschi welcomed the far-reaching decision "for the defense and spread of Catholicism in Germany and in the north."[142] Lamormaini informed Barberini of the emperor's "one and only thought, to restore to the Catholic faith and church his provinces and kingdoms and all Germany" and of his own desire that Urban as "pastor of the universal church" have a part in this grand design.[143] Vitelleschi assured Contzen that he would work to convince Urban VIII to support the return of this ecclesiastical property "in the way you have suggested."[144] To Ziegler he indicated with enthusiasm that he would speak with those who he hoped would persuade the pope to support the measure.[145] The confessors wanted a sign that the pope stood behind the venture. Vitelleschi already did.

138 Bireley, *Maximilian von Bayern*, 84–5.
139 An electoral convention, as the term indicates, was a meeting of the seven electors, or their representatives, often with the emperor. Electoral conventions became more prominent after it became increasingly clear that agreement could not be reached at a diet, and they show the growing importance of the electors within the imperial constitution.
140 Memorandum of Contzen, undated but before Sept. 7, 1627, HStA, KSchw 773; Maximilian to Mainz, Sept. 7, 1627, ibid.; see Bireley, ibid., 77–8.
141 Bireley, ibid., 83–4.
142 Vitelleschi to Ziegler, Dec. 25, 1627, Rhen. Inf. 6, f. 224.
143 Lamormaini to Barberini, Dec. 21, 1627, BL 6944, ff. 28–9.
144 Vitelleschi to Contzen, Oct. 9, 1627, ARSJ, Germ. Sup. 6, f. 23.
145 Vitelleschi to Ziegler, Aug. 5 and Sept. 9, 1628, ARSJ, Rhen. Inf. 6, ff. 241, 244'.

The proposed restitution of church lands elicited further deliberation at the Catholic courts. It would constitute a massive transfer of property from Protestant to Catholic hands. It would weaken some German Protestant principalities substantially – Württemberg in the southwest, for example, where the Catholics soon claimed fourteen large monasteries and thirty-six convents[146] – and incite Protestant opposition, but it would also provide the resources to finance a Catholic restoration, including Jesuit colleges in Protestant areas. The moderate party in Vienna that included the three privy councillors, Peter von Stralendorf, Trautmannsdorf, and Abbot Anton Wolfradt of Kremsmünster, were wary of pursuing "absolute victory"; new victories would only incite more attempts to curtail imperial power.[147] But according to the nuncio in Vienna Carlo Carafa, Lamormaini spoke of the "glorious enterprise" to be undertaken by Ferdinand, a term reminiscent of the Spanish Armada.[148] The prospect was opening up, Vitelleschi wrote Contzen, "that the dark clouds of heresy having been scattered, the splendor of the orthodox faith would illumine not only Germany but the whole of the north."[149] To Lamormaini he promised that he would have 2,500 Masses offered each week by the Jesuits for the major decision soon to be made by the emperor and his council.[150] Yet as Lamormaini's plans became more expansive, to include the formation of a new Saxon Province, a note of caution entered his correspondence, and Vitelleschi admonished Lamormaini gently about making plans for the future without consulting the provincial.[151]

Finally, on March 26, 1629, under date of March 6, the Edict of Restitution was published, calling for the return to the Catholics of the disputed ecclesiastical property. The measure showed clearly the religious nature of the war. "No Roman Pontiff has received such a harvest of joys from Germany since the time of Charlemagne," Lamormaini proclaimed in his letter to Francesco Barberini.[152] Vitelleschi appeared restrained when he learned the news. At first, he hoped for great things from it for the church, "provided the strength for implementing it is not lacking," especially given the situation in Italy, he noted, ominously alluding to the incipient conflict over Mantua between Spain and France.[153] Later, he was more optimistic.[154]

146 Bireley, *Religion and Politics*, 86.
147 Ibid., 59 and n. 52.
148 Carafa to Barberini, Dec. 22, 1627, BL 6944, ff. 26–7.
149 Vitelleschi to Contzen, Dec. 11, 1627, ARSJ, Germ. Sup. 6, f. 39.
150 Vitelleschi to Lamormaini, Jan. 15, 1628, ARSJ, Aust 3II, f. 954.
151 Vitelleschi to Lamormaini, Feb. 12 and May 13, 1628, ibid., ff. 976, 1008.
152 Lamormaini to Barberini, Mar. 28, 1629, BL 7054, f. 72.
153 Vitelleschi to Lamormaini, Apr. 21 and 28, 1629, ARSJ, Aust. 4I, ff. 95–6, 98–9.
154 Vitelleschi to Lamormaini, ibid., June 23, 1629, ibid., f. 123.

A factor that helped the Edict surmount the last-minute doubts at the Catholic courts about its juridical correctness was the anonymous "Dillingen Book," or *Way to Peace*,[155] of the Jesuit canonist Paul Laymann. The book argued a strong legal case for a strict Catholic interpretation of the Peace of Augsburg and was to the Edict as theory to practice. It made clear to the Protestants what to expect from the militants if the Catholics continued to hold the upper hand. Vitelleschi instructed the provincial in Munich to weigh the pros and cons of its publication with prudence and care before he allowed it to appear, lest the book cause "grave offense."[156] But it then appeared without the approval of Jesuit censors. The Dillingen Book became an arsenal of legal weapons for the militants but a book of infamy for the Protestants. After the great shift in the fortunes of war, Gustavus Adolphus was said to desire to hang three Jesuits whose name began with *L*, Lamormaini, Laymann, and Laurentius Forer, another polemicist who assisted Laymann with the *Way to Peace*. Later, fellow Jesuits called Laymann to account for the book's publication.[157]

Papal policy toward the Edict was complex and opaque. A distinction needs to be made between what Vienna thought it was and what it was in reality. Urban's brief of May 5, 1629, warmly congratulated Ferdinand on the far-reaching measure.[158] The nuncio Pallotto and his successor in 1630, Ciriaco Rocci, both favored the Edict personally. Ferdinand had every reason to believe that Urban stood behind him. But the pope's primary concern was for the juridical position of the church. Despite several enthusiastic pronouncements, Urban VIII seems never to have given unambiguous support to the Edict of Restitution. To do so would have meant an implicit endorsement of the Peace of Augsburg, of which the Edict was an interpretation. The papacy had not protested the Peace of Augsburg, but it had also scrupulously avoided endorsing it. Rocci was instructed to give no indication that the popes had ever approved it.[159] Full support for the Edict would also have compelled the pope to much greater financial aid for the emperor than he was willing to provide.[160] Unlike his predecessor, Urban did not share the militant,

155 *Pacis compositio inter principes et ordines Catholicos atque Augustanae Confessionis adhaerentes in Comitiis Augustae a. 1555 edita* (Dillingen, 1629).

156 Vitelleschi to Mundbrot (provincial), Jan. 13, 1629, ARSJ, Germ. Sup. 6, f. 129.

157 Robert Bireley, "The Origins of the 'Pacis Compositio' in 1629: A Text of Paul Laymann, S. J.," AHSJ 42 (1973): 106–27.

158 Urban VIII to Ferdinand II, May 5, 1629, Hans Kiewning, ed., *Nuntiaturberichte aus Deutschland nebst ergänzenden Aktenstücken*. Section 4: *Siebzehntes Jahrhundert, Nuntiatur des Pallotto* 2 (Berlin, 1897): no. 102.

159 Barberini to Rocci, Aug. 10 and 17, 1630, Konrad Repgen, *Die römische Kurie und der westfälische Friede* 1, 2 (Tübingen, 1965) no. 16, 17: 43–7.

160 Bireley, *Religion and Politics*, 81–4, 127–8.

providentialist theology despite his occasional resort to its rhetoric.[161] Later, after the great reversal of fortune in 1631, Urban claimed that he never supported the Edict, to Vienna's consternation.[162]

Pope and emperor remained at loggerheads over the ecclesiastical jurisdiction of the patriarchate of Aquileia and control of the University of Prague, frequent items in Vitelleschi's correspondence with Lamormaini. In addition, there were disputes over the disposition of church lands recovered from the Protestants in Bohemia.[163] The nuncio Carafa, at first a Jesuit supporter, had reversed his position in 1626 and complained that with Lamormaini as confessor the Jesuits had become intolerable in Vienna. Through their influence with Ferdinand, they excluded other orders from any matters spiritual or political in which they had an interest. Even the imperial ministers needed their favor.[164] Vitelleschi, while deploring the machinations of the Society's enemies in Prague, gently admonished Lamormaini not to stoop to similar measures.[165]

But at the end of 1627 the fate of Mantua suddenly became the most crucial issue for pope and emperor as well as Spain and France. On Christmas day of that year the Gonzaga duke of Mantua died without a direct heir. As fiefs of the empire this north Italian principality and the marquisate of Montferrato with which it was permanently linked fell ultimately under Ferdinand's suzerainty. The two were crucial for control of the peninsula, and both Spain and France had prepared their candidates for the event of the duke's demise. Duke Charles of Nevers, the French candidate, seized control of Mantua on January 17, 1628. Four months later the Spanish governor of Milan, Don Gonzalo de Córdoba, invaded Montferrat and soon began to besiege its mighty fortress of Casale. Meanwhile, Ferdinand placed both duchies under sequester until he could adjudicate the dispute between the two claimants. Spain had long supported the imperial cause in Germany but had never received from the emperor the aid in The Netherlands to which it felt entitled. Now it put heavy pressure on Vienna for assistance in north Italy, especially because it foresaw, correctly, eventual French intervention to support the French candidate.

Urban VIII for his part wanted at all costs to keep war out of Italy, where German imperial troops might spread heresy and where memory

161 For a nuanced characterization of the differences between the policies of Gregory XV and Urban VIII, see Lutz, *Kardinal Giovanni Francesco Guidi di Bagno*, 371–86.
162 Bireley, ibid., 184.
163 Bireley, ibid., 61.
164 Carafa to Barberini, Nov. 25, 1626, BL 6949, ff. 118–24.
165 Vitelleschi to Lamormaini, Dec. 11, 1627, ARSJ, Aust. 3II, ff. 933–4.

of the Sack of Rome of 1527 remained alive. Nor did he want the expansion of Spanish power in Italy that control of the duchies would bring. A new, extraordinary nuncio, Giovanni Battista Pallotto, was dispatched to Vienna. He was a good friend of the Society, Vitelleschi informed Lamormaini, and he was expected to replace the present nuncio.[166] Carafa was recalled a few months later, largely because he could not get along with Lamormaini. Pallotto brought with him a brief for the confessor, in which Urban pointed up the opportunity for Ferdinand to obtain glory by preserving Italy from war.[167] Lamormaini's position was that both sides should await the judgment of the emperor. By invading Montferrat Spain had failed to do this even though it claimed merely to be implementing the emperor's order of sequestration.[168] The papacy's desire for Lamormaini's assistance in the matter of Mantua inclined it to show more support for Ferdinand's plans to restore ecclesiastical lands in Germany.

Spain and the Spanish party in Vienna, which included Eggenberg, were furious with Lamormaini, who according to nuncio Pallotto, was the chief obstacle to imperial intervention on the side of Spain.[169] They feared that he would hold it up long enough for Louis XIII and Richelieu finally to take the Huguenot fortress of La Rochelle, which they had been besieging for nearly a year, and then to march into Italy themselves, thus frustrating the Spanish grab for Montferrat. In a stormy interview of July 1628 with the Spanish ambassador, the marquis of Aytona, Lamormaini claimed that Spanish policy was unjust. Eggenberg threatened to resign, a move Ferdinand refused to consider.[170] Hearing how deeply offended the Spanish ambassador had been by Lamormaini's attack on Spanish policy in his presence, Vitelleschi cautioned the confessor lest his forthright speech cause problems for others, presumably the Jesuits in Spain.[171] By now Lamormaini had earned Madrid's enduring hostility. Through the imperial ambassador there, Franz Christoph von Khevenhiller, Olivares accused him of interfering in Italian affairs unduly and speaking and writing against the king of Spain. The interview with Aytona was particularly insulting.[172]

166 Vitelleschi to Lamormaini, Apr. 15, 1628, ARSJ, ibid., f. 997.
167 Urban VIII to Lamormaini, Apr. 15, 1628, BL 2198, ff. 47′–8.
168 Bireley, ibid., 71–2.
169 Pallotto to Barberini, Jul. 22, 1628, Kiewning, ed., *Nuntiaturberichte* 1 (Berlin, 1895), no. 52.
170 Bireley, ibid., 72.
171 Vitelleschi to Lamormaini, Aug. 24, 1628, ARSJ, Aust. 4I, f. 12.
172 Lamormaini to Khevenhiller, Jan. 3, 1629, ASV, Nuntiatura Germaniae 118, ff. 31′–3′; see Bireley, ibid., 246, n. 37, for the various versions of this letter. I have not found Olivares's letter, which was dated either Nov. 7 or 17.

In reply to Olivares, Lamormaini set forth his view of the Italian situation through Khevenhiller. After protesting his loyalty to the king of Spain as a native of Luxembourg, he maintained that he had not taken sides but merely advocated that both parties await an imperial decision. Implicitly, of course, this position criticized the Spaniards, who had invaded Montferrat, even if they had done so under the pretense of implementing the sequester for the emperor. Lamormaini then went on to relate that in his talks with Ferdinand he advised the emperor to consider the words not only of the lawyers and politicians but also of the theologians who spoke on behalf of the divine law. Even if military intervention could be justified, it was better to seek a peaceful solution so as not to divide the Catholic powers. Lamormaini shared the papal goal of a united Catholic front against the heretics. A war of Spain and/or the emperor against France would only undermine the effort against the heretics. This was the higher justice before God.[173]

Lamormaini's letter pleased Urban VIII and Barberini, and they let Lamormaini know this through the nuncio Pallotto.[174] Vitelleschi was more cautious. He found the letter "prudently and religiously written." But he went on to note that in Rome, on the basis of eyewitness accounts of Jesuits and others, the word circulated that he had claimed that the king of Spain invaded Montferrat "against every law and tyrannically," that Gonzalo da Cordoba was "a most impudent tyrant," and so on. In light of this, he considered it unlikely that many would believe his assertion to Khevenhiller that he had never spoken against the king of Spain, though he, Vitelleschi, certainly did. In a typical sentence he wrote, "I am not able not to fear that not all the hostility stirred up in Spain against Your Reverence and the Society will be dissipated by your response." Lamormaini should be careful not to say anything that might be misinterpreted.[175] Not long before this, as the Mantuan crisis first erupted, the superior general had bidden all the Spanish provincials to foster that universal love that embraced all parties, even those at odds with each other.[176]

Olivares in his response to Lamormaini of late June 1629 contended that Spanish theologians and lawyers approved the invasion of Montferrat and pointed out that the duke of Nevers now refused to recognize imperial authority.[177] Ferdinand prohibited Lamormaini

[173] Ibid.; Bireley, ibid., 73.
[174] Barberini to Pallotto, Jan. 27, 1629, Kiewning, ed., *Nuntiaturberichte* 2: no. 22.
[175] Vitelleschi to Lamormaini, Mar. 3, 1629, ARSJ, Aust. 4I, ff. 70–1.
[176] Vitelleschi to the Spanish provincials, May 29, 1628, ARSJ, Hisp. 86, ff. 133–4.
[177] Galleazzo Gualdo Priorato, *Historia delle guerre di Ferdinando II e Ferdinando III imperatori, e del ré Filippo di Spagna contro Gustavo Adolfo . . . e Luigi, ré di Francia, successe*

from answering once again as the confessor wanted to do, lest the exchange get out of hand.[178] By this time French troops, having crossed the Alps in the dead of winter, had marched into Italy and raised the siege of Casale. That April of 1629 imperial troops began to clear the Alpine passes in preparation for an invasion, and Lamormaini blessed the venture, because Ferdinand could not allow the French to dictate for Italy.[179] But Lamormaini still hoped to forestall any fighting. The Edict of Restitution had just been issued, and Ferdinand would need troops north of the Alps to enforce it.

Vitelleschi helped defuse tensions between Vienna and Munich over the controversial imperial general Wallenstein. As he remarked to Lamormaini in September 1626, Ferdinand and Maximilian were the two columns "on which rested all hope for restoring religion and ending heresy in Germany and almost the whole of the north."[180] At Maximilian's suggestion, Ferdinand had started to raise an imperial army to meet the challenge from Denmark and its allies. Wallenstein's force was the result. The existence of a powerful imperial army lessened Ferdinand's dependence on the League and Maximilian. Soon disputes began to develop over strategy and over Wallenstein's tactic of supplying his troops off the land. Initially, Lamormaini and Wallenstein got on well. The general was a generous benefactor of the Society, and in 1628 Vitelleschi at Lamormaini's behest named him a Founder of the Society, a dignity accorded outstanding benefactors that entitled them to a special share in the prayers of the Society.[181] Earlier in 1626 Esaias Leuker, a Bavarian agent in Vienna, had accused Lamormaini of fomenting discord between Maximilian and Ferdinand because of his attachment to Wallenstein. Contzen brought this to Vitelleschi's attention, who in turn passed it on to Lamormaini, who in the meantime cleared himself with Maximilian. Vitelleschi stressed the "singular as it were and more than fraternal charity as well as mutual communication of plans in full confidence" that ought to prevail between the two confessors.[182] This was not always to be the case. Two years later, after the general had been granted nearly complete control over the imperial military and had been invested with the duchy of Mecklenburg, Maximilian and the

dall'anno 1630 sino all'anno 1640 (n.p., c. 1640), 245–7; Franz Christoph von Khevenhiller, *Annales Ferdinandei* 11 (Leipzig, 1726), 600–4, where it is dated June 27, 1629. Both are translations from a presumably Spanish original.

178 Khevenhiller, 11: 604.

179 Bireley, ibid., 73.

180 Vitelleschi to Lamormaini, Sept. 26, 1626, ARSJ, Aust. 3II, f. 746.

181 Vitelleschi to Lamormaini, June 3, 1628, ibid., f. 1012; see Bireley, ibid., 48.

182 Vitelleschi to Contzen, Sept. 26 and Oct. 10, 1626 (citation), ARSJ, Germ. Sup. 5, ff. 450′, 453; Vitelleschi to Lamormaini, Sept. 26, 1626, ibid., Aust 3II, f. 746.

electors viewed his ascent with fear, especially because he reportedly disdained the electors. Once again Vitelleschi passed on Maximilian's and Contzen's complaints about Wallenstein to Lamormaini.[183] Ferdinand then reduced the number of troops Wallenstein had under arms, and Contzen reported, too optimistically, that the issue had been resolved.[184] Whether this was due to the actions of the Jesuits is not clear.

Back in France, the government's conflict with the Huguenots resumed in 1627. In September royal forces began the siege of La Rochelle, the Huguenot bastion on the Atlantic, which held out until the end of October 1628. Louis, Richelieu, and Suffren remained on the scene during most of this long stretch, which saw the population of the fortified city shrink from 27,000 to 8,000.[185] Its surrender on October 28 broke the back of the Huguenots as a political and military force. In the aftermath Louis and Richelieu sought reconciliation with the defeated. The surviving La Rochelle Huguenots were spared their lives and their property, and they were granted limited liberty to practice their religion. But the government did hope for their conversion, and several religious houses were founded in the city, one of them a Jesuit house that developed into a college by 1630, when it opened its doors for its first students. The initiative for the college in La Rochelle came from Richelieu.[186]

Suffren preached the sermon in the cathedral of La Rochelle on November 1, All Saints Day, when Louis made his triumphal entry. He compared Louis to David, "the patron and model of all kings." Just as David dealt with the Philistines, who were disobedient to God's design, so Louis put down the rebellious citizens of La Rochelle. Suffren emphasized their disobedience, not once speaking the word "heretic," and thus underplaying the religious element in the conflict. Now Louis would show them mercy, a virtue in which he surpassed all other rulers. But they had to commit themselves to loyalty to him. Louis himself, Suffren reminded the king, owed his victory ultimately to God, not to his arms or his strategy.[187]

Louis and Richelieu both received letters from Vitelleschi congratulating them on the triumph of La Rochelle. The cardinal merited a good portion of the praise for the success of the long campaign, Vitelleschi wrote Richelieu. It was most useful for young Louis to have "his Nestor,"

183 Vitelleschi to Lamormaini, July 29, 1628, ibid., Aust. 4I, 2–3.
184 Vitelleschi to Contzen, Oct. 28, 1628, ibid., Germ. Sup. 6, 123; Bireley, ibid., 67.
185 A. Lloyd Moote, *Louis XIII, the Just* (Berkeley, 1989), 197.
186 Fouqueray 4, 215–18.
187 Jean Suffren, *La reduction de la Rochelle, avec l'entrée victorieuse du Roy, et le sermon du P. Souffrant de la Compagnie de Jesus* (Nyort, 1628), 10–12.

upon whose counsel and ability he could draw. Vitelleschi's letter struck the note of victory over heresy and the triumph of Catholicism more than had the sermon of Suffren.[188] The following month the general thanked Richelieu effusively for arranging for the foundation of the college in La Rochelle, and he expressed his appreciation for the cardinal's support in difficult times for the Society, an allusion to the events of 1625/26. To Suffren he remarked about the "incredible clemency" of the king toward the rebellious city.[189]

That winter of 1628/29, in what amounted to a military feat, Louis and Richelieu organized an army of 38,000, crossed the Alps in February, took Susa in Savoy on March 5, forced the duke of Savoy to abandon his alliance with Spain, and relieved the crucial fortress of Casale in Montferrat from the Spanish siege. They then returned to France, reduced the remaining Huguenot strongholds in southeastern France, and on June 28 concluded with the Huguenot leaders the Peace of Alais. The agreement formalized the status of the Huguenots, ending their situation as "a state within a state" and allowing them considerable freedom to practice their religion.[190]

Through Suffren, Vitelleschi congratulated Louis on the taking of Susa. In words that the Spaniards might well have contested, he recognized that Louis brought peace to Italy.[191] Certainly this was the view of the papacy. Suffren was invited to Rome for a personal visit with Vitelleschi, but the rigors of the campaign had taken their toll on his health, and he had to decline. Besides, Suffren was not able to leave the king.[192]

It is unlikely that Richelieu would have permitted Suffren to undertake a journey to Rome. The cardinal saw Suffren as representing him with Louis when the two were separated and thus as a factor in maintaining his close relationship with the king. When Richelieu was absent from court, he and Suffren seem to have corresponded regularly. From Valence during the Huguenot campaign following the return from Italy, the confessor wrote the cardinal that he had been expected fifteen days now. "The King recognizes by your absence how much your presence is necessary for him. . . . I beseech you, by the zeal you have for the glory of God and the well-being of all this state, not to deprive the king any longer of your life and your wise and disinterested counsel, so that this state

188 Vitelleschi to Louis XIII, Dec. 9, 1628, ARSJ, Epist. Gen. 2, f. 340; Vitelleschi to Richelieu, Dec. 13, 1628, ibid., Gallia 46I, ff. 117′–18; see also Vitelleschi to Suffren, May 3, 1629, ibid., Francia 5I, f. 292′.

189 Vitelleschi to Richelieu, Jan. 24, 1629, ARSJ, Gallia 4I, f. 118; Vitelleschi to Suffren, Jan. 24, 1629, ARSJ, Francia 5I, f. 282′.

190 Moote, 201–5.

191 Vitelleschi to Suffren, Apr. 1, 1629, ARSJ, Francia 5I, f. 291′.

192 Vitelleschi to Suffren, Apr. 29 and June 14, 1629, ibid., ff. 292′, 294.

lamenting is not constrained to say: hominem non habeo."[193] Richelieu also counted on Suffren to foster the relationship between Louis and his wife, which it was hoped would lead to a child, to preserve peace between Louis and his mother, and to look out for his, the cardinal's, interests with both women. Suffren reported to Richelieu that summer that the queen was speaking well of the cardinal. The confessor had reminded Louis of how much the cardinal did for the state, and the king agreed. He also spoke to the queen-mother of the cardinal's benefits to the state.[194]

In the summer of 1629 Richelieu renewed his efforts to secure allies among the German princes; especially desirable were Catholic allies because they would defuse the charge of Richelieu's enemies that he was aiding the German Protestants in his efforts to weaken the Habsburgs. Because of its fear of the Habsburgs, the papacy fostered Richelieu's initiative with Bavaria, and the nuncio in Paris, Bagno, communicated to Munich in deepest secrecy the draft of a defensive alliance. Most of Maximilian's councillors evaluated the draft proposal positively; they feared the growing ascendancy of Wallenstein and were unhappy with the emperor's venture into Italy.[195] Contzen also favored the proposal, but mostly for other, militant, expansionist reasons. He saw in an agreement with France not only a means to maintain the traditional structure of the empire in the face of a perceived threat from Vienna but more importantly the start of a broad Catholic alliance that would bring France into the German war on the Catholic side in the effort to implement the Edict of Restitution.[196] Henceforth, the militants Contzen and Lamormaini hoped to win over French support for their program in Germany. This was not so far-fetched as one might think, given the pressure Richelieu remained under from the *dévots*. The papacy had long aimed at such a union of the Catholic powers to include Spain, too, while remaining wary of the Habsburgs. The French initiative bore no fruit at this time because Maximilian did not want to jeopardize his relationship with Vienna. Vitelleschi seems to have had no knowledge of Franco-Bavarian contacts, and Lamormaini certainly did not.

193 Suffren to Richelieu, May 9, 1629, Richelieu, Les papiers. *Section politique intérieur* 4 (Paris, 1983), no. 258: 277–8.
194 Suffren to Richelieu, Aug. 17, 1629, ibid., no. 522: 545–6.
195 Albrecht, 208–32.
196 Bireley, *Maximilian von Bayern*, 108–14.

CHAPTER 4

The Clash of Catholic Interests, 1629–1631

FROM the summer of 1629 to the summer of 1631 the differences among the Catholic courts widened and, with this, divisions among Jesuits. These differences became particularly evident during the Electoral Convention of Regensburg, which met from July 3 until November 11, 1630. Although strictly speaking a meeting of the imperial electors with the emperor, in fact it amounted to a small-sized European peace conference with every major European state plus many of the German and Italian ones sending representatives. Jesuits were also in evidence; more than thirty visitors stretched the hospitality of the college in Regensburg.[1] Vitelleschi attempted to moderate the strains among them. His goal was unity within the Society and among the Catholic powers.

Lamormaini continued to work for peace in Italy, where his efforts eventually failed, and he made plans for the implementation of the Edict of Restitution. Both Cardinal Barberini and Pope Urban showed their gratitude for his attempt to preserve peace in the peninsula. Urban, according to Vitelleschi, thought that he deserved the gratitude of all Italy, and the pope encouraged him to promote the union of the Catholic powers against heretics and pagans. Vitelleschi also passed along the suggestion of a "major figure" in Rome that the pope be requested to mediate the dispute over Mantua, as in fact he was eventually to do.[2] But Lamormaini realized that he could not hold back the forces for war much longer. Vitelleschi instructed him that he ought not think of resignation if war did break out, a prospect Lamormaini evidently had mentioned. Rather, he should bear the cross of the office to which God had assigned him, "in a brave and constant spirit."[3]

1 Reinhard Ziegler to Johannes Busaeus (German Assistant, Rome), July 15, 1630, ARSJ, Boh. 94, f. 275.
2 Vitelleschi to Lamormaini, June 30 and July 14, 1629, ARSJ, Aust. 4I, ff. 125–6, 129–30.
3 Vitelleschi to Lamormaini, Aug. 4, 1629, ibid., ff. 138–8′.

In September 1629, 38,000 imperial troops made their way over the Alps and they laid siege to Mantua in December. They were repulsed, but they took the fortified city by storm in July 1630 and sacked it just as the electoral convention was getting under way. To the west, a French army again headed by Louis and Richelieu returned to Italy in the spring, took the fortress of Pinerolo in Savoy, and then occupied much of Savoy. But the Spaniards were not inactive; they seized control of most of Montferrat. To the north, in early July 1630 Gustavus Adolphus, King of Sweden and Lion of the North, supported by Richelieu, landed threateningly with an army on the island of Usedom off the Baltic Coast. An agent of the cardinal had mediated a truce in 1629 between warring Sweden and Poland in order to free Gustavus to invade the empire. Richelieu hoped to hurl the forces of the Protestant king against the emperor.

That winter of 1629/30 Lamormaini responded, with the approval of Ferdinand, to an initiative of his counterpart in Paris, Jean Suffren, in the hope of promoting peace. Their exchange of letters belongs in the context of other contacts between Vienna and Paris that were taking place as Spain was pressuring the emperor to intervene in Italy. In January 1629 Ferdinand had congratulated Louis on his reduction of La Rochelle, asserting that he and Louis made war in "nearly the same cause" and that they both experienced the powerful right arm of God in their support. He hoped that in the future "joined in spirit as befitted great kings and princes by the friendship and bond between them, they would look to the peace and tranquillity of the Christian world."[4] So Ferdinand, undoubtedly encouraged by Lamormaini, hinted at an alliance or at least cooperation with France. Maximilian of Bavaria attempted to mediate between Paris and Vienna in the Mantuan question, and Louis sent a French diplomat, Melchior de Sabran, to Vienna in late July, but neither of these initiatives proved fruitful.[5]

Suffren's letter, dated September 26, 1629, has been lost. It could only have been sent with Richelieu's knowledge. Lamormaini considered

[4] Ferdinand II to Louis XIII, Jan. 27, 1629, Armand-Jean du Plessis, cardinal de Richelieu, *Les papiers: Correspondance et papiers d'état: Section politique extérieur, empire allemand*, ed. Adolf Wild, 1: *1616–1629* (Paris, 1982): no. 266: 509–10. See also letters of the same date to Queen Anne, no. 264: 508, and to Marie de Medici, no. 265: 508–9, and the instructions of Ferdinand to his agent in Paris, Mätthaus Werdeman, to congratulate Louis on earlier victories over the Huguenots, Apr. 22, 1628, ibid., no. 241: 472–3.

[5] Dieter Albrecht, *Die auswärtige Politik Maximilians von Bayern* (Göttingen, 1962), 288–91; Robert Bireley, *Religion and Politics in the Age of the Counterreformation: Emperor Ferdinand II, William Lamormaini, S.J., and the Formation of Imperial Policy* (Chapel Hill, NC, 1981), 95, 97.

it a much belated response to his letter to Suffren four years before. Vitelleschi mediated the exchange between the two confessors. It revealed profound differences between them, not only regarding the political situation but also about the role of Jesuits, and especially confessors, in politics.

Lamormaini opened his letter by welcoming the communication from his counterpart in Paris about a pact of peace among Christian princes lest Satan drive a wedge between the Imperial Majesty and the Most Christian King. Both certainly championed piety and religion. Yet Lamormaini regretted that an earlier letter of his to Suffren had gone unanswered. Evidently, Lamormaini had sought once before to foster a relationship between Ferdinand and Louis, probably at the start of his tenure as confessor; we saw above Ferdinand's letter of April 15, 1624, calling Louis to a common front against the heretics.[6] Suffren now requested a suggestion as to what the two confessors might presently do to create understanding between the two princes. Lamormaini replied that first of all it was necessary that Louis be aware of Ferdinand's intentions and that Ferdinand be convinced of the justice and piety attributed to Louis by so many and of Louis's unwillingness to attempt anything against the emperor, his rights, or his jurisdiction. Ferdinand for his part had no intention of violating the rights of any prince. His whole purpose was to restore Catholicism in his hereditary lands and kingdoms and, to the extent this was possible within the bounds of the imperial constitution, in the empire. In this venture he would like to associate the Most Christian King as a reliable friend, and he was prepared to welcome the Most Catholic King as well into an alliance.

Lamormaini went on to indicate that Ferdinand was not at all happy that Spanish ministers – he was careful not to say the king – had approved the invasion of Montferrat and that, if his troops had not been engaged in fighting the heretics in the north, Ferdinand would have sent troops himself to raise the Spanish siege of Casale. Nor was Ferdinand displeased with Louis's dispatch of troops to Casale's relief. These statements would obviously infuriate Spanish authorities should they learn of them, and they did. On the other hand, the emperor was unhappy with Nevers's refusal to honor the sequestration, with Louis's failure to consult with the emperor before he sent troops into provinces where Ferdinand was suzerain, and with the king's sending an envoy to the imperial court who displayed only bluster and threats. This was a reference to the mission of Sabran to Vienna in July 1629.[7]

6 See above, 84.
7 Bireley, 95.

Ferdinand realized, the letter continued, how the conflict over Italy harmed the Catholic cause. If Nevers submitted to imperial jurisdiction and the French king interceded for him and if Louis disavowed the mission and manner of Sabran, Ferdinand would grant Louis's request and invest Nevers with the duchy of Mantua. So Lamormaini outlined the settlement that actually did take place in the Peace of Cherasco two years later. Then the way would be open, the confessor continued, for the two of them to respect each other's rights, to form an alliance, and to cooperate in the defeat of iniquity and the advancement of the kingdom of Christ. The king of Spain would also be invited to join the alliance. Lamormaini concluded his letter with a passionate plea for peace. "Reverend Father, Europe is crowded with so many and such large peoples. Unless we expand beyond [Europe], unless we lead so many armies that have been raised, who have become accustomed to idleness, war, and pillage, into the expansive kingdoms and provinces of the infidels and draw them to the faith of Christ, we will be consumed by one another, to the dishonor of God, loss to the Catholic faith, and the danger of eternal damnation, from which God deliver us." So Lamormaini looked beyond Europe to a crusade against the Turks, a venture that still stirred enthusiasm in Christendom. Indeed, Richelieu's confidant, the Capuchin Father Joseph, had long promoted a crusade to be led by the duke of Nevers.[8]

Lamormaini transmitted his answer to Suffren through Vitelleschi, who despite his remark to Lamormaini that it would certainly promote understanding between the two princes passed it on with no comment at all, probably because he feared intruding into French foreign policy.[9] The general also brought Lamormaini's efforts to the attention of Cardinal Barberini and the pope, who welcomed them. But while encouraging Lamormaini in his attempts to bring the two princes together, Vitelleschi was not optimistic about the prospects for success, though one never knew what God in his providence might bring about, he added.[10]

Suffren's reply, dated January 9, probably never reached Lamormaini. As late as mid-March Vitelleschi conjectured that the French confessor

[8] Lamormain; to Suffren, Nov. 24, 1629, Richelieu, no. 301: 577–80. On Father Joseph's plans for a crusade, see L. Dedouvres, *Politique et apôtre, Le P. Joseph de Paris* 1 (Paris, 1932).

[9] Vitelleschi to Lamormaini, Jan. 5, 1630, ARSJ, Aust. 4I, ff. 201–2; Vitelleschi to Suffren, Jan. 8, 1630, ARSJ, Francia 5I, f. 306. The date of Vitelleschi's letter to Suffren and the date of Suffren's response to Lamormaini, Jan. 9, indicate that Lamormaini's letter must first have been sent to Suffren by some other route.

[10] Vitelleschi to Lamormaini, Jan. 19, 1630, ARSJ, Aust. 4I, f. 206.

may have decided not to respond at all because he thought that there was little he could do in the cause of peace and he preferred to leave Lamormaini up in the air rather than admit this.[11] Suffren's response was surprising, because he had initiated the exchange and requested Lamormaini's ideas about what they might do for the cause of peace. While recognizing Lamormaini's zeal and good intentions, Suffren now severely criticized Jesuits who withdrew from ministries proper to their vocation, like preaching, teaching, and hearing confessions, and became involved in politics. This led them into activities less consonant with their vocation, where they were easily deceived and manipulated because of their inexperience. Clearly, this was the case with Lamormaini's report of the French emissary Sabran, about whose mission Lamormaini admittedly learned only from others. Suffren, who knew him personally, vouched for his integrity and proper conduct. If Jesuits showed so little skill when they dabbled in politics, there was danger that this would undermine credibility for their normal ministries. Suffren understood the role of the Jesuit confessor differently from Lamormaini.

Lamormaini, the French Jesuit contended, praised the fine qualities of Ferdinand, which was all to the good, but he ignored his shortcomings. Everyone knew that the duke of Nevers possessed the best title to Mantua and Montferrat. Why was there any need for a sequester? Why did Ferdinand not issue the only possible judgment and support Nevers against the Spanish? Louis had no choice but to come to the aid of his client Nevers in the pursuit of justice. Ferdinand then sent an army into Italy that wreaked havoc among the civilian population and brought Calvinism in its wake. No wonder infidelity triumphed! If the emperor really sought peace and truly deplored the damage done to church and religion by the conflict over Italy, then he had to act with justice. Otherwise, a bitter war was likely. Suffren fully supported Richelieu's position.[12] Indeed, Richelieu may have instigated the confessor's letter to try to find out what concessions the emperor was willing to make on the Italian question.

Subsequently, Vitelleschi learned that Lamormaini's letter with its sharp criticism of Spanish policy was being read publicly in Jesuit dining rooms in France. For this he reprimanded Suffren but then later accepted the French Jesuit's explanation that this was done without his knowledge.[13] Olivares soon learned of Lamormaini's letter. The result was a further effort on his part to curtail the confessor's influence in Vienna, as we shall see. One might surmise that Lamormaini's letter was

[11] Vitelleschi to Lamormaini, Mar. 16, 1630, ibid., f. 243.
[12] Suffren to Lamormaini, Jan. 9, Richelieu, ibid., no. 306: 586–9.
[13] Vitelleschi to Suffren, Mar. 25 and Sept. 7, 1630, ARSJ, Francia, 5I, ff. 312, 324–5.

leaked, as it were, to stir mistrust between Vienna and Madrid. Later Vitelleschi admonished Lamormaini to exert greater caution in his political correspondence.[14]

The Electoral Convention of Regensburg opened officially on July 3, 1630. Besides Lamormaini, four Jesuits accompanied the imperial party: Lucas Fanini, confessor of Empress Eleonora; Heinrich Philippi, confessor of the emperor's son, Ferdinand, now the young king of Hungary; the Spaniard Peñalosa, instructor in Spanish of the king of Hungary; and Johannes Weingartner, a court preacher. During the early days of the convention Lamormaini spent a day at Amberg, a day's journey from Regensburg, with Contzen, Ziegler, and Georg Schröttel, confessor of Archbishop-Elector Ferdinand of Cologne, Maxmimilian's brother, and Hermann Baving, provincial superior of the Lower Rhenish Province.[15] This seems to be the only time that Lamormaini and Contzen met face-to-face, at least while they served as confessors. Vitelleschi regularly asked all the confessors to keep him posted on what was transpiring in Germany.

Ziegler was not sanguine. Everyone spoke of peace, he wrote to Rome, "but it will be difficult to arrive at this goal if the Catholics yield nothing of their rights."[16] Anselm Casimir of Mainz, different from his predecessor Georg Friedrich von Greiffenklau, was to be the most conciliatory of the Catholic princes during the coming years.

Optimism characterized Lamormaini about what could be achieved in Regensburg for the advancement of Catholicism. Among other things, he had in mind the transfer to the Jesuits of church lands, especially former women's monasteries, which were to be recovered by the Edict of Restitution and to be used to endow colleges. Some Jesuits in Regensburg, including Baving, had assembled to discuss this issue, especially with regard to Lower Saxony. Lamormaini's plans were expansive. As a New Year's gift in 1630 he had presented to Ferdinand a list of ninety locations for possible Jesuit colleges in north Germany, in four newly created Jesuit provinces: the Westphalian, Lower Saxon, and Upper Saxon, which all lay in Electoral Saxony, and a Baltic Province in Brandenburg.[17] Recovered church lands would finance these. Lamormaini sent a copy of the list to Vitelleschi, who seems to have considered the confessor's plan too ambitious, but asked him to tell Ferdinand "that I continue to have offered to the Lord each week one

14 Vitelleschi to Lamormaini, Oct. 18, 1631, ARSJ, Aust. 4I, ff. 532–4.
15 Lamormaini to Busaeus, July 22, 1630, ARSJ, Boh. 94, f. 276.
16 Ziegler to Busaeus, July 29, 1630, ibid., f. 279.
17 Eustachius Sthaäl, "Vita Lamormaini," ARSJ, Vitae 139, ff. 56'–8.

thousand Masses and four thousand Rosaries for the succesful progress of his pious efforts."[18] Lamormaini's design was not quite so fantastic as it first sounds if one keeps in mind that many of these colleges were foreseen initially as mere missionary outposts. His grand plan also helps explain his unwillingness to see concessions on the Edict made to Saxony and Brandenburg.[19]

Both Lamormaini and Contzen served as go-betweens for the communication of confidential information. One of the issues at the convention was the future of the Palatinate. Here Maximilian stood in opposition to the other Catholic electors. All of them had agreed that some territory might be restored to the Elector Palatine in the interests of a peace settlement, provided he accepted certain conditions. Maximilian then informed Ferdinand through Lamormaini that he did not share the opinion presented in the name of the Catholic electors. "He judges," wrote Lamormaini to the emperor, "that no restitution would ever be in the interest of religion."[20] The refusal of the representative of the Elector Palatine to make concessions made the difference between Maximilian and the other electors moot.

The first major issue brought to the table by the electors at Regensburg was the reform of the imperial military. By this they meant not only the dismissal of Wallenstein but a reduction in the number of troops under arms and a consequent lessening of the financial burden of supporting the imperial army. This was to take place just as Gustavus embarked ominously on his campaign in the north. Maximilian and Contzen long had envisaged the removal of the dominating generalissimo, though Maximilian hesitated to press the issue with the emperor. Despite some differences with Wallenstein, Lamormaini along with several imperial ministers advocated the dismissal only because they feared that otherwise the Catholic electors would break with the emperor. Under considerable pressure Ferdinand yielded on August 13 to the electors. But who was then to lead the imperial army? The Catholic electors proposed Maximilian as the new commander-in-chief of the imperial forces and the retention of the League army as a separate entity. Eventually, Maximilian, again with a view to preventing a split between

18 Vitelleschi to Lamormaini, Mar. 2, 1630, ARSJ, Aust. 4I, f. 240.

19 For a discussion of the prolonged dispute over the "monastery question," that is over the proposal of Lamormaini and other Jesuits to use lands of the monastic orders to be recovered by virtue of the Edict of Restitution to finance Jesuit colleges, see Bireley, 133–50.

20 Lamormaini to Ferdinand II, Sept. 18, 1630, Beda Dudik, "Korrespondenz Kaiser Ferdinands II und seiner erlauchten Familie mit P. Martinus Becanus und P. Wilhelm Lamormaini, kaiserl. Beichtväter S.J.," *Archiv für österreichische Geschichte* 54 (1876): 337–8; Robert Bireley, *Maximilian von Bayern, Adam Contzen S.J. und die Gegenreformation in Deutschland 1624–1635* (Göttingen, 1975), 115.

the Catholic electors and the emperor, withdrew his candidacy, and a clumsy compromise was reached. Both armies were to remain as currently constituted, with regular conferences to take place between imperial and League officials to coordinate their efforts. Subsequently, Tilly was placed in charge of both armies, being responsible to Maximilian for the League troops and to Ferdinand for the imperial forces.[21] But before the compromise was attained, there began bitter and resentful exchanges between Munich and Vienna that continued well after the conclusion of the convention.

Contzen with his acid pen exacerbated the rising tensions between the two courts. Vitelleschi had to intervene. From Regensburg Contzen complained to the superior general of unnamed Jesuits who along with various Austrian councillors incurred the displeasure of the electors. Vitelleschi responded with a request for names, but Contzen does not seem to have delivered them.[22] One was certainly Lamormaini. Ferdinand himself in a note to Lamormaini asked him to make an effort to alter Contzen's opinion of Eggenberg, his chief minister, whom Contzen and Maximilian considered too favorable to Spain.[23] Contzen's position at Regensburg on the army issue can be gleaned from an anonymous manuscript attributed to him; it reflected thoughts that another Jesuit later asserted to have heard from Contzen's own mouth.[24] The manuscript responded to a Latin paper circulating at Regensburg titled "Twelve Arguments or Reasons Why the Emperor of the Romans Ought Not Confer Supreme Command or Charge of the Imperial Army on the Elector of Bavaria."[25] The author, a Spaniard or member of the Spanish party in Vienna, warned of the dangerous increase in power that command of the imperial army would give Bavaria, justified the Spanish claim to a voice in imperial affairs on the basis of Spain's support of the Catholic forces, and referred to the Wittelsbachs as a "House of an inferior sort." Deep resentment in Munich was the result.

Contzen, who cannot have written without Maximilian's approval, accused the Spaniards in his "Response" of exploiting the empire for their own purposes and certain ministers in Vienna of profiting from the war. That the emperor took orders from a foreigner was unbearable. The Spaniards might claim that the dismissal of his general Wallenstein had

21 Bireley, *Religion and Politics*, 116–20.
22 Vitelleschi to Contzen, Nov. 9, 1630, ARSJ, Germ. Sup. 6, f. 302.
23 Ferdinand to Lamormaini, dated only Regensburg, 1630, Dudik, 273.
24 Balthazar Cordier to Vitelleschi, Mar. 25, 1632, ARSJ, Aust. 21, ff. 80–2.
25 "XII Argumenta sive rationes quibus Romanorum Imperator motus, quominus Electori Bavariae supremem exercitus Caesarei directorium sive regimen censuerit conferendum," HStA, KSchw 6764, 2–5'; other copies, ibid., 12765, 15022, and a German copy in ibid., Jesuitica 704, ff. 25–9.

humiliated the emperor, but in fact it was his long tenure in the post that besmirched Ferdinand's reputation. Contzen played on an old theme when he reminded his readers that Bavaria had rescued Ferdinand in his hour of need. Now out of resentment Maximilian was being treated as the victorious David was treated by the envious Saul. It was not Maximilian who needed to be held in check, as the Spaniards affirmed, but the emperor and the king of Spain, who were undermining the imperial constitution.[26]

Contzen was only uncovered in late 1631 as the author of the "Response." But in the meantime he continued to vie with Vienna, at a time when he knew that after long negotiations, papal mediation, and with Contzen's own enthusiastic encouragement Maximilian had finally concluded with France the highly secret mutual defense Treaty of Fontainebleau on May 8.[27] In a letter of June 8 to Lamormaini, after asserting the need for cooperation between Munich and Vienna, he went on to rehash the army issue, accusing imperial officials of unreliability and corruption. Had it not been for the League, the Swedes would have long ago occupied Prague. Now was not the time to dissolve the League, as Lamormaini had advocated.[28] Alerted about Contzen's letters, Ferdinand advised Lamormaini not to answer, because Contzen always came up with a further response so that there would be no end to the exchange. He suggested that Lamormaini ask Vitelleschi to have Contzen moderate his "nature and style."[29] Lamormaini did respond to Contzen's charges, not to Contzen but to another Munich Jesuit, Caspar Hell, where he admitted that at Regensburg he had initially advocated dissolution of the League army but soon changed his mind on the issue. He added, with a view to Contzen's charge of corruption in Vienna, that only Count Fürstenberg could be bribed to act against the Catholic religion.[30]

Lamormaini complained about Contzen's activity to Vitelleschi, who raised the matter with Contzen in a typical manner. "I am compelled

[26] "Ad XII Argumenta seu rationes . . . , Responsio fidelissimi consiliarii Caesareani ex officio demissione oblata Sacrae Caesareae Majestati," ibid., Jesuitica 704: 15–22. Albrecht, 272, n. 37, and Bernhard Duhr, *Geschichte der Jesuiten in den Ländern deutscher Zünge* 2, 2 (Freiburg, 1913): 253, attribute the "Responsio" to Laurentius Forer, S.J. He may have participated in writing it, so that Contzen could later deny full responsibility for it to Vitelleschi. But the style, the content, and Vitelleschi's correspondence point to Contzen.

[27] Bireley, *Maximilian von Bayern*, 167–9.

[28] Contzen to Lamormaini, June 8, 1631, HStA, Jesuitica, ff. 23–4.

[29] Ferdinand II to Lamormaini, Oct. 16, 1631, Dudik, 273–4.

[30] Lamormaini to Casper Hell, June 25, 1631, HStA, Kriegsakten, 212, ff. 36–7. Fürstenberg's name was written in cipher. Notes on the letter in Contzen's hand were meant to assist Hell in a reply.

to ask Your Reverence to clear yourself as diligently as possible from certain calumnies spread by malevolent tongues, convinced as I am that they are false." It was question of a "stinging and biting" manuscript attributed to him in Vienna that profoundly upset the emperor, the king of Spain, and the whole House of Austria. At first the emperor did not think that such a piece could stem from a Jesuit, but now he began to suspect that it did. It was imperative that Contzen explain himself to the emperor and the king of Spain, where the Society already faced trouble because of Lamormaini's anti-Spanish position in Vienna and because of Vitelleschi's refusal to acquiesce in the bestowal of a bishopric on Father Salazar.[31] Contzen did succeed in clearing himself with Vitelleschi, who was eager to accept any explanation to be able to respond to Vienna and Madrid. Whether Contzen denied any part in the composition of the "Response" is not clear.[32] The emperor was ready to let the matter rest, and Francisco Aguado, the confessor of Olivares, satisfied Madrid regarding Contzen.[33] But Lamormaini was not at all content with Contzen's explanation.[34]

Back to the Convention of Regensburg. The war in Italy further divided the emperor and the electors. For the electors it represented an instance of the subordination of German affairs to Habsburg interests, especially when it drew troops away from the north where Gustavus Adolphus now threatened. Lamormaini shared the electors' view, also because he envisaged the Catholic powers coming together against the Protestants. The presence of two French representatives in Regensburg, one Richelieu's Capuchin associate Father Joseph of Paris, opened up the possibility of negotiations there over the Italian conflict. Only two days after their arrival, despite the fact that their instructions called for them to contact only the electors, Father Joseph met with Ferdinand and Lamormaini.[35] Soon talks began in earnest with imperial officials. Lamormaini was optimistic.[36] On October 13, 1630, the Peace of Regensburg was signed. As Lamormaini had suggested in his letter to Suffren, Nevers would submit to the emperor, who agreed that at the behest of Louis XIII and Pope Urban he would invest Nevers with Mantua and Montferrat within three months. Complicated articles regulated the withdrawal of French and imperial forces from Italy. Spain was not a party to the treaty, but the Spaniards were expected to leave Casale

31 Vitelleschi to Contzen, Dec. 20, 1631, ARSJ, Germ. Sup. 6, f. 411–12.
32 Vitelleschi to Contzen, Feb. 7, 1632, ibid., f. 427.
33 Vitelleschi to Aguado, Oct. 6, 1632, ARSJ, Tol. 9, f. 264'.
34 Vitelleschi to Lamormaini, Feb. 25, 1632, ARSJ, Aust. 4II, f. 583.
35 Bireley, *Religion and Politics*, 121–2.
36 Vitelleschi to Lamormaini, Oct. 12 and 25, 1630, ARSJ, Aust. 4I, ff. 334–5, 346–8.

to Nevers. Another provision required both France and the emperor to desist from aiding each other's enemies either directly or indirectly. Principally because of this last provision, Richelieu refused to ratify the treaty, because it meant that France would have to surrender its policy of supporting allies or client states in the empire against the emperor.[37]

But this only temporarily held up a settlement in Italy. Negotiations continued through the spring with the help of papal mediation, and on June 19, 1631, Ferdinand ratified the less favorable Peace of Cherasco, which did not contain the provision objectionable to Richelieu, to the satisfaction of the electors and Rome and to the anger of the Spaniards.[38] For Lamormaini it was a step toward mobilizing Catholic forces against the German heretics and now Gustavus Adolphus.

During the Convention of Regensburg Father Joseph also negotiated with Maximilian's representatives toward the eventual secret mutual-defense Treaty of Fontainebleau of May 8, 1631, between France and Bavaria.[39] Maximilian explicitly secured the recognition of his obligations to the emperor, but when news of the treaty leaked out Vienna was bound to see it as directed against the emperor, as indeed Maximilian's original goals in the negotiations were protection against a Vienna dominated by Wallenstein and security in his position in the Palatinate. Now it was aimed more to secure French assistance against the advancing Swedes. Contzen continued to see in the treaty a step toward bringing France into the German war on the Catholic side. For him Maximilian had "sinned greviously" by not aligning himself with France earlier out of fear of Vienna.[40] Both Contzen and Lamormaini looked to France for assistance to the German Catholics, but from different perspectives. Richelieu, for his part, saw the Treaty of Fontainebleau in tandem with the Treaty of Bärwalde of January 23, 1631, whereby he formally undertook to subsidize the Swedish advance into the empire, mistakenly thinking that he could manipulate Gustavus Adolphus. His treaties with Sweden, Bavaria, and German Protestant states aimed to construct an anti-Habsburg party in the empire. For this he needed a Catholic partner in Germany, also to disarm critics at home who accused him of aiding the Protestants in a religious war.

The Edict of Restitution emerged as the most important item for discussion at Regensburg. Should the Catholics maintain it, or should

37 Bireley, ibid., 122.
38 Ibid., 162–3.
39 Ibid., 128.
40 Contzen to Busaeus, May 22, 1631, ARSJ, Boh. 94, ff. 303–3'. Contzen could not resist asking Busaeus whether he should send Lamormaini a list of complaints against the imperial army that he appended.

they modify it in light of the protests of the Protestant states, especially Saxony and Brandenburg, and of the ominous Swedish advance? To compromise on the Edict would make possible a united German front against the Swedes. Militants and moderates clashed. Contzen and Lamormaini strongly influenced the decision to remain firm on the Edict, and Vitelleschi stood behind them. At this point the religious, and holy, nature of the war came most clearly into focus.

The Edict had provoked a wave of protests from Protestant princes immediately after its issuance. Of these the most important were the two electors who hitherto had maintained their allegiance to the emperor, Saxony and Brandenburg, and of these Saxony, which came to see itself as the advocate of the moderate Protestant states. The Catholics realized the need to keep Saxony on the emperor's side and not drive him into the arms of Gustavus Adolphus, but how could this be done without unacceptable concessions on the Edict, which they claimed to be merely the clear meaning of the Peace of Augsburg? The most the Catholic electors and the emperor would grant Saxony was a confirmation of a guarantee made back in 1620, at the time of the suppression of the Bohemian rebellion, that no action would be taken toward the recovery of the church lands it held without a new legal process, that is, not by virtue of the Edict itself. This amounted to a temporary suspension of the Edict. It was the most that the Jesuit theologians would allow, Contzen in Munich and Lamormaini along with three colleagues in Vienna, and the princes were unwilling to go beyond this.[41]

Contzen and Keller in Munich took a hard line in a paper requested of them in preparation for the Convention of Regensburg. If people were ready to make sacrifices for peace, they wrote, so all the more should they be prepared to make them for complete victory, "which consists in the restitution of the ecclesiastical lands." They held out to the Catholics the example of the heroic Maccabees of the second century before Christ, who led the Jewish resistance against the attempts of Syrian kings to suppress Judaism. Reference to the Books of the Maccabees would become a topos. "In a cause as holy as was that of the Maccabees, it was necessary to hope rather for a favorable outcome of war than to surrender body and soul to the heretics and endanger posterity."[42]

Early in August in Regensburg deputies of the Catholic electors met with the three electoral confessors, Contzen, Ziegler, and Schröttel, to

[41] Memorandum of Contzen, HStA, KSchw 70, 139–40; see BA 2, 4: no. 289: 368–70, and Bireley, *Maximilian von Bayern*, 124; Memorandum of Lamormaini and colleagues, HHStA, Trautmannsdorffisches Familienarchiv 102, ff. 18–18', 27; see Bireley, *Religion and Politics*, 88.

[42] Memorandum of the Bavarian Theologians, undated, BA 2, 5: no. 170: 419–23.

talk about possible concessions to Saxony. The question for the confessors was: Would it not be wiser to surrender claims to some ecclesiastical lands for the sake of peace and the unity of the empire rather than to persist in the war in the attempt to impose a settlement on the Protestants? This was the moderate position. All three confessors agreed that concessions might be made in cases of necessity, with Contzen reminding the others of the need for papal approval. But the question was: When was necessity at hand? Contzen, Lamormaini, and others who were convinced that the Catholic princes had been entrusted with a divine mission and could count on God's help were not ready to admit easily that such a desperate situation had been reached. This was especially the case when they anticipated that France would come to the aid of the German Catholics once the Peace of Regensburg was concluded.[43]

Not all theologians held to the militant position. A long, anonymous theological memorandum prepared for the elector of Cologne – probably by the Spanish Dominican Cosmas Morelles, a theology professor at the University of Cologne and representative of the Inquisition there – stated clearly the theological position that the moderates consistently took during the coming years. It drew heavily on Thomas Aquinas. According to Morelles, the Catholics could in good conscience hand over ecclesiastical lands permanently to the Protestants, whereby he had in mind above all the bishoprics claimed by Saxony. First, he argued from natural law. Law itself was meant to serve the common good. Both the empire and the church stood to benefit more from the peace and stabilization of the Catholic position in the empire to be gained by the surrender of the church lands than from continued war. Canon law did not stand in the way because it always allowed for exceptions. Nor was there need to have recourse to the pope in this emergency situation; the emperor's approval was adequate. Morelles admitted that in most cases people generally would follow the religion of the ruler. If the church lands in question were populated mostly by Catholics, then their surrender would not be permitted. But as it was, the population of the bishoprics was largely Protestant. Above all, the Dominican rejected the militant claim that God called the Catholic princes to restore Catholicism in Germany and promised his assistance in the effort. He also denied outright the parallel with the Hebrews in the Old Testament, especially with the Maccabees, that the militants liked to draw. God had given the Hebrews a special revelation, but there was no such revelation given the Catholic princes in the current situation as the militants

[43] Bireley, *Maximilian von Bayern*, 133–4.

were in effect arguing. Decisions had to be made on the basis of human prudence, not on appeals to providence and special revelations.[44] This was not a holy war.

On September 3, John George of Saxony notified the emperor that he planned to convoke a conference of Protestant states to discuss their common grievances. This scared the Catholic princes and stimulated further discussions about possible concessions on the Edict, or at least its implementation. A position paper was drawn up by a group of moderate Protestant states headed by Hesse-Darmstadt and so called the "Hessian Points."[45] Saxony and Brandenburg did not endorse it. The paper was presented to Mainz on October 1. Mainz in turn took the lead in preparing a "Catholic Response," which was ready on October 22.[46] Momentum seemed to be building for a compromise.[47] Lamormaini was worried, as Vitelleschi's response to his letters shows. The general reassured him that one thousand Masses and four thousand Rosaries were still being offered each week for his intentions.[48]

But Maximilian, then, acting against the advice of most of his councillors, stemmed the momentum. He could not agree, so his delegate to the conference of the Catholic electors on October 21 asserted that the state of necessity, which the theologians claimed was necessary to justify concessions on the Edict, had in his case been reached. If the other Catholic states thought that for them a state of necessity did obtain, then he had no choice but to go along with them. But he would not take the initiative. Precisely at this conference Maximilian launched the plan for a compromise on the army issue; a week before, the Peace of Regensburg had been concluded. Maximilian and Ferdinand seemed to be closing ranks behind the Edict. Over the next few days in joint conferences of delegates of the electors with imperial ministers, Mainz continued to advocate concessions on the Edict for the sake of peace in the empire. Ferdinand's chief minister, Prince Eggenberg, agreed. Ferdinand himself, then, consented to further contacts with the Protestants, but he made it clear that he did not favor a new Peace of Religion or a modification of the Edict. The Catholic electors then decided that they would restrict their talks with the Protestants to proposals about further discussions, with Mainz suggesting February 3 in Frankfurt. So the

44 "Consilium Theologicum Cuiusdam Monachi Dominicani et Celebris Professoris," 1630, HStA, Kriegsakten 242, 22 folios.

45 "Articuli Acatholicorum, welche sie zu Regensburg ubergeben," or "Hessische Puncten," BA 2, 5: no. 170: 680–5.

46 "Gegenerclerung uf die proponirte mittel zur gutlichen vergleichung der religionsstrittigkeiten," ibid., pp. 685–90.

47 Bireley, *Maximilian von Bayern*, 134–5.

48 Vitelleschi to Lamormaini, Nov. 23, 1630, ARSJ, Aust. 4I, f. 355.

convention ended without any compromise on the Edict. The militants had won.[49]

Maximilian, in a memorandum drawn up later during negotiations leading to the Peace of Westphalia, conceded that at Regensburg, against his better political judgment, he sided with the militants. The confessors, he alleged, made the consciences of the Catholic princes "unquiet and heavy," and they spoke of ecclesiastical penalties in the event of compromise. They assured the princes of the full restoration of Catholicism in the empire if only they trusted in God. So an opportunity for compromise had been lost, the war expanded with the intervention of foreign powers, the salvation of many millions of souls endangered, and terrible destruction visited upon Germany. Maximilian was wrong about the possibility of compromise at Regensburg. Examination of the "Hessian Points" and "Catholic Response" shows that the moderates on both sides were still far apart. So one cannot fairly lay the blame for the failure of an agreement on the Edict solely on the Catholic militants. But Maximilian clearly supported them.[50]

The outcome of Regensburg contented Lamormaini. The Edict stood, and with it his plans for Jesuit colleges in north Germany. An agreement had been reached with France over Italy; Richelieu refused to ratify it, but a new peace, less favorable to be sure, would soon be concluded freeing imperial troops for transfer to Germany. A major source of division between emperor and electors had been removed with the dismissal of Wallenstein, and basic agreement on military organization had been reached. Vitelleschi shared Lamormaini's satisfaction. To the confessor, the superior general wrote that he had also heard from Ziegler and Contzen, but that Lamormaini saw matters in a broader perspective.[51] Yet Lamormaini worried about what might happen at the talks with the Protestants now tentatively scheduled for Frankfurt in February.[52]

Meanwhile, back in France, in early 1630 Louis determined to renew the French campaign in Italy, in support of the duke of Nevers and with a view to relieving Casale. The tension between Marie de Medici and Richelieu festered; she resented Richelieu's influence over her son, and she considered the cardinal ungrateful after he had risen through

[49] Bireley, ibid., 135–8; id., *Religion and Politics*, 123–7.

[50] "Discurs uber des Reichs statum," published in Albrecht, 379–81 (appendix). Contzen confirmed Maximilian's stand with the militants at Regensburg in his letter to Franz Wilhelm von Wartenberg, s.d., Konrad Repgen, *Die römische Kurie und der westfälische Friede* 1, 2 (Tübingen, 1965): no. 26: 63–4.

[51] Vitelleschi to Lamormaini, Dec. 14, 1630, ARSJ, Aust. 4I, ff. 473–4.

[52] Lamormaini to Barberini, Jan. 11, 1631, BL 7054, ff. 78–9.

her patronage. Generally, she favored the policy of the *dévots*. The king's health was fragile. Marie opposed his taking the lead of the French troops in Italy, as he was eager to do. At issue here was also the succession. Louis and Anne as yet had no children, and Louis's flighty, irresponsible brother, Gaston, stood next in line for the throne. Suffren attempted to maintain harmony among the king, Marie, and Richelieu.

In early June, Louis and the cardinal journeyed back from their position with the army for five days in Lyons, where the two queens had taken up residence. There Michel de Marillac, a *dévot* recently promoted to keeper of the seals, argued against the war and against Louis's participation in the campaign, especially given now the spread of the plague among the troops. Marillac advocated peace in the face of a threatening European war, relief for the poor whom he thought war taxes were likely to incite to rebellion, and a vigorous campaign to convert the Huguenots. But Louis remained determined on war, and he rode back to the front, where his presence was needed to rally the soldiers who were deserting at a record pace.[53]

Eventually, Louis did take sick, and he was compelled to return once again to Lyons, where from July 25 to August 23 he remained separated from Richelieu and cared for by the two queens and surrounded by courtiers partial to the *dévots*. Negotiations were now under way for a truce in Italy, mediated by the papal representative Giulio Mazarini, later to succeed Richelieu as chief minister in France. With Louis was Suffren, who wrote Richelieu on August 8 that he was seeking the reconciliation for which the king hoped between Richelieu and Marie, a goal that was "one of the most important goals necessary for the well-being of this state." "We continue to raise our hands to heaven," he went on, "for a favorable result for the matters that God has placed in your hands." The fortunes of war wavered, and aware of Richelieu's own indecision he prayed that God's will be done. That was the only path to genuine peace of heart.[54] Ten days later Suffren expressed a keen desire for the cardinal's presence, so necessary for the king and for the proper management of affairs. Richelieu, under great strain, seems to have intimated an intent to retire, to which Suffren replied, "Your absence confirms me in my opinion never to consent to the execution of the resolution [to retire] that you have taken and have communicated to me. God has made use of you, makes use of you now, and will make use of you for the good of the church and of his state; it is

53 A. Lloyd Moote, *Louis XIII, the Just* (Berkeley, 1989), 211.

54 Suffren to Richelieu, Aug. 8, 1630, Armand-Jean du Plessis, cardinal de Richelieu, *Le papiers: Correspondance et papiers d'état, Section politique intérieur*, ed. Pierre Grillon, 5 (Paris, 1982): no. 491: 497–8.

necessary to cooperate with the design of God and not to stand in its way."[55] Claude le Bouthiller, a royal secretary and one of the cardinal's men, praised Suffren to Richelieu as "veritably, one of the finest men on earth."[56]

Once Richelieu and Louis were reunited at Lyons in late August, the quarrels between the cardinal and Marie heated up. At this time, Father Joseph and Charles Brûlart de Léon were dispatched to Regensburg to search for a diplomatic solution for the war in Italy. The French position there was weakening, with Louis perhaps now more intent on carrying on the war than the cardinal. Before Richelieu joined him, the king had authorized the continuation of subsidies to the Dutch. Louis's health recovered in early September, but at the end of the month it then deteriorated drastically. Fever brought him to the brink of death.[57] Suffren described the course of Louis's crisis in two letters to the provincial superior of the Paris Province.

On September 27, after a fifth bleeding, and fearing that the king might not survive the anticipated onslaught of fever that night, the confessor wrote, he began to prepare him for confession and Holy Communion. But not wanting to alarm the king, he used the pretext of the king's birthday that day for the celebration of the sacraments. Louis himself realizing the seriousness of his illness, then requested Viaticum, or communion for the dying. After receiving it from the hands of the cardinal of Lyons, the king summoned his mother and before the nearly one hundred persons present sought pardon for the pain he had caused her in the course of his twenty-nine years. All Lyons prayed for him. That evening he requested Extreme Unction, or the last rites, but the doctors did not judge that the time had arrived for this. Suffren remained with the king at Louis's request, and Marie and Anne stayed late into the night.[58]

There followed a brief respite, but then during the night of September 29/30 the king grew extremely weak, and the doctors now recommended the last rites. Suffren confirmed for him that the end seemed near. Louis made his confession, with great devotion and without showing any fear of death, according to Suffren. The cardinal of Lyons again brought him Holy Communion. At the king's behest, because Louis could now scarcely speak, Suffren asked pardon on his

55 Suffren to Richelieu, Aug. 18, 1630, ibid. no. 531: 542–3.

56 Bouthiller to Richelieu, Lyons, Aug. 16, 1630, cited in Armand-Jean du Plessis, cardinal de Richelieu, *Lettres, instructions, et papiers d'état*, ed. Denis-Louis-Martial Avenel, 3 (Paris, 1861): 864, n. 1

57 Moote, 213–15.

58 Suffren to Barthélemy Jacquinot (provincial), Sept. 28, 1630, Richelieu, *Les papiers: Section politique intérieur* 5: no. 567: 580–2.

behalf for any way in which he may have offended any of those present. Louis then summoned Richelieu to his bedside and spoke a few words to him, and then others followed for a final word with the king. But, to the surprise of all, before the last rites, during a final bleeding, an abscess broke. Hope for the king's life revived, and his strength began to return. He took some food, then rose to walk a bit around the room. By six the next morning the crisis had passed.[59]

The intrigues of the court quickly resumed. Richelieu's enemies, and he had many, stirred up Marie's enmity toward him. The two queens looked after the king in Lyons, and they accompanied him as he began the journey back to Paris on October 18. When news of the Treaty of Regensburg reached the traveling party, Louis immediately rejected it, and a council meeting in Roanne on October 26, with Richelieu presiding, confirmed this. The negotiators had exceeded their instructions. Marillac alone opposed this decision.[60]

By early November the royal entourage arrived back in Paris. On November 10 Marie relieved Richelieu of the offices he held for her household. The scene was now set for what has been called the "Day of Dupes." The next evening Louis and his mother were in conversation in her palace of the Luxembourg, when Richelieu, having come to make the courtesy visit required by the relinquishment of his offices, walked in on the pair and asked that he be allowed to defend himself against the charges of his enemies. Marie was beside herself, told her son that she could not work with the cardinal, and insisted that Louis would have to choose between them. The king, embarrassed by the scene, excused himself and made for his hunting lodge at Versailles. There he summoned the cardinal. Nearly all the court, including Marie and Richelieu, sensed that this meant his disgrace. At Versailles Louis and Richelieu talked long into the night. The upshot was that the cardinal's enemies were sent away from Marie's entourage, and Marillac was relieved of his position as keeper of the seals and imprisoned. When Marie requested to come to Versailles, Louis informed her through Suffren that if it was about Marillac, there was no need to make the trip. Cardinal Richelieu returned to Paris in the royal carriage alongside the king.[61]

In the weeks following, Richelieu made use of Suffren to calm Marie down and to pursue a policy of reconciliation. But the efforts to establish harmony failed. On December 23 the nuncio Bagno arranged a conversation between Richelieu and Marie at Marie's Luxembourg

59 Suffren to Jacquinot (provincial), Oct. 1, 1630, ibid., pp. 582–6.

60 Moote, 216.

61 Moote, 216–19; Henri Fouqueray, *Histoire de la Compagne de Jésus en France* 4 (Paris, 1925): 390.

Palace, along with Louis, Suffren, and Bagno himself. But Marie received the cardinal coldly, and nothing positive resulted. Three days later at the queen-mother's initiative, Richelieu accompanied by Suffren visited her once again. This time the cardinal set a negative tone by declining to accept the seat Marie offered him. Suffren attempted to soften Marie's earlier remarks by attributing them to an anger that had gotten the better of her. But the cardinal retorted that he had given her no grounds for anger. Marie then refused to reveal clearly the reasons for her deep dissatisfaction with Richelieu. So the conversation ended.[62]

Vitelleschi, too, was chagrined by the protracted alienation of Richelieu and Marie. Both had been good to the Society, but the superior general believed that it was necessary to take the cardinal's side. He recognized, he wrote Suffren, that the confessor on the scene knew best how to operate in the situation. But he asked Suffren to do two things. First, he should approach the cardinal and offer him in Vitelleschi's name the services of the whole Society, because of all that Richelieu had done for the Jesuits, and he should assure the cardinal of the singular affection of all Jesuits for him, an affection that was "so great that it could scarcely be greater." In addition, Suffren should frequently express to Richelieu how much the Society owed him. Vitelleschi obviously wanted Richelieu to know that the Jesuits supported him wholeheartedly. Second, Suffren should urge Marie to reconciliation with the best arguments he could muster.[63] Virtually the same message was communicated to the provincial of the Paris Province, whom Vitelleschi also asked to visit Richelieu and Marie.[64] That same day Suffren wrote from Paris that the cardinal's affection for the Society grew daily; on the Feast of the Circumsion, New Year's Day, Richelieu celebrated the main Mass in the Jesuit church and left a substantial donation.[65] But the confessor began to grow despondent in the conflicted situation in which he found himself; Vitelleschi encouraged him and summoned him to confidence in providence.[66]

In February Louis took his mother and his wife along with Suffren to Compiègne outside Paris, where he attempted to convince his mother to cooperate with the cardinal. This he did only after his brother Gaston publicly renounced his oath of loyalty when the budget of his entourage was drastically reduced; Marie was believed to be implicated in his action, which accurately foreshadowed rebellion.[67] Suffren again

[62] Fouqueray 4: 392–3.
[63] Vitelleschi to Suffren, Jan. 11, 1631, ARSJ, Francia 5I, f. 333.
[64] Vitelleschi to Jacquinot (provincial), Jan. 11, 1631, ibid.
[65] Suffren to Vitelleschi, Jan. 11, 1631, ARSJ, Francia 47, ff. 84–4'.
[66] Vitelleschi to Suffren, Feb. 16, 1631, ARSJ, Francia 5I, f. 335.
[67] Moote, 222–3.

mediated, drawing up an agreement by which the queen-mother would promise to abandon her association with Richelieu's enemies. She rejected this as excessively harsh. Richelieu, then, at Louis's request, prepared alternatives to break the impasse at a council meeting on February 23. One was his own retirement, another Marie's provisional exile from court. Louis, faithful to his minister, chose the latter, and early the next morning Louis and Anne departed from Compiègne. Suffren was instructed to inform Marie of Louis's profound regret for leaving without a proper farewell. Soon many of Marie's supporters were either in prison or exiled.[68] Louis never saw his mother again.

Louis left Suffren with Marie, at first provisionally and then indefinitely, to assist her and, it was hoped, to convince her to move to one of the residences further from Paris and the court that were offered to her. She refused to budge. Gaston fled to Lorraine, a move that implied that he was in cahoots with the duke of Lorraine, a Habsburg ally. Enemies of the Jesuits spread the rumor that Suffren encouraged Marie in her stubbornness. The confessor wrote Richelieu of rumors that he would soon be replaced as the king's confessor, adding that he spent a couple of hours with Marie each day trying to console her with readings from the Gospel.[69] But Richelieu reassured the Jesuit that he discounted the rumors and trusted his friend.[70] But three weeks later, on April 2, the cardinal informed Suffren through an intermediary that the king would have to choose another confessor for himself if Suffren was to remain with Marie as Louis wanted. To this message the cardinal added that "it pained him greatly to let him [Suffren] know that the king was not overly happy with his last sermon."[71] This referred to a sermon Suffren had delivered in the church at Compiègne in which he allegedly spoke of Marie as being persecuted and of the cardinal as the persecutor. Suffren vigorously denied making any such implication, and it is difficult to determine the extent to which the sermon may have contributed to his release.[72] In any event, he obviously could no longer serve as confessor to both Louis and his mother.

The first two Jesuit confessors who followed Suffren in France kept a low profile and were of negligible political importance. They seemed to confirm the words of the eighteenth-century Jesuit historian Griffet,

68 Moote, 222–4; Fouqueray 4: 393–5.

69 Suffren to Richelieu, Mar. 8, 1631, Richelieu, *Les papiers: Section politique intérieur* 6: no. 120: 144–5.

70 Fouqueray 4: 397.

71 "Instruction pour M. de Saint-Chamond envoyé en mission auprès de la reine mère," Dijon, April 2, 1631, Richelieu, *Les papiers: Section politique intérieur* 6: no. 173: 208–12.

72 Fouqueray 4: 397–8; Henri Griffet, *Histoire du règne de Louis XIII* (Paris, 1758), 2: 160–1.

that "the cardinal always paid close attention to give this task [of royal confessor] to men who were incapable, either by character or by inclination, to enter into court intrigues or to become involved in government affairs."[73] Marie de Medici, now in exile, remained a threat to Richelieu. Chosen to succeed Suffren was Charles Maillan, then provincial of Lyons. So Richelieu with Louis's consent reached outside the circle of Paris for the next confessor. Richelieu had known him in 1618 when the future cardinal was living in exile in Avignon, where Maillan was then rector of the college.[74] Though surprised by it, Vitelleschi confirmed the selection.[75] Always aware of the importance of the position for the Jesuits in France, he effusively expressed his gratitude to Richelieu, and once again he placed the Society at the service of the cardinal.[76] Earlier, Vitelleschi had notified Richelieu that Gaston, currently in Nancy in Lorraine, had been ill with a fever.[77] So the general helped supply information to Richelieu about his enemies, having learned of this presumably from the Jesuits there.

Suffren remained at Marie's side for the rest of his life, accompanying her to the Spanish Netherlands, Holland, England, and dying on September 15, 1641, in the Spanish Netherlands just after Marie and her party had crossed the channel en route to Cologne, where she died less than a year later on July 3, 1642. Altogether he served as her confessor for twenty-six years. She seems not to have consulted him on political matters, and he did not attempt to influence her politics, apart from his efforts to create harmony within the royal family, which of course had political implications. His last years in particular were not easy ones for Suffren. As he wrote Vitelleschi from Compiègne, "It is not a small work to live at the court of Marie de Medici in such a way as to satisfy the court of Louis XIII, for their desires and tendencies are often in opposition, and it is not up to me to judge where right and fairness are to be found. Until now, thanks to God, nothing has happened to prejudice either the king or his mother against me; nevertheless, in such slippery territory it is very easy to take a false step."[78] Loneliness afflicted the

73 Griffet, ibid., 3: 7.

74 Camille de Rochemonteix, *Nicolas Caussin, Confesseur de Louis XIII, et le Cardinal de Richelieu* (Paris, 1911), 25, n. 2.

75 Vitelleschi to Maillan, May 30, 1631, ARSJ, Francia 5I, f. 345.

76 Vitelleschi to Richelieu, May 31, 1631, ARSJ, Gallia 46I, f. 129′.

77 Vitelleschi to Richelieu, May 13, 1631, Richelieu, *Les papiers: Section politique intérievr* 6: no. 256: 294.

78 Suffren to Vitelleschi, June 24, 1631, cited in Henri Fouqueray, "Jean Suffren à la cour de Marie de Médicis et Louis XIII d'après le mémoires du temps et les documents inédits, 1615–1643," *Revue des questions historiques* 68 (1900); also published separately at Paris, 1900. I cite the latter, p. 63.

Jesuit, having lived many years outside a community of the Society and facing the prospect of more years of the same.

Marie's initial intention was to remain at Compiègne, awaiting hopefully a reversal of fortunes at court. But the days dragged on. On July 19, 1631, she fled to the court of Archduchess Isabella in the Spanish Netherlands, where she found a warm welcome. The flight was improvised at the last moment, and Suffren was not part of the group that departed. Soon Marie wrote summoning him to follow. With less than a day to make up his mind, and unable to consult his superior in Paris, he followed her call. One of his concerns was that by his conduct he compromise the Society in the eyes of Louis or Marie. He laid the whole matter out to Vitelleschi, who in a letter of September 13 completely approved his actions.[79] Suffren remained apart from the continual intrigues and plots stemming from Marie, her entourage, and frequently Gaston, in which, sometimes allied with Spain, they provoked minor civil wars in France, all with the purpose of overthrowing the hated cardinal. But he seemed gradually to take the side of Marie against Richelieu as her exile became more painful and her situation more humble. Richelieu instructed the sieur des Roches, who journeyed on the king's behalf to Marie in Brussels in 1633, that should Suffren or any others want to discuss all that had happened, he should remind them that they knew well enough that the queen-mother had brought her ill-fortune upon herself.[80]

Marie made several efforts to return, promising to stay out of politics, but Richelieu did not trust her resolve. With Louis's consent, he laid down harsh terms for her, especially the requirement to deliver up to his justice some of her courtiers. This probably would have meant death for them.[81] Louis's later confessor, Nicholas Caussin, attempted to intercede for her directly with the king, and he did succeed in touching Louis's conscience. The result was his dismissal, as we will see. Under pressure from the government of the Spanish Netherlands to leave once Spain and France were at war, Marie headed through Holland to England, where her daughter and son-in-law, Queen Henrietta Maria and King Charles I, received her enthusiastically. Here Suffren carried on conversations with several English clergymen and made a number of conversions, and from here he also still pursued reconciliation between Marie

[79] Suffren to Vitelleschi, Mons, Aug. 1, 1631, cited in Fouqueray, ibid., 65–6; Vitelleschi to Suffren, Sept. 13, 1631, ARSJ, Francia 51, f. 352.

[80] "Instruction selon laquelle Le Sieur des Roches, Capitaine de Chevaux Lègers, se conduira au voyage que le Roy l'envoie faire vers la Reyne, Sa Mère, Fontainebleau, June 2, 1633, Richelieu, *Lettres, instructions diplomatiques et papiers d'État*, ed. Avenel, 4: 468–9.

[81] Fouqueray, "Jean Suffren," 75–6.

and the cardinal.[82] Life in England among the Protestants proved difficult. In August 1641, as England lurched toward civil war, Marie crossed back over the Channel, and it was then that Suffren died. Louis died less than a year after Marie, on March 8, 1643. On his deathbed he professed profound regret for his treatment of his mother, and he instructed his secretary to include this sentiment in his testament for all France and Europe to know.[83]

The Frankfurt Conference, where Catholics and Protestants were to resume their discussion on the Edict of Restitution, originally scheduled for February 3, 1631, was postponed until August 3. Chiefly responsible for this delay was the meeting called by Saxony at Leipzig, where delegates of more than forty Protestant states deliberated from late February until early April. The conference issued a vigorous protest against the Edict, demanding not only cessation of its enforcement but the return of all church property already reclaimed by the Catholics by virtue of it. Led by Saxony and Brandenburg, the assembled Protestant states refused to supply the imperial army any further with men, money, or quarters, and they announced their intention to raise their own army of 40,000. This set off alarms. The Swedes continued to advance, and by June 20 compelled Brandenburg to ally with them. The Franco-Swedish Treaty of Bärwalde stipulated that the Swedes would not attack those states of the Catholic League that remained neutral, a provision that aimed to direct the Swedish forces against the emperor. In addition, the Swedes agreed to allow the practice of Catholicism in the Catholic lands they occupied.[84] The other side of Richelieu's program was the aforementioned secret defensive Treaty of Fontainebleau with Bavaria of May 30, 1631, which provided for mutual aid in event of an attack by a third party and was to last for eight years.[85] For Contzen it signaled that France was moving toward the Catholic side in Germany.

What about Spain? The Spaniards aimed to form a Habsburg League, a project that they had promoted since 1625, to comprise Spain, the emperor, the Spanish Netherlands, Archduke Leopold, and as many German states, Protestant as well as Catholic, as it could recruit. It was aimed against Sweden and especially France, and it envisioned a united Germany opposing these two powers, eventually coming to

82 Richelieu to Suffren, c. Mar. 23, 1641, and Suffren to Richelieu, April 1641, Richelieu, ibid., 6: 762–4, 764 n.
83 Fouqueray, ibid., 85–6.
84 Geoffrey Parker, *The Thirty Years War*, 2nd ed. (London, 1997), 104–6, 111.
85 Bireley, *Maximilian von Bayern*, 167–8.

the aid of Spain in The Netherlands. The Spaniards quietly opposed the Edict, because it divided Germany at a time when a united German front was necessary against Sweden and France. Philip IV suggested directly to Ferdinand that he "find a more opportune outlet for his piety and zeal."[86] On June 19 the Treaty of Cherasco ending the war in Italy for the emperor, and France delivered another blow to the Spaniards.

In January Lamormaini along with two militant bishops, Heinrich von Knöringen of Augsburg and Franz Wilhelm von Wartenberg of Osnabrück, beseeched Cardinal Barberini in Rome to have Pope Urban write the Catholic electors to urge them fully to uphold the Edict at the coming negotiations at Frankfurt. Lamormaini's letter was prompted as he put it by the "zeal which God has implanted in me, despite my unworthiness, for the renewal and restoration of the Catholic religion in Germany and all the country of the north." Emperor Ferdinand had said, he reported, that his mind was such that "he would rather imperil his provinces, kingdoms, himself and his own than yield to the heretics anything against justice, religion, or the Edict, provided all the Catholic electors, or at least the elector of Bavaria should the others vacillate, stood by him with constancy and assisted him." Words of holy war followed: "God promises us the victory in a short time; his cause drives [us]. God can easily grant us victory whether we are weak or whether we are strong. Let the giants, the sons of Enoch, or Goliath not strike fear in us; with God's assistance we will devour them. Let us stand firm, and he will fight for us." Lamormaini adverted to the negotiations over Italy then in progress. If peace were established there, the heretics would see how France was coming over to the Catholic side. Unity was necessary.[87]

Urban responded with a flurry of briefs to the emperor, the Catholic electors, and many others, including the empress and the king of Hungary, imploring them not to compromise the interests of the church. Rocci the nuncio was instructed to cooperate closely with Lamormaini. But there was no threat of papal protests or denunciations should the Catholics make concessions. Papal priorities were revealed by the slim financial aid accorded the emperor and the Catholic League: for three years half the revenues from devastated church lands recovered from the Protestants or still to be recovered from them.[88]

86 Philip IV to Ferdinand, June 19, 1631, Heinrich Günter, *Die Habsburgerliga, 1625–1635, Briefe und Akten aus dem General-Archiv zu Simancas* (Berlin, 1908), no. 48.

87 Lamormaini to Barberini, Jan. 11, 1631, BL 7054, ff. 78–9; see also Lamormaini to Barberini, May 10, 1631, ibid., ff. 81–2.

88 Bireley, *Religion and Politics*, 152–3.

The instruction for the imperial delegates to the Frankfurt Conference, dated January 29, maintained the hard line on the Edict, though it did allow for discussion of procedures for enforcement. Lamormaini and Lucas Fanini, confessor of Empress Eleonora endorsed it. Vitelleschi announced that both he and Barberini were relieved when they heard this from Lamormaini.[89] At this point Eggenberg left the court in Vienna for his home in Graz, disillusioned by Lamormaini's ascendancy. The final version of the instruction, dated July 8, showed only minor changes. Maximilian and Mainz endorsed the instruction only on July 28, after the rescheduling of the conference.[90]

During the period between the close of the Electoral Convention at Regensburg in November and the opening of the Frankfurt Conference in August 1631 an intense battle was fought out between militants and moderates in Munich and Vienna. Contzen triumphed over the moderates in Munich in the preparation of the instruction for the Bavarian delegates to the Convention of the Catholic League in Dinkelsbühl in early May. Privy councillors in a meeting in late March recommended "to seek peace without delay on whatever conditions we can secure." It was not possible to prevail by military force.[91] Contzen's position emerged from his letter to Busaeus in Rome of May 22. "All the Catholics are filled with great hope; in a short while we will be equal to the enemy in terms of human strength," he wrote, alluding, it would seem, to the imperial troops to return from Italy after the conclusion of peace there and to prospective French aid. "Because of the goodness of our cause, we are superior. We hope that divine assistance will be with us, especially since everywhere we undertake the penances that are accustomed to propitiate God."[92] But later Contzen took note of the struggle in Munich, "Many Catholics resist, angry to the death with the theologians. It is not safe to write about them."[93]

A manuscript circulating in Munich stemming not from Contzen but from another unidentified Jesuit declared that the fundamental difference between the "politicians" (*politici*) and the theologians (*theologi*) – for our purposes the moderates and the militants – was their different evaluation of the roll of trust in God. His conclusion was that because it was nearly impossible to participate in the coming negotiations

[89] Vitelleschi to Lamormaini, Mar. 29, 1631, ARSJ, Aust. 4I, ff. 439–40.
[90] Bireley, ibid., 153–4.
[91] Notizbuch Richels (Notebook of the Bavarian vice-chancellor, Bartholomaeus Richel), Mar. 29, 1631, HStA, KSchw 5973, f. 108'.
[92] Contzen to Busaeus, May 22, 1631, ARSJ, Boh. 94, f. 303.
[93] Contzen to Busaeus, July 17, 1631, ibid., 309.

without making concessions unacceptable to conscience, it would be better for the theologians to wash their hands in innocence and leave the judgment between them and the politicians up to God.[94]

Laymann rather than Contzen was the principal author of a militant position paper dated July 11, 1631, drawn up by the Munich theologians in preparation for the approaching Frankfurt Conference. Contzen in appended remarks returned to familiar themes. We must look, he wrote, "to the justice of the Catholic cause, to the aid that God has provided the Catholics throughout this whole war, powerfully and in an ordinary fashion," that is, not through miracles but through his normal providence, "and that he is prepared in the future to give to the Catholics who trust in him, unless the dissent itself of some Catholics on this point compel God as it were to withdraw the right arm of his divine power and to permit us at last to descend to that necessity which we hope to escape through an agreement [with the Protestants]."[95] Maximilian followed Contzen.[96]

Over in Vienna, Lamormaini found himself at odds with Ferdinand's leading councillors, Stralendorf, Trautmannsdorf, and Abbot Anton, who had now become bishop of Vienna, and especially with Eggenberg and others of the Spanish party at court.[97] They had favored modification of the Edict at Regensburg, especially with regard to Saxony and Brandenburg, and they continued to do so. That winter there arrived at court the Spanish Capuchin Diego de Quiroga as confessor of the Infanta Maria Anna, who married the king of Hungary in February. One of his assignments was to counter the influence of Lamormaini,[98] and he was to remain a significant figure at the court until the end of the war, especially after the succession of Ferdinand III. Reinforced by Quiroga, the Spanish party opposed the peace then being negotiated in Italy, but on this point most councillors sided with Lamormaini because of the need to retain the support of the Catholic electors and to free the soldiers for service in the north against Gustavus Adolphus.[99]

[94] "Rationes octodecim cur theologi sinceri et religiosi metuant pacem novam religionis promovere malintque rem totam laicis permittere," 1631, HStA, Jesuitica 700, f. 35–8; see Bireley, *Maximilian von Bayern*, 154.

[95] HStA, Kriegsakten 264, ff. 19–28.

[96] For a recent discussion of the situation in Munich at this time, see Dieter Albrecht, *Maximilian I von Bayern, 1573–1651* (Munich, 1998), 770–4, who does not see Maximilian as siding with the militants as clearly as I do.

[97] Bireley, *Religion and Politics*, 157–8.

[98] On Quiroga, see Buonaventura de Carrocera, "El Padre Diego de Quiroga, diplomatico y confessor de reyes, 1574–1649," *Estudios Francescanos* 50 (1949): 71–100.

[99] Bireley, ibid., 162.

At one point Spain considered an attempt to win Lamormaini over or at least to remove him from court with the offer of a cardinal's hat.[100] Then the Spaniards began to put pressure on Vitelleschi in Rome. The Spanish Cardinal Gaspar Borja y Velasco called on the superior general to complain that Lamormaini, who was a subject of Philip IV by virtue of his birth in Luxembourg, regularly countered Spanish interests in Vienna. Vitelleschi reported to Lamormaini that he had defended him against the rather vague charges of the cardinal, but he indicated that it would help if Lamormaini would send him a letter in his own defense to the cardinal.[101] Spanish pressure on Vitelleschi then intensified.

One of the charges now brought against Lamormaini was that at Regensburg he had stood in the way of young Ferdinand, king of Hungary, being elected king of the Romans and so formally guaranteeing his succession in the empire. This was a far-fetched accusation. Before the Convention of Regensburg the emperor decided not to put this issue on the agenda. In its course, then, when it appeared that Mainz's intervention might lead to a compromise on the Edict, Eggenberg raised it informally with the Catholic electors,[102] probably thinking that agreement among all the electors on the Edict would lead to a unity that would make possible the election of the king of the Romans and, not incidentally, prepare the way for emperor and electors to aid Spain against France and in The Netherlands. Lamormaini, then, opposed concessions on the Edict, none of significance were made, and the division between Catholic and Protestant electors persisted. The Spaniards usually hesitated overtly to oppose the Edict, so instead of challenging Lamormaini on it, they accused him of preventing the election of the king of the Romans. But their tactics backfired. Vitelleschi, in addition to keeping Lamormaini abreast of renewed charges, wrote directly to the emperor notifying him of the Spanish accusations and requesting that he vouch for Lamormaini with Philip IV.[103] Both Ferdinand then and the king of Hungary testifed to Lamormaini's loyalty, forcing Cardinal Borja to back down, for the time being.[104]

In a letter of September 27 Vitelleschi also recommended that Lamormaini secure a testimonial from Eggenberg, but in a postscript

100 Philip IV to Cesare Gonzaga, duke of Guastalla, Apr. 22, 1631, Günter, no. 43. Guastalla was serving as an extraordinary Spanish ambassador in Vienna at the time.

101 Vitelleschi to Lamormaini, July 12, 1631, ARSJ, Aust. 4I, f. 488.

102 Bireley, *Religion and Politics*, 113, 119, 126.

103 Vitelleschi to Lamormaini, July 26, 1631, ARSJ, Aust. 4I, 490; Vitelleschi to Ferdinand II, July 26, 1631, ARSJ, Germ. 113II, f. 460.

104 Vitelleschi to Cardinal Borja, Sept. 28, 1631, Hisp. 70, f. 257; Vitelleschi to Ferdinand II, Oct. 25, 1631, Germ. 113II, f. 467; Vitelleschi to the king of Hungary, Oct. 25, 1631, ibid., ff. 466–7.

he withdrew this recommendation, indicating that he would explain in his next letter.[105] Eggenberg, Vitelleschi elaborated in a long communication of October 18, had proven to be a major source of Philip IV's complaints against the confessor.[106] Lamormaini was in no way to let it be known that Vitelleschi had informed him of this, nor was the superior general free to divulge his source of information. Eggenberg accused him, Vitelleschi wrote the confessor, of speaking out too freely on the Italian war and of informing Maximilian of the emperor's plans. Many in Vienna did not approve of the correspondence Lamormaini stored in cabinets in his room marked "Italian," "Spanish," "French," or "Belgian." Most significantly, according to Eggenberg, Lamormaini considered to be matters of conscience affairs that were merely political; not only this, but when councillors disagreed with him, he attempted to persuade them of his position. Often then there arose a conflict of views in Vienna that rendered the emperor "uncertain and perplexed." For this reason Eggenberg had indicated a desire to resign from court. As we have seen, he did leave Vienna in February, but he then returned in June when summoned by a handwritten note from Ferdinand.[107] This was evidently, Vitelleschi noted, a tactic to secure Lamormaini's dismissal.

These were serious charges, most basic the allegation of undue interference in politics. Vitelleschi stated that he did not write to reprimand the confessor. Nor did he attempt to clarify what issues to avoid as purely political because for him Lamormaini's activities all promoted the restoration of Catholicism in Germany. What was then to be done? First, Lamormaini should not think about seeking release from his office; this would only distress the emperor and hinder the common good, which Vitelleschi implicitly identified with the policy of Catholic restoration that the confessor was pursuing. Second, if these charges were true, or approached the truth, could the confessor at least refrain from obstructing Spanish goals if he could not positively foster them. Third, he ought to be careful not to say or especially to write anything that could be construed as hostile to the intentions of the king of Spain, "insofar as the nature of your office permits." This caution asked Lamormaini to square the circle, because the policy he advocated stood in stark contrast to Spain's. In this context Vitelleschi mentioned Lamormaini's errant letter to Suffren, which had fallen into Spanish hands. Finally, Vitelleschi recommended that Lamormaini seek to improve his standing in Madrid through the offices of the imperial

105 Vitelleschi to Lamormaini, Sept. 27, 1631, ARSJ, Aust. 4I, f. 523.
106 Vitelleschi to Lamormaini, Oct. 18, 1631, ibid., 532–3.
107 Bireley, *Religion and Politics*, 165.

ambassador there, who would dispel any suspicions about his attitude toward the monarchy. Vitelleschi hoped that no Jesuit would incur the disfavor of the king of Spain, who merited so much from the Society because of his many benefits to it. We do not have Lamormaini's response to this letter, but his and Vitelleschi's troubles with Spain were hardly over. The whole political and military situation was about to change drastically.

Muzio Vitelleschi, superior general of the Society of Jesus from 1615 to 1645. From Arnold van Westerhout, *Imagines Praepositorum Societatis Jesu* (Antwerp, 1748). Courtesy of Cudahy Library, Loyola University Chicago.

Contemporary satirical engraving with text showing the expulsion of the Jesuits from Bohemia and Hungary in 1618/19 as a pilgrimage to two spurious saints in Amsterdam, where they will be jailed; the carriage driver is the well-known enemy of the Jesuits, the French *parlementaire* Antoine Arnauld (1560–1619). Among the passengers is Lucas Fanini, later confessor of Empress Eleonora, wife of Ferdinand II. Courtesy of the Germanisches Nationalmuseum, Nuremberg.

Pierre Coton, S.J., preacher and confessor of Henry IV and Louis XIII of France is protected by the Virgin Mary and her Son from the attack of a heretic assailant. From Matthias Tanner, *Societas Jesu apostolorum imitatrix* (Prague, 1694). Courtesy of Cudahy Library, Loyola University Chicago.

Christ speaks to Ferdinand II from the cross. This illustration represents the legend that in 1619, at the time of an enemy attack on Vienna, Christ reassured the future emperor, "Ferdinand, I will not desert you." From Franz Christoph von Khevenhiller, *Annales Ferdinandei*, vol. 11 (Leipzig, 1726). Courtesy of the Newberry Library, Chicago.

This marvelous title page of Adam Contzen, *Ten Books on Politics* (Mainz, 1621), reveals the comprehensive nature of the work. Courtesy of the Newberry Library, Chicago.

Jerónimo de Florencia, S.J., preacher to Philip III of Spain, attends the king on his deathbed, 1621. From Matthias Tanner, *Societas Jesu apostolorum imitatrix* (Prague, 1694). Courtesy of Cudahy Library, Loyola University Chicago.

The university church and the Jesuit college in Vienna about 1630; an engraving by Salomon Kleiner and H. Sperl, 1724. Lamormaini obtained the funds for the buildings and oversaw their original construction. Courtesy of the Institut für Kunstgeschichte der Universität Wien, Vienna.

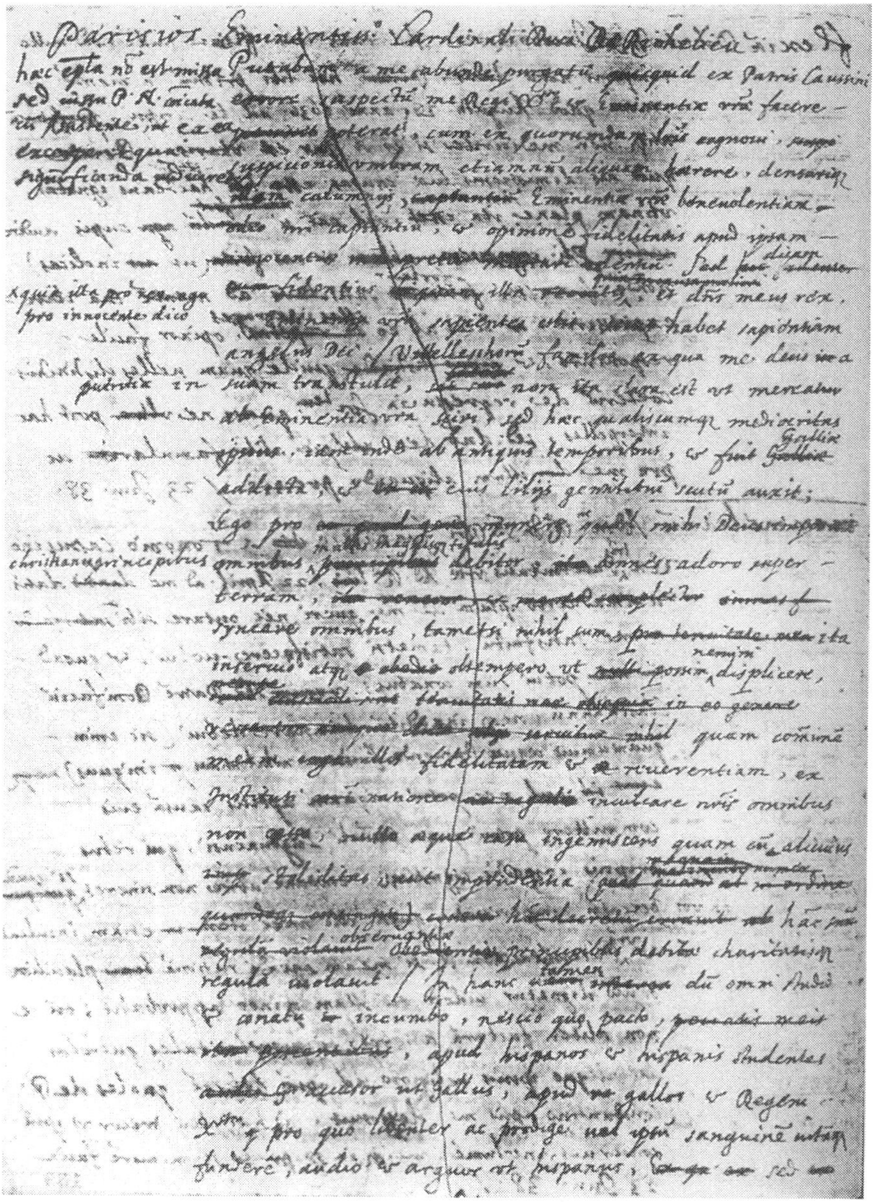

Draft copy of the first page of the letter from Vitelleschi to Cardinal Richelieu, dated June 23, 1638. The letter was not sent. Courtesy of the Archivum Romanum Societatis Jesu, Rome.

The caption to this illustration reads "The Society is attacked in vain by its enemies." From the *Imago primi saeculi* (Antwerp, 1640). Courtesy of Cudahy Library, Loyola University Chicago.

The Jesuit church of St. Louis on the rue Saint-Antoine in Paris. Cardinal Richelieu celebrated the first Solemn Mass in this newly constructed church on May 10, 1641. From Martin Zeiller, *Topographia Galliae* (Frankfurt, 1655). Courtesy of the Newberry Library, Chicago.

CHAPTER 5

Collapse and Recovery in Germany, 1631–1635

GUSTAVUS Adolphus's resounding victory over Tilly at Breitenfeld near Leipzig on September 17, 1631, reversed the course of the Thirty Years War. The fortunes of war that hitherto had accompanied the Catholic armies suddenly switched sides. Under enormous pressure from the Swedes and impelled by the Catholics' refusal to modify the Edict of Restitution, Saxony went over to Gustavus Adolphus on the eve of Breitenfeld. John George's army now marched into Bohemia and seized Prague, while the Swedes advanced through the bishopric of Würzburg to celebrate Christmas in Mainz in the Rhineland. The Swedish king was to be no mere tool of Richelieu. The following year the Swedes occupied much of southwest Germany and Bavaria, including Munich, compelling Maximilian to transport his court to Salzburg and Braunau. Hastily recalled by the emperor, Wallenstein challenged Gustavus Adolphus at Lützen in Saxony in November 1632. Neither side carried off the victory, but the Swedish king fell on the field, thus depriving the Swedish forces of their charismatic leader.

Gradually, the Catholic forces recovered, and the victory of combined imperial, League, and Spanish forces over the Swedes at Nördlingen to the west of Regensburg on September 6, 1634, reestablished a military balance. This prepared the way for the Peace of Prague on May 30, 1635, whereby Saxony returned to the imperial side. Ferdinand and John George intended to incorporate most of the German states into the peace, so that united they could expel the Swedes from Germany and pacify the empire. The Peace of Prague provided for major concessions to the Protestants on the Edict of Restitution, and it ended the aggressive campaign for Catholic restoration in the empire. Meanwhile, Wallenstein was removed from office for insubordination and eventually executed February 25, 1634. The king of Hungary, the future Ferdinand III, stepped into his boots as supreme commander of the imperial forces.

The months following the disaster at Breitenfeld turned out to be the most trying of his years as confessor for Lamormaini. Spanish influence at court grew dramatically as the emperor became more dependent on Spanish aid, and Wallenstein was again in the ascendant. Both developments boded ill for Lamormaini. In early December 1631 Cardinal Peter Pazmany, primate of Estergom and a former Jesuit colleague of Lamormaini in Graz, noted that nearly the whole kingdom wanted him removed from office.[1] A month later the superior of the professed house in Vienna reported to Rome that many folks, common people as well as nobility, held the Jesuits responsible for the war and resulting calamities, though this did not seem to affect the Society's pastoral ministry in the city.[2] Lamormaini's influence at court diminished greatly. He was excluded from a group of six theologians secretly assembled by imperial ministers to discuss possible concessions to Saxony and Brandenburg.[3] For much of the late winter and spring of 1632 Lamromaini lay sick in bed. But Vitelleschi stood by him, if not fully uncritically. He signaled this in his first communication to the confessor after news of Breitenfeld reached Rome. To be sure, the disaster might seem to end the hope for the restitution of all the church lands and the advance of the restoration, he wrote, but there was no reason to lose courage.

> Up to this point and in the midst of the greatest dangers, the divine mercy has in such wonderful ways defended His Imperial Majesty and the other champions of the church. We cannot doubt that in the future [he] will once again take up arms and defend his cause and his servants who have not feared to expose to the enemy all that they possess for the sake of his glory, after he has permitted us to be humiliated for a time and has taught us to place all our hope in him alone.[4]

A handwritten note from Ferdinand dated January 21, 1632 showed that he too stuck with the confessor. "I hope in my God," he wrote, "and I await the confusion of his enemies and all the political councillors."[5]

Fellow Jesuits in Vienna criticized Lamormaini to Vitelleschi. The Spaniard Peñalosa, long resident in Vienna, regarded Lamormaini

[1] Pazmany to Hmira Janos, Tyrnau, Dec. 5, 1631, Peter Pazmany, *Epistolae Collectae* 2 (Budapest, 1911): no. 697.

[2] Nicholas Jagniatorius to Vitelleschi, Jan. 3, 1632, ARSJ, Aust. 21, f. 55.

[3] Robert Bireley, *Religion and Politics in the Age of the Counterreformation: Emperor Ferdinand II, William Lamormaini, and the Formation of Imperial Policy* (Chapel Hill, NC, 1981), 172.

[4] Vitelleschi to Lamormaini, Nov. 8, 1631, ARSJ, Aust. 4I, f. 542.

[5] Ferdinand II to Lamormaini, Jan. 21, 1632, Beda Dudik, "Korrespondenz Kaiser Ferdinands II und seiner erlauchten Familie mit P. Martinus Becanus und P. Wilhelm Lamormaini, kaiserl. Beichtväter, S.J.," *Archiv für österreichische Geschichte* 54 (1876): 275.

highly as a Jesuit, but thought that he trusted in his own conscience excessively. In addition, Lamormaini ought to seek out the Spanish ambassador at court to explain his position to him; as it was, the confessor avoided the company of the Spaniards. Those Jesuits also came in for Peñalosa's criticism, who spoke ill of Lamormaini to non-Jesuits, who then used their words against the confessor.[6] Lucas Fanini, confessor of Empress Eleonora, urged the superior general to convince Lamormaini to resign. Vitelleschi's responded that he could not do this without a list of particulars that Fanini did not supply. Also, it would be only fair to allow Lamormaini to respond to any charges against him; otherwise he could claim that he was condemned unheard. Vitelleschi, who always desired information, requested Fanini to keep him informed of developments without using Lamormaini's name in his correspondence. He would know who was meant.[7]

Vitelleschi's response to Tommaso Politio, an Italian Jesuit in Vienna, is instructive because it shows that he did understand clearly the fundamental objections of the Spaniards to Lamormaini. The reasons for their dissatisfaction with him, wrote Vitelleschi, were basically three: He worked for peace in Italy, he supported the Edict, and he refused a compromise with the Protestants. All the rest were of no account. Vitelleschi obviously stood with Lamormaini on these. What did pain the superior general was the way some Jesuits failed to support the confessor, their brother.[8]

That spring of 1632 the scheduled congregation of procurators in Rome was called off because of the war and a wave of the plague. Rumors flew about that the congregation was really canceled lest it turn into a forum for complaints about Lamormaini's activities. Vitelleschi had to write the provincial of the Austrian Province that this was not the case. Apparently more Jesuits had written Rome about the confessor, accusing the general of serving as the confessor's defender. What am I supposed to do, Vitelleschi countered, condemn him unheard?[9] The following April at the Austrian provincial congregation some delegates broke out in criticism of Lamormaini. Vitelleschi later confirmed the provincial in his decision to cut off such discussion, because it did

6 Ambrosío Peñalosa to Vitelleschi, Jan. 10, 1632, ARSJ, Aust. 21, ff. 62–4.

7 Vitelleschi to Fanini, Jan. 27, 1632, ARSJ, Germ. 111, f. 147. This was a response to a letter of Fanini addressed to the superior general "*soli*," that is, for his eyes only. This was a category separate from the normal correspondence.

8 Vitelleschi to Tommaso Politio, Feb. 14, 1632, ibid., Germ. 111, f. 148. This was also a response to a *soli* letter.

9 Vitelleschi to Georg Forer (provincial), May 1, 1632, ARSJ, Aust. 4II, 626–7.

not belong in the congregation, and he reminded Lamormaini that many fathers spoke in his defense.[10]

The Spanish government stepped up its campaign to pressure Vitelleschi to remove Lamormaini from office or to moderate his activity. Olivares peremptorily called to Madrid seven leading Spanish Jesuits including three provincial superiors. There they assembled in mid-November 1631. The count-duke explained to them the king's complaints against an ungrateful Society. First, the imperial confessor as well as unnamed others – Contzen was also out of favor in Spain at the time – advocated policies harmful to the emperor, to Spain, and even to the Catholic faith. Vitelleschi himself then came in for strictures. When Spanish objections to Lamormaini had been communicated to him, Vitelleschi informed the emperor that the king wanted Lamormaini dismissed, whereas he had only asked that the confessor's activities be moderated. Olivares interpreted the general's letter to Ferdinand as an attempt to drive a wedge between Vienna and Madrid. Furthermore, in order to secure the goodwill of the pope, Vitelleschi favored France. It might be worthwhile for him to consider whether papal favor was as valuable as the support of the king of Spain whose territories encompassed twenty-four provinces of the Society. Vitelleschi could have remedied this situation, but he had taken no effective action to do so. Olivares then added complaints about improper treatment of several Spanish Jesuits. Vitelleschi had ordered withdrawn from circulation a book by Father Hurtado de Mendoza arguing that one could not in conscience aid the Dutch rebels against Spain, but he had permitted a volume by a French Jesuit that made the case for French aid to the Dutch.[11]

The king, Olivares told the fathers, wanted to leave the correction of this situation up to the Jesuits themselves. But he threatened several measures. One was a prohibition that any Spanish ministers or officials make their confession to a Jesuit, because the Society used the confessional to impose its views. The other measures involved the constitutional structure of the Jesuits and recalled efforts of Philip II to control the Spanish Jesuits:[12] the establishment of a commissioner general with wide authority over the Jesuits in Spain; the requirement that alternate superior generals be Spaniards; and regular visitation of the houses in Spain by the superior general.

[10] Vitelleschi to Lamormaini, July 2, 1633, ARSJ, Aust. 4II, 832–3.
[11] For the book of Hurtado de Mendoza, see below, 169–70.
[12] On Philip II's efforts to introduce changes in the Jesuit Constitutions, see William V. Bangert, S.J., *A History of the Society of Jesus* (St. Louis, 1972), 98–9.

Luis de La Palma, reporting for the group to Vitelleschi, stressed the seriousness of the situation, and he recommended in their name that the superior general either accede to the king's wishes or explain clearly why he could not do so.[13]

Vitelleschi's response to the Spanish charges came in a letter to the Spanish provincials. As we might expect, he recognized the Society's profound indebtedness to the king of Spain, and he assured the provincials that he knew of no Jesuit who failed in his obligation of gratitude. If in the past some including the imperial confessor did lapse in this regard, he had corrected them. This remark probably referred to his letter to Lamormaini following the charges attributed to Eggenberg, and it may have also pointed to his reproof of Contzen for his manuscript critical of Spanish plans for the Catholic military after the Convention of Regensburg. With regard to his letter to the emperor, he had understood that Philip IV wanted Lamormaini removed. Perhaps he had erred in this, he acknowledged, but his intention was certainly not to create enmity between Vienna and Madrid. Of the book by a French Jesuit justifying French aid to the Dutch rebels, he was not aware, but he would attempt to locate it.[14] Nothing was said explicitly either by Olivares or by Vitelleschi about the basic issues of the Italian peace or the Edict.

Vitelleschi's response did not satisfy Olivares; in particular, he would have preferred that Vitelleschi write directly to him rather than communicate through the provincials and Aguado, his confessor. But the count-duke did not force the issue any further at this point.[15]

Even before he received Vitelleschi's recommendation that he write to explain himself to the king of Spain, Lamormaini took up his pen to do so. He acted at the suggestion of the marquis of Cadereyta, a new, second Spanish ambassador in Vienna, who obviously made an effort to reach out to the confessor. Lamormaini made three points in his letter. First, he dismissed the charge of obstructing the election of young Ferdinand, king of the Romans, as ridiculous, as it was from his perspective. Then he contended, perhaps somewhat disingenuously, that he could not have opposed the designs of the king because he did not know them. Previous Spanish ambassadors, and he named them all, never communicated with him. How could he have opposed their plans?

[13] Jean Marie Prat, "Philippe IV, roi d'Espagne et la Compagnie de Jésus: Épisode historique, 1631," *Précis historique*, series 3, vol. 3 (Paris, 1894): 208–17. Prat prints the letter of de la Palma to Vitelleschi, without a date, that reports the whole incident.

[14] Vitelleschi to the provincials of Toledo, Castile, and Andalusia, Feb. 7, 1632, ARSJ, Tol. 9, ff. 214–14′.

[15] Vitelleschi to Aguado, Aug. 24, 1632, Tol. 9, ff. 255′–6.

Here we touch on the other side of Peñalosa's complaint to Vitelleschi, that Lamormaini did not seek contact with the Spanish representatives in Vienna. Cadereyta seems to have opened communications to a degree. Perhaps Lamormaini also recognized the role Spain was inevitably to play in Vienna after Breitenfeld. The confessor admitted that he opposed the war in Italy, but so had others in Vienna and Madrid, as Ferdinand himself told him. The most serious charge against him, according to the confessor, was that he aided and abetted the enemies of the House of Habsburg, whose natural subject he was. This he vigorously denied as he pointed out that to his mind the Habsburgs were "the staunchest advocates and propagators of the Catholic Church." He closed by beseeching Philip to protect him and the whole Society from such false charges and calumnies and to show them his grace and favor.[16]

Lamormaini's letters to the king of Spain and Olivares pleased Vitelleschi, and he showed them to critics of the Society in Rome.[17] But now he wrote Lamormaini at length listing criticisms of the confessor that he had received without necessarily identifying himself with them, as was his style. Some overlapped with those of Eggenberg that he had communicated earlier, but nothing was said now directly, as it was earlier, about undue intrusion into political affairs under the guise that conscience was at stake. Vitelleschi never accused Lamormaini of this, because he himself shared the confessor's understanding of the relationship between religion and politics.

Lamormaini, the first criticism went, when consulted on matters of major moment by the emperor or ministers, not only gave them his opinion but took the matter up with others whom he aggressively sought to persuade of the rightness of his view. So he both violated proper confidentiality and inappropriately canvassed for his opinions at court. This practice seems to have first alerted the Spaniards to his opposition to their positions. Also courtiers often took advantage of his willingness to talk in order to secure information about the government's designs. In this context one thinks of the earlier accusation that he communicated information to Maximilian. Second, there was his extensive political correspondence that he kept in files in his room, to which even the emperor took exception. Vitelleschi could find no fault with this, because the confessor received many letters to which he had to respond if he were not to give offense. Yet so many people complained of this, that the confessor ought, at least, to relocate the files or conceal them behind

[16] Lamormaini to Philip IV, Mar. 2, 1632, in Eustachius Sthaäl, "Vita Lamormaini," ARSJ, Vitae, ff. 62–2'.

[17] According to the "Vita Lamormaini," ibid., the king was pleased with the letter. The confessor also wrote Olivares, but I have not found the letter.

a curtain. Third, neither Ferdinand nor fellow Jesuits were happy with his practice, when he was asked to consult with other Jesuits on a matter, of attempting to convince those who held another view to subscribe to his or to prevent theirs from reaching the emperor. Here Vitelleschi called attention to the Instruction for Confessors of Princes, which prescribed that the views of all those consulted be related to the prince, and he suggested the whole Instruction for Lamormaini's perusal once again. A final criticism pointed to a sore point with both imperial councillors and fellow Jesuits, that is, Lamormaini's tendency to discount and discredit the ideas of others and to cling to his own. "Whether this or the other points that I have raised are all true I cannot say," Vitelleschi concluded typically, "but because they have been passed on to me by prudent men worthy of confidence, I send them on for your consideration and the better performance of your office."[18]

Matters continued to turn worse for the Catholics in Germany in the course of 1632. The deteriorating state of affairs drew from Vitelleschi a highly personal letter to Lamormaini in which the general for the only time addressed him in the familiar "*tu*" form.[19] "What are we to do, my father? The Catholic religion perishes throughout nearly all Germany, all Belgium, and after a time – would that I am deceived – will perish similarly in Italy," he wrote, alluding to the widespread fear that Gustavus Adolphus would cross the Alps. "And we with dry eyes stand unmoved and quietly look on. May the God of mercies avert such an evil. Allow me, freely to open up to you what I have in my heart [and have not revealed] to any other mortal. Last month at Tivoli while I was reflecting frequently on these matters and looking at them from different angles so that I might find some remedy, finally I determined that two things were completely certain." The first was that unless the pope and the Catholic King drew together in a bond of genuine love, the condition of the Catholic religion would continue to worsen. Second, there was no one more suited to bring about this unity of pope and the crown of Spain than Ferdinand devoted son of the church that he was, and what glory this would bring him along with victory over all his enemies. "This is the sum of what I beseech you, good Father, that in your zeal and love for God and his church, you put your hands to this task, than which no greater can be conceived, with a great spirit confident in the divine mercy, and to the extent that you are able, bring it to the desired end." Vitelleschi was well aware of the difficulties to be overcome, but, as he interestingly cited "our Seneca," "we do not

[18] Vitelleschi to Lamormaini, Apr. 3, 1632, ARSJ, Aust. 4II, ff. 605–7.

[19] Vitelleschi to Lamormaini, Oct. 16, 1632, ARSJ, Germ. 111, f. 4. This letter is found in the *soli* correspondence, not in the regular correspondence.

venture [to undertake] things because they are difficult, but they are difficult because we do not venture [to undertake] them." The Lord of Hosts will certainly assist your efforts, and who can resist him. "For this cause I daily offer my life and my blood to God at his altar."

Shortly afterward, but without the same degree of personal feeling, Vitelleschi encouraged Aguado, Olivares's confessor, to work toward that same union of pope and Spanish king, indicating also that he had written to Lamormaini to the same effect.[20] So Vitelleschi looked to a union of pope with the two Habsburg rulers. There was no word of the Most Christian King. Both Lamormaini and Contzen continued to look to Paris too. As we shall see, Urban VIII was about to initiate a diplomatic offensive to bring all three Catholic rulers together. Was Vitelleschi more realistic about France, or did he hesitate to interfere in France for fear of crossing Richelieu? Meanwhile, Lamormaini interpreted the death of Gustavus Adolphus at Lützen as a further sign of God's special providence toward Ferdinand and his mission in Germany.[21]

The months after Breitenfeld marked the darkest period of the war for Maximilian too. Vitelleschi encouraged Contzen to hope in the wake of Breitenfeld. "Neither the sad [news related by Contzen] nor the severe setbacks already received nor those yet to be feared have by any means been able to destroy the confidence that I long ago conceived about a favorable outcome of this war.... The Lord of Hosts will be with us."[22] As with Lamormaini in Vienna, Contzen was subjected to sharp criticism even by his fellow Jesuits for his role in advocating a hard line on the Edict. Vulnerable as Bavaria was after Tilly's defeat at Breitenfeld, Maximilian looked for assistance from Vienna. But the return of Wallenstein and the desperate military situation of the emperor precluded effective aid from that quarter. So he eventually accepted Richelieu's offer of a neutrality agreement based on the Treaty of Fontainebleau. Negotiations with the veteran French diplomat Hercule de Charnacé in Munich from December 3 to 24 resulted in terms that would obtain neutrality not only for Bavaria but for its allies in the Catholic League. Charnacé then left for Mainz to secure Gustavus Adolphus's acceptance of the conditions. Should the Swedish king refuse, Charnacé assured Maximilian, France would break with Sweden. Maximilian considered himself justified in entering this

20 Vitelleschi to Aguado, Nov. 2, 1632, ARSJ, Tol. 9, f. 280.
21 Girolamo Grimaldi (extraordinary nuncio in Vienna) to Barberini, Dec. 11, 1632, BL 6978, ff. 212–18.
22 Vitelleschi to Contzen, Nov. 15, 1631, ARSJ, Germ. Sup. 6, f. 401.

agreement, which in his view was in the best interests of the empire in the long run, though he was well aware that Vienna would not see it so.[23]

Contzen, who was twice consulted on the neutrality agreement, approved of it reluctantly. "Yet if necessity compels extreme [measures], let it be," he wrote.[24] At the same time, he influenced the instruction of December 25, 1631, for the Bavarian delegates to a League Convention in Mühlhausen so that they were less likely to take an initiative toward concessions. Significant was a change introduced into the instruction that revealed the friction between militants and moderates. The draft contained a short, polemical passage that took up a point made in the position paper drawn up for Regensburg by an unidentified Dominican, namely, that the design of God in the war was unknown. It was presumptuous to depend on miracles for the Catholic cause; the only responsible way to proceed was to calculate on a rational basis the means at hand to continue the war. Contzen complained of the lack of confidence in God that the passage revealed. Certainly, the Maccabees did not act presumptuously when at God's command they took the field against overwhelming odds. To be sure, Contzen did not count on a miracle but rather on God's normal providence, with an eye toward France. But he did not exclude the former. Maximilian ordered the passage objectionable to Contzen deleted.[25]

Meanwhile, from Vitelleschi and from Maximilian's Roman agent, Francesco Crivelli, Munich learned of rumors spread by the Spanish party in the Eternal City. They insinuated that, like Solomon in his old age, the elector had grown ambitious and, in pursuit of the imperial title for himself, he had concluded a treaty that would ruin the Habsburgs. The reference was to the negotiations with France about a neutrality agreement with the Swedes. Both Maximilian and Richelieu were followers of Machiavelli, Spanish charges asserted, and they called into question Maximilian's reputation as a champion of the faith, which was a highly sensitive point with him.[26] The elector turned to Contzen for a response for the pope's benefit.

In his draft of Maximilian's letter to Urban VIII, Contzen vigorously defended the elector's negotiations with France, pointing out tactfully that an agreement would help protect Italy from an onslaught

[23] Robert Bireley, *Maximilian von Bayern, Adam Contzen, S.J., und die Gegenreformation in Deutschland 1624–1635* (Göttingen, 1975), 170–4.
[24] Memorandum of Contzen, s.d., HStA, Kriegsakten 283, f. 51.
[25] Bireley, *Maximilian von Bayern*, 176.
[26] Vitelleschi to Contzen, Jan. 3, 1632, ARSJ, Germ. Sup. 6, f. 418; Bireley, *Maximilian von Bayern*, 179–80.

by Gustavus Adolphus, which was widely feared at the time. Furthermore, Richelieu was committed to break with Sweden if Gustavus rejected the terms of neutrality. The letter expressed the hope that the Catholic states would form a common front against the heretics. This was scarcely a new idea, but Maximilian now made it his own, and it was to stimulate a new diplomatic initiative in Rome.[27] Contzen's own letter to Vitelleschi made a point that he omitted in the draft for the pope, that the nuncio in Paris, and so the curia itself, urged the neutrality with Sweden. That the nuncio in Paris, Alessandro Bichi, had recommended a neutrality agreement is true, but the curia by this time, in light of the advance of Gustavus Adolphus, no longer strove to split Maximilian from Vienna but wanted to reconcile the two.[28] Contzen persisted in seeing in the Treaty of Fontainebleau the means of bringing France over to the Catholic side in Germany. Precisely at this time, ministers in Vienna were complaining of his pro-French statements. At the end of January 1632, along with a letter to Barberini, Maximilian sent a treatise, "A Theologico-Political Plan concerning the State of Europe and a Remedy for its Evils" drawn up for him by Contzen.[29] The confessor beseeched Urban as the Vicar of Christ to mediate between the Most Christian and the Most Catholic Kings, so that jointly they would come to the aid of the German Catholics. Otherwise, the empire would perish, unless a miracle intervened. Already the Swedes were recruiting guides for their march over the Alps, Contzen informed the Romans. Urban should now commission extraordinary nuncios for the major Catholic courts, to begin negotiations to reconcile their differences and form an alliance against the heretics. As we shall see, Urban responded to this plea.

In a dramatic scene in Mainz, Gustavus rejected the terms of neutrality, and despite further negotiations with Paris and to the consternation of Contzen and Maximilian, Richelieu refused to break with the Swedish king. Gustavus's action was also a defeat for the French cardinal. Richelieu learned that he could not manipulate the king, who now was firmly ensconced just to the east of the French border. That spring and summer Swedish troops devastated extensive areas of Bavaria, and from mid-May to early June Gustavus held court in Munich. Maximilian was compelled to look back toward Vienna and eventually to Spain for assistance.

27 Maximilian to Urban VIII, s.d., HStA, Kriegsakten 283, ff. 14–15'.

28 Contzen to Vitelleschi, Jan. 22, 1632, HStA, Kriegsakten 283, ff. 57–60, 62; Bireley, *Maximilian von Bayern*, 172.

29 "Consilium theologopoliticum de praesenti statu Europae et malorum remedio," s.d., ibid., ff. 8–12' (also in BL 6709, ff. 11–14'); Maximilian to Barberini, Jan. 29, 1632. ibid., ff. 9–10.

Contzen wrote Vitelleschi frequently during this period, often three or four letters for each one he received. The Jesuits came under fire in Munich, too, from friend and foe as responsible for the current ills of Germany. Vitelleschi expressed surprise that the provincial superior of Upper Germany had not arranged for a public response to charges against the Society, and he commissioned both Adam Tanner and Andreas Brunner, who was then working for Maximilian on a multivolume history of Bavaria, to undertake the task.[30] Neither completed it. Tanner died in the course of 1632, leaving a manuscript incomplete, and Brunner was among a group of hostages taken by the Swedes and held in Augsburg for two years.

So Contzen took up the task on his own, preparing a lengthy manuscript in his and the Society's defense that never saw the light of publication, "A Consideration on the Persecution of the Church of Christ throughout Germany."[31] To the charge that the hard-line confessors were to blame for the failure to reach an accommodation with the Protestants at Regensburg, he responded, correctly, that a wide gap had separated the moderate Catholics from the moderate Protestants, and the latter did not even have the support of Saxony or Brandenburg. One might counter, of course, that a readiness for minor concessions on the part of Contzen and like-minded colleagues might have initiated a dynamic that would have eventually generated further agreement. Contzen attempted to explain theologically why God allowed his champions to be routed. This brought him to the issue of suffering in the Christian life. God permitted it as a test of faith, as a means of detachment from the world, as penance for sin. The real cause of the catastrophe, as often in a holy war, was sin, the sin of the Catholics and especially of the clergy whose failings Contzen described in some detail. Penance for sin and conversion of life were needed. Should someone object that the Protestant victory seemed to demonstrate that God favored them, his response was that God punished the Catholics as a father his child, whereas he rejected the Protestants as apostates. Contzen was not at all prepared to give up on the war, but he insisted on moral and religious reform. God would not permit a just cause to be defeated in the long run, and the recovery of the ecclesiastical lands was clearly such a cause.

Jesuit censors in Rome refused to allow the publication of the manuscript as it stood. They found Contzen's account of the sins of the German Catholics exaggerated and his descent into detail offensive,

30 Vitelleschi to Anton Welser (provincial), Feb. 21, 1632, ARSJ, Germ. Sup. 6, ff. 434–5.

31 "De persecutione Ecclesiae Christ per Germaniam consideratio," HStA, Jesuitica 81, ff. 126–226.

and they questioned whether the emperor and princes would be happy if the account of negotiations at Regensburg were made public. Another objection was that in his plan for reform, he attributed too large a role to the princes, to the disadvantage of ecclesiastical authorities.[32] Rather than make the changes required for publication, Contzen preferred to circulate the manuscript as it stood among a restricted audience.[33]

During that fateful spring of 1632 Contzen at Vitelleschi's urging was smoothing the feathers that he had ruffled in Vienna and Madrid by his remarks growing out of the dispute over military reorganization at Regensburg. That April, a week after his letter to Lamormaini, Vitelleschi called to Contzen's attention "that not only in Paris but in many other places men of the Society and especially the confessors of some princes in Germany are accused of meddling excessively in political affairs, of repeatedly speaking and writing too freely about them and the words and deeds of princes, sometimes with little regard for prudence and circumspection." After his typical disclaimer, "not that I think you to be particularly in need of this recommendation, but that I might satisfy those who regularly exhort me that I admonish all confessors of princes about their duty," Vitelleschi beseeched Contzen that at a time when the eyes of nearly all seemed fixed on the Jesuits and their ears alert to their words, he watch himself with special care and make every effort to allow nothing to escape him that could offend any Catholic prince or render him less benevolent toward the Society. Only recently there had been complaints about him from the emperor. The general did not believe that they were justified; still the confessor should take even greater care not to write or say anything that could confirm the empty charges of "I don't know who." Vitelleschi was pleased, he added, with Contzen's manuscript defending the Society, but he did not venture to reverse the judgment of the censors.[34] All in all, the superior general did not seem so alarmed about the activities of the confessors as pushed into correcting them by Jesuits in Rome and in the provinces. Contzen's reaction to his admonition satisfied him, and again he praised the confessor's defense of the theologians considered to be too rigid.[35]

Yet in the provincial congregation held in Munich June 5–12, 1633, there was more discontent with Contzen expressed than with Lamormaini in Vienna. The assembly voted against the convocation of a general congregation, but one reason given in favor of convoking one was to deal with the various charges and calumnies about Jesuit

[32] Censors' Report, s.d., ibid., 704, ff. 37–8.
[33] Vitelleschi to Contzen, May 1 and Aug. 28, 1632, ARSJ, Germ. Sup. 6, ff. 458, 482.
[34] Vitelleschi to Contzen, Apr. 10, 1632, ibid., ff. 448–9.
[35] Vitelleschi to Contzen, Aug. 7, 1632, ibid., f. 476.

involvement in politics. The provincial congregation also proposed to Rome that "since the whole Society suffers seriously at the hands of nearly every type of person as if it mingled excessively in the secular affairs of states and princes," the superior general consider whether further remedies needed to be taken to meet the situation. In his official response Vitelleschi asserted that Jesuits now were less involved in politics than ever before, and he attributed the charges against the Jesuits chiefly to the ill will of enemies. Princes generally agreed with this, he wrote. But if the fathers had a specific instance in the province in mind, he requested that they inform him of it.[36] Vitelleschi's response only makes sense if we exclude from politics matters that touch upon both religion and politics as Vitelleschi was wont to do. Jesuits' critics did not do this.

Following up on the Bavarian recommendation, on March 29, 1632, Urban VIII announced the mission of three extraordinary nuncios to Vienna, Paris, and Madrid. Their goal was to reconcile the three Catholic courts and to prepare the ground for a Catholic alliance.[37] This effort remained a cornerstone of papal policy for the remainder of the war. The announcement came only three weeks after a dramatic scene in Rome where in consistory the Spanish Cardinal Borja openly protested papal policy in Germany, especially the pope's failure to take forceful action against the French support of heretics.[38] The papal initiative heartened Lamormaini, who continued to look to France for eventual assistance to the German Catholics. When Girolamo Grimaldi, the extraordinary nuncio, arrived in Vienna in late June, Lamormaini paid him a visit, but this time there was no papal brief for the confessor, diminished as was his status at court.[39] Contacts were kept alive between Vienna and Paris, sometimes mediated by the nuncios. Peter von Schwarzenberg traveled to Paris as an emissary of Ferdinand in the spring of 1632, and Nicolas de Charbonnière went to Vienna as a permanent French resident in February 1633.[40]

But the Spanish party in Vienna remained dominant, reinforced by Quiroga. Their hand was greatly strengthened by the French renewal of the Treaty of Bärwalde with Sweden in April 1633 and then by French support of the Heilbronn League of German Protestant states headed

36 ARSJ, Cong. 62, ff. 198′, 204–5′.
37 Ludwig von Pastor, *The History of the Popes* 28: *Greqory XV and Urban VIII 1621–1644*, trans. from the German (London, 1938): 293–4.
38 Ibid., 287–90.
39 Bireley, *Religion and Politics*, 186.
40 Ibid., 178, 193.

by Sweden the following September. The Spaniards in Vienna pushed the emperor toward negotiations with Saxony to entice it and then other German Protestant princes back to the imperial side. Mediated at first by the landgrave of Hesse-Darmstadt, they began at Leitmeritz in Bohemia, were transferred to Breslau, and, after the fall of Wallenstein, to Pirna in Saxony.

The Hungarian Cardinal Pazmany arrived in Rome in late March 1632 with a twofold mission from Ferdinand. He first aimed to obtain funds for the hard-pressed imperial forces, and in this he achieved modest success. Grimaldi brought with him 80,000 talers for the emperor and 50,000 for the League, and regular subsidies were maintained. Pazmany then tried to convince the pope to join the nascent Habsburg Alliance between Ferdinand and Philip IV, which had been provisionally concluded on February 14. But Urban as *padre commune* of Christendom and wary of Habsburg power always refused to take this step. Ferdinand and many in Vienna could not fathom why Urban hesitated to condemn France for its blatant support of heretics and to join the alliance. But the most the pope would ever do was to urge the French to cease their assistance to the Protestants. He feared a French schism. Urban's criticism of the Edict now angered Vienna even more. Pazmany in his attempt to pry funds from the pope reminded him that the emperor was fighting a religious war over the ecclesiastical lands, which Urban had enthusiastically endorsed. The pope denied that he had ever supported the Edict, "unless perhaps (which he said was accustomed to happen often) the secretaries had written something more [than they should have]."[41] To be sure, if one read the texts of the papal briefs with great care, one might discover a reservation about the Edict. But neither the nuncios nor the communications of Francesco Barberini showed any sign of it.

Maximilian and Contzen took some hope from the papal initiative, but the French treaties with Sweden and the Heilbronn League discouraged them. Both turned more to Spain. In 1633 Olivares determined to send an army under the duke of Feria up from Milan into Alsace to protect the vital Spanish Road, to dislodge the Swedes on the Upper Rhine, and if necessary to deal with the French who were threatening there. The Spanish diplomat and literary figure Diego Saavedra Fajardo appeared at the Bavarian court in exile in Braunau in July to promote the project, and he remained for nearly ten years in residence at the Bavarian court. Both Maximilian and Contzen favored the Spanish project, which turned out to be a success, and Contzen and Saavedra came to talk frequently.[42]

41 Pazmany to Ferdinand II, Apr. 10, 1632, Pazmany 2: no. 727; Bireley, *Religion and Politics*, 183–4.

42 Bireley, *Maximilian von Bayern*, 199, 203.

Oddly, there was little follow-up from Vitelleschi to the papal initiative with the three extraordinary nuncios. His correspondence with the French confessor or with French officials after the flight of Marie de Medici in 1631 amounted to little. Analogously to Urban VIII, who refused to intervene against Richelieu's policy, Vitelleschi hesitated to attempt to influence it. He perceived the French sensitivity to interference in their affairs, and he feared the impact alleged Jesuit involvement in politics might have on the whole French Society. He did ask the French confessor, Maillan, to welcome and assist the extraordinary nuncio in Paris, but this perhaps as much because he was close to the pope and had a brother who was a Jesuit.[43] As we saw, in October 1632 he implored Lamormaini to convince the emperor to undertake to reconcile the pope and the king of Spain, but he did not mention France. For the Habsburg Alliance of February 1632 he expressed enthusiasm, and he hoped that it would come to encompass more states.[44] Lamormaini he encouraged to accommodate the new Spanish ambassador in January 1633.[45]

The Wallenstein issue came to the surface again in early 1632 and filled Vitelleschi's correspondence with Lamormaini for the next two years. The imperial general had returned to service following Breitenfeld on terms that equipped him with widespread, undetermined powers over the military and for negotiations with the enemy. He was in a strong bargaining position, well aware of Ferdinand's dependence on him. Wallenstein considered the Edict to be disastrous for the emperor and his cause and Lamormaini to be responsible for it, and he knew that the confessor had advocated his dismissal. Now Eggenberg assured him that neither Lamormaini nor other political ecclesiastics would be permitted to interfere with his activity. Their influence at court was to be reined in.[46]

Lamormaini tentatively reached out to Wallenstein once he was back in harness. A New Year's greeting for 1632 wished the general "the wisdom of Joshua, the sword of Gideon, the bravery and piety of Judas Maccabaeus, the spirit and confidence in God of David the warrior according to the heart of God, the religion, zeal, and the standard of Constantine the Great." But these words with their connotation of holy warriors probably did not impress the general. Lamormaini admitted that at Regensburg he had advocated the general's dismissal, but

43 Vitelleschi to Maillan, Mar. 31, 1632, ARSJ, Francia 3I, f. 367.
44 Vitelleschi to Lamormaini, Mar. 29, 1632, ARSJ, Aust. 4II, ff. 599–600.
45 Vitelleschi to Lamormaini, Jan. 22, 1633, ibid., f. 739.
46 Bireley, *Religion and Politics*, 175–6.

he explained, he favored this only because he thought it necessary to maintain harmony between the emperor and the electors. Certainly the general would not hold this against him now. Neither this nor a similar greeting at Easter drew any response from Wallenstein.[47]

Vitelleschi advised Lamormaini to rebuild his bridge with the general. After the Battle of Lützen, with the prospect of the recovery of church lands again in sight, Vitelleschi suggested that Lamormaini cultivate his relationships with ministers and generals who would have a say in the allocation of these properties, and especially with Wallenstein. Perhaps, Vitelleschi suggested, Ferdinand himself would put in a good word for Lamormaini with the general. In order to do his part, Vitelleschi enclosed a letter congratulating Wallenstein on his recent victory and acclaiming him as God's instrument for the restoration of Catholicism. Lamormaini should forward it as he thought best. Buoyed by the outcome of Lützen with the death of Gustavus, the superior general still expected the victory of the Catholic cause in Germany.[48]

Maximilian felt uneasy about Wallenstein's renewed generalate while aware of its necessity. He had led the campaign to have the general dismissed at Regensburg. Increasingly, Wallenstein's failure to attack the enemy as the elector expected, his neglect to respond to Maximilian's desperate calls for military assistance, and his secret contacts with the enemy awakened the elector's fears. But he was too vulnerable to oppose Wallenstein openly. So he turned to Contzen. That January 1633 Contzen informed Vitelleschi of Maximilian's complaints about Wallenstein, and especially of Wallenstein's alleged resort to astrologers in decision making. Vitelleschi cautioned Contzen that no one should know of his letter in response. Only because of the service he owed Maximilian did he become involved in the matter. Key words of the letter were in cipher.[49]

The next week a letter sped from Rome to the confessor in Vienna. The superior general long had hesitated to raise this issue, he wrote, but the persistence of those writing to him had convinced him that it deserved Ferdinand's attention. He then related the charges that Wallenstein's reliance on astrology impaired his military effectiveness. It was said to be the work of demons. Vitelleschi carefully avoided taking a position on the truth of the accusations, but his unnamed correspondent asserted

[47] Lamormaini to Wallenstein, Jan. 2, 1632, in Beda Dudik, *Waldstein von seiner Enthebung bis zur abermaligen Übernahme des Armee-Ober-Commando* (Vienna, 1858), 194.
[48] Vitelleschi to Lamormaini, Jan. 1, 1633, ARSJ, Aust. 4II, ff. 733–4.
[49] Vitelleschi to Contzen, Feb. 12, 1633, ARSJ, Germ. Sup. 6, f. 521.

vehemently their truth.[50] Several weeks later Vitelleschi again exhorted Lamormaini to seek reconciliation with Wallenstein. In words redolent of holy war and Ferdinand's mission, he continued:

> I am also in no way able to be persuaded that Divine Providence will abandon the efforts by which His Imperial Majesty has labored up to this point to restore the Catholic religion in all Germany. Nor am I able to fear that God will desert the cause, which up to now he has championed not so much through human plans or resources as through the wonderful guidance of his wisdom and his extended right arm, and which divine power has defended beyond nearly all expectation when human powers have failed; nor [am I able to fear] that he will permit that the fruit of so many victories be corrupted by an unjust peace.[51]

So he continued at length, encouraging the confessor not to flag in his holy campaign.

Soon Vitelleschi learned from Lamormaini that the confessor could do nothing about Wallenstein. The superior general passed this information on to Contzen while exhorting him to continue to foster harmony between the two pillars of the Catholic cause in Germany.[52] Vitelleschi's letter congratulating Wallenstein on his victory at Lützen, Lamormaini determined, would be better left undelivered.[53]

In July 1633 Maximilian sent his vice chancellor Bartholomew Richel to Vienna to protest Wallenstein's inactivity, but he hesitated to call for his replacement because he feared reprisals.[54] Opposition to Wallenstein mounted in the fall as a result of the general's long truces and secretive negotiations with Saxony. The Spaniards broke with him when he opposed the expedition of the duke of Feria's army from Milan into Alsace, and the veteran diplomat Oñate, back in Vienna as an extraordinary ambassador, turned against him. In November Bernard of Weimar captured Regensburg and started to ravage Bavaria. Wallenstein resisted Ferdinand's command to come to Maximilian's aid. This was insubordination. Wallenstein also planned to quarter troops that winter on Habsburg lands after giving assurances that this would not be necessary. Maximilian now ordered Richel back to Vienna to pursue Wallenstein's removal along with Oñate, Lamormani, and others known to be hostile to him. Wallenstein's shattered health forced him to spend long periods in bed. Rumors flew about concerning his dependence on astrology and especially his ultimate intentions. By late December Ferdinand had

[50] Vitelleschi to Lamormaini, Feb. 19, 1633, ARSJ, Aust. 4II, f. 765.
[51] Vitelleschi to Lamormaini, Mar. 12, 1633, ibid., ff. 782–3.
[52] Vitelleschi to Lamormaini, Apr. 26, 1633, ibid., f. 799; Vitelleschi to Contzen, Mar. 26 and Apr. 12, 1633, ARSJ, Germ. Sup. 6, ff. 538, 552.
[53] Vitelleschi to Lamormaini, Mar. 26 and May 21, 1633, ARSJ, Aust. 4II, ff. 791–2, 807–8.
[54] Bireley, *Maximilian von Bayern*, 198.

decided to dismiss Wallenstein once again because he threatened his rule.[55]

Lamormaini's correspondence with Vitelleschi diminished significantly during the fall of 1633. For a time Vitelleschi wondered why, and he encouraged the confessor to write bad news as well as good.[56] But eventually he figured out that something was happening about which the confessor could not communicate, and he promised prayers.[57]

Events now moved toward a climax. Sensing trouble, Wallenstein summoned his leading officers to Pilsen on January 13, where he demanded of them an oath of allegiance to himself. This action was given the worst possible interpretation in Vienna in light of the rumors about his intentions. Ferdinand realized he had to act. He deputed three privy councillors to review all the material on Wallenstein and to recommend measures to be taken. This amounted to a trial of sorts. Of the three councillors, two had been closely associated with Wallenstein: Eggenberg and the bishop of Vienna; the third was Trautmannsdorf. They decided on January 24 that the general should once again be dismissed from office. He was then to be brought to Vienna to be given a hearing. Should this not be possible because of his resistance, as the councillors thought likely, then those sent to arrest him might take his life. He would be executed for treachery.[58]

That evening Ferdinand sent a handwritten note to Lamormaini. "The bishop of Vienna will inform Your Reverence of a matter of great moment, and this under the highest seal of conscience and confession, the observance of which I know to be safe with Your Reverence; let the bishop know your mind without much reflection, since there is great danger in delay."[59] So Lamormaini was given a veto over the verdict. He clearly supported Wallenstein's removal from office and the verdict of execution that was likely to be carried out. Though once again he realized the need for the dismissal to preserve harmony between Habsburg and Wittelsbach and he opposed Wallenstein's efforts to conciliate the Protestants, his principal reason now was the conviction that Wallenstein sought to "ruin the emperor, uproot the House of Austria, take possession of the Austrian lands and kingdoms himself, and distribute the lands and property of the emperor's faithful ministers to his fellow conspirators," as he wrote Vitelleschi in an extended letter that

[55] Bireley, *Religion and Politics*, 200–1.
[56] Vitelleschi to Lamormaini, Oct. 8, 1633, Jan. 24, 1634, ARSJ, Aust. 4II, ff. 873, 912.
[57] Vitelleschi to Lamormaini, Feb. 25, 1634, ibid., Aust. 4II, f. 917.
[58] Bireley, *Religion and Politics*, 202.
[59] Ferdinand to Lamormaini, Jan. 24, 1634, Dudik, "Korrespondenz Kaiser Ferdinands II," 276–7.

described in detail the events of January and February and remains one of the principal sources for the climax of the Wallenstein affair.[60]

For nearly a month Ferdinand and his councillors prepared in great secrecy for the arrest of Wallenstein, taking care, successfully, to forestall any mutiny of the troops. Only on February 22 was the order for his arrest published. Wallenstein fled with several close aides from Pilsen to Eger. There they were all killed by a detachment of Irish and Scottish soldiers in imperial service. "Truly the Wallenstein comedy came to a tragic end (*Tragicus profecto exitus Friedlandiae comoediae*)," as Lamormaini wrote. "Behold how God summoned from the outer borders of Europe those who would defend the emperor, who both worked with God and trusted in him, and who would exterminate the traitors."[61]

Reflecting the views of both Lamormaini and Contzen, both of whom had informed him of Wallenstein's end,[62] Vitelleschi rejoiced and praised God at the frustration of the conspiracy against Ferdinand and the empire itself. It surely answered the many prayers and Masses offered for the emperor. The Lord had intervened on Ferdinand's behalf once again.[63] The superior general thanked Contzen for his part in foiling the traitors and for his report of the events.[64] But to Lamormaini he also recommended a further investigation of the conspiracy, both to ensnare others who might have been involved in it and, more importantly, to make fully clear the legal basis for the emperor's action. For the emperor's reputation it was important to demonstrate the guilt of the conspirators.[65] To Ferdinand the defeat of the plot against him seemed a response to a vow he had made, and he proceeded to endow the Jesuit novitiate of St. Anna in Vienna so richly that Lamormaini needed to curtail his generosity.[66]

Maximilian frequently employed Contzen to push his case for more financial support from Rome. Weekly letters of the confessor during July 1633 complained of the lack of papal subsidies for Maximilian who was defending the church in Germany. Many in Rome greatly admired the prince, Vitelleschi answered, but still wondered why instead of

60 Lamormaini to Vitelleschi, Mar. 3–4, 1634, Heinrich Ritter von Srbik, *Wallensteins Ende*, 2nd ed. (Salzburg, 1952), 381–3.

61 Ibid.

62 According to Vitelleschi to Barberini, Mar. 28, 1634, BL 6515, f. 66, the general sent the cardinal four letters about the death of Wallenstein, two from Contzen, one from Georg Spaiser, superior in Halle, and one from Lamormaini. Only Lamormaini's has survived.

63 Vitelleschi to Lamormaini, Apr. 1, 1634, ARSJ, Aust. 4II, ff. 923–4.

64 Vitelleschi to Contzen, Apr. 1, 1634, ARSJ, Germ. Sup. 7, f. 639.

65 Vitelleschi to Lamormaini, Apr. 22 and 29, ARSJ, Aust. 4II, ff. 931, 934.

66 Bireley, *Religion and Politics*, 204.

complaining about the lack of subsidies, he simply did not raise more troops on his own. They were convinced, and here "they" meant papal officials, that the prince's aerarium, or secret treasury, certainly contained adequate funds. "I would more wish this were true," Vitelleschi remarked about the alleged funds, "than dare to believe it." So the general distanced himself from the rumors, but he then asked Contzen for guidance about how to deal with them and so to protect Maximilian's reputation in Rome.[67] Later Vitelleschi acknowledged Maximilian's gratitude for the assistance that the superior general had given in the prince's pursuit of funds for the Catholic League.[68]

With Lamormaini, Vitelleschi raised the issue in 1634 of the prohibition against the Jesuits owning land in Hungary. He suggested that an effort might be made to have this rescinded at the upcoming Hungarian diet. But when Lamormaini responded that the emperor, Cardinal Pazmany, and the palatine of Hungary all counseled against this and pointed out that the prohibition was not enforced in practice, he acquiesced in their judgment.[69]

Negotiations with Saxony picked up after the fall of Wallenstein. The conflict between the moderates and the militants persisted in Vienna and Munich, with the position of the former steadily improving. In early 1633 Cardinal Pazmany had been inclined to accept nearly any peace agreement in the empire that maintained the position of the church in the Habsburg lands, and two other major ecclesiastical figures, the bishop of Vienna and Cardinal Dietrichstein, joined him in this. For them the interest of the nascent Habsburg monarchy predominated over the empire. The two nuncios Rocci and Grimaldi supported Lamormaini, and they were reinforced by a papal brief of July 9, 1633, which exhorted the emperor to steadfastness while avoiding the rhetoric of holy war and any threat of ecclesiastical punishment.[70] Ferdinand in his talks with Lamormaini brought up the contrary position of the three ecclesiastics, but Lamormaini continued to exercise a powerful influence on him.[71]

But even the moderates recognized that there could be no viable peace agreement in the empire until a military balance was struck between the two sides. The Bavarian councillor Wilhelm Jocher in a

[67] Vitelleschi to Contzen, Aug. 13, 1633, ARSJ, Germ. Sup. 6, f. 539.
[68] Vitelleschi to Maximilian, Jan. 21, 1634, ARSJ, Germ. 113II, f. 546.
[69] Vitelleschi to Lamormaini, Jan. 14 and Mar. 25, 1634, ARSJ, Aust. 4II, ff. 901, 922.
[70] Urban VIII to Ferdinand II, July 9, 1633, Konrad Repgen, *Die römische Kurie und der westfälische Friede* 1, 2 (Tübingen, 1965): no. 59: 114–16; Bireley, *Religion and Politics*, 196–7.
[71] Bireley, *Religion and Politics*, 191–2.

memorandum of late June 1633 vigorously condemned the theology of Contzen but acknowledged the unacceptability of the terms offered by the Protestants.[72]

Following the death of Wallenstein, cooperation picked up between Spain and the emperor. The king of Hungary assumed the command of the imperial forces as well as formal responsibility for the peace negotiations. Then at Nördlingen on September 6, 1634, the Catholics won the military victory for which they had hoped. The combined forces of the king of Hungary and Don Fernando, the cardinal infante of Spain, who led another Spanish army up from Milan, soundly defeated the Swedes and drove them out of southwest Germany. This greatly enhanced the Catholic bargaining position at Pirna, the Saxon town whither negotiations had been moved. But the Swedes' defeat also convinced Richelieu that in order to achieve his goals in Germany, he would have to enter the war openly. So the French became more aggressive in the west of the empire and were less inclined than ever to agree to an arrangement with Madrid.

Emperor Ferdinand in commissioning his son as commander of the imperial army as it opened the campaign that led to Nördlingen listed as one of the campaign's objectives the safety and preservation of the Society of Jesus in Germany. So he showed persistent confidence and trust in the Jesuits, for which Vitelleschi thanked him profusely.[73]

Nördlingen then elicited from Vitelleschi renewed enthusiasm and confidence in the Catholic cause. Exuberant letters found their way to the emperor, the king of Hungary, and Maximilian, which echoed anew the themes of holy war. "The Lord of Hosts has manifested his power, horse and rider he has cast into the sea," he exulted in biblical terms. He congratulated Ferdinand on a momentous victory, "in which a judgment was made over the most important matters: the imperial crown and dignity, the preservation of the ancient religion, the fortune and glory of the House of Austria, and if it is permitted to add to these great matters something humble and little, the life and preservation of our Society engaged as it is with a ferocious foe." The king of Hungary he compared to David; others, like Saul, had slain their thousands, the king had slain his tens of thousands. The Jesuits now had the prospect of recovering their houses in southwest Germany and perhaps beyond. To Maximilian, Vitelleschi seemed to take up the theme of Contzen's treatise, "A Consideration on the Persecution of the Church in Germany."

[72] BA 2, 8: no. 128: 191–209.
[73] Vitelleschi to Ferdinand II, June 3, 1634, ARSJ, Germ. 113II, ff. 560–1.

After their initial victories God became angry with the Catholics for their sins; now, however, his favor had returned.[74]

But Contzen and Lamormaini were once again at odds. It is not clear what the issue was; it probably was associated either with the allotment of papal funds for Munich and Vienna or with the relative credit for the victory at Nördlingen. Illness had overtaken Contzen, making him unusually testy; after his death in June 1635 a large gallstone was taken from his body that must have caused acute pain.[75] Lamormaini complained again of the bitter pen of the Bavarian confessor whose missives were circulating in Vienna. Vitelleschi exhorted Lamormaini to patience and told him that he could not possibly expel Contzen from the Society, a measure that Lamormaini must have suggested, and he reminded him of Contzen's illness. Lamormaini ought to try to suppress the letters from Munich rather than to show them to Ferdinand and his ministers. Contzen Vitelleschi called to task for "the sharp and pointed letter" he sent to Vienna. His own function, Vitelleschi wrote, was not to resolve the issue between them but to encourage them both to work for harmony among the two princes.[76]

The three imperial negotiators returned from Pirna on December 7, 1634, with the "Pirna Points," the draft of a treaty with Saxony that foresaw the incorporation of most German Catholic and Protestant states into the agreement. The draft represented a compromise on the Edict and thus a retreat from the militant plan for a Catholic restoration in the empire. The hope was to unite the German states in order to drive out the foreigners, the Swedes and, increasingly, the French. The Spaniards were enthusiastic.

The normative date for the possession of church lands, imperial or territorial, as well as for the enjoyment of ecclesiastical privileges such as freedom of worship, was to be fixed at November 12, 1627. The status as of that date would endure for forty years; at that time the emperor's jurisdiction over the issues would revive, but he was to make a decision only after hearing the views of a body composed equally of Catholics and Protestants and sworn to fairness. Though in the nature of things the Catholic surrender of lands and privileges was likely to become permanent, it was not officially so, and this feature made the terms

[74] Vitelleschi to Ferdinand II, Oct. 21, 1634, ARSJ, Germ. 113II, f. 572; Vitelleschi to the king of Hungary, Oct. 21, 1634, ibid., ff. 573–4; Vitelleschi to Maximilian, Oct. 21, 1634, ibid., ff. 576–7.

[75] Bireley, *Maximilian von Bayern*, 202.

[76] Vitelleschi to Lamormaini, Oct. 21, Nov. 11, and Dec. 9, 1634, ARSJ, Aust. 4II, ff. 985–6, 995, 1008–9; Vitelleschi to Contzen, Nov. 11 and Dec. 9, 1634, ARSJ, Germ. Sup. 7, ff. 694, 700.

much more acceptable. The settlement meant that the Catholics would retain or regain most of their church lands in south and west Germany, and even in the northwest, but they would surrender their claims in the north, especially in Saxony and Brandenburg, as well as in areas of Franconia and Swabia. But there were many exceptions. Highly favorable to the emperor was the recognition that he could determine the religious settlement in the Habsburg lands independently of the norm. Final settlement of the Palatinate question was left open, though John George of Saxony indicated that he would yield to Maximilian if all the other terms were accepted. A new imperial army was to be created, in which Saxony would have a major command, and all military alliances were dissolved, that is, the Catholic League. Full amnesty was granted to those German states that had taken up arms against the emperor in 1630 at the time of the invasion of Gustavus Adolphus or later. One major weakness of the treaty was the failure to make any territorial concessions to Sweden, which would not be satisfied after five years of war with the monetary compensation offered it.[77]

There now began an intense struggle over ratification in Vienna that pitted the moderates against the militants. The imperial councillors favored the treaty, and so did the Spaniards. Against it were Lamormaini and to a degree the new papal nuncio, Malatesta Baglione, who arrived in late November warmly recommended by Vitelleschi as a friend of the Jesuits.[78] Papal policy remained ambiguous. The departing nuncio Rocci had been instructed in October to support Lamormaini but "with prudence."[79] Mainz and Cologne had sent Mainz's confessor Ziegler to Rome in the summer of 1634, to inquire whether they might surrender ecclesiastical lands to the Protestants. This was precisely the question Urban did not want to be asked directly. The pope refused formally to approve any concessions to the Protestants; his goal remained the maintenance of the church's juridical position. But he had no intention of subsidizing the German Catholics more generously or of threatening them with church penalties. In effect, he was telling them, as some in Vienna realized, to make the best arrangement they could but not to expect him to sanction it officially.[80] Papal diplomacy still worked at the reconciliation of the three crowns; but this became even more unlikely after the French renewed their commitment to the Heilbronn League on November 1, 1634, and then began to occupy areas on the Upper Rhine evacuated by the Swedes.

77 Bireley, *Religion and Politics*, 209–11.
78 Vitelleschi to Lamormaini, Apr. 29 and Jun. 3, 1634, ARSJ, Aust. 4II, ff. 934, 940–1.
79 Barberini to Rocci, Oct. 21, 1634, cited in Repgen 1, 1 (Tübingen, 1962): 335, n. 121.
80 Bireley, ibid., 211–12.

The imperial privy council argued a strong case for ratification of the peace in a paper read before the emperor on January 20, 1635. The greater good of church as well as empire demanded its acceptance. The resources simply were not there to continue the war. Concessions were to be made to the Protestants, but they were more than offset by the gains. Another factor now was the fear of an interregnum in the empire. Ferdinand's health deteriorated steadily; if he died before his son were elected king of the Romans and the succession regulated, Saxony as first imperial vicar would govern provisionally, and there would be ample opportunity for the French to fish in the waters of the empire as they had frequently attempted. Nearly everyone favored the peace, the paper went on, including "High Cardinals," a reference to Pazmany and Dietrichstein. At the close the paper described vividly the sufferings of the common people: families ruined, women raped, churches destroyed, schools closed. These could not be permitted to continue. War was barbarizing the people to the detriment of all religion. Then, certainly with an eye to Lamormaini, the paper emphasized that the decision had to be based on "human reason," not on an alleged revelation. Ferdinand's advocacy of religion and justice did not guarantee him victory. Instances in scripture showed that God had sometimes ordered a holy war and then punished the Hebrews with defeat for their sins.[81]

But there was to be no final decision yet. The Catholic electors had to be heard from. In addition, Ferdinand now commissioned Cardinal Dietrichstein to convoke a conference of theologians to assess the terms of the Pirna Points; were they acceptable to conscience? They deliberated from February 5 to 16 in Vienna. Twenty-four took part, religious from different orders and one diocesan priest. They were to discuss the peace among themselves, but there was to be no common opinion; each individual, or group from an order, was to prepare an assessment. Three Capuchins, including Quiroga, constituted one group. Quiroga and his confrere Basilio d'Aire, an Irishman who represented Cardinal Harrach of Prague, argued that the emperor not only could accept the terms but that he was bound to do so in the circumstances under pain of mortal sin.[82]

The largest faction was made up of Lamormaini and four of the other seven Jesuits. Lamormaini did not write up an opinion, but he spoke more than any other at the conference, as can be seen from the protocol. He beseeched his colleagues to answer only that for which they could take responsibility at the judgment seat of Christ. He did not believe

[81] HHStA, Friedensakten 11a, ff. 48–58.
[82] Bireley, ibid., 215–16.

that a state of necessity justifying the terms existed, and he still held out hope for French aid. With Lamormaini's endorsement, Ludwig Crasius, professor of theology at the Jesuit academy at Olomouc in Moravia, asserted that we should not doubt "that God, who up to this point has rescued our most pious Emperor from so many dangers, in this extremity will also show us the way either to continue the war or to obtain a better peace."[83] Three Jesuits were ready to authorize yielding to necessity, with reservations. The Spaniard Peñalosa sided with the Capuchins. God would show his special care for Ferdinand, he contended, by enabling him to make the right decision. Several participants went out of their way to challenge the myth that God had called Ferdinand to restore Catholicism in Germany. Ignacio a Santa Maria, a Portuguese and the only Augustinian present, stressed that it would be presumptuous to rely on divine assistance for victory absent a clear revelation as in the case of Gideon in the Book of Joshua. For a number of the theologians, papal permission would normally be required for the surrender of church property, but most added that time would not allow this or that the pope was bound to assent to a reasonable request. All in all, thirteen of the sixteen written opinions approved the peace in the current circumstances.[84]

Just as the theological conference ended, the long expected opinions of the Catholic electors arrived. But contrary to past experience, they were divided. Ferdinand of Cologne, Maximilian's brother, rejected the peace, influenced perhaps by the protection the French had provided his lands from the Swedish invader. Recent Catholic victories gave solid ground for hope, he affirmed. Anselm Casimir of Mainz, on the other hand, approved the terms if the alternative were war. He cited two dicta in support of his position: No one was bound to the impossible, and the lesser of two evils was to be chosen. His people suffered at the hands of the Swedes, and he spoke of French efforts to dismember the empire. Like his brother Ferdinand, Maximilian had long refused concessions on the Edict because he feared to sin by rejecting God's call, and he did not want to compromise the Wittelsbach reputation as a champion of the faith. But at this point he broke with the militant position. He accepted the terms for essentially the same reasons as the imperial councillors. The greater benefit for church, Bavaria, and empire lay in peace. The stand of Mainz also influenced him; he could safely follow an ecclesiastical elector. Contzen by this time was seriously ill, and gradually his place was being taken by another Jesuit, Johannes

83 HHStA, ibid., f. 218.
84 Bireley, ibid., 216–19.

Vervaux, confessor of Maximilian's wife, Elizabeth of Lorraine, and as we shall see, a moderate. He, too, may have influenced the elector.[85]

Now Ferdinand called together eight "intimate" councillors, including Lamormaini, the two Cardinals Pazmany and Dietrichstein, Bishop Anton of Vienna, Stralendorf, and Trautmannsdorf for a final decision on the Pirna Points in light of the views of the theological conference and the electors' opinions. Lamormaini stood alone. The arguments scarcely changed. The majority insisted once again on the need to base policy on reason and not on anticipated miracles. Finally, at this point Ferdinand came down on the side of the majority. But the negotiators were to seek to insert a number of amendments into the agreement, among them permanent possession of the Palatinate electoral title and lands on the east bank of the Rhine for Maximilian. Saxony proved to be surprisingly pliant on this and other issues.[86]

On May 30 the imperial and Saxon delegates signed the Peace of Prague in the city on the Moldau. So Ferdinand broke with the myth long upheld by Lamormaini and others, including Vitelleschi, that his mission to restore Catholicism in Germany guaranteed him victory with divine aid and forbade concessions to the Protestants beyond what the Peace of Augsburg had granted them. Maximilian turned away from an analogous form of the myth. With this departure from a long-held position on the part of the two pillars of Catholicism in the empire, the Thirty Years War lost its character as a holy war on the Catholic side. This did not mean that for either of them religion became any less important. Rather, it indicated that for both of them the good of religion was better served by some concessions for the sake of peace. Religion continued to be a significant factor in the war. But the formal declaration of war by Catholic France on Spain eleven days before the conclusion of the Peace of Prague gave the war a new character and further reduced its religious nature. Death removed Contzen from the scene on June 24, 1635. Lamormaini's political influence in Vienna declined rapidly after the peace, but he remained personally close to Ferdinand until the emperor's death in early 1637. Pope Urban's reaction to the peace turned out to be much more favorable than Vienna anticipated; religion came off much better than he expected. A brief of July 22 lauded Ferdinand's efforts for the church, but it avoided any statement that might be interpreted as juridical assent to the concessions to the Protestants.[87]

85 Ibid., 219–20.
86 Ibid., 220–5.
87 Ibid., 225–6.

Critics in Spain leveled two charges against Vitelleschi in the months following the Peace of Prague. One was the familiar claim that he favored France over Spain. To substantiate it, they contended that the French ambassador regularly visited Jesuit headquarters in Rome for conversations with the superior general. A Spanish agent must have been keeping an eye on who went in and out of the Jesuit curia. Second, they charged that he had attempted to undermine the negotiations leading up to the Peace of Prague. This he did, allegedly, at the behest of Pope Urban and Cardinal Barberini, through letters to Ferdinand II and to Lamormaini.

To refute these charges, Vitelleschi addressed a letter directly to Olivares. He flatly denied any partiality toward France in light of the immense debt of gratitude that the Society owed to the king of Spain for his innumerable benefits. As was customary at the arrival of a new ambassador in Rome, the superior general had paid the French ambassador a visit, and the ambassador had, as was normal, reciprocated with a visit to the superior general. Periodically, it was true, the ambassador did come to hear Sunday Mass at the Jesuit curia, and he sometimes remained to chat openly with the French assistant and others from France. But there was nothing of politics to it.

Vitelleschi also denied that he had, either directly or indirectly, sought to influence Ferdinand, Lamormaini, or any other person against accepting the Peace of Prague or that he acted at the curia's urging. He did admit that in several letters to Lamormaini he indicated that it would be a consolation to him if the peace were concluded on conditions that upheld the reputation and served the benefit of the House of Austria.[88] In the context, especially of his belief in Ferdinand's mission, this could only mean a peace without compromise on the Edict. Vitelleschi and his Spanish critics were of starkly different views of what promoted the reputation and well-being of the House of Austria.

Vitelleschi's letter to Lamormaini of January 13, 1635, which in the normal course would have arrived in Vienna toward the end of the conference of theologians, had read in fact:

It has now come to the point that the public good is to be determined in matters of the highest moment, for the sake of which this long, memorable and nearly lethal war has been fought, and on which the foundation and preservation of the whole commonwealth and the Catholic church depend. I doubt that there is anyone who thinks that peace ought to be concluded with those who seek peace under false pretext or do not know how to preserve a stable peace. I

[88] Vitelleschi to Olivares, Aug. 31, 1635, ARSJ, Hisp. 70, ff. 322′–3′; Vitelleschi to Lamormaini, June 21, 1635, ARSJ, Aust. 4II, f. 1073.

doubt that the most pious emperor will concede anything easily that would in any way blemish with posterity his most praiseworthy zeal for preserving and propagating religion. This will not happen, if he observes the holy practice that he has observed up to now, that he consider religion before all his kingdoms and all human matters.[89]

Lamormain could scarcely have read this letter without seeing in it an exhortation to stand firm on the Edict. Similar sentiments that pervaded three other letters into early April urged Lamormaini to persevere in the face of odds. The confessor should speak out freely when the future of the church and the salvation of millions of souls were at stake.[90] French intervention also remained a possibility for Vitelleschi. Still, he did acknowledge at one point in January the argument for peace from necessity and disavow the capacity to pass a judgment on its merit. This he had to leave to others competent in the matter.[91] A change in his thinking was starting to take place.

But that he ran into opposition ought not surprise the confessor. This he would encounter no matter what position he took; as Vitelleschi explained in his letter of March 17, he himself had recently experienced it, referring to the charges already emanating from Spain. Though he had "no part" in deciding the issue, suspicions were falling on him as if he had fostered war rather than peace. He did desire peace, but one that he saw as causing no harm to religion, piety, and justice, built not on "political" but on "divine and eternal" laws.

[89] Vitelleschi to Lamormaini, Jan. 13, 1635, ARSJ, Aust. 4II, ff. 1020–1.
[90] Vitelleschi to Lamormaini, Mar. 3 and 17 and Apr. 7, 1635, ibid., ff. 1046–7, 1053–4, 1063.
[91] Vitelleschi to Lamormaini, Jan. 27, 1635, ibid., f. 1025.

CHAPTER 6

France and Spain until the Demise of Richelieu and Olivares, 1635–1642/43

ON May 19, 1635, France declared war on Spain in dramatic fashion. Richelieu dispatched a herald to proclaim the challenge to conflict in the marketplace of Brussels. So the Most Christian King and the Most Catholic King initiated a combat that endured beyond the Peace of Westphalia until the Peace of the Pyrenees of 1659. Ever since the Treaty of Vervins in 1598 between Henry IV and Philip II, a series of lesser conflicts had broken out between the rival monarchies, including the struggles over the Valtelline and then from 1628 to 1631 over Mantua and Montferrat. They served as a prelude to the protracted war that now erupted. On December 30, 1635, after some hesitation and under pressure from Madrid, Emperor Ferdinand II joined his Habsburg cousin and agreed to undertake military operations against the French. But he always refused to allow the publication of a formal declaration of war against France under his name, despite the urging of his son, the king of Hungary. This would have belied the desire for peace that he confirmed by naming his delegate to the peace conference that the pope hoped to convene at Cologne.[1] One cannot help but speculate that Lamormaini had a role in this attitude. Yet despite the efforts of the peacemakers, the three Catholic crowns had now taken to arms. This development greatly diminished the religious character of the Thirty Years War.

The Spaniards enjoyed military successes at first. The Army of Flanders under the cardinal infante invaded France in 1636; its scouts reached Corbie about sixty miles north of Paris, striking fear into the

[1] Hildegard Ernst, *Madrid und Wien 1632–1637: Politik und Finanzen in den Beziehungen zwischen Philipp IV and Ferdinand II* (Münster, 1991), 197–9, 296–313; Klaus Malettke, "France's Imperial Policy during the Thirty Years' War and the Peace of Westphalia," in *1648: War and Peace in Europe*, eds. Klaus Bussmann and Heinz Schilling, 1: *Politics, Religion, Law and Society* (Münster, 1999), 182–3. The king of Hungary, subsequently Ferdinand III, did publish a declaration of war in September 1636.

Parisians, but the drive petered out as did an imperial attack to the south in Burgundy. Two years later the Spaniards raised the French siege of their border fortress of Fuenterrabbía at the western end of the Pyrenees, a victory that was celebrated wildly in Madrid. But the imperial loss of the crucial fortress of Breisach on the Rhine in December 1638 to the army of Bernard of Weimar, who had entered French service after 1635, marked a turning point to the west. Then the following October a Spanish fleet was destroyed by the Dutch at the Battle of the Downs off the northwest tip of France. Catalonia responded to Olivares's desperate efforts to raise funds through new taxes with a rebellion in May 1640 that would, with French support, continue until 1652. Portugal followed the Catalan example with its own rebellion in December 1640 that led to independence once again, but only in 1668. Spain seemed to be coming apart.

The outbreak of war between Spain and France discouraged Pope Urban, but the papacy continued its efforts to reconcile the three crowns and to work for a European peace. Shortly after the outbreak of the Franco-Spanish War, Urban secured agreement in principle from France, Spain, and the emperor that they would send delegates to the peace congress that he envisioned for Cologne. In October 1636 Cardinal Martio Ginetti arrived in the Rhenish city as papal legate to the conference, but he was to return to Rome exactly four years later with the conference never having gotten underway. Difficulties over passports – that is, over who was to attend the conference and on what terms – kept the parties apart, especially the French effort to secure the full participation of the German states and so to undermine the position of the emperor in the empire.[2]

Meanwhile, other negotiations were carried on, often in secret, between France and Spain during the 1630s.[3] Both states were strained to the limit. Peasant revolts rocked France in 1636 and 1639. "The peace of Christendom" was a phrase frequently on the lips of both Richelieu and Olivares,[4] but each ultimately hoped for victory on his own terms. The Spaniards were almost desperate for peace in 1640, but a new obstacle always appeared to frustrate it. By the end of that year the direction of events was becoming clear. The French won their first great victory over a Spanish army at Rocroi in northeast France on May 19, 1643. By that time both Richelieu and Olivares had departed from the scene. Richelieu died on December 4, 1642, to be followed the following May by

[2] Konrad Repgen, *Die römische Kurie und der westfälische Friede*, 1, 1 (Tübingen, 1962): 394–6.
[3] Auguste Leman, *Richelieu et Olivares: Leur négociations secrètes de 1636 à 1642 pour la rétablissement de la paix* (Lille, 1938).
[4] Ibid., 51, 89.

Louis XIII. Olivares's long term as Philip IV's favorite and chief minister came to an end with his fall from power on January 17, 1643.

Polemical exchanges had accompanied the rivalry between France and Spain since the early decades of the century, and they often overlapped with the intense contest for public opinion within France between the *bons français* and the *dévots,* who were sympathetic to the Spanish Habsburgs as champions of Catholicism. Opponents challenged Richelieu's policies once their direction became clear, especially his alliance with Protestants, and the cardinal mobilized a phalanx of writers in his defense. Spanish polemics intensified after war broke out in 1635; the Spanish literary figures Saavedra Fajardo and Francisco de Quevedo both published responses to the French declaration of war.[5] Two Jesuits took up the pen for Spain before and after 1635 and so created problems for Vitelleschi and especially for the Society in France. At the same time, Contzen's pen was embroiling him with the Spaniards, another concern for the superior general, as we have seen.

The two Spanish Jesuit authors involved were Pedro Hurtado de Mendoza, whom we have met before involved in government service, and Claudio Clemente, both teachers at the Colegio Imperial in Madrid. Vitelleschi's reaction to their imprudent publications makes clear once again his awareness of the fragile status of the Society in France. In 1630 Hurtado de Mendoza published the treatise *On the Three Theological Virtues.*[6] Normally, one would think that a volume like this had little potential to offend princes or governments. But at a point in his discussion of charity, Hurtado de Mendoza criticized French support of the Dutch heretics. The French Jesuits protested. Vitelleschi immediately complained to the Spanish provincials; their French brothers would suffer for it, he stressed, and revealing his fears added that they might even be subject to banishment.[7] To the provincial of Paris he lamented the imprudence of Hurtado de Mendoza and the negligence of superiors. He assured him that he was taking measures to see that all copies were located, bought up, and consigned to the flames.[8] When word arrived that a French Jesuit planned a response, Vitelleschi vigorously discouraged it, because this would only keep the embers warm, but he allowed

5 See Michel Dévèze, "1635, Le heurt idéologique franco-espagnol," *Actes du 94e Congrès National des Sociétés Savantes* (Pau, 1969), 1: 23–38, and José María Jover, *1635: Historia de una polémica y semblanza de una generación* (Madrid,1949).

6 *De tribus virtutibus theologicis.*

7 Vitelleschi to Francisco de Prado, Valladolid (provincial of Castile), July 11, 1631 (duplicated on August 15), ARSJ, Hisp. 70, f. 251'; Vitelleschi to the Spanish provincials, July 18, 1631, ibid., f. 252.

8 Vitelleschi to Barthélemy Jacquinot (provincial), July 12, 1631, ARSJ, Francia 5I, f. 347'.

later that if copies reached Paris, the French would have no choice but to respond.[9] His letter to Richelieu told of the difficulty monitoring all Jesuit publications, assured him of the measures to locate and destroy the books, and implored him not to hold the matter against the whole Society.[10]

The matter of Hurtado de Mendoza resulted in a letter of Vitelleschi to all the provinces of the Society in December 1631 instructing superiors to tighten their watch over publications of Jesuits and not to approve "those [books] which reproach princes whoever they are, or their subjects [presumably nations] whoever they are, nor mention with disdain either princes or subjects, whether they be living or dead." He went on to prohibit Jesuits from writing on current topics that were likely to raise storms of protests.[11] Less than a year later an even stronger communication followed to all the provinces, prohibiting Jesuits under pain of excommunication from writing or publishing anything, even obiter remarks, "that could cause offense, including prefaces, dedicatory letters, even the most brief," as well as the verses sometimes addressed to the reader at the start of a book, without first sending the material to Rome and waiting for Rome's response.[12]

This second letter was prompted by still another book, this time published anonymously, with the imaginative title *Gesta Impiorum per Francos* (*Deeds of the Impious [committed] by the French*), a clear allusion to the medieval *Gesta Dei per Francos* (*The Deeds of God Worked through the French*). In 1632 the superior general notified Miguel Pacheco, the provincial of Toledo, that it had been brought to his attention that in a public service a member of the Colegio Imperial community in Madrid had criticized the king of France and was about to publish in Antwerp a book in the same tone with the above title. Pacheco was to determine who the author was, prevent publication of the book, and assign the author a severe penance, perhaps even dismissal from the Society.[13] By August Vitelleschi had seen the book himself and knew the author's identity.[14] The culprit turned out to be Claudio Clemente, born in the Free County of Burgundy about 1594, who had taught rhetoric at Dôle and Lyons before moving to the Colegio Imperial in

9 Vitelleschi to Jacquinot (provincial), July 26, 1631, ibid., f. 340; Vitelleschi to Louis de la Salle, Oct. 9, 1631, ibid., f. 354.
10 Vitelleschi to Richelieu, July 19, 1631, ARSJ, Gallia 46I, f. 131.
11 Vitelleschi to All Provinces, Dec. 14, 1631, ibid., 38, f. 26′.
12 Vitelleschi to All Provinces, Sept. 18, 1632, ibid., f. 31.
13 Vitelleschi to Miquel Pacheco (provincial), May 4, 1632, ARSJ, Tol. 9, f. 234′; Hugues Didier, "Un Franc-Comtois au service de Espagne: Claude Clement S.J. (1594?–1642)," AHSJ 44 (1975): 260, dates this letter June 10.
14 Vitelleschi to Pacheco (provincial), Aug. 24, 1632, ibid., f. 259′, cited in Didier, 261.

Madrid. As a native Burgundian he had inherited an aversion to the French and an intense Habsburg allegiance.[15] Clemente must not realize, Vitelleschi assumed, the dangers in which his book placed the Jesuits in France. Rumor reported that the author had a similar book in progress, Vitelleschi added, and he instructed Pacheco to make certain that it was not published. But some in Madrid, who obviously were familiar with French *dévot* writing, defended Clemente, contending that there was nothing in his book that was not found in French authors. Vitelleschi would not allow this justification, and he wrote *"in secreto"* of his fear that the Jesuits be expelled from France. To the charge that "I am French," which some Spaniards advanced, he replied that he was only carrying out his duty as general.[16]

Vitelleschi apparently succeeded in keeping the *Deeds of the Impious [committed] by the French* out of French hands. The confessor in Paris was instructed to excuse the Society with Richelieu and the king, but the name of the book was never mentioned.[17] But the volume does seem to have found its way to Vienna, where it was read at recreation, to the great delight of the Jesuit community, and it even stimulated a short piece mocking Louis and the cardinal that was posted on the community bulletin board. Informed of this, Vitelleschi reprimanded Lamormaini and at the same time lamented the delicate situation in which he found himself and the Society, in the midst of princes with such different interests and goals. How was it possible to avoid offending one or the other and bringing harm to the Society?![18] The book cannot be located today in European libraries; the efforts to suppress it may have been successful.[19]

But there was more to come from Clemente. The volume he was rumored to be writing in 1632 appeared at Madrid in 1636, a year after the outbreak of hostilities between Spain and France. Its abbreviated title read *Machiavelli Strangled by the Christian Wisdom of Spain and Austria*. The next year a second Latin and a Spanish edition were published at Alcalà.[20] The book was in the Antimachiavellian tradition, and Clemente aligned himself explicitly with Aquinas, Ribadeneira, Scribani, Contzen, and others. But essentially it constituted a panegyric to the Christian policy of the Habsburgs. Since the days of Charles V they stood out as the genuine champions of the church and the embodiment of a Christian

15 On Clemente, see especially Didier, 254–64.
16 Vitelleschi to Pacheco (provincial), Dec. 6, 1632, cited in Didier, 262–3.
17 Vitelleschi to Maillan, Oct. 20, 1632, ARSJ, Francia 5I, f. 385'.
18 Vitelleschi to Lamormaini, Dec. 15, 1635, ARSJ, Aust. 5I, 70.
19 Didier, 264.
20 *El machiavelismo degollado par la Christiana sabiduría de España y de Austria.*

reason of state. Philip IV, to whom the book was dedicated, and Olivares came in for high praise. Neither France nor Richelieu was mentioned explicitly. But it was evident that the references to alliances with heretics and with Turks pointed to them. They put into practice the maxims of the atheistic Machiavelli. Yet no one in Rome seems to have taken note of this book.

Vitelleschi clashed with Olivares frequently from 1629 until 1635 over the part played by Lamormaini in Vienna and to a lesser extent Contzen in Munich. The role at court of Father Hernando de Salazar, the confessor of Olivares, also continued to be a source of conflict between Vitelleschi and Madrid. As we have seen, Salazar seems to have withdrawn to a degree in 1627 after remonstrances from Vitelleschi about his involvement in secular matters. Yet that year and the next he and several other Jesuits were asked by the superior general to intercede with the king for the princess of Piombino, a small Italian client principality of Spain, so that she could regain the territory and keep her other lands.[21] Olivares then began to seek a bishopric for Salazar, despite the prohibition against the acceptance of ecclesiastical office by Jesuits found in their Constitutions. The king named him bishop of Malaga in 1630. Vitelleschi had four Spanish provincial superiors travel to Madrid to protest the appointment, and the pope refused to grant the necessary dispensation.[22] Philip IV and Olivares then aimed to appoint him archbishop of Charcas in Bolivia, and the nuncio in Spain agreed to this on several conditions. One was that he not be consecrated until he arrived in the Indies. Thus, he could not collect the revenues if he remained in Spain.

Vitelleschi now mobilized Ferdinand II, through Lamormaini, to protest the appointment in Rome and with Philip IV.[23] So Olivares had another source of complaint against Vitelleschi and Lamormaini.[24] Eventually, through negotiations behind Vitelleschi's back, Olivares obtained for Salazar the title "archbishop-elect of Charcas," which enabled him to receive some revenues. But Urban VIII assured Vitelleschi in person that he would permit consecration only in the Indies.[25] Vitelleschi, then, acquiesced in the title of archbishop-elect and allowed Salazar,

[21] Vitelleschi to Fathers Florencia, Salazar, Albornoz, and Pedro Gonzalez de Mendoza, July 7, 1627, ARSJ, Hisp. 70, f. 203; Vitelleschi to Salazar and Albornoz, May 31, 1628, ibid., f. 210.

[22] J.H. Elliott, *The Count-Duke of Olivares* (New Haven, CT, 1986), 427; Antonio Astraín, *Historia de la Companía de Jesús en la Asistencia de España* 5 (Madrid, 1916): 220–1.

[23] Vitelleschi to Ferdinand II, Nov. 2, 1630, ARSJ, Germ. 113I, ff. 428, 433.

[24] Vitelleschi to Olivares, Oct. 20, 1631, ARSJ, Tol. 9, f. 195.

[25] Vitelleschi to Pacheco (provincial), Mar. 23, 1634, Madrid, Real Academia de la Historia, Legajo 9/7259.

exempt from obedience and community life, to continue to live in his quarters in the community of the Colegio Imperial in Madrid, until fellow Jesuits complained about his style of life, so that he moved into his own house in 1639. The provincial was instructed to secure the approval of the king and Olivares before requesting Salazar to move.[26]

During this time Salazar remained active for the government, especially in matters of finance. He and the royal confessor, the Dominican Antonio Sotomayor, both sat on a committee to evaluate proposals for raising the funds of which the government was always in need. In 1631 he was made a member of the Council of the Inquisition, and shortly thereafter, in order to give full attention to these duties, he resigned his position as confessor of Olivares. The Venetian ambassador reported that Salazar was the closest political confidante of Olivares.[27]

Finance remained Salazar's principal area, and he was credited with the idea for the papel sellado, a highly unpopular stamp tax. His role in the development of taxes made him "one of the most unpopular figures in Spain,"[28] and he was satirized at the Madrid Carnival of 1637.[29] According to the nuncio, Salazar was the soul of the anti-Roman faction in Madrid.[30] He allegedly shared the count-duke's conviction that the church failed to contribute adequately to the war effort, and in 1631–32 he served prominently on a committee that drew up a report on the "Abuses of Rome and the Nunciature" and that worked out a position on church–state relations highly favorable to the crown. He generally defended the right of the government to impose taxes, including the stamp tax, on the church without the consent of the pope.[31] Vitelleschi feared the impact of Salazar and one or two other Jesuits on the reputation of the Society in Spain, but he was at a loss about what action to take.[32] After the fall of Olivares in 1643 Salazar also dropped from notice, but Francisco Aguado, his successor as Olivares's confessor and a delegate to the general congregation following the death of Vitelleschi, brought his case up during the assembly's discussion of the role of Jesuits in politics.[33]

[26] Vitelleschi to Hernando de Valdés (provincial), Dec. 11, 1638, ibid.; Astrain 5: 227–30.
[27] Report of Alvise Mocenigo III, read on Mar. 16, 1632, *Relazioni di ambasciatori veneti al Senato*, ed. Luigi Firpo, vol. 9: *Spagna, 1602–1631* (Turin, 1978): 641–2.
[28] Elliott, 556.
[29] Astrain 5: 228–30.
[30] Elliott, 428.
[31] Quintín Aldea Vaquero, "Iglesia y estado en la época barroca," *Historia de España Ramón Menéndez Pidal* 25 (Madrid, 1982): 37–40, 54, 210. See also id., "Iglesia y estado en la España del siglo XVII (Ideario político ecclesiatico)," *Miscelanea Comillas* 36 (1961): 177–94, 378.
[32] Vitelleschi to Alonso del Cano (visitor to the Toledo Province), ARSJ, Tol. 8II, 261'.
[33] Astrain 5: 230; see below, p. 230.

Aguado replaced Salazar as confessor of the count-duke of Olivares during the summer of 1631. Vitelleschi thanked the count-duke for honoring the Society by choosing his confessor from its ranks once again.[34] But Aguado's appointment represented a significant change in the character of the confessor. Whereas Salazar actively participated in government as a councillor and lived in a style lavish for a religious, Aguado remained apart from government, lived modestly, and was well known as a spiritual writer and director. From his first years as a priest he held responsible posts within the Society's own governing structure. His choice may have been dictated not so much by Salazar's increasing duties as by Olivares's desire for a confessor more at home in the ways of the spirit.

Born in 1572 of impoverished nobility in Torrejon, not far from Madrid, Aguado entered the Jesuits in 1589.[35] Shortly after his ordination to the priesthood he was appointed assistant to the master of novices. In 1603 the novitiate moved from Alcalà to Madrid. There Ana Feliz de Guzman, marquesa of Camarata, the aunt of Olivares, established the house on a firm financial footing.[36] This initiated a contact between the Guzman family and Aguado that would grow. She continued to take an interest in the novices, "her children" as she called them, during his term as master of novices from 1606 to 1616. Father Florencia preached at Aguado's final profession in the Society in 1605 and again at the dedication of a new chapel in the novitiate, a ceremony that drew many members of the court to the house.

In 1616 Aguado began a term as secretary to the provincial of the Toledo Province. During this period he journeyed to Rome as provincial delegate to the congregation of procurators in 1619, where he had the chance to meet Vitelleschi personally. After his return he became rector of the major seminary in Alcalà and following that rector of the Colegio Imperial in Madrid, where he vigorously supported its expansion into the Estudios Reales.[37] In 1627 he became provincial himself, and following the completion of his three-year term he became superior of the professed house in Madrid, where most of the Jesuits associated with the court resided. While there he was named a court preacher and then confessor of the count-duke.

[34] Vitelleschi to Olivares, Sept. 24, 1631, ARSJ, Tol. 9, 191.

[35] Biographical data here are drawn from two overlapping sources: Alonso de Andrade, *Vida del Venerable P. Francisco Aguado, S.J.* (Madrid, 1658), and id., *Varones ilustres de la Compania de Jésus* 6 (Madrid, 1667).

[36] According to Andrade, *Aguado*, 103, she was Olivares's mother, but Elliott, p. 11, notes that his mother died when he was seven and that this was his aunt.

[37] Andrade, *Varones ilustres*, 672.

Two of Aguado's books in particular help us to understand the mentality that he brought to his task as confessor. The first was *The Wise Christian*, published in Madrid in 1633 and reissued in 1635 and 1638. The book was dedicated to Olivares for two reasons, according to Aguado. The first was the strength that the count-duke drew from the reading of spiritual books, a practice to which he turned after the death in 1626 of his daughter and only child and that grew out of a new seriousness about religion.[38] The second reason was connected with the purpose of the book. Aguado noted in his general preface that he had already authored the book *On the Perfect Religious* and had been contemplating a second volume on the same topic. Then, stimulated by his appointment as confessor, we might surmise, he realized the need for a book showing that the full Christian life could be lived in the world and pointing the way to how this could be done. So he, too, contributed to this genre popular during the Catholic Reform, of which Francis de Sales's *Introduction to the Devout Life* (1607) was the most prominent example. Though aware of the charge of flattery to which he opened himself, Aguado put Olivares forward as exemplifying the Christian wisdom necessary for the man of faith struggling to respond to God's call in the world. The book contained a short section on the office of *privado*, or favorite and chief minister, which Olivares occupied with Philip IV. It offered standard pieces of advice – for example, that the favorite must avoid flaunting his position and influence; such conduct only stirred anger and resentment and stimulated the formation of factions aimed at his downfall.[39]

Aguado's *Various Exhortations, especially Doctrinal*, completed in 1639 and published in Madrid in 1641, contained a selection of "conversations" (*pláticas*) that he conducted for the court; the book was dedicated to Doña Ines de Zúñiga, wife of the count-duke, who organized the conversations. They were intended for "busy persons."[40] One conversation was titled "In Time of War," and it offered a short theology of war.[41] "Why so much din of war," asked Aguado, "why such accumulation of arms and gathering of munitions, why such racket of battles? What does God Our Lord intend for his kingdom, so Catholic as it is where his name is esteemed, his religion fostered, his faith reigns, when it is everywhere engulfed by wars and harried by enemies?." In other words, why in God's providence was Spain so often at war? Aguado looked first to the Hebrew scriptures for an answer. One reason was that

38 Elliott, 278–9.
39 *El cristiano sabio*, 149–50.
40 *Exhortaciones varias, dotrinales*, 183.
41 J.H. Elliott first suggested to me that this passage contained a theology of war. I am grateful to him for this tip.

wars kept people from growing soft and yielding to evil habits, which were more harmful and pernicious than "the Dutch and the French." For this he cited Augustine's *City of God* (1, 30). The passage even sounded like Machiavelli, especially after Aguado reminded his readers of Scipio's words to the effect that Rome needed Carthage to bring out its best in terms of readiness and courage. But clearly God's principal purpose with war was to teach his people, whether the Hebrews or the Spaniards, dependence on God and confidence in him and to instruct them in patience. Both David and Judas Maccabaeus learned to trust in God through the experience of conflict. "The more we trust in God, the more we are able to assure the success of our arms, and only lack of confidence is able to hand this invincible crown over to its enemies." God fights alongside his people.

This presupposed, according to Aguado, that the wars were defensive, that Spain neither provoked nor initiated them, as was certainly the case he thought. It also required that the people observed God's commandments and lived lives of virtue. Obedience to God compelled the Lord, as it were, to stand by his people. Constant prayer was also required, seeking God's help on the battlefield. As with the Israelites, sin could bring defeat. War, then, called forth prayer, faith, and reform of life.[42]

Noteworthy here and so different from Contzen or Lamormaini was the total absence of confessional or religious war. There was not a word about fighting heretics or championing the cause of the church in war. The enemies of Spain in the eyes of Aguado were the Dutch and especially the French. His views, not surprisingly, reflected those of the count-duke. For Olivares the Thirty Years War was not a religious war, or certainly not principally so. At one point in 1625 Spain briefly gave support to the French Huguenots.[43] More significantly, neither Olivares nor Aguado hesitated to ally Spain with Lutheran Saxony when this was necessary to unite Germany to face the challenge from France.[44] For them there was no need to subordinate all to a Habsburg mission to restore Catholicism in Germany and to the maintenance of the Edict of Restitution. Rather, this policy obstructed the goals of Spain. Hence, the count-duke's opposition to Lamormaini and his attempts to have him removed from office.

Writing continued to occupy Aguado as confessor. In addition to *The Wise Christian* and the *Various Exhortations*, he published at least

[42] Aguado, *Exhortationes varias, dotrinales*, 424–34. The publication date is 1641, but the censor's approval is dated July 17, 1639, so the manuscript was completed by then.
[43] Elliott, 227.
[44] Ibid., 232.

one other devotional book while serving as confessor, *The Most Holy Sacrament of the Faith, the Treasure of the Christian Name* (Madrid, 1640).[45] Besides the "conversations" he conducted at court, he introduced the regular reservation of the Blessed Sacrament in the royal chapel and the monthly observance there of the Forty Hours Devotion.[46] Administrative duties within the Society still had a claim on him. He held three offices all for the second time: first superior of the main Jesuit residence in Madrid, then rector of the Colegio Imperial, and finally provincial from 1640 to 1643. This last he accepted only with the understanding requested by the count-duke that he restrict his visitation of the houses so as to be available for consultation when he was needed.[47]

While serving as confessor of Olivares, Aguado kept out of political affairs and court matters, as his biographer claimed, avoiding attachment to parties and not serving on committees as Salazar had. He simply gave his opinion when asked for it on issues of conscience. The king did consult him on appointments to bishoprics. Aguado even refused to intercede for various persons when asked to do so by Vitelleschi and others.[48] To be sure, it was to Aguado that Vitelleschi turned when Lamormaini and Contzen caused problems for the Society in Spain in 1631–32 and again in 1635. He seems to have been successful in smoothing the waters; certainly, none of the measures threatened against the Society were taken, and the Jesuits seem to have suffered in no other way. In 1632–33, when Urban VIII sent extraordinary legates to the three courts and Vitelleschi urged Lamormaini to encourage the emperor to work for harmony between Madrid and Rome, the superior general asked Aguado to advance this intention with Olivares.[49] But there is no record of any effective action by the confessor. Four years later Vitelleschi asked Aguado to intercede at court on behalf of the Upper Rhine Province of the Society. Some lands in the Lower Palatinate had been awarded to it, but the Spanish commissioners refused to hand them over.[50] A follow-up by Vitelleschi over a year later indicated that nothing had happened.[51]

Recommendations continued to come regularly from Vitelleschi to Aguado, usually for Italian noblemen. One instance of 1638 illustrates the dilemma sometimes faced by Vitelleschi with regard to these

45 *Sumo sacramento de la fe, tesoro del nombre cristiano.*
46 Andrade, *Aguado*, 283–4.
47 Ibid., 281.
48 Ibid., 268, 270–1, 275.
49 Vitelleschi to Aguado, Nov. 2, 1632, and Jan. 16, 1633, ARSJ, Tol. 9, ff. 280–80′.
50 Vitelleschi to Aguado, Aug. 8, 1637, ARSJ, Hisp. 70, f. 363′–64.
51 Vitelleschi to Aguado, Aug. 31, 1638, ARSJ, Tol. 8II, 353.

requests. First, there was a straightforward letter of recommendation to Aguado on behalf of Juan Cesar de Colonna, prince of Carbanno. Four days later there followed another letter, in which the superior general confessed that he did not know the nature of the prince's business in Madrid. He supposed that it might well deal with affairs that were prohibited to Jesuits. If this were the case, his recommendation was to count for nothing. Aguado would know how to deal with the situation, because there had been similar instances in the past.[52] Two days later a letter went out to another Jesuit in Madrid. Vitelleschi stated that he wanted to be able to show a letter of recommendation for the prince to the ambassador of the grand duke of Tuscany in Rome and so oblige him, but he did not want to violate Jesuit decrees.[53]

Another Jesuit, the theologian Juan Martinez Ripalda, took over as the count-duke's confessor after his dismissal as first minister. Ripalda may have had a hand in the composition of the "*Nicandro*," a spirited and notorious defense of his policy that Olivares issued in response to charges brought against him after his removal from office and enforced retirement to the small town of Toro. His confessor remained with him until he died in 1645.[54]

In 1631 Richelieu chose to succeed Suffren as Louis's confessor Charles Maillan, then provincial of Lyons and a former acquaintance of the cardinal during his year of exile from the court in Avignon back in 1618.[55] Both he and his successor proved docile to the cardinal. Vitelleschi again thanked Richelieu profusely for drawing the confessor from the Society,[56] though it is unlikely that Louis would have permitted otherwise. Several months later he gave Maillan a cryptic instruction about political matters. "With regard to matters of state," he wrote, "the Society does not prohibit [your dealing with] those affairs that pertain to the direction of the king's conscience and which are included in the office of confessor."[57] This was both broad and vague; it did not attempt to delineate clearly what were matters of state, and it gave no examples. Nor was there any mention of the Instruction for Confessors of Princes. The confessor was not expected to handle all the business of the Society at court, but it would be helpful if he were to assist with the

[52] Vitelleschi to Aguado, Oct. 16 and 22, 1638, ARSJ, Hisp. 70. 385', 386'–7.
[53] Vitelleschi to Juan de Montalvo, Oct. 24, 1638, ibid., 387'.
[54] Elliott, 657.
[55] Camille de Rochemonteix, *Nicolas Caussin, confesseur de Louis XIII et le cardinal de Richelieu: Documents inédits* (Paris, 1911), 25, n. 2.
[56] Vitelleschi to Richelieu, May 31, 1631, ARSJ, Gallia 46I, f. 129'.
[57] Vitelleschi to Maillan, May 30 and Oct. 9, 1631, ARSJ, Francia 5I, ff. 345, 355.

more important affairs. He ought not be perceived as importunate by the king's ministers. The following year Vitelleschi permitted Maillan to keep for his use the carriage and horses that Richelieu made as a gift to him. This was unusual for a confessor – Vitelleschi frowned on it for Salazar in Spain – and he may have permitted it because he did not want to offend the cardinal, whose beneficence he once again lauded.[58]

The years 1632 and 1633 saw the occupation by the Swedes of much of southwest Germany where many Jesuit houses were to be found. Vitelleschi regularly requested Maillan to secure Louis's intervention with the Swedes on behalf of the German Jesuits who were subject to mistreatment and to exactions that were impossible to pay. Maillan's intercession for the Jesuits in Dillingen and Augsburg succeeded in alleviating their situation.[59] Vitelleschi's letter of gratitude to Richelieu proclaimed how the cardinal assisted the Jesuits not only in France but now in Germany too.[60] Louis showed a "truly paternal providence and care" toward the German Jesuits, Vitelleschi remarked after requesting Maillan's assistance on behalf of the Jesuits in Mainz.[61] Later the king sent a legate to the Swedes to urge that ecclesiastics be allowed to return to the occupied towns, as was called for by the Franco-Swedish Treaty of Bärwalde.[62]

The Treaty of Bärwalde had been concluded in early 1631, and it quickly became public knowledge. During the 1630s prior to its declaration of war on Spain, France edged closer to intervention in the conflict. The nuncios encouraged Maillan to raise with Louis the issue of conscience about his support of the heretics in Germany, especially the Swedes.[63] But Vitelleschi appears not to have done so, probably fearful of antagonizing Richelieu. The most the superior general did was to send Maillan a perfunctory recommendation of Francesco Adriano Ceva, the extraordinary nuncio sent to Paris by Urban VIII as part of his new peace initiative in 1632.[64] Later in 1634 some Frenchmen in Rome complained that the journey to Rome by Reinhard Ziegler, the confessor of Mainz, had a goal inimical to French interests. In reality it had two purposes: to ascertain whether Urban VIII would approve the surrender of ecclesiastical lands if the German Catholics could not obtain better

[58] Vitelleschi to Maillan, June 3, 1632, ibid., f. 372.
[59] Vitelleschi to Maillan, April 21 and July 15, 1633, ibid., ff. 403, 407.
[60] Vitelleschi to Richelieu, July 15, 1633, ARSJ, Francia 46I, f. 138.
[61] Vitelleschi to Maillan, Sept. 8 and Dec. 30, 1633, ARSJ, Francia 5I, ff. 412', 418.
[62] Vitelleschi to Maillan, Mar. 10, 1634, ibid., f. 421.
[63] Henri Fouqueray, *Histoire de la Compagnie de Jésu en France* 5 (Paris, 1925): 6–7.
[64] Vitelleschi to Maillan, Mar. 31, 1632, ARSJ, Francia 3I, f. 367.

conditions from the Protestants, and to urge the pope to pursue more vigorously the effort to reconcile the two Catholic powers, France and Spain.[65] Vitelleschi assured Maillan that he had seen Ziegler's instruction and that there was nothing in it harmful to French interests. If there were, he would never have permitted it.[66]

Maillan died on October 4, 1635, after a long illness. Nicholas Caussin, soon to be Louis's confessor and, as we shall see, perhaps not an unbiased observer, passed judgment on Maillan and implicitly on Vitelleschi himself. Toward the end of his life, Caussin wrote, Maillan became aware that his moderate counsel produced "horrendous" effects. In other words, his failure to oppose the cardinal with the king was responsible for the great expansion of the war, the victories of Gustavus Adolphus in Germany, and the suffering of the French peasantry, who were taxed to pay for the war. Maillan became so disillusioned, according to Caussin, that he no longer wanted to continue living. He began to bring the war up with the king, to reassure his own conscience. But he became preoccupied with his imminent death, and he was outmaneuvered by the cardinal. His fellow Jesuits knew of the fear of judgment that gripped him on his deathbed, even though he was a man of great innocence of life.[67]

Upon learning of the death of Maillan, Vitelleschi wrote the provincial Armand that he found consolation in the thought that the cardinal, so well-disposed toward the Society as he was, would with divine guidance find another Jesuit suitable for the task of confessor.[68] Shortly afterward he congratulated Jacques Gordon on his selection.[69] Gordon, a Scotsman, had entered the Society way back in 1573 in Rome and had now reached the age of eighty-two. He had taught moral theology in Rome, Bordeaux, and then at the College of Clermont. Perhaps his publication of a comprehensive moral theology in Paris in 1634 drew Richelieu's attention to him; the volume treated perfunctorily the controversial issues of toleration of heretics and the just war, and it severely condemned any form of tyrannicide.[70]

In March 1636 Vitelleschi directed a letter to Gordon at the insistence of Pope Urban himself and invoked the confessor's obedience.

65 Instruction of the Elector of Mainz for P. Ziegler, Mar. 24, 1634, BA 2, 8: no. 354: 671–5.
66 Vitelleschi to Maillan, July 3, 1634, ARSJ, Francia 5I, f. 432'.
67 Caussin to Vitelleschi, Quimper, Mar. 7, 1638, B.N., 25054, f. 66.
68 Vitelleschi to Ignace Armand (provincial), Nov. 8, 1635, ARSJ, Francia 5II, f. 467.
69 Vitelleschi to Gordon, Dec. 5, 1635, ibid., f. 472.
70 *Theologia moralis universa octo libris comprehensa* (Paris, 1634); see Book 5, Question 4, Chapter 4 (pp. 837–8) on tyrannicide; Book 6, Question 12, Chapter 2 (pp. 1323–4) on heresy; and Question 19, Chapters 8–10 (pp. 1390–5) on the just war.

The incredible slaughter and spilling of Christian blood that the war generated greatly saddened the pope, Vitelleschi wrote. The general implored the confessor in the pope's name that he request the king out of compassion for the people to end the delays with which France was obstructing the opening of the peace congress that Urban had called for Cologne. Otherwise, the devastation and loss of life would only continue. The pope, it would seem, wanted to circumvent Richelieu. But Vitelleschi's last lines frustrated this. Gordon was not to say a word of this or take any action without first consulting the cardinal and showing him the letter. Richelieu in his "most perspicacious wisdom" would know what ought to be done.[71]

A stroke forced Gordon to give up the office of confessor on March 11, 1637. Old and enfeebled as he was, he did not act on this letter, as far as we know, nor on another letter that, according to Caussin, he received from an anonymous religious. The letter warned him that if he did not alert the king to the true state of his conscience because of the wars he was waging, he would draw down upon himself the wrath of God. Stricken by his stroke shortly afterward and smitten by pangs of conscience, he passed on to Caussin, his successor, the paper he had drawn up for the king. Caussin assured him that he would carry out the duties of his office, even should it cost him his life.[72] He was to challenge Richelieu.

Shortly before Maillan's death and just as Louis XIII declared war on Spain in May 1635, the representatives of the clergy gathered in Paris for their decennial assembly, which continued until the following May. The Jesuits had been at the center of the previous Assembly of the Clergy in 1625/26, with the uproar over their publications. The war effort now gobbled up funds, and the clerical assembly for the first time conceded monies on a large scale for an official purpose other than a war on heretics.[73] But this grant was only made after substantial discussion. One paper arguing in its favor was submitted by the Jesuit theologian Michel Rabardeau, who asserted the government's right by virtue of natural law to draw funds from the clergy to finance a war even if the war was not a religious one.[74] Imposts on clerical landed revenues also fell on religious orders, including the Jesuits. This prompted Vitelleschi to request a particular favor from Richelieu. In a letter flattering the

[71] Vitelleschi to Gordon, Mar. 2, 1636, ARSJ, Francia 5II, f. 488.
[72] Caussin to Vitelleschi, Quimper, Mar. 7, 1638, B.N., 25054, ff. 66–7; Rochementeix, 76–7.
[73] Pierre Blet, *Le clergé de France et la monarchie: Études sur les assemblés générales du clergé de 1615 à 1666* (Rome, 1959) 1: 476–7.
[74] Pierre Blet, "Jésuites gallicans au XVIIe siècle?" AHSJ, 29 (Rome, 1960), 66–7.

cardinal for his munificence toward and assistance of the Society, he begged for another benefit, which Father Séguiran, now superior of the professed house in Paris, would suggest to him.[75] This turned out to be exemption for the Jesuits from the payments on rents imposed on religious orders. Louis through a private decree had granted this request even before Vitelleschi's letter could have arrived. Again an effusive and grateful letter went out from Rome to the cardinal.[76]

Vitelleschi also sent off a letter of gratitude to François Sublet de Noyers, the newly appointed secretary of war and a creature of Richelieu, whose counsel, Vitelleschi wrote, undoubtedly helped Louis to decide to concede this exemption.[77] Periodically, the superior general corresponded with ministers at the French court who were sympathetic to the Society. Sublet de Noyers was one, Cardinal de La Rochefaucauld another. Born in 1588, Sublet de Noyers had been brought along by Richelieu as a royal commissioner and intendant before the fact. After his appointment as secretary of war in 1636 he undertook major military reforms, and the cardinal allowed him to administer the army's affairs. The initiative for the royal press that was created in 1640 seems to have come from him, and one of its first publications was an edition of the *Spiritual Exercises* of Ignatius Loyola.[78] Sublet de Noyers was known to be close to the Jesuits, and after the death of his wife, he was thought to have taken vows in the Society.[79] Vitelleschi's first letter to him dated from 1627 after the fathers in Paris had written the superior general about his goodwill.[80] Later, Vitelleschi expressed the Society's reliance on him, especially in legal matters, when the Jesuits faced so many enemies.[81] Another figure with ties to the Society and an occasional correspondent of Vitelleschi was Pierre Seguier, who was named keeper of the seals in 1633 and then, in 1635, chancellor, the highest judicial official in the kingdom, a position he held until 1672. Sublet de Noyers was dismissed from office shortly after the death of Richelieu, his patron, but Seguier remained as a support for the Society at court. In 1635 Vitelleschi suggested that a formal record of all his benefits to the

75 Vitelleschi to Richelieu, Dec. 2, 1636, ARSJ, Gallia 46I, ff. 168′–9.
76 Vitelleschi to Richelieu, Jan. 1, 1637, ibid., ff. 170′–1.
77 Vitelleschi to Sublet de Noyers, Jan. 1, 1637, ibid., f. 170′.
78 *Exercitia spiritualia S.P. Ignatii Loyolae* (Paris: Typographia regia, 1644). Geoffrey Treasure, *Mazarin: The Crisis of Absolutism in France* (New York, 1995), 54, 329.
79 François Hannibal d'Estrées, *Mémoires*, ed. P. Bonnefon (Paris, 1910), 187; on Sublet de Noyers, see Orest Ranum, *Richelieu and the Councillors of Louis XIII: A Study of the Secretaries of State and Superintendents of Finance in the Ministry of Richelieu, 1635–1642* (Oxford, 1963), 100–19.
80 Vitelleschi to Sublet de Noyers, Dec. 30, 1627, ARSJ, Gallia 46I, f. 112′.
81 Vitelleschi to Sublet de Noyers, June 15, 1630, ibid., f. 123′.

Society be maintained, lest the Jesuits forget his many gifts and favors for them.[82]

Jacques Gordon's period as confessor corresponded roughly to the most difficult years of the Thirty Years War for the French. The advance of the Spanish army sent the Parisians into panic and escalated the profound dissatisfaction with Richelieu, who was blamed for the war. The king's determination to remain in the capital during the crisis did much to strengthen the backbone of the population. Unrest in the countryside raised its head in 1635, increased threateningly in 1636 in Poitou and the Limosin, and again in 1637, especially in Périgord. A force of 12,000 took up arms against the government, many of them former soldiers, with nobles joining them. An attempt to kidnap Richelieu at Amiens in October 1636, during the siege of Corbie, failed when at the last minute neither Gaston d' Orléans nor the count of Soissons gave the prearranged signal.[83]

This was the situation into which Nicholas Caussin walked when he took over as confessor in late March 1637. Caussin notified Vitelleschi of his appointment on April 3, and he indicated that the provincial had shown him the general's instructions regarding court confessors, which presumably comprised Acquaviva's Instruction as well as the guidelines worked out in 1626.[84] Vitelleschi congratulated him duly on his appointment but made no comment about the instructions.[85] Some in Paris doubted his suitability for the office. Once they learned of Richelieu's prospective choice, the provincial Étienne Binet and the superior of the professed house in Paris, Séguiran, sought an interview with the cardinal. There they suggested that Caussin's prudence and experience in human affairs did not measure up to the task of confessor. But the cardinal stuck by his choice, perhaps because he figured that Caussin's inexperience would make it easier to control him.[86]

Nicholas Caussin saw the light of day in Troyes in 1583. His father was a medical doctor, and it was said that Nicholas acquired his sympathy for the poor from accompanying his father to treat them in their hovels. From the start he stood out as a student, especially in the three languages of Latin, Greek, and Hebrew. He studied for the priesthood and then, shortly before ordination, at age twenty-four, entered the Jesuits. From

82 Vitelleschi to Seguier, June 8, 1635, Paris, Bibliothèque de l'Institut de France, Collection Godefroy 15, f. 139. See Pierre Blet, "Le chancelier Seguier protecteur des Jésuites, et l'Assemblée du Clergé de 1645," AHSJ 26 (Rome, 1957), 177–98.

83 Jean-Marie Constant, *Les conjurateurs: Le premier libéralisme politique sous Richelieu* (Paris, 1987), 122–5.

84 Caussin to Vitelleschi, Apr. 3, 1637, ARSJ, Francia 47, f. 106.

85 Vitelleschi to Caussin, May 10, 1637, ibid., Francia 5II, f. 532'.

86 Rochemonteix, 28–9, 34–5.

1609 to 1614 he taught rhetoric at the college of Rouen, and then after ordination in 1615 he taught it first at La Flèche and then at Clermont. Quickly, his reputation as a preacher spread, and in 1620 he moved to the professed house in Paris, where he lived with the Jesuits associated with the court: Coton, Séguiran, Suffren, and others. Here, in addition to making preaching tours throughout the kingdom, he devoted himself to writing: books of devotion, controversial works, dramas, and essays on rhetorical theory.[87]

His book *The Holy Court* made him famous. It first appeared in Paris in 1624 and underwent many editions, growing fatter as they expanded, and translations into the major European languages, including Czech and Polish.[88] Henry Lamormaini, William's brother, translated two parts of the work into Latin (Vienna, 1636). Yet Caussin had little actual experience of the court, so that the book often seemed distant from reality.[89] Caussin was a disciple of Francis de Sales, and he published a book on spiritual direction according to the Bishop of Geneva.[90] Like Francis, Aguado, and so many authors of the period, his purpose was to show that the full Christian life could be lived in the world, in this case at court. As he put it in his dedications of the *Holy Court* to the king and to the nobility of the realm, he desired to show them the way to virtue so that they would sanctify the whole kingdom. The first volume dealt with the court in general, and the second turned to four main types of personage at court: the prelate; the nobleman-soldier; or cavalier; the man of politics, or ruler and councillor; and the lady. The book proceeded largely through the use of narrative examples drawn from every historical period from the ancient to the contemporary. Its frequently extravagant style suited the times, and it was to have an influence on French classical drama.[91]

Caussin lauded the military virtues in his treatment of the cavalier. The Lord of Hosts himself was a warrior, he claimed, but he then spiritualized the term by emphasizing God's campaign against the heart of man. Sacred scripture glorified David and Judas Maccabaeus, he noted, and contradicting Machiavelli in the manner of the Antimachiavellians, he argued that Christians made the best soldiers. But he carefully avoided the assertion that virtue produced worldly success. This was patently

[87] Ibid., 3–21; for Caussin's bibliography, see Carlos Sommervogel, *Bibliothèque de la Compagnie de Jésus* 2 (Brussels/Paris, 1891; rpt. 1960): 902–26.
[88] See Sommervogel, ibid., 906–17.
[89] See the evaluation of Volker Kapp, "La théologie des réalités terrestres dans *La Cour Sainte* de N. Caussin," in *Les Jésuites parmi les hommes* (Clermont-Ferrand, 1987), 141–52.
[90] *Traité de la conduite spirituelle selon l'esprit du B. François de Sales* (Douai, 1643).
[91] Kapp, ibid.

not always the case, he recognized. There was considerable treatment of how one ought to fight in war, the *jus in bello*, but there was virtually nothing on the just war. At one point he drew a parallel between Charlemagne's conquest of heathens and Louis XIII's defeat of the heretics. Still, neither holy nor religious war was a major topic of the book.[92]

Caussin first heard the confession of Louis XIII on March 25, 1637. The previous day Cardinal Richelieu had summoned him to his residence at Reuil, where the two met for the first time. The cardinal alerted Caussin to the king's relationship with a seventeen-year-old member of the queen's entourage, Marie Louise de La Fayette. Richelieu himself had initially encouraged the bond between Marie Louise and Louis, whose marriage with Anne lacked strong mutual affection and who was prone to emotional attachments to individual male and female courtiers. These always worried the cardinal, who feared that they would spill over into politics and endanger his position, as they sometimes did. But he also attempted to use them to stay informed of the king's moods and attitudes, especially toward himself. The previous favorite, Marie de Hautefort, had refused to bend to the cardinal's purpose, and so he engineered her fall from favor.[93] But neither would Marie Louise allow herself to be used by the cardinal to keep tabs on the king's thinking, so that Richelieu became fearful that others would exploit her to undermine his position with the king. The relationship was, according to Richelieu, innocent but dangerous, and he encouraged the confessor to try gradually to persuade the king to break it off. Caussin was put on his guard by this attempt to interfere in the confessor's office.[94]

Coming from an illustrious family of the Auvergne, Marie Louise had appeared at court as a fifteen-year-old, where she served as a maid of honor to Queen Anne.[95] Attractive, intelligent, tactful, devout, she won the hearts of those at court, especially the heart of the king. At court events Louis engaged in extended conversations with her, and soon people noticed. He took her with him on hunting expeditions. Toward the end of 1636, "the year of Corbie," Louis, "finding in her security and virtue as much as beauty," increasingly opened his heart to her, lamenting his dependence on the cardinal and other frustrations,

[92] *La cour sainte* 2 (Paris, 1628): 10–11; and 2 (Paris, 1664): 118; and "Les cavaliers," 386–444.

[93] Victor Cousin, *Madame de Hautefort: Nouvelles études sur les femmes illustrés et la société de xviie siècle,* 4th ed. (Paris, 1874), 20.

[94] Caussin to Soeur Louise Angelique de La Fayette, 1638, BN 25054, f. 10′ (Marie Louise took as her name in the convent "Louise Angelique."); Henri Griffet, *Histoire du règne de Louis XIII* (Paris, 1758) : 8.

[95] Adolphe Sorin, *Louise Angelique de La Fayette: La Cour–La Cloître* (Nantes, 1892), 1–17, 29.

according to one memorist.[96] She in turn confided to him her intention to enter the religious life in the near future, which the king opposed. Louis granted her favors, such as ready access to him for her uncle, François de La Fayette, bishop of Limoges and chaplain to the queen. The two became good friends.[97]

Frequently, either just before or just after the actual confession, Louis brought up matters of conscience to his confessor. He did not do this with Caussin at his first confession, either because he saw nothing improper with his relationship with Marie Louise, Caussin assumed, or because he suspected that Caussin was "the cardinal's man" and did not yet trust him. Caussin did not think it proper for him to question Louis about it.[98] But when Caussin did not report anything to Richelieu after his second meeting with Louis, the cardinal sent Sublet de Noyers late one night to impress upon him the need to end the king's relationship with Marie Louise and to inform Caussin of La Fayette's intent to enter the convent. Moreover, the girl was a "schemer" and could be a source of political trouble. Caussin replied noncommittally that he would do what he thought best.[99]

The next day the king told Caussin outside confession of his affection for Marie Louise and of his sadness at her desire to enter the convent. She then asked to talk to Caussin privately about a matter of conscience. After first securing the king's permission, he agreed, and she told him of her desire to pursue a religious vocation. Caussin was convinced that it was not a sudden impulse but a genuine call that she had felt already as a young girl. Yet by this time, having learned that her views of royal policy corresponded to his, he had started to form a plan to ask her to support him in gradually persuading Louis to move toward peace. So he was not eager to see her enter the cloister immediately, as Richelieu wanted. The next day, when Caussin saw the king at his rising ritual, Louis assured him that wrenching as it was for him, he would not stand in the way of Marie Louise's vocation. Marie Louise now determined to wait no longer, prompted it seems according to Madame de Motteville, who heard it years later from Marie Louise herself, by an uncharacteristic advance by Louis.[100] Hers was the only dry eye when she took her leave

[96] Françoise Bertaut de Motteville, *Mémoires sur Anne d'Autriche et sa cour*, new ed., ed. M.F. Riaux (Paris, 1886), 1: 59.
[97] Griffet 3: 6–7.
[98] Caussin to Soeur Louise Angelique, 1638, ibid., ff. 10′–11.
[99] Ibid., f. 11; Griffet 3: 8–9. Richelieu probably learned of Marie Louise's intention to enter the convent from the Dominican Père Carrè, who was spiritual director of many women at court as well as an informer for the cardinal; Sorin, 45.
[100] Motteville 1: 63–4.

of Louis, Queen Anne, and the court. She entered the convent of the Visitation on the rue Saint-Antoine in Paris on May 19, 1637.[101]

Melancholy overtook the king. After a while Caussin reminded him that though his feelings showed his deep humanity, the time had come for reason to assume control. But he then proposed that the king might visit Marie Louise in the convent, a suggestion that he made with the clear design of using her for the benefit of the "public good."[102] Carried on through the monastic grill and with companions nearby on both sides but out of earshot, their conversation lasted three hours. Caussin, who had now become the spiritual director of Marie Louise, had not known of the visit beforehand; and when he heard of it, he immediately sent a note to Sublet de Noyers disclaiming any knowledge of it. The cardinal, clearly upset that Louis had not told him of the planned visit either, summoned Caussin the next day to discuss the matter. He claimed that Caussin was not as forthcoming as other confessors had been. Shortly afterward, the cardinal called Caussin in again, this time, according to Caussin, offering him and his family anything they wanted in exchange for a "close understanding" with the cardinal, of which the king would not be told. Caussin replied that he would be as open as his conscience and reason allowed him, and he advised the cardinal not to disrupt a relationship in which the king seemed to find such contentment.[103] Louis's periodic visits to the convent continued, his conversations with Marie Louise lasting three to four hours and even more and, of course, not going unnoticed by ambassadors, who remarked about them in their reports.[104]

Only now that Marie Louise was settled in the convent did she and Caussin develop a full mutual trust as well as intent. Until then she suspected that he might not keep her confidences from the cardinal, and he was not assured of her prudence and maturity. Both saw themselves as wishing the best for a king uncertain of himself and dominated by Richelieu. Caussin later remembered Marie Louise once saying, "I assure you, Father, I would consider myself blessed to lay my head on the scaffold to secure the salvation of the king and the liberty of France." Caussin revealed his hope to her that they would work together to convince the king to end the war that so burdened the people and caused such terrible devastation. They also aimed at a reconciliation of Louis with his mother as well as a closer relationship between Louis and Anne.[105]

101 Caussin to Soeur Louise Angelique, 1638, ibid., ff. 13–16, 21′; Griffet 3: 8–12.
102 Caussin to Soeur Louise Angelique, 1638, ibid., f. 23.
103 Ibid., ff. 30′–4′; Caussin to Vitelleschi, Mar. 7, 1638, ibid., f. 46; Griffet 3: 16.
104 Rochementeix, 158–9.
105 Caussin to Soeur Louise Angelique, 1638, ibid., ff. 34′–6.

In fact, it was after his last visit to the convent on December 5, 1637, that Louis spent the night with Anne, when she probably conceived the future Louis XIV, their first child after twenty-two years of marriage.[106] Vitelleschi encouraged Caussin to work "prudently" for peace, though it is doubtful that the confessor told him of Marie Louise.[107]

The young La Fayette took the habit and the religious name "Louise Angelique" on July 22 in a ceremony at which Caussin preached and Queen Anne was present. Louis could not bear to come.[108] Afterward, the queen approached Caussin to tell him that he was in conscience bound to speak to the king about the suffering of the people as a result of a war being waged only because of the ambition of Richelieu. The cardinal prevented the king from hearing any other views, and he kept the royal family divided. Caussin remained in generalities in his answer. In the course of the summer, then, Louis learned of a secret correspondence that Anne had carried on for four years with members of her family, especially her brother, the cardinal infante and governor of the Spanish Netherlands. Richelieu had discovered and tracked it for some time. Anne had recourse to Caussin, and he was present at two long interviews Richelieu conducted with the queen over the matter.[109] The correspondence, common enough among ruling families, revealed nothing treasonous or the betrayal of any state secrets, though it did contain occasional anti-French sentiments. The inquiry into the correspondence ended in an agreement that Anne would henceforth refrain from secret communications and then in a warmer relationship between the two spouses that probably contributed to Anne's pregnancy.[110]

Louis's visits to the convent continued after Marie Louise took the habit. By this time suspicious of the extensive conversations Louis was carrying on with Marie Louise and with Caussin, Richelieu had taken to keeping a file on the confessor's activities. Twice, according to this account, Caussin assured the cardinal that the king spoke only favorably of him.[111] But both La Fayette and Caussin gradually spoke more forcefully to the king about the war, its devastation, and the French alliance with the Swedes and the consequent persecution of the church in Germany. After one such conversation with her the king left abruptly, but he later sent word through Caussin that he regretted this and would

106 Rochementeix, 173–4.
107 Vitelleschi to Caussin, Sept. 16, 1637, ARSJ, Francia 5II, f. 587.
108 Caussin to Soeur Louise Angelique, 1638, ibid., f. 24.
109 Griffet 3: 17–8, 48–50, 57.
110 A. Lloyd Moote, *Louis XIII, the Just* (Berkeley, 1989), 278–81.
111 "Journal de R.P.C. (Caussin), July 15, 1637–February 1638," Armand-Jean du Plessis, cardinal de Richelieu, *Lettres, instructions et papiers d'état*, ed. Denis-Louis-Martial Avenel, 5 (Paris, 1871): 805–16; Griffet 3: 103–5.

return again.[112] Vitelleschi encouraged Caussin to work to gain French participation in the projected papal peace congress in Cologne. "I beseech you," he wrote, "through your prudence, authority, and zeal, to employ all your strength in such a divine work."[113] Caussin must have believed that he enjoyed Vitelleschi's full support. In late November the king bestowed the bishopric of Mans on a candidate recommended by Caussin without consulting Richelieu, as he normally did. The cardinal, sensitive as he was to his role in the appointment to benefices, took further alarm at this, whereas Caussin seems to have interpreted it as confirmation of his increasing authority with the king.[114]

All this led up to a decisive interview with Louis before confession on December 8, 1637, the Feast of the Immaculate Conception. Caussin has left us an account of this in his letter to Vitelleschi of March 7, 1638, written from his exile.[115] Well prepared beforehand, he forcefully put before the king the case for a change in policy and consequently in government. Conscience required it. He began by impressing upon the king that royal rule was meant to imitate divine government, its goal was to lead subjects to their well-being through religion and justice. The king was to be their shepherd, not their hangman, obviously an allusion to Richelieu's harsh policies. Goodness and clemency provided the solid basis for government that won the support of the people. The king was to foster the church and to honor the Holy Father. Caussin then turned to love of neighbor and first of all to love of family. At this point he handed the king a long and moving letter that Marie de Medici had written in her own hand and then smuggled to the confessor.[116] The letter implored her son to treat her with the justice due a subject and with the love due a mother, and it requested that Louis restore her revenues and allow her to return to France. Marie promised not to seek involvement in government, and she indicted Richelieu for deliberately dividing the royal family so that he could maintain his own authority.

According to Caussin, the letter touched the king deeply; the issue of his mother remained a source of continued guilt feelings. Emboldened by the king's reaction, the confessor went on to encourage Louis to invigorate his relationship with Anne, thus continuing a theme raised by Marie Louise. Next, Caussin turned to the great issue of peace in

112 Griffet 3: 17.
113 Vitelleschi to Caussin, Oct. 26, 1637, ARSJ, Francia 47, f. 109.
114 Griffet 3: 105–6.
115 Caussin to Vitelleschi, Mar. 7, 1638, ibid., 49′–53′; this letter is the principal source for the account that follows.
116 Griffet 3: 109; this letter of Marie is not mentioned explicitly in Caussin's letter to Vitelleschi of March 7.

Christendom. He urged the king to pursue it with vigor and to take upon himself the task of government, thus implying dismissal of the cardinal. Nor ought the king make decisions on such major issues as war or peace without consulting with leaders of the realm, who presumably would convene in an Assembly of Notables or even in a meeting of the Estates General. So the confessor expressed a desire for a more limited government that was shared by some members of the aristocratic opposition to Richelieu.[117] Caussin accused the government of plotting an alliance with the Turks against the emperor, and he severely criticized Richelieu's alliances with the Dutch and the Swedes. The evidence seems to indicate clearly that there was at the time talk in Paris about an alliance with the Turks, which, however, Louis himself never permitted.[118] The king defended alliances with the Dutch and the Swedes, alliances that he asserted had been approved in writing by theologians, including Jesuits. But Caussin's point was not alliances in themselves with heretics, which were permissible, but the particular alliances Richelieu entered for France. Terms of the treaties did call for respect for the Catholic religion, but these were not observed; and, in fact, the church in parts of Germany was undergoing horrendous devastation. Finally, Caussin pleaded eloquently on behalf of the people – the year had seen severe peasant uprisings – subject to confiscatory taxes and in parts of the country to the quartering of troops.

Louis then made his actual confession to Caussin, who then said Mass for him in the chapel of the chateau San Germain. At the time of Communion, holding the host before the king, the confessor addressed him in a dramatic fashion, returning to high points of their conversation and urging Louis to be true to his duty as a monarch. "All this I have said so that I might unburden your and my conscience. You have an immortal soul which some day will come before the divine tribunal. Think of what you will respond to your and my judge, and tremble at the voice of the wisest king, who said that 'the powerful will suffer more intense torments.'" The king, according to Caussin, was "profoundly moved" by this prayer.[119]

Another account of this conversation overlapped to a degree with Caussin's, but it reported much greater resistance to the confessor on

[117] See Constant, esp. 117–23, 262–3.

[118] Rochementeix, 206–8; see below, n. 123. Shortly afterward, in 1639, Richelieu was attempting to persuade the Venetians to ally with the Turks and launch an offensive against the emperor; see Anja Victorine Hartmann, *Von Regensburg nach Hamburg: Die diplomatischen Beziehungen zwischen dem französischen König und dem Kaiser vom Regensburger Vertrag (13. Oktober 1630) bis zum Hamburger Präliminarfrieden (25. Dezember 1641)* (Münster, 1998), 421.

[119] Caussin to Vitelleschi, Mar. 7, 1638, ibid., 53′–4′.

the part of Louis and, in general, a defense of the cardinal's policy and role in government. According to Léon le Bouthillier, count of Chavigny, secretary of state, and close to Richelieu, it stemmed from the king himself the next day.[120] This account emphasized that Louis almost walked out resentful of Caussin's threat of damnation.[121] He was angered by Caussin's interference in matters of politics about which the confessor was ill-informed, and he disputed the confessor's statements about alliances with the Turks and with the Dutch and the Swedes. Louis ridiculed Caussin's alleged statement that he rely on the affection of his people, who would know how to defend him in time of need. The assertion showed how little Caussin understood of politics.

The morning after his session with Caussin the king seemed visibly shaken. Courtiers noticed, and they reported it to Richelieu. When Caussin saw Louis that day, according to the confessor's account, the king told him that their conversation had deeply affected him, but that he feared to bring the issues up to the cardinal. But if Caussin would do so, the king would support him in the cardinal's presence. The two agreed that Caussin would seek an appointment with Richelieu later that afternoon at the cardinal's residence at Reuil without letting the cardinal know that Louis ordered him to do so. Louis would then turn up at the cardinal's residence, fortuitously, as it were, as he often did. Caussin hesitated, explaining to the king that this would expose him to the cardinal's wrath, but he finally agreed.

That evening Caussin was admitted to an audience with Richelieu when he arrived at his residence. The two talked, with Richelieu taking the opportunity to instruct Caussin about the danger of women meddling in politics. When the king's carriage pulled up, Richelieu asked Caussin to step into a side room, because it would not be wise to let the king see them together. Caussin acquiesced, figuring that the king would ask for him. When he did, Richelieu informed him that Caussin had departed, which he did after waiting a long time to be called in

120 Richelieu, *Lettres* 5: 811–14. It seems to have been drawn up in response to Caussin's letter of Dec. 17 to Sublet de Noyers defending himself from his exile, ibid; this account is followed in *Mémoires de cardinal de Richelieu sur le regne de Louis XIII depuis 1610 jusqu à 1638*, in *Nouvelle collection des Mémoires rélatifs à L'histoire de France*, eds. Michaud and Poujoulat, 23 (Paris, 1857): 225.

121 Griffet 3: 106–9. According to this account in Griffet, at least once, Louis, worn by the torrent of words, indicated his desire to continue the conversation another time, but he quickly expressed regret for doing so. Also, in Griffet's account, Caussin dealt first with broader political issues and then with family matters.

A principal source known to Griffet and to Madame de Motteville, but since lost, is a "Mémoire" of Caussin. This was an account of his disgrace drawn up by de Lezeau, dean of the council of state and a friend of Caussin, after the confessor's return from exile in 1643, and then approved by Caussin himself; see Rochementeix, 246.

to the conference. Richelieu, then drawing on his formidable rhetorical powers, reviewed with the king all the issues that Caussin had raised, explaining that the reason for Caussin's departure was the realization that he could not respond to the cardinal's position. The next day, when Caussin went to see the king, he found access difficult; and when he was admitted, Louis asked where he had been the previous evening. Caussin began to explain, and Louis to grow interested, when Sublet de Noyers and Chavigny entered and distracted the conversation. Richelieu then dispatched a note to the king requesting his release from service.[122] The threat of resignation was a tactic to which the cardinal resorted at critical moments.

Forced to choose between the cardinal on the one hand and Caussin and an eighteen-year-old religious on the other, Louis, not surprisingly, chose the cardinal. This was the end for Caussin. There was really no other possibility. Louis did not consider himself competent to conduct the government himself, as did, for example, Maximilian of Bavaria, and he had no other person to whom to turn who could take the helm of government as France struggled through the first years of war with Spain. This is perhaps the best argument to show that Caussin was not part of a cabal. He had no one to put forward as a replacement for the cardinal; if he had been active in attempting to organize a new set of ministers, then he would have been guilty of direct involvement in politics. Later on, Caussin was accused of offering the position of first minister to the duke of Angoulême, at least by implication, but he vigorously denied it, adding that if he had proposed someone to take the cardinal's place at the head of the government, it certainly would not have been the said duke.[123] Caussin's intervention did not completely fail of an impact on the king. On December 11, the very day that Caussin would go into banishment, he instructed all the French bishops that they were to hold public prayers "for the peace of Christendom."[124] Furthermore, as Richelieu pointed out in his Political Testament, Louis never agreed to an alliance with the Turks against the emperor, even though his predecessors had taken this step and the cardinal himself considered it justified.[125] Caussin undoubtedly confirmed him in this resolution.

122 Caussin to Vitelleschi, Mar. 7, 1638, ibid., f. 55; Caussin to Richelieu, Quimper, n.d., ibid., 449–52. Griffet 3: 115–18 has a slightly different account; Richelieu, *Lettres* 5: 1067, n. 4.

123 Rochemonteix, 136–50, discusses this question at length and concludes that Caussin did not make the offer to the duke; see also Griffet 3: 111–15.

124 Leman, 51.

125 Richelieu, *Testament politique*, ed. Françoise Hildesheimer (Paris, 1995), 83.

Caussin and Marie Louise cannot simply be reckoned to the ranks of the *dévots*, though they shared some of their goals. The two showed no interest in religious wars or crusades, either domestic or foreign, and they advocated limits to what they considered the tyrannical government of Richelieu. Caussin saw himself as confronting the king as the conscience of both required. He considered himself a voice for the poor of the kingdom and the victims of the war, a prophet called by God to speak out on their behalf, and he likened Marie Louise to the biblical Esther, who saved her people in time of crisis.[126] We might question whether Caussin showed prudence in confronting Louis so forcefully and dramatically on so many issues at once. It was precisely prudence that Caussin's superiors found lacking in him. But his actions took great courage in the circumstances. Caussin did not believe that he had unduly overstepped his bounds into political matters, as he argued in a later letter to the cardinal.[127] Those issues he addressed involved conscience and so fell within the range of his office.

The day after the miscarried confrontation at Richelieu's palace, the cardinal sent Sublet de Noyers to the Jesuit provincial Binet with a letter ordering that Caussin be sent away to the college at Rennes immediately. His books and papers were to be seized, and he was to talk to no one before his departure. Binet informed Caussin of the decision, and the next morning, December 11, the confessor was in a carriage on his way to Rennes. Richelieu called in Binet and Séguiran to explain his action. Neither one of them questioned it, and they both recognized Caussin's guilt. Both had considered him unfit for the task of confessor in the first place. When Caussin defended himself in a letter to Sublet de Noyers, the cardinal became furious and spoke of exiling him to the wild forests of Canada, but he finally settled for the college of Quimper at the far northwest corner of Brittany.[128] Richelieu also placed in the official *Gazette de France* a notice humiliating Caussin. The confessor was dismissed

> because he did not govern his conduct as he ought, and his conduct was so bad that everyone and his whole order were so much the more astonished that he remained in his post as long as he did before he was removed from it. The displeasure that those of his own order have for his fault is proportioned to the great and sincere passion that they feel for the state and the service of the king.[129]

[126] Caussin to Soeur Louise Angelique, 1638, ibid., ff. 26–9.
[127] Caussin to Richelieu, Quimper, n.d., Auguste Carayon, *Documents inédits concernant la Compagnie de Jésus* 23 (Paris, 1886): 452–7.
[128] Rochementeix, 262–3, 299–308, 310–12.
[129] Dec. 26, 1637, cited in Rochementeix, 309–10.

So Richelieu made it clear that the Society vigorously disavowed Caussin, and in a note written at the same time to the two Jesuit superiors he reassured them that the affair of Caussin had diminished neither the king's nor his own affection for the Society.[130] Binet praised Richelieu's understanding and benevolence toward the Society in light of Caussin's serious offense, and his letter elicited from the cardinal another testimonial of Richelieu's continued benevolence toward the Jesuits.[131] Caussin himself bore up well but was understandably resentful of the way that his fellow Jesuits, and especially Séguiran and Binet, failed to defend him or even to hear his side.[132] From Quimper, he would take up the cause of his defense.

Richelieu sought to secure the transfer of Soeur Louise Angelique to a convent in Savoy, but the king would not permit it, even though he never did visit the convent again. After being named novice-mistress at the age of twenty-four, Soeur Louise Angelique became one of the founders of a new convent in Challiot in 1651 and was later named superior there, where she died in 1665. The cardinal did see to the removal from court of the bishop of Limoges, her uncle, as well as several others in the queen's entourage who were known to be unfavorable to him.[133]

Throughout the fall of 1637 Caussin had kept Vitelleschi informed of his efforts for peace. On December 8 Vitelleschi acknowledged these but reminded Caussin to confer with "those concerned," which certainly meant the cardinal.[134] Apparently, the first person to inform the Roman Jesuits of the affair was the prince of Condé, a friend of the Society whose son, the future Grand Condé, was then being tutored by Caussin as he began his military studies at the Academie Royale. He took the side of Richelieu and reported the king's approval of the procedure of Binet and Séguiran.[135] Binet, when he reported to Vitelleschi, emphasized the continued benevolence of Louis toward the Society, which his selection of another Jesuit as confessor demonstrated, "although he felt deeply the error of Father Caussin. We are greatly indebted to Richelieu that the Society has not endured a serious persecution; thus he is not only a patron of the Society but truly a father [to it]." Sublet de Noyers also merited the Society's gratitude; in fact, the Jesuits seemed never to have

130 Richelieu to the Jesuit superiors, end of December 1637, Richelieu, *Lettres* 5: 106–9.

131 Binet to Richelieu, Jan. 15, 1638, cited in Rochementeix, 342–3; Richelieu to Binet, Jan. 30, 1638, Richelieu, *Lettres* 6: 6–8.

132 See Caussin to Binet, Dec. 17, 1637, Sorin, 137.

133 Rochemonteix, 312–14.

134 Vitelleschi to Caussin, Dec. 8, 1637, ARSJ, Francia 5II, f. 565ʳ.

135 Henri II de Bourbon, prince of Condé to Étienne Charlet (French assistant), Jan. 1, 1638, cited in Rochementeix, 338–9; ibid., 337.

had so many friends in parlement.[136] Leading Jesuits in France manifested no sympathy for Caussin. In Spain, however, when the news from France arrived, they thought otherwise. As one Spanish Jesuit close to the court noted, Caussin, exiled in Brittany for his courage in speaking out, could not have acquired greater honor than if they had bestowed on him the largest church in France. The author of the *Gesta impiorum per Francos* would certainly take consolation in seeing that a French Jesuit thought as he did.[137]

Vitelleschi reacted to the situation in three letters, to Séguiran, to Binet, and then to Richelieu himself, all dated February 6. To the two superiors he expressed his profound sorrow over the incident. A passage in the letter to Séguiran was deleted, where he claimed that had he been consulted on the matter he would not have approved Caussin for the position. Vitelleschi backed Binet in his assigning Caussin to the college at Quimper, as well as his prohibiting Caussin's preaching or writing books and his depriving him of the right to vote or be elected to office in the Society. This punishment signaled how severely the Society disapproved of Caussin's conduct, he wrote. Shortly afterward, when he learned that Caussin instead of acknowledging his errors was defending himself, the superior general instructed Binet by special courier to tell the cardinal that if he wanted it, the Society would order Caussin to leave France.[138] Vitelleschi's letter to Richelieu revealed his continued deference to the cardinal:

After the grave error or rather guilt of Father Caussin, I dare to approach Your Eminence, for fathers are accustomed to undergo acute anguish for the sins of their sons and the head is compelled to suffer humiliation and sorrow for the shameful and sad misfortune of one part. I cannot say how profoundly I am afflicted by the notorious and dangerous imprudence of that father when I hear said things which it horrifies the mind to conceive and about the likely results of which, without the order of Your Eminence [on behalf of the Society] one could not even dream. I lay dejected for a long time until I learned through reliable reports that the much tried mercy of the Most Christian King was exercised toward us as a result of the constant goodness and wisdom of Your Eminence, and that all the rest would not be stained unknowingly by the guilt of one. May God reward the singular providence and excess of mercy of Your Eminence toward us and adorn your most prudent counsels with blessed success.

136 Binet to Vitelleschi, Jan. 12, 1638, ARSJ, Francia 47, f. 111.

137 Sebastian Gonzalez, Madrid, to Rafael Pereyra, Seville, Feb. 2, 1638, *Cartas de algunos PP. de la Compañía de Jesús sobre los sucesos de la monarquía entre los años 1634 y 1648*, Memorial Histórico Español 14 (Madrid, 1865): 312–13.

138 Vitelleschi to Séguiran, Feb. 6, 1638, ARSJ, Francia 5II, f. 572'; Vitelleschi to Binet, Feb. 6 and 21, 1638, ff. 573, 575.

Vitelleschi notified the cardinal of the punishment he had meted out to Caussin and added that he was ready to add any the cardinal would want. "Would that as a result of this lapse both he and all the others will emerge more cautious in the future and more observant [of the limits] of their office."[139] A letter to Sublet de Noyers asked him to intercede with Richelieu and the king in the Caussin affair.[140]

Subsequently, rumors circulated in France that Vitelleschi himself had encouraged Caussin in his effort to foster peace on terms unacceptable to Richelieu. Vitelleschi dealt with these charges in a letter to Richelieu dated June 23, 1638, which he drew up but then did not send. He pointed out that his family, the Vitelleschi, had always been partial to France and had even placed the fleur-de-lys on its coat of arms. But his office as superior general required him to respect equally all princes. Indeed, the French often considered him Spanish, and the Spanish accused him of being French. He had already sent all his correspondence with Caussin during his period as confessor up to Binet, to show to the cardinal if necessary. His talks with Cardinal Barberini here in Rome about peace involved "nothing other than the common desires of peace which I knew from common knowledge and the letters of Father Caussin that the Most Christian King and Your Eminence shared." Vitelleschi then cited his letter to Gordon of March 12, 1636, in which he had urged the confessor to influence the king toward peace but to do nothing without the knowledge and approval of the cardinal. Vitelleschi was determined to clear himself and the Society from any implication in Caussin's project.[141] But on the advice of the assistant, he committed the matter to the provincial Binet and remained in generalities until specific allegations might be made against him.[142]

From the far reaches of Quimper during his six-year exile Caussin made efforts to defend himself through letters to fellow Jesuits, to friends, and to authorities, including Louis XIII, Richelieu, and Urban VIII.[143] Most significant was a letter of pamphlet length to Vitelleschi of March 7, 1638, which found its way into print that year.[144] It was Caussin's apology, and it provided a detailed narrative of events

[139] Vitelleschi to Richelieu, Feb. 6, 1638, ARSJ, Gallia 46I, ff. 182–2′.
[140] Vitelleschi to Sublet de Noyers, Feb. 6, 1638, ibid., 182′.
[141] Vitelleschi to Richelieu, June 23, 1638, ibid., ff. 189′–90. (not sent).
[142] Vitelleschi to Binet, July 1, 1638, ARSJ, Francia 6I, f. 10.
[143] Most of these twenty-five letters are undated; today they are found in manuscript copies in a bound volume in the Mediathèque in Louviers; see Rochemonteix, xiv–xvii. I have usually used published or manuscript copies from the BN when they were available.
[144] N. Caussin, *Epistola ad P. Mutium Vitelleschi*, s.l., 1638, is listed in the catalogue of the Staatsbibliothek in Munich, but the library staff could not locate it when I was there.

on which I have drawn. The author complained about his abandonment and persecution by his fellow Jesuits, especially his silencing and punishment without any opportunity to defend himself. There was no answer from Vitelleschi, who, it will be recalled, in dealing with Lamormaini's critics insisted on the need to give the confessor an opportunity to present his side of the case. What most incensed Caussin was a letter circulated by the provincial Binet indicating his errors and justifying the measures taken against him. This letter has not been found, but Caussin summarized the charges against him at the end of his letter to Vitelleschi before responding to them in detail.[145]

The first charge was that he did not consult with his superiors about his dealings with Louis. The Instruction for Confessors of Princes called for this at least when complicated matters were at issue, and Vitelleschi admonished Lamormaini for neglecting this consultation. Caussin's first response to this was that he needed to respect the seal of confession. But as we have seen, many of Caussin's conversations with the king took place outside confession. Caussin's response to this was that the king was sensitive to discussion of his private affairs. In any event, the case was obvious to him; he was only following the Gospel in his call for peace and for reconciliation within the royal family. And if he were to consult, with whom would he do so? With Binet or with Séguiran, whom he knew to be a minister of the cardinal? This was the nub of the issue. Caussin did not talk with either of his superiors because he suspected, with good reason, that they would relate all that he told them to Richelieu. According to a royal official writing in 1638 to Philippe de Béthune, the former ambassador in Rome, this was the fundamental reason for his dismissal.[146]

The second charge was that Caussin did not follow the position of his predecessors regarding alliances with "infidels." As we have seen, he did not object to alliances with heretics in principle, but because in practice they were ruining the church in Germany. How many times had Vitelleschi implored protection from the devastation of the Swedes? Caussin did persistently accuse Richelieu of pursuing an antiimperial alliance with the Turks. Louis disputed this in the crucial interview of December 8, and he himself never permitted it, but there were advocates of it at court.

Caussin considered the third charge the most serious one, that he had attempted to secure the dismissal of the cardinal and the overthrow of the government. He readily admitted that he and Marie Louise

[145] Caussin to Vitelleschi, Mar. 7, 1638, BN, 25054, ff. 61–73.
[146] Saumery to Béthune, n.d. (1637/38), Paris, Bibliothèque de l'Institut de France, Collection Godefroy 15, f. 376.

attempted to reverse the government's policy on the war. This was a matter of conscience to him, and he must have realized that it implied the dismissal of the cardinal. He urged Louis to take the government in hand himself, and he asserted that the king should consult with leading figures of the realm on major issues of war and peace. The laws of the kingdom required this. On the other hand, Caussin convincingly denied that he was involved in any conspiracy to form a new government. As he wrote Binet shortly after his enforced departure from Paris, the search of his papers would find nothing of the sort.[147] In this respect a certain political naiveté shows. The king had no one to replace Richelieu.

The final charge against Caussin was rooted in the fundamental ambiguity of the Society's various directives for the confessors of princes. Caussin stood accused of incurring the censures of the Fifth and Seventh General Congregations that prohibited political activities. This issue had been a concern of Binet as superior of the professed house in Paris in the case of Arnoux nearly twenty years before. Caussin's response, of course, was that he was dealing with profound matters of conscience, which the Society's legislation certainly permitted.

Toward the end of the letter Caussin placed himself in the tradition of the prophets of the Hebrew scriptures and the Fathers of the Church: Athanasius, John Chrysostom, and Ambrose. They did not fear to speak out against injustice, and neither did he. His letter to Urban VIII, written later, between the deaths of Richelieu and Louis XIII, breathed the same spirit of resistance to the unjust power of Richelieu. Caussin remained convinced of the righteousness of his position as he petitioned the pope to compel the superior general to appoint a commission to provide for his rehabilitation.[148]

Shortly after the death of Louis XIII in 1643 Queen Anne summoned Caussin back to Paris from exile. There he took up residence once again in the professed house, apparently to the acclamation of at least some of his fellow Jesuits. Vitelleschi joined the rejoicing, but he gently admonished Caussin to moderation and humility while agreeing that should either king or queen choose him as confessor he might have all the privileges of the office.[149] Caussin must have suggested this possibility to him. The former confessor took up his pen right away and by the end of 1643 published an *Apology for the Religious of the Society of Jesus*.[150] Dedicated to Anne of Austria, this was a defense of the Society against their

147 Caussin to Binet, Dec. 17, 1637, Sorin, 137.
148 Caussin to Urban VIII, Feb. 10, 1643, BN, 25054, ff. 73–5'.
149 Vitelleschi to Jean Filleau (provincial), July 1, 1643, ARSJ, Francia 6I, f. 197; Vitelleschi to Caussin, Sept. 15, 1643, ibid., f. 202'.
150 I have used the *Apologie pour les religieux de la Compagnie de Jésus*, 2nd ed., (Lyons, 1644).

enemies of the nascent Jansenist movement, who according to Caussin felt free to raise their voices now that Louis, well known as a protector of the Jesuits, had left the scene. Despite the unfair treatment that he had received from his companions, Caussin defended the Society with vigor.

Caussin published two further books with eloquent pleas for peace before his death in 1651. By then the Peace of Westphalia had been concluded, but his *Angel of Peace* had been written, it seems, just before or after his return from exile and was held up by the censors until 1650, probably because of remarks about individual rulers.[151] France still remained at war with Spain and itself was caught up in the upheaval of the Fronde. The author addressed the *Angel of Peace* to all Christian princes. His moving expression of the profound desire for peace among the peoples of Europe accounted for the book's wide dissemination.[152] He was not a pacificist, Caussin declared, and he recognized the teaching of Augustine and Thomas Aquinas on the just war. But many wars, also according to Augustine, were in fact unjust, especially wars of Christians against Christians. Some princely ministers, he contended in a passage that certainly pointed to Richelieu, maintained their countries in war for their own benefit and profit from the conflict. For them everything that benefitted the prince's interests was licit. Populations were fed up with this attitude and the wars that it generated. They looked now to the young Louis for peace. Caussin's *The Kingdom of God or Elaborations on the Books of Kings*, which was published in 1650, expanded on elements of the *Holy Court*. It took peace once again as a main theme. Caussin criticized those "who seek by whatever means to expand the kingdom of the French and who determine that the one way to glory and riches leads through continual foreign wars." They justified this by the example of Rome and never experienced the horrors of the battlefield themselves. Rather, seated in their armchairs "they philosophize at leisure" on wars.[153]

Shortly after Caussin's departure into exile at Quimper, with the consent of the king, Richelieu appointed another Jesuit, the seventy-eight-year-old Jacques Sirmond, the new royal confessor. In his *Mémoires* the cardinal relates that he briefly thought to follow the counsel of others and go outside the Society for Louis's confessor. But because of Louis's and

151 *Angelus pacis: Ad principes christianos* (Paris, 1650); Vitelleschi to Caussin, Oct. 1, 1643, ARSJ, Francia 6I, f. 204.

152 For the many editions and translations, see Sommervogel, ibid.

153 *Regnum Dei seu dissertationes in libros regum in quibus quae ad institutionem principum illustriumque virorum, totamque politicen sacram attinent insigni modo tractantur* (Paris, 1650), 115–16.

his father's long-standing custom of a Jesuit as confessor and because of the harm that the choice of other than a Jesuit at this time would do to the reputation of the Society, he determined to stick with a Jesuit.[154] One might add that Louis himself probably would have insisted on a Jesuit. Moreover, the choice of a member of the Society brought it further into the cardinal's debt.[155] Sirmond, a highly respected savant and member of the Republic of Letters, had spent his whole life among books. His experience left him completely unprepared for the task, but his reputation and his docility suited him for it. Sirmond seems to have demurred at first and then assumed the position reluctantly out of obedience. Vitelleschi congratulated him and expressed the hope that his virtue and prudence would help to overcome the ill feeling that recent events had brought to the Society in France.[156]

Richelieu realized that he made a mistake when he did not provide a set of instructions for Caussin, whose character he had badly misjudged. He did not repeat the error. He now drew up new instructions for the confessor, which Louis approved. They encouraged him regularly to read over the Society's own rules for court confessors, thus implying that the cardinal's instructions merely reiterated them. To be sure, there was considerable overlap with Acquaviva's Instruction as well as with the cardinal's instructions for Suffren in 1626. But there were differences too. The instructions were prefaced with the remark that three types of conduct had undone Caussin. First, he maintained contact with too many people at court and too readily believed what they told him. Second, he was too inclined to become involved in worldly matters, and third, he spent much more time at court than was necessary.[157] Richelieu's guidelines urged Sirmond to occupy his time more with prayer and his books than at court. They advised him to stay out of business matters, and especially the sensitive disposition of benefices. One source of Richelieu's anger with Caussin had been the king's bestowal of a bishopric in November 1637 on the advice of the confessor without Richelieu's knowledge. According to the cardinal, a religious did not have the experience or contacts necessary to judge the qualifications of candidates and, in fact, in recent years, that is, during his ministry, the quality of episcopal nominations had improved, a statement with which modern scholarship agrees.[158] The earlier instructions

[154] Richelieu, *Mémoires*, ibid., 227.
[155] Fouqueray 5: 97.
[156] Vitelleschi to Sirmond, Feb. 6, 1638, ARSJ, Francia 5II, f. 573.
[157] Richelieu, *Mémoires*, ibid., 229.
[158] Joseph Bergin, "Richelieu and the Bishops," in Joseph Bergin and Lawrence Brockliss, eds., *Richelieu and His Age* (Oxford, 1992), 176–202.

for Suffren allowed the confessor to remonstrate with the king in order to prevent the nomination of an unsuitable candidate. That provision was not found in the instruction for Sirmond. Richelieu reflected Acquaviva's Instruction when he prescribed that the confessor come to court only when he heard the king's confession or when some significant cause required his presence.

What about issues of state? Acquaviva's Instruction ordered that the confessor stay out of "political matters," but these had been difficult to define, and Vitelleschi had frequently admitted the obvious overlap of political affairs and matters of conscience. Richelieu's instructions allowed the confessor, when he questioned the morality of government policy, to approach the cardinal himself or other ministers and to make known his questions and remarks to them. If they were not able to satisfy him, then both he and they were to approach the king together to request a joint consultation in the king's presence with leading experts of the realm. The confessor was then bound in conscience to support the king's decision. But he was not to take his objections directly to the king. This was a new and severe limitation on the confessor's activity. Acquaviva's Instruction stipulated as a condition of accepting the post of confessor that the confessor have access to the king to raise questions about government and policy. Yet the Instruction also encouraged the prince to consult other theologians in the event of a difficulty with the confessor's opinion, and the confessor was expected to abide by their opinion. In Louis's case, of course, the cardinal would select the experts or theologians to be consulted. Caussin, when he learned of this condition, addressed to Sirmond a highly critical and, in the circumstances, unfair letter.[159] His successor had agreed, Caussin charged, to separate Louis de Bourbon from Louis XIII, king of France, and to serve as confessor only to the former.

Vitelleschi accepted the new rules Richelieu laid down for the confessor, in the hope that their observance would render the Society more acceptable to the king and the cardinal after the troubles with Caussin.[160] He also suggested reserve with regard to the letters of recommendation that he, Vitelleschi, sent to Sirmond. These could not be completely avoided, but the confessor should exercise his own judgment and not undertake anything that might offend the cardinal or the king.[161] Much of the correspondence with Sirmond dealt with assistance to the Jesuits in areas of Germany held by the French or their allies. In June 1639, for

[159] Caussin to Sirmond, n.d., Louviers ms., 235–50; see Rochementeix, 330–1.
[160] Vitelleschi to Binet (provincial), Feb. 6, 1638, ARSJ, Francia 5II, f. 573.
[161] Vitelleschi to Sirmond, Feb. 20, 1638, ibid., f. 574'.

example, Vitelleschi thanked Sirmond for interceding on behalf of the Jesuit college in Freiburg im Breisgau, but six months later the college faced new problems.[162] Early the next year it was the fathers in Trier and Coblenz who were in need.[163] Louis even sought to shield the Jesuits in Swedish-occupied Bohemia.[164]

The nuncio Ranuccio Scotti noted in his final relation of 1641 after two years in Paris that the Jesuits kept their distance from him, "so as not to lose [their position] with the royal ministers." The one exception was François Puigeolot, a professor of physics at the College of Clermont who had known the nuncio when the Italian studied in Rome.[165] Sirmond also kept a low profile during his term as confessor, which lasted until after the death of the cardinal on December 4, 1642. By that time the tide had turned clearly in the war against the Habsburgs. But revolts, particularly in Normandy in 1639–40, showed the continued unhappiness of large segments of the population. One event of great signficance for the Jesuits was the opening of their new church of Saint Louis on the rue Saint Antoine in Paris in May 1641. The cardinal contributed generously to its construction, and in an event that according to one account transcended all description, he celebrated the first Mass in the new edifice with the king, the queen, and many dignitaries in attendance.[166] Vitelleschi mourned his death as one who esteemed and favored the Society, ordered that one hundred Masses be said for the repose of his soul, and instructed the French Jesuits to recognize in a public fashion his benevolence to the Society.[167]

Louis died on May 14, 1643, outliving the cardinal by less than six months. In the interval between Richelieu's death and his own, Louis performed a final act of filial piety toward his recently deceased mother, Marie de Medici. He saw to the solemn transfer of her remains from Cologne to a place beside her husband, Henry IV, in the church of Saint Denis outside Paris and the placement on April 12 of her heart with her spouse's in the chapel of the Jesuit college at La Flèche.[168] Finally, Marie returned to France.

162 Vitelleschi to Sirmond, June 15 and Dec. 15, 1639, ibid., Francia 6I, ff. 58, 74'.
163 Vitelleschi to Sirmond, Jan. 25, 1640, ibid., 78'.
164 Vitelleschi to Jacques Dinet (provincial), July 8 and Nov. 15, 1639, Francia 61', ff. 61', 73.
165 *Correspondance de nonce en France Ranuccio Scotti (1639–41)*, ed. Pierre Blet (Paris/Rome, 1965), 606.
166 See the description of the ceremony dated May 10, 1641, ARSJ, Francia 33II, ff. 283–4; Vitelleschi to Richelieu, June 1, 1641, ARSJ, Gallia 46I, ff. 225–5'.
167 Vitelleschi to Jean Filleau (provincial), Jan. 26, 1643, and Vitelleschi to Louis Le Mairat (superior of the professed house), Jan. 26, 1643, ARSJ, Francia 6I, ff. 183'–4.
168 Fouqueray 5: 444–51.

Meanwhile, Sirmond, by now enfeebled, was dismissed by Louis as confessor two months before the king's death and replaced by Jacques Dinet, who was at the time the provincial superior.[169] The reason for Sirmond's dismissal seems to have been his advocacy, along with that of Sublet de Noyers, of a more influential position for Anne of Austria on the planned council of regency than the dying king was willing to accord her.[170] This helps explain Anne's later refusal to consider Dinet for the position of confessor to the young Louis XIV. Dinet attended Louis on his deathbed and has left an account of the experience.[171] So the Jesuits remained involved in the affairs of Louis, Marie de Medici, and Anne of Austria until the king's death and were often divided over them. Throughout his life Louis remained a friend of the Society, an attitude he inherited from his father. Having learned on his sickbed that some troublemakers were insulting the Jesuits in the streets of Paris, he ordered that the magistrates intervene immediately and that "it be made known to everyone that he loved the said Jesuit fathers, took them under his protection, and would arrest and punish anyone who said or did any evil against them."[172] Like his father, he willed his heart to the Jesuits, in his case to their magnificent new church of St. Louis in Paris. What would be the status of the Society under the new regime that began to take shape as the king lay on his deathbed?

[169] Dinet to Vitelleschi, Mar. 27, 1643, ARSJ, Francia 47, f. 120.

[170] Pierre Chevallier, *Louis XIII, roi cornelien* (Paris, 1979), 636; see also Ruth Kleinman *Anne of Austria, Queen of France* (Columbus, OH, 1985), 129–43, and Griffet 3: 599.

[171] *L'idée d'une belle mort ou d'une mort Chrestienne de la fin heureuse de Louis XIII surnommé le Juste* (Paris, 1656).

[172] April 15, 1643, Eugène Griselle, *Profils de Jésuites de XVIIe siècle* (Lille/Paris, 1911), 28–33.

CHAPTER 7

The Empire after the Peace of Prague, 1635–1645

As a result of the Peace of Prague of 1635, the war lost its character as a holy war, and it became much less a religious conflict within the empire. The peace laid down principles, such as a normative year for the enjoyment of religious rights and privileges, that would carry over into the Peace of Westphalia, and it led to the reconciliation of most German Protestant states with the emperor. This was an achievement. The Electoral Convention of Regensburg of 1636/37 capped it then, as it were, with the election of young Ferdinand, king of the Romans, on December 22, 1636, and he succeeded his father as Emperor Ferdinand III after Ferdinand II's death on February 15, 1637.

But the overt entrance of France into the war, while greatly reducing its religious nature, expanded the conflict into a genuine European war, with the Franco-Hispanic contest central to it. Any settlement in the empire would have to take into account now the claims of the two allied foreign powers, France and Sweden. This the Peace of Prague did not do. Moreover, some German territorial rulers – in particular, Amalia Elisabeth of Hesse-Kassel and the regent for Karl Ludwig, the son of Frederick of the Palatinate (d. 1632) – rejected the terms of Prague. Others, like the duke of Württemberg and the dukes of Brunswick-Luneberg, accepted the terms, but only reluctantly, because of particular burdens that the peace imposed on them and of which they hoped to be relieved. The integration of the Bavarian and Saxon forces into the imperial army never worked out smoothly, and in effect the Bavarian and the imperial armies operated as separate forces whose activities were only coordinated with difficulty. The war took an increasingly high toll on the population. Members of an English delegation en route to the Electoral Convention of Regensburg in 1636 reported the utter desolation of the territory along the Main River as they traveled from Mainz to Frankfurt. Hunger had so overcome some people in Mainz that they could scarcely crawl to receive the alms offered them by the traveling party. Pillage had eighteen times in two years visited one village that the delegation passed through along the Danube. Berlin's population sank from 12,000 to 7,500 during 1618–38, and in some rural areas the decline reached 40 percent.[1]

Even before France entered the war openly, negotiations had begun to end the conflict, and they continued on and off in one way or another until 1648. Urban VIII took the initiative with his call in late 1634 for a peace conference, in Rome or at some other neutral site, to involve the three Catholic crowns and their allies, and he persevered in this effort even after the French declaration of war.[2] After their loss of Breisach in December 1638, the military tide began to turn against the imperial forces, as we have seen. This helped stimulate renewed efforts to unite the German states, first at the Electoral Convention of Nuremberg starting in February 1640 and then at the Diet of Regensburg, which opened in early September 1640, supplanting the Electoral Convention. So the diet convened for the first time since before the war in 1613, and it continued in session until October 1641. At one point during its course the Swedish General Baner threatened to take Regensburg.

The efforts to unite the German states raised the issue once again of concessions to the Protestants. Thus, there resulted another contest between militants and moderates within the Catholic camp and within the Society of Jesus itself, especially within the South German Province. The division among the Jesuits after 1635 manifested itself even in their theater productions: Pieces that dealt with the war were frequently avoided because of their potential for controversy.[3] Vitelleschi became concerned about the conflict between the moderates in Munich and the militants in Dillingen at the university and at the court of Prince-Bishop Heinrich von Knöringen of Augsburg, who had been the patron of Laymann's *Way to Peace* in 1629.[4] But the moderates now occupied a commanding position. The two new Jesuit confessors in Vienna and Munich, Johannes Gans and Johannes Vervaux, respectively, belonged to the moderate camp. Vitelleschi himself, who as we have seen despite his later denials seemed to support Lamormaini during the negotiations prior to the Peace of Prague, now came over to the moderate position, under the influence of the two new confessors and their princes, with a nudge from Cardinal Barberini.

1 Geoffrey Parker, ed., *The Thirty Years War*, 2nd ed. (London, 1997), 146–8.

2 Auguste Leman, "Urbain VIII et les origines du Congrès de Cologne," *Revue d'histoire ecclésiastique* 19 (1923): 370–1.

3 Jean-Marie Valentin, *Le théâtre des Jésuites dans les pays de langue allemande (1554–1680): Salut des âmes et ordres des cités* (Bern, 1978), 2: 757–61.

4 Vitelleschi to Wolfgang Gravenegg (provincial), July 20, 1641, ARSJ, Germ. Sup. 7, f. 1110.

Papal policy remained complex. Popular suffering and widespread devastation horrified the pope. Yet the papacy refused formally to recognize or even deal directly with heretics, in order to preserve its juridical position. This policy limited its political effectiveness, but it did not prevent all mediatory activity and indirect contact with Protestants, for example, encouragement of the emperor to allow France to bring its Protestant allies to the projected conference in Cologne.[5] Quietly dropped was the notion that the desired reconciliation of the three crowns served as a prelude to a united campaign against the Protestants.

Lamormaini's political influence tumbled drastically in Vienna after the conclusion of the Peace of Prague. But his personal relationship with Ferdinand remained close, and Vitelleschi maintained his correspondence with the confessor. The general's letters now aimed to secure the emperor's support for the projected papal peace conference. Precisely at this time Vitelleschi was urging Maillan, Gordon, and then Caussin in Paris to push the cause of peace with Louis, though not without first consulting Richelieu. In December 1635, writing to Lamormaini explicitly at the behest of Cardinal Barberini, the superior general lauded the emperor for already naming his delegates to the conference and for suggesting locations for it. Vitelleschi now asked Lamormaini to pursue two goals with Ferdinand. The first was to name cities along the Lower Rhine appropriate for the conference. Thus far, for the sake of their Dutch allies, the French had insisted on either Cologne or Liège, two cities that Vienna had hitherto rejected as hostile to the Habsburgs and too distant from Vienna. Nor was Vienna eager to allow the French to dictate the site of the conference. The second request was to convince the king of Spain to send delegates to the conference. France had already agreed to do so.[6] Interestingly, Vitelleschi did not write Aguado, Olivares's confessor, and perhaps Cardinal Barberini did not ask him to do so. Rather, Vitelleschi attempted to reach Philip IV through the emperor.

Three months later, after Spain had named its delegates, Vitelleschi once again exhorted Lamormaini to get Ferdinand to agree to a site for the conference, Cologne or perhaps Liège, he now intimated. Vitelleschi knew Ferdinand to be "most desirous of universal peace, and that his piety was moved by nothing more than such extensive devastation of territories, massacres of peoples, and spilling of human blood."[7] Two

[5] Konrad Repgen, *Die römische Kurie und der westfälische Friede* 1 (Tübingen, 1962): 397–9.
[6] Vitelleschi to Lamormaini, Dec. 15, 1635, ARSJ, Aust. 5I, ff. 72–3; Leman, 381.
[7] Vitellschi to Lamormaini, Mar. 15, 1636, ibid., ff. 110–12.

weeks later Vitelleschi added that Lamormaini must have understood that what he had written about the location for the conference had been written only because "others" had requested it of him, probably the pope at the behest of the French, who continued firm in their insistence on these two cities. But Vitelleschi reiterated his own personal commitment to peace as the only alternative to "enormous evils for us and for the Christian commonwealth."[8]

In July Lamormaini heard from Vitelleschi that the pope and the French had agreed on Cologne as the site, and he was asked to incline Ferdinand to accept this decision. In fact, as the nuncio Baglione reported, Lamormaini had already had a hand in convincing Ferdinand to yield on this point.[9] Both the emperor and the king of Spain did send delegates to Cologne in the spring of 1637, but largely because of the dispute over the terms on which their Swedish and Protestant allies would be admitted to the conference, French delegates never did appear, so that the conference never got off the ground and the site was later moved to Münster in Westphalia.[10]

Vitelleschi continued to seek Lamormaini's intervention on behalf of Italian clients. One was the brother of Pietro Aldobrandini, cardinal-nephew of Clement VIII; like other members of the Aldobrandini family, Vitelleschi noted, he had served with distinction in the imperial military. According to reports, the spoils of the Bohemian rebels were now being distributed. Certainly, the Aldobrandini family merited a share after having played a part in the suppression of the rebellion. The Society was also much indebted to the generosity of the cardinal.[11]

In the spring of 1636 the upcoming Electoral Convention of Regensburg was the focus of attention more than a projected general peace conference sponsored by the pope. Along with Ferdinand II, the future Ferdinand III, and the bishop of Vienna, Lamormaini received a papal brief encouraging him to look to the good of "religion and public peace" at Regensburg. Urban VIII firmly endorsed the election of Ferdinand III, despite Richelieu's attempts to sway him.[12] Rome may

[8] Vitelleschi to Lamormaini, Mar. 29, 1636, ibid., f. 118.

[9] Vitelleschi to Lamormaini, July 5, 1636, ibid., f. 157; Leman, 382. Baglione, cited by Leman, wrote to Rome on May 17 that without certain secret interventions, he would have despaired of securing the emperor's agreement to Cologne. I attribute these interventions to Lamormaini.

[10] Konrad Repgen, "Negotiating the Peace of Westphalia: A Survey with an Examination of the Major Problems," *1648: War and Peace in Europe*, eds. Klaus Bussmann and Heinz Schilling, 1 (Münster, 1999): 356.

[11] Vitelleschi to Lamormaini., Aug. 18, 1635, ARSJ, Aust. 5I, f. 25.

[12] Urban VIII to Lamormaini, May 10, 1636, Repgen 1, 2 (Tübingen, 1965): no. 158: 243, n. 4; Auguste Leman, "Le Saint-Siège et l'élection imperiale du 22 Décembre 1636," *Revue d'histoire ecclésiastique* 34 (1938): 543, 549.

not have been aware of Lamormaini's diminished status. The confessor did accompany Ferdinand to Regensburg, but he played a minimal role at the convention. Its principal achievement was the election of Ferdinand III; it also dealt with other issues, including the Palatinate, but without any specific result.[13] The previous spring Vitelleschi, who always sought to aid the English Catholics, had asked Lamormaini in an unusual confidential letter to do what he could to foster the interests of an English delegation to Vienna on behalf of the Elector Palatine, in the hope that this would benefit the English Catholics. But he was to do this without in any way offending Maximilian or prejudicing Catholic interests. This was a difficult order.[14] Lamormaini did meet with the head of the English delegation, Thomas Howard, earl of Arundel, and they seem to have gotten along well. Lamormaini advised Arundel to be honest and forthright in his dealings with the imperial ministers, but beyond that he was not able to assist him.[15]

On January 25, while staying over in Straubing in Bavaria on the return trip from Regensburg, the emperor suffered a stroke. At his request, Lamormaini dispensed him from his customary hour of prayer so that he did not have to rise at four in the morning. The end was approaching for Ferdinand, and he expired in Vienna on February 15, 1637, attended by Lamormaini, who had spent the previous day at his side. One of Lamormaini's first projects after the emperor's death was a multivolume biography of Ferdinand, a venture that found the hearty endorsement of Vitelleschi.[16] Of this he published in 1638 the final and the only volume that appeared, but it became a Baroque classic as *The Virtues of Ferdinand II, Emperor of the Romans*.[17] From 1639 to 1643 he served another term as rector of the college in Vienna, and he continued to advance Catholic claims to church lands in the empire, especially in Württemberg, and to formulate plans for the foundation of Jesuit colleges as far afield as Pomerania and Brandenburg.[18] After the sudden

13 Dieter Albrecht, *Maximilian I von Bayern, 1573–1651* (Munich, 1998), 958–9.
14 Vitelleschi to Lamormaini, Apr. 12, 1636, ARSJ, Germ. 111, f. 249.
15 Eustachius Sthaäl, "Vita Lamormaini," ARSJ, Vitae 139, 51′–2. Sthaäl notes that Count Arundel, who came from a distinguished Catholic family, was "*semi-Catholicus*" and welcomed religious instruction from Lamormaini. For an account of Arundel's mission, see Francis C. Springell, *Connoisseur and Diplomat: The Earl of Arundel's Embassy to Germany in 1636* (London, 1963); on Lamormaini, 64.
16 Vitelleschi to Lamormaini, Mar. 14 and 21, 1637, ARSJ, Aust. 5I, ff. 242–3, 254.
17 *Ferdinandi II imperatoris Romanorum virtutes* (Vienna, 1638).
18 On the latter, see Vitelleschi to Lamormaini, Mar. 20, 1638, ARSJ, Aust. 5I, f. 350. For Lamormaini's efforts to maintain the church's claims to lands in Württemberg, see Heinrich Günter, *Das Restitutionsedikt von 1629 und die katholische Restauration Altwirtembergs* (Stuttgart, 1901), 287–93, 308.

death of the Austrian provincial in 1643, he held this office briefly before he died in the year of the Peace of Westphalia.

In the course of the Electoral Convention of Regensburg, the Jesuit Heinrich Philippi died. For twelve years he had served as confessor to the king of Hungary, now to become Emperor Ferdinand III. Selected to replace him was Johannes Gans, then a preacher to the king. Born in Würzburg in 1591, as a young Jesuit he had volunteered for the China Mission and actually journeyed as far as Portugal in 1619 before Vitelleschi recalled him to Austria due to a change in circumstances. First a preacher in Graz, he was assigned to Vienna in the early 1630s, to preach in St. Stephen's Cathedral. Soon he was attached to the court as preacher of the king of Hungary, also accompanying him on his campaigns. In the summer of 1635 Vitelleschi in a letter to Philippi acknowledged that life in camp was freer than in a religious house, but he requested Philippi tactfully to encourage Gans to moderation in food and drink.[19] Vitelleschi congratulated Gans on his appointment as confessor, which signified that young Ferdinand shared his father's affection and benevolence toward the Society.[20] To Gans's request for guidance, Vitelleschi called attention to Acquaviva's Instruction for the Confessors of Princes and exhorted him to ponder it frequently.[21]

Gans represented a sharp contrast with his predecessor Lamormaini in both style of life and conception of the role of imperial confessor. Austerity characterized Lamormaini, whereas Gans obviously enjoyed a fine meal along with several beers in company with members of the court. Vitelleschi cautioned him to a modest diet, urbanity of manner, and seriousness of conversation.[22] Altogether at this time twelve Jesuit priests ministered at court as confessors or preachers with six lay brothers to assist them.[23] Complaints soon reached Rome about dissension at the professed house in Vienna, where the court Jesuits resided, and about Gans and a court preacher accompanying the court, in secular dress, on hunting expeditions. Vitelleschi instructed the provincial superior to take measures, tactfully but firmly, to remedy the situation.[24] Gans initially does not seem to have received the correction well.[25] Later

[19] Vitelleschi to Philippi, July 28, 1635, ARSJ, Aust. 5I, ff. 16–17; Bernhard Duhr, *Geschichte der Jesuiten in den Ländern deutscher Zunge* 2 (Freiburg, 1913), 2: 232–4.

[20] Vitelleschi to Gans, Jan. 10, 1637, ARSJ, Aust. 5I, f. 219.

[21] Vitelleschi to Gans, Feb. 7, 1637, ibid., ff. 231–2.

[22] Ibid.

[23] Duhr, ibid., 236, n. 1.

[24] Vitelleschi to Gregor Rumer (provincial), Nov. 5, 1639, and Apr. 7, 1640, ARSJ, Aust. 5I, ff. 516, 558.

[25] Vitelleschi to Gans, Aug. 18, 1640, ibid., 590.

he was accused of having insulted the bishop of Laibach by calling him "Crassus Carinthus," and the rector of the college there wanted him removed from his position.[26] When the new superior general Carafa tried to appoint another confessor in his place in 1646, he failed because of the emperor's opposition, as we shall see.

The distance between Gans and Lamormaini opened wider when it came to their understanding of the office of confessor and of imperial politics. At the Diet of Regensburg in 1641 Gans assigned the principal responsibility for the troubles of the empire to the Edict of Restitution, the product of a few zealous and well-intentioned but politically inept imperial advisors. So Gans evaluated the centerpiece of his predecessor's program for the restoration of Catholicism.[27] The nuncio Baglione's secretary, Tinti, relying partly on an Italian Jesuit at court, Pietro Negroni, sized up the situation accurately in a letter to the secretary of state, Cardinal Ceva, of March 7, 1637, shortly after Gans's appointment. Lamormaini, he wrote, influenced the emperor by seeing everything as a matter of conscience. Ferdinand III had declared that he did not intend to proceed in this way.[28]

After several months in office Gans wrote Vitelleschi that many difficulties could be overcome if a different procedure were followed in dealing with the court, to which the superior general answered that he would gladly learn where errors had been made in the past and how they might be corrected.[29] But Gans never responded directly to this. The confessor continued to have access to the emperor, but he was excluded from political deliberations and was not on good terms with Trautmannsdorf, who became Ferdinand III's principal councillor.[30] Gans accepted this exclusion, if reluctantly at times, and he certainly never advocated a program as had Lamormaini. Occasionally, he did speak out against abuses in government – for example, in 1639 when he criticized Ferdinand III as well as Trautmannsdorf and the bishop of Vienna for dabbling in alchemy.[31] Diego de Quiroga, the Capuchin confessor of the Empress Maria Anna and a member of the Spanish party, long wielded more influence than did Gans.[32] But overall, under Ferdinand III ecclesiastics exercised less influence than under his father.

[26] Vitelleschi to Rumer (provincial), Dec. 13, 1642, Aust. 5II, f. 763.
[27] Duhr 2, 1 (Freiburg, 1913): 473–4.
[28] Repgen 1, 1: 418, n. 108.
[29] Vitelleschi to Gans, Oct. 31, 1637, ARSJ, Aust. 5I, ff. 316–17.
[30] Repgen 1, 1: 408, n. 108.
[31] Duhr 2, 2: 235.
[32] Ludwig Steinberger, *Die Jesuiten und die Friedensfrage in der Zeit vom Prager Frieden bis zum Nürnberger Friedensexekutionshauptrezess, 1635–1650* (Freiburg, 1906), 17–18.

Gans corresponded much less regularly with Vitelleschi than had Lamormaini, and of this correspondence little was political in character, not even, for example, during the Diet of Regensburg in 1640–41, when he was consulted on major issues. However, he did receive Vitelleschi's normal requests for favors from the imperial court. While he was at Regensburg, the superior general requested that should the current imperial representative in Rome resign, as some expected, Gans put forward to replace him the name of Prince Nicholas Ludovisi, a relative of Cardinal Ludovisi, nephew of Gregory XV, who had been especially good to the Jesuits. But Gans was not to mention Vitelleschi's name in this regard.[33]

Johannes Vervaux, Contzen's replacement in Munich, also differed greatly from his predecessor, but in different respects. He enjoyed at least as much influence in Munich as had Contzen, and he inclined toward France even more than his predecessor. But he also periodically participated in sessions of the privy council and even undertook at least one major diplomatic mission, tasks never required of Contzen. Unlike Contzen, he belonged to the moderate party and so represented a profound change. Vervaux finally completed the history of Bavaria, the *Annals of the Bavarian People*, on which several Jesuits worked at Maximilian's behest. It was published in 1662, the year after Vervaux's death, under the name of the councillor Johannes Adlzreiter because Jesuit superiors feared the backlash from some positions taken in the book especially regarding Ludwig IV, the fourteenth-century Wittelsbach emperor whom the pope excommunicated.[34] The third volume of the *Annals* dealt with Maximilian's reign. In his treatment of the Electoral Convention of Regensburg of 1630, Vervaux sharply criticized the militant councillors, including Contzen, though not by name, for their rigid position, and he also blamed them for the subsequent problems of the empire.[35] Vervaux was not responsible for Maximilian's shift to a moderate position, but he fit well with it and evidently fostered it. He was to encounter severe opposition from some fellow Jesuits, but Vitelleschi, who now found himself in the moderate camp, consistently upheld him.

Vervaux came from the town of Xivry-le-Franc in Lorraine, where he was born in 1586. Already a priest, he entered the Lower Rhine Province of the Jesuits in 1618, and he found his ministry for a time in Trier as a professor of moral theology and director of the Marian

33 Vitelleschi to Gans (Regensburg), June 20, 1640, ARSJ, Aust. 5I, f. 576.

34 Andreas Kraus, "Altertumswissenschaft und Geschichte," *Handbuch der bayerischen Geschichte* 2, 2nd ed., eds. Max Spindler and Andreas Kraus (Munich, 1988): 913–14.

35 J. Adlzreiter (Vervaux), *Annales boicae gentis* 3 (Munich, 1662): 220–2 (XV, 30–42).

Congregation. By 1629 he was on loan to the Province of Lorraine to assist in a campaign to recatholicize the area around Saarwerden. His activity there brought him to the attention of Elizabeth of Lorraine, Maximilian's wife; and when her confessor died in 1631, she requested Vervaux as his successor. Vitelleschi, as was his custom, acquiesced, and so Vervaux ended up in Munich.[36] He began to write Vitelleschi, like Contzen, on an almost weekly basis, and the general noted already in 1633 that though they both often reported the same facts they frequently deduced from them "a different hope or fear for the future."[37]

Elisabeth of Lorraine died at Christmastime 1634, having born the prince no children. Vitelleschi gave Vervaux permission to return to the Lower Rhine Province, but then reversed himself when it became evident that Maximilian wanted to retain him at court in Munich.[38] Vervaux accompanied Maximilian and his party to Vienna in June 1635, where the elector married his new wife, Maria Anna, daughter of Ferdinand II and sister of the king of Hungary. By the end of the year Maximilian let it be known that he could think of no one other than Vervaux as his confessor, and so Vitelleschi approved the choice.[39] Shortly afterward, in 1637, Maximilian's first child and successor, Ferdinand Maria, was born. Vervaux was destined to play a part in his education, and the confessor almost certainly authored the *Paternal Admonitions* that outlined Maximilian's conception of the good prince and served as the most prominent of his political testaments.[40] The confessor enjoyed Maximilian's full confidence.

In the spring of 1636 Vitelleschi wrote Vervaux as he had Lamormaini in Vienna encouraging him to support the English mission to Vienna on behalf of the Count Palatine. An English Jesuit, Father Henry Silisdon, who resided in Liège and served as an informant for Maximilian on English affairs,[41] had already been to Munich to discuss possibilities. Vitelleschi himself does not seem to have been in the clear about what was transpiring, but he was intent on securing any sympathy he could from the English government for the Catholics there. The overriding priority, however, was Maximilian's interest, and nothing should be

36 Duhr 2, 2: 256–7.

37 Vitelleschi to Vervaux, Mar. 26, 1633, ARSJ, Germ. Sup. 6, f. 537.

38 Vitelleschi to Vervaux, Feb. 3 and Mar. 2, 1635, ibid., ff. 710, 729.

39 Vitelleschi to Vervaux, Dec. 29, 1635, ibid., f. 802.

40 Heinz Dollinger, "Kurfürst Maximilian und Justus Lipsius," *Archiv für Kulturgeschichte* 46 (1964): 227–36. The "Monita Paterna" were published in the *Annales boicae gentis* and have been edited by Friedrich Schmidt, *Geschichte der Erziehung der bayerischen Wittelsbacher*, Monumenta Germaniae Paedagogica 14 (Berlin, 1892): 102–41.

41 On Silisdon, see *English and Welsh Jesuits 1555–1650*, ed. Thomas J. McCoog, 2 (London, 1995): 294.

undertaken that would undermine it. Vitelleschi sent on a copy of his April 12 letter to Lamormaini, to be shown to Maximilian if necessary, so that no misunderstandings could arise with the elector.[42] Later Vitelleschi expressed his satisfaction with the way Vervaux handled the matter, and he beseeched him to keep secret his mild intervention on behalf of the English mission.[43] At the Electoral Convention there was no progress made on the Palatinate question, but in private discussions between Bavarian and English delegates Maximilian does seem to have at least considered an eventual alternation of the electoral dignity. The issue had supposedly been resolved by the Peace of Prague. But Maximilian realized that no solution would be final until it was accepted not only in Germany but by the other major European states.[44]

After the setbacks of 1638, including the loss of Breisach and the renewal of the Franco-Swedish alliance, it became evident to moderate Catholics that concessions beyond those of the Peace of Prague would have to be made to gain or to retain support of German Protestants for the emperor and for peace. They hoped to win over Countess Amalia Elisabeth, who governed Calvinist Hesse-Kassel for her minor son and who was allied with France and Sweden. To bring her over to the imperial side would require allowing Calvinists to be included within the Religious Peace of Augsburg, a concession strongly opposed by Catholic, and some Lutheran, princes until then. They now yielded.

On September 14, 1639, when the new nuncio Gasparo Mattei was received in audience by Ferdinand III, he exhorted the emperor not to make the rumored concessions to Hesse-Kassel, prejudicial as they were to the church. Mattei was both more visible at court and more aggressive in promoting papal policy than his predecessor.[45] Ferdinand replied to him that he had discussed the matter with his councillors, with his theologians, and with Bavaria and Mainz, who was an ecclesiastic and a theologian. They all approved the measure. Mattei expressed his surprise and suggested that the emperor give the matter more thought. A subsequent interview with Trautmannsdorf that day proved even less satisfactory. Two days later Mattei spoke with Gans, who responded elliptically that "these are trifling matters; it is greatly to be doubted that more universal [concessions?] will be made."[46] So he

42 Vitelleschi to Vervaux, Apr. 26, 1636, ARSJ, Germ. Sup. 7, f. 837.

43 Vitelleschi to Vervaux, July 5, 1636, ibid., f. 869.

44 Albrecht, 958–60.

45 Repgen 1, 1: 401–5.

46 "Istae sunt nugae; universalia possunt expectari valde dubitandum." This direct citation of Gans by Mattei is not perfectly clear.

seemed to make light of the matter. Mattei indicated that he would continue to pursue the question with Gans.[47] Several weeks later Mattei and Gans talked again. Gans, Mattei noted, spoke more as a "politico" than as a religious in the matter of Hesse-Kassel, and he went on to remark that the Jesuits were good religious but tended to take the side of princes when princely interests were involved. He intended to maintain his contacts with Gans.[48]

Negotiations with Hesse-Kassel broke down on other matters, so that the concession produced no positive result at this point. Significant to note is that nothing about this issue appeared in the correspondence of either Gans or Vervaux with Vitelleschi; they were more independent of him than were their predecessors, and he himself seems to have had no objection to this.

In early May 1639 Mainz summoned an Electoral Convention for June 20 in Frankfurt. Eventually, it convened on February 3, 1640, not in Frankfurt but in Nuremberg. Its program was to overcome the hindrances to peace both within and beyond the empire, to provide for the conduct of the war in the meantime, and to determine a policy for the event that neither military efforts nor negotiations brought peace. Maximilian stood behind this initiative. In addition, despite his anger over France's alleged betrayal of the German Catholic princes during the 1630s, he once again saw negotiations with France as the key to peace, and he supported the talks with Sweden in which the emperor was engaged in Hamburg. In late 1639 he once again inaugurated secret contacts with Paris. Richelieu, he was now aware, would demand as the price of peace territorial concessions from the Habsburg lands in the west of the empire, especially in Alsace, and a break between Vienna and Madrid so that France could continue its war with a Spain bereft of assistance from its Habsburg cousin in Vienna and other German states. Of great importance to the elector was the maintenance of his hold on the Palatinate electoral title and as much of the territory as possible. For this, too, he hoped for French support. Maximilian planned to expand the Electoral Convention to include other German princes, especially representatives of the imperial circles, in order to put pressure on Vienna to be more open to negotiations with France.

Ferdinand III was conscious of Maximilian's intent. At the time he rejected territorial concessions to France and any break with his Spanish cousin. He planned rather to make a separate peace with Sweden, with whom he was negotiating, and so split it from France, and then

[47] Mattei to Barberini, Sept. 17, 1639, cited in Repgen 1, 1: 403, n. 54.
[48] Mattei to Barberini, Oct. 8, 1639, cited in Repgen 1, 1: 417.

to mobilize the empire to join the war with France alongside Spain. Though he consented to the electoral convention, he began to point toward the convocation of a diet, where all the German princes would gather and where he as emperor would naturally play a predominant role that he would not at an electoral convention. With the support of Anselm Casimir of Mainz, who consistently sided with the emperor, he called on May 26 for a diet in Regensburg. It eventually convened on September 13, thus superseding the electoral convention that dissolved in July without reaching any significant decisions. The diet's program called for treatment of the same issues as the convention.[49]

Formidable difficulties stood in the way of conducting a diet in the midst of the war. Swedish General Baner, as we have seen, threatened Regensburg in January 1641. Many princes, instead of appearing themselves, sent delegates because of the wartime dangers and because of the expense of maintaining themselves in an appropriate fashion while in Regensburg. But Ferdinand came in person, thus expanding his influence by his presence, arriving already in early June. With him came his confessor Gans as well as the papal nuncio Mattei. Maximilian remained in Munich and Vervaux with him.

Maximilian favored further limited concessions to the Protestants for the sake of uniting the German states more effectively against the foreign enemies. Ferdinand III, Mainz, and Cologne all came around to this position by February 1641.[50] At issue was an amnesty for two groups of Protestant states, those that had not accepted the terms of the Peace of Prague, like Hesse-Kassel and the Palatinate, and those like Württemberg that accepted the Peace but were excluded from some of its benefits. The church property that Duke Eberhard of Württemberg stood to regain from an amnesty constituted one-third of his territory.[51] The moderate Catholics sought through an amnesty to win over the Protestant rulers along with their armies to the imperial side. The diet eventually approved the amnesty in October 1641, but this action did not succeed in persuading either Hesse-Kassel or the duke of Württemburg to change sides, and it had little effect on the progress of the war. It is significant for our purposes because it occasioned a further conflict between moderates and militants within the Catholic camp and, indeed, within the Society of Jesus, a conflict that caused problems for Vitelleschi and then for Carafa until the end of the war.

The militant opposition to the amnesty was led by the nuncio, Mattei, who did not always enjoy the full backing of his superiors in Rome,

[49] Kathrin Bierther, *Der Regensburger Reichstag von 1640/1641* (Kallmünz, 1971), 25–62.
[50] Ibid., 130–1, 179.
[51] Ibid., 147, n. 52.

Bishop Heinrich von Knöringen of Augsburg, and several abbots whose orders claimed extensive church lands in Württemberg. Associated with them were Jesuits at the University of Dillingen, the residential city of Knöringen, and in particular two, Laurentius Forer and Heinrich Wangnereck. Forer, born in Lucerne in 1580, taught theology first at Ingolstadt and then for many years at Dillingen, where for twenty-seven years he was confessor to the prince-bishop. He authored numerous militant controversialist works. Shortly before and after the Peace of Prague he had submitted several memoranda to Bavarian and imperial councillors, including Lamormaini, which he realized had not been well received.[52] More prominent and more prolific still was the volatile Heinrich Wangerneck. Born of a prominent Munich family in 1595 and related on his mother's side to the renowned Bavarian theologian and Luther opponent, Johann Eck, he taught at Dillingen from 1625 to 1664, apart from four years at the mission in Lindau on Lake Constance. He was a brilliant polemicist and extremist Catholic,[53] who became persona non grata in Munich.

On July 10, 1640, nuncio Mattei reported from Regensburg on recent talks with Ferdinand III and with Gans. The emperor he had reminded of his oath to protect religion, and he spoke in particular of the need to exclude from the diet the Protestant administrators of (arch)bishoprics, an issue that had provoked the dissolution of the last diet in 1613. In fact, they were not allowed to take seats in 1640.[54] Mattei exhorted Gans to see that the emperor not stain his conscience with concessions to heretics, in particular two that it was rumored he would make: first, the admission of Calvinism in the empire, and second, the allowance of liberty of conscience in the Habsburg lands, on which in fact Ferdinand never considered yielding. Gans replied that he was doing all that he could and added that it would be advantageous if there were an ecclesiastic on the council. When Mattei suggested that no one was more suitable than Gans himself, the confessor replied that Ferdinand had said that the councillors did not want an ecclesiastic among them.[55]

The first discussions at the diet over the amnesty issue took place in October. As they were starting, Mattei hosted a dinner to enable Gans to meet the militant representatives of the bishop of Augsburg, who asked the confessor to bring their case before the emperor. But his intervention

[52] Carl Conrad Eckhardt, *The Papacy and World Affairs* (Chicago, 1937), 171–3. Three of these memoranda are found in HStA, Jesuitica 704, ff. 45–8′, 52–9′, 61–3′, along with other materials of Forer.

[53] Steinberger, 15; Duhr 2, 1: 472.

[54] Bierther, 54.

[55] Repgen 1, 1: 417–18, and n. 108.

if it took place at all must have been unsuccessful. When Mattei next saw the emperor, Ferdinand told him that "the priests ought not handle political matters," to which the nuncio replied that it was impossible for him to avoid politics when it was so intertwined with religion. He excused his interventions with Ferdinand, but he was compelled to carry out his mission as nuncio.[56]

Maximilian advocated the amnesty among the Catholics. But he qualified his support with two weighty conditions. First, the amnesty would not apply to the Count Palatine, because it would then undermine Maximilian's position on the Palatinate issue, and second, it would not take effect until all the Protestant states in question accepted it and came over to the emperor's side. In the fall of 1640 the elector hoped to secure Württemberg's support for the Bavarian contingent of the imperial army.[57] He castigated his delegates in Regensburg when for tactical reasons they did not make his position adequately clear, and he emphasized that the Munich theologians – who had to include Vervaux and probably Wolfgang Gravenegg, provincial of the Upper German Province – had sanctioned the amnesty for the sake of peace.[58] Vitelleschi undoubtedly knew that Gravenegg was a moderate. The superior general had ordered him to Regensburg for the diet and forestalled any hesitation that he might have about dealing with "matters of state."[59]

The Bavarian delegates sent Gravenegg to Mattei to explain to him the elector's policy, but Mattei characterized him as "completely Bavarian."[60] At one point the Bavarian vice chancellor Richel confronted Mattei; he blamed France for the need to make concessions on religion and severely criticized Rome for not taking measures against France. Richel later let it be known that Francesco Barberini himself, who maintained a long-standing confidential correspondence with Maximilian, had approved Maximilian's action. Barberini weakly denied this subsequently, but a look at his letter to Maximilian would allow for the Bavarian interpretation.[61] One sees here again the ambivalence of papal policy: on the one hand, the strict upholding of a juridical position, which Mattei was doing, and at the same time, a tacit recognition of political reality as represented by Barberini's carefully worded letter. Nor did Rome ever remonstrate directly with Maximilian over his policy or

56 Mattei to Barberini, Oct. 16, 1640, cited in Repgen 1, 1: 453, n. 234; ibid., 452–3.
57 Albrecht, 967, 970.
58 Bierther, 88 and n. 69 citing Maximilian to his delegates, Nov. 27, 1640.
59 Vitelleschi to Wolfgang Gravenegg (provincial), Feb. 29, 1639, and Aug. 25, 1640, ARSJ, Germ. Sup. 7, ff. 1027, 1078.
60 Mattei to Barberini, Oct. 23, 1640, cited in Repgen 1, 1: 483–4, n. 345.
61 Barberini to Maximilian, Nov. 24, 1640, Repgen 1, 2: no. 151: 216; ibid. 1, 1: 454 and n. 238, 478–83, 491–5.

make an effort to influence either Mainz or Cologne, who had not yet taken a clear position, to oppose the amnesty. This made it difficult, of course, for the nuncio in the field, Mattei.

Sometime before December 25, at Knöringen's request, Wangnereck sent to Regensburg two manuscript copies of a polemical booklet against the amnesty titled "A Difficult Question, Is the Peace which the Protestants Want of Itself Illicit?"[62] They were intended for nuncio Mattei and for Georg Stengl, rector of the university at Dillingen, whom Knöringen had sent to Dillingen in November to bolster the opposition to the amnesty and whom Gravenegg, his provincial superior, ordered back to Dillingen in February.[63]

Clearly written and effectively argued, "A Difficult Question" contended that the proposed amnesty violated natural, divine, and ecclesiastical law. The concessions infringed on the church's rights, they violated the oaths of Catholic princes to protect religion, and they endangered souls in that they surrendered lands from which Catholic clergy ministered to and evangelized local populations. Wangnereck objected especially to the permanence of the concessions envisioned by the amnesty; the surrender of church lands in the Peace of Prague had been, strictly speaking, only for forty years, after which claims could be legally reasserted. Wangnereck blamed the theological councillors, often his fellow Jesuits, for approving the concessions, not the princes for wanting to make them. He also defended the theologians who had prohibited concessions at Regensburg in 1630. Those who supported the amnesty were "worthy of eternal death."

Yet nothing here breathed the holy war ideology of Contzen or Lamormaini. One of Wangnereck's goals was to prevent the Catholics from acting "*intempestive*," that is, from further resort to arms. If the emperor and the leading Catholic states accepted the amnesty, the other Catholic states ought not resist its passage and seek to continue the war. They could act thus without burdening their consciences because they could not be blamed for what they could not prevent. Wangnereck recommended rather a subsequent protest or reservation of rights similar to the protest of Cardinal Otto von Truchsess of Augsburg against the Peace of Augsburg of 1555,[64] and his advice pointed to the

62 "Quaestio ardua, An pax quam desiderant protestantes, sit ex se illicita, ex regulis naturalis, divini, et christiani juris, secundum quas fas et nefas discerni debet, recens elucidata. Anno Christi 1640," Repgen 1, 2: no. 156: 225–40, with some unimportant omissions.

63 Repgen 1, 1: 476, 483 and n. 345. In 1636 Vitelleschi had prohibited the publication of a manuscript by Stengl because it was too incendiary against the Protestants; see Vitelleschi to Anton Welser (vice-provincial), Aug. 9, 1636, ARSJ, Germ. Sup. 7, f. 878.

64 On the protest of Truchsess, see Repgen 1, 1: 74–5.

eventual Roman policy toward the Peace of Westphalia. Wangnereck's manuscript was originally not intended to be circulated generally but to be kept within a small Catholic group, but this restriction evidently failed.[65]

Members of the moderate party in Regensburg, or perhaps Vervaux in Munich, must have alerted Vitelleschi to Wangnereck's "A Difficult Question." "The argument was exceedingly dangerous, and likely to provoke charges against the Society," Vitelleschi wrote the author. He instructed Wangnereck not to allow the booklet to come into the hands of anyone until he – that is, Vitelleschi – had seen and approved it. Typical of his manner, he advised Wangnereck that he would have issued a more severe order had he not known the readiness of his correspondent to obey.[66] Once he had read the booklet, the superior general does not seem to have objected to Wangnereck's argument. "Nevertheless," he instructed Wangnereck, "I do not want it circulated for any reason or to come into the hands of others lest it provoke hatred and subsequent harm for the Society, which could all too easily happen. Not every truth has to be indiscriminately championed by Ours, when there were not lacking those who ex officio were responsible to do so," presumably an allusion to the nuncio.[67] Interestingly, Vitelleschi went on to explain that this was a matter of circulation of the manuscript and of the welfare of the Society; he was not attempting to interfere in the direction of a conscience, whether of the prince-bishop or anyone else. It is not clear to what extent "A Difficult Question" did influence the nuncio Mattei in his decision to lodge a formal protest against the amnesty on April 18, 1641.[68]

The Bavarians continued to promote the amnesty. Gans told Mattei in January, disingenuously it would seem, that he had remonstrated with the Bavarian ministers about it, but that the emperor could do little to oppose it, especially if the ecclesiastical electors and in particular Mainz supported it. Gans blamed Maximilian and the imperial councillors.[69] Maximilian's brother, Ferdinand of Cologne, committed himself to the amnesty on February 2.[70] Then when the delegates of Mainz consulted Gans in early February about whether Elector Anselm Casimir could approve the loss of the monasteries in Württemberg entailed by

65 Steinberger, 32, 169–71.
66 Vitelleschi to Wangnereck, Feb. 9, 1641, ARSJ, Germ. Sup. 7, ff. 1091–2.
67 Vitelleschi to Wangnereck, Apr. 6, 1641, Steinberger, Document 1: 195.
68 Repgen 1, 1: 451, 499.
69 Mattei to Barberini, Jan. 22, 1641, Repgen 1, 2: no. 163: 251–2; ibid. 1, 1: 482 and nn. 341, 343.
70 Bierther, 130–1.

the amnesty without burdening his conscience, the imperial confessor replied in the affirmative. It was a question of choosing the lesser of two evils. Better to surrender the church lands in question and so facilitate cooperation and peace among Catholics and Protestants in the empire than to insist on holding on to the lands and so widening the differences between the two religious parties and prolonging the war. Gans considered acceptance of the Peace of Prague by the theologians a clear precedent for his decision. In 1635 they had sanctioned surrender of ecclesiastical territories for the sake of winning Protestant states over to the emperor's side. Gans did not note that the Peace of Prague allowed the Catholics to challenge legally Protestant possession of the lands in question after the lapse of forty years, whereas the amnesty surrendered them permanently. Whether this distinction made much difference in practice or not, it remained of importance for the militants. After considerable hesitation, and following Cologne, Mainz made the Bavarian position its own in early March.[71]

Emperor Ferdinand inclined to support the amnesty by early January, but he only had to make a final decision in July, after the princes and electors sanctioned it. Following the example of his father prior to the Peace of Prague, he summoned a council of theologians to evaluate it. Four of them took part in the consultation: Gans; Sebastian Denich, who was dean of the Cathedral of Regensburg; Quiroga; and another, unnamed, Spanish Capuchin. All voted in favor of it, despite the warnings of Mattei, who had already lodged a protest against it. Gans in his memorandum of July 16 saw the amnesty as a logical development beyond the Peace of Prague, as he had in his opinion for Mainz during the winter. He thought that the pope should be notified but that there was no need to seek papal permission for the amnesty. It was in this memorandum that he made the statement that the Edict of Restitution fostered by his predecessor instigated the troubles of Germany. Gans also encouraged Denich to approve the amnesty, though the dean seems to have already shared the confessor's view.[72] Ferdinand III formally approved the amnesty on August 20, and it was incorporated into the final resolution of the diet of October 10, 1641.

The amnesty did not persuade any major Protestant states to change sides, and it had little practical effect.[73] The further renewal of the

[71] Bierther, 132–4, who cites at length in n. 236 the account of the Mainz delegation about their conversation with two Jesuits, Gans and "Thullern," whom I have been unable to identify.

[72] Repgen 1, 1: 516–17 and n. 457; Steinberger, 36–7; Duhr 2, 1: 473–4; see also two opinions of Denich, n.d., and July 16, 1641, HStA, Jesuiten 704, ff. 235′–7′ and 239–48.

[73] Bierther, 183–4; Albrecht, 972.

Franco-Swedish Alliance on June 30, 1641, greatly diminished the outlook for the split between the two foreign powers that the emperor hoped to provoke. Some states had wanted to take up at the diet the religious *Gravamina*, or complaints, of both Protestants and Catholics that revolved around questions of the interpretation of the Peace of Augsburg and that contributed greatly to the outbreak of the war back in 1618. But this was put off until a later convention and eventually only was regulated in the Peace of Westphalia. The diet also called for the start of negotiations with the two foreign powers: France and Sweden. The Treaty of Hamburg, then, of December 25, 1641, involving France, Spain, Sweden, and the emperor determined that these would be transferred from Cologne and Hamburg to the Westphalian cities of Münster and Osnabrück. But it would take several years before negotiations began there in earnest.[74]

During the Diet of Regensburg, complaints reached Vitelleschi from Germany about Vervaux's moderate position from fellow Jesuits and other militants, but he generally backed Vervaux. Some complained that Maximilian's confessor did not adequately consult with other theologians before advising the prince. This was a familiar complaint against confessors, and from Vitelleschi's perspective, the failure to consult helped to bring down Caussin. Discussion of matters with others, Vitelleschi wrote Vervaux on June 15, 1641, would give his advice more authority if not with the prince then with those less sympathetic to the Society who were unhappy with Maximilian's policy.[75] The superior general also lauded the provincial Gravenegg for calling Father Simon Felice to Munich to assist Vervaux.[76] A month later Vitelleschi listed three propositions regarding the amnesty that Vervaux allegedly had defended at a meeting in Freising: that an action that was intrinsically evil was allowable in case of necessity; that the monks of Württemberg, if permitted to recover their monasteries in the territory of a heretical prince, were likely to abandon the faith and take wives; that the protest of the nuncio against the amnesty contradicted papal policy and even the earlier conduct of the nuncio himself.[77] The last charge may have grown out of the ambiguity of papal policy that we have periodically noted. As usual, Vitelleschi made it clear that he did not believe these charges himself but needed an explanation.

74 Bierther, 185–95, 249–50.
75 Vitelleschi to Vervaux, June 15, 1641, ARSJ, Germ. Sup. 7, f. 1105; see also Vitelleschi to Gravenegg (provincial), Feb. 23, 1641, HStA, Jesuiten 651.
76 Vitelleschi to Gravenegg (provincial), June 15, 1641, ARSJ, Germ. Sup. 7, f. 1105.
77 Vitelleschi to Vervaux, July 20, 1641, ibid., f. 1109.

Vervaux had little trouble in clearing himself. First, he sent the names of the other theologians he consulted about the matters in question.[78] There was no lack of moderates in Munich. The prince-bishop of Freising then testified that Vervaux did not defend the propositions attributed to him at the meeting.[79] Vervaux also provided Vitelleschi with a paper defending his position on the amnesty, which the superior general promised to read when he had time.[80] The theological issues themselves did not interest Vitelleschi so much as did the impact on others, especially princes, of the positions that Jesuits took on the issues.

Early the next year Vitelleschi gave Vervaux an unusually wide berth in response to the confessor's own apparent doubts about what was permitted him. There was no need, Vitelleschi wrote, to change the rule prohibiting Jesuits from dealing with political affairs, so that he could help the prince form his conscience. No decree forbade a Jesuit to concern himself with matters of state and even to be present at council meetings when a proper moral judgment and formation of conscience required it. But at the meeting the confessor was not to speak or to participate in a vote. These words Vervaux "could take as a rule [of conduct] in this whole business."[81]

Wangnereck remained a serious problem for superiors and for Vitelleschi. By 1642 he had become an agent for Bishop Knöringen of Augsburg in disputes with the city of Augsburg and with Maximilian over the possession of the county of Mindelheim, and he was correctly rumored to be the real author of a pamphlet laying out the bishop's argument in the latter case, which was to be published under the name of Knöringen's chancellor. His activities clearly violated the Society's prohibition against participation in secular affairs – religion was not a factor – and threatened to anger Maximilian. Gravenegg the provincial was to look into these matters and to take them up with Knöringen; under no circumstances was Wangnereck's pamphlet to be published by the press of the Jesuit University of Dillingen.[82] Several months later, writing directly to Wangnereck, Vitelleschi ordered him to desist from his activities. Responding to a letter from Knöringen defending Wangnereck, Vitelleschi explained the Society's position on participation in secular affairs and showed how Wangnereck's activities were bound to involve the Jesuits in conflicts between princes. If the bishop had fully understood the Society's regulations and the dangers to which

78 Vitelleschi to Vervaux, July 27, 1641, ibid., f. 1110.
79 Vitelleschi to Vervaux, Aug. 31 and Oct. 19, 1641, ibid., ff. 1114, 1116.
80 Vitelleschi to Vervaux, Sept. 7, 1641, ibid., f. 1115.
81 Vitelleschi to Vervaux, Feb. 3, 1642, ibid., f. 1127.
82 Vitelleschi to Gravenegg (provincial), Jan. 31, 1643, ibid., ff. 1162–3.

Wangnereck's activities exposed the Jesuits, he certainly would never have employed him as he did. The bishop undoubtedly could turn to other lawyers and theologians to advise and act for him in these matters.[83]

Maximilian continued to see negotiations with France as the key to peace for the empire and the preservation of his position in the Palatinate. This implied the exclusion of Spain from the peace and concessions to the French west of the Rhine, both of which Ferdinand III opposed. Swedish and French victories early in 1642, especially the French defeat of the imperials at Kempen in January, pushed the elector further in this direction. In a meeting in April and early May, Bavaria, Cologne, and Mainz determined on a mission to Rome to urge the pope to convince the French of the desire of the German states for peace. But imperial objections forced the cancellation of the project, as they also undercut an attempt of Maximilian to join with Saxony in a common mission to Paris. Ferdinand himself sent the Dominican Georg von Herberstein to Paris at the end of 1642, right at the time of Richelieu's death, to sound out the situation, but four conferences with the new first minister, Cardinal Mazarin, produced nothing.[84]

While at the same time mounting a military offensive in the southwest against the French, Maximilian persisted in his attempts to negotiate with France despite the reservations of some of his own ministers.[85] Early in 1643, undoubtedly at Maximilian's request, Nicasius Widuman, provincial of the Upper German Province, inquired of the rector of the Jesuit professed house in Paris whether Vervaux would be welcome there as an emissary of Maximilian. The rector contacted Sublet de Noyers, who responded that he would not be welcome; echoing Mazarin, Sublet de Noyers saw the venture as an attempt to split France from its ally Sweden.[86] Military success against the French, especially at Tuttlingen on November 24, 1643, did not bring them to the negotiating table. In the spring of 1644 Maximilian approached Paris through Cardinal Bichi, the former nuncio in Paris now in Rome, and the current nuncio in Paris Grimaldi. Mazarin decided at this point to receive a mission from Maximilian. Vervaux was to be Maximilian's agent. The elector chose him probably because of his confidence in Vervaux and the

83 Vitelleschi to Wangnereck, May 9, 1643, ibid., ff. 1175–7; Vitelleschi to Heinrich von Knöringen, bishop of Augsburg, May 16, 1643, ARSJ, Germ. 113II, ff. 904–5.

84 Hans Wagner, "Einleitung: Die kaiserlichen Instruktionen," APW 1: *Instruktionen* 1: *Frankreich, Schweden, Kaiser* (Munster, 1962): 332–3; Albrecht, 981–7.

85 Albrecht, 987–90.

86 Wagner, ibid., 334, n. 2; Steinberger, 41.

confessor's facility in French. The provincial Widuman was enthusiastic about Vervaux's journey to Paris, but neither his local superior nor a now declining Vitelleschi seem to have known of it. The French stalled a long time on the passes necessary for Vervaux; they did not arrive until mid-February 1645.[87] In the meantime, the military situation deteriorated for Maximilian and the emperor, and serious negotiations had begun in Münster and Osnabrück in Westphalia. The delay on the part of the French seems to have been caused by disagreements between Mazarin and the French delegates at the peace negotiations over whether to deal with Maximilian outside the conference.

Vervaux arrived in Paris on April 3, 1645. A great Swedish victory at Jankow in Bohemia on March 6, 1645, gave a decided advantage to the Franco-Swedish allies just then, and it resulted in a last-minute change in the confessor's instructions. He was to seek first a separate armistice between the empire and France, apart from Spain or Sweden; toward this end he was to try to find out what France's specific territorial demands were and, if they were reasonable, to agree to pass them on to Ferdinand. If Mazarin disclaimed interest in this, then he was to suggest an armistice for Bavaria, Cologne, and the states of the three southwest circles of the empire. If this option found no favor with the French, then he could go on to raise the possibility of French "protection" for Bavaria and the other states, a peculiar legal status similar to an earlier "protectorate" that Richelieu had applied to Trier and other territories lying between France and Germany. But neither Maximilian nor his allies were to be committed to any aid against the emperor. Vervaux was allowed considerable leeway in which to maneuver because, as the instruction read, "he himself would know how far his lord could go with a good conscience in this respect." Another goal of the mission was to establish contact with Mazarin.[88]

Twice, on April 5 and again on April 11, Mazarin received Vervaux, whom he characterized as "open enough and sincere."[89] The French minister worried that he give the impression that he was negotiating behind the back of his Swedish allies. He showed little interest in a peace without Spain or Sweden, and he referred Vervaux to Münster. In

[87] Albrecht, 991–3; Steinberger, 40–2; Gerhard Immler, *Kurfürst Maximilian I. und der westfälische Friedenskongress: Die bayerische auswärtige Politik von 1644 bis zum Ulmer Waffenstillstand* (Münster, 1992), 62.

[88] Instruction for Vervaux, Mar. 22, 1645, *Dokumente zur Geschichte von Staat und Gesellschaft in Bayern*, Section 1: *Altbayern vom Frühmittelalter bis 1800*, vol. 3, *Altbayern 1550–1651*, ed. Walter Ziegler, 2 (Munich, 1992): 1179–87, citation on 1187; Immler, 69–73.

[89] Mazarin to the French plenipotentiaries at Münster, Apr. 7, 1645, Jules Mazarin, *Lettres de cardinal Mazarin pendant son ministère, recueillies et publiées*, ed. M.A. Chereul, 2 (Paris, 1874): no. 60: 147.

their second session, Vervaux received a vague promise to see to it that the Catholic religion did not suffer in areas occupied by the Swedes or French and agreement to support Maximilian on the Palatinate issue if the elector supported French aims. From others in Paris, Vervaux learned of the specific French territorial demands: Alsace and the fortresses of Breisach and Philipsburg on the Rhine. Mazarin rejected Vervaux's suggestion that he stay on for future negotiations. The cardinal clearly preferred Münster as the place for these. All in all, Vervaux had little to show for his mission, though discussions did continue at Münster about a possible armistice.[90] For our purposes Vervaux's trip to Paris is significant as the one major diplomatic mission undertaken by a Jesuit confessor for the four courts under discussion.

Later in 1645 Maximilian made use of Laurentius Forer to attempt to obtain French support for the German Catholics through recourse to the new Pope Innocent X, who unfortunately was at odds with Mazarin from the beginning of his pontificate. The Upper German Province elected Forer as a delegate to the Eighth General Congregation, which after the death of Vitelleschi convened in Rome in late November. Before he departed for the south, Forer was summoned to a conference with Maximilian himself and Vervaux, where he was entrusted with a supplicatory memorial to be delivered into the hands of the pope. The memorial affirmed that the war in Germany was "a religious war," and it emphasized the losses the church would suffer if the Ecclesiastical Reservation were surrendered permanently. Maximilian pleaded with the pope to do all in his power to bring France to the aid of the German Catholics. As Forer later wrote, the elector spoke with tears in his eyes as he entrusted the Jesuit with this task so as to satisfy his conscience that he had done his utmost on behalf of the Catholic cause in the empire. Forer succeeded in delivering the memorial personally to the pope in an audience of December 30, 1645. But the most he was able to secure from him or from the cardinals with whom he met was a noncommital "We'll see," (*Videbimus*), nor was his attempt to pry funds loose from the papal treasury any more successful.[91]

Vitelleschi's health began to deteriorate in 1643 as he completed his eightieth year and his twentieth-eighth as superior general. One can note a falling-off in the amount of correspondence in his last year. On

[90] Albrecht, 992–6; Immler, 72–83; Steinberger, 40–4.

[91] "Memoriale in manus oblatum S.D.N. Innocentio X nomine et iussu Serenissimi Maximiliani Electoris Bavariae . . . a Laurentio Forero Societatis Jesu, anno 1645," HStA, Jesuiten 704, ff. 64–70 (a second copy, ff. 156–61'); Forer to Leopold Manzino, S.J., Munich, June 22, 1655, ibid., f. 71.

September 3, 1644, he named as his vicar Carlo Sangrio of the Naples Province, who relieved him of some of his duties and would assume the temporary direction of the Society after his death on February 9, 1645.

The triennial provincial congregations of 1639 and 1642, in Vitelleschi's later years, had manifested a growing sentiment for a general congregation. There had never been such a long hiatus without one. Two Spanish provinces, Toledo and Castile, voted for one in 1639, and two French provinces, Lyons and Aquitaine, in 1642, and significant minorities called for one in other provinces.[92] The reasons that generally carried the day against a general congregation were the difficulties of conducting one during the war and the lack of any real crisis within the Society. Excessive national feeling and attachment to princes were cited both in favor of and against the convocation of a general congregation. The minority favoring a general congregation in the Austrian Province in 1639 saw it as an opportunity to foster the fraternal unity within the Society that had characterized its early years and to prevent Jesuits from becoming too closely identified with their princes, and in the Upper German Province a minority considered it a likely means to harmony and understanding, not only among Jesuits, but beyond the Society among princes and states.[93] But the majority in both provinces thought otherwise, those in the Upper German Province fearing requests from princes that would infringe on the Society's freedom but be difficult to deny. The Province of Aquitaine also argued against a general congregation on the grounds that it would turn into a forum where princely conflicts would be played out. In 1642 the two Rhenish Provinces, the Upper and Lower, made the same point.[94] But the minority in the Toledo Province saw in a general congregation a useful way to foster harmony among nations through example.[95]

In 1639 the Upper German Provincial Congregation endorsed a significant memorial drawn up by Laurentius Forer, who brought it to Rome as a provincial delegate. It represented a clear departure from Contzen's militance on the part of the province. "From so many unhappy events of the war," it stated, "it seems that it does not please God that the Catholic religion be propagated in Germany by [force of] arms, so that another method of resisting heresy must be taken up." One way was to counter Protestant books more effectively. They kept publishing new works, whereas Catholics tended to stick with Bellarmine and other standard authors. Needed were more-effective responses to ongoing

92 ARSJ, Cong. 67, ff. 2, 28; 69, ff. 335, 360.
93 Ibid., 66, ff. 107', 127.
94 Ibid., f. 302; 69, ff. 264, 276.
95 Ibid., 68, ff. 82–3'.

Protestant publications. But Forer emphasized apostolic preaching, that is, the sending out of missionary preachers into both Catholic and non-Catholic areas. So the Society operated in England, Ireland, Holland, India, and China, that is, in non-Catholic areas. Boniface and Willibrord had planted the faith in Germany in this way. Those German Jesuits who desired to go to the Indies would find plenty of missionary challenges at home. Perhaps even some Jesuits from England could be invited over to instruct the German Jesuits in their methods, the memorial suggested. The Society could gather financial support for such endeavors from the Catholic princes, but it would have to reckon with hardship and even some martyrs. But what would be more in the spirit of Ignatius and the early Jesuits, the paper asked. According to Forer, the bishops of Augsburg and Constance had asked for such missionaries, and two priests had undertaken such preaching with success for two months, but there had been no follow-up.[96]

In 1642 a minority in the Lower Rhine Province thought that a general congregation would be the place to take stronger measures against Jesuits mingling in politics. But this issue did not appear in the Upper German Province, where the confessors had been most active, nor in other provinces.[97] There was much more concern generally with the allied problem of Jesuits being caught up in national feeling and contests among princes, sometimes by their taking up the pen to advance a princely cause. A particular issue for the Lower German Province in 1642 was how Jesuits ought to conduct themselves in cities occupied by the Swedes or the French. Sometimes friends would confide to Jesuits plans to rise up against the occupying forces in consort with a besieging army; not to report this information was considered a crime by the occupying authority.[98] To this Vitelleschi's response was to avoid political conversations with non-Jesuits.

The death of Vitelleschi made it necessary to summon the Eighth General Congregation to elect his successor. Prior to this, provincial congregations were held in the course of 1645, to elect delegates to the general congregation and to submit propositions for the general

[96] Ibid., 66, ff. 141–2', and another memorial in the same sense, f. 139. One conjectures that the chief reason for not openly sending missionaries into Protestant territories of Germany to evangelize the population was that it challenged the right of reformation conceded princes by the Peace of Augsburg and invited an influx of Protestant preachers into Catholic territories. Catholic priests were tolerated or operated clandestinely in some Protestant areas, especially cities; see, for example, Hermann Tüchle, ed. *Acta S.C. de Propaganda Fide Germaniam spectantia: Die Protokolle der Propaganda Congregation zu deutschen Angelegenheiten 1622–1649* (Paderborn, 1962).

[97] Ibid., 69, ff. 249–63, 266; 70, f. 49.

[98] Ibid., 69, f. 272; Duhr 2, 1: 442–3.

congregation or call attention to issues that needed to be addressed. Again, some provincial congregations deplored extreme national feeling. This came out most vigorously in the words of the Upper Rhine Province, which comprised Mainz, a prince-archbishopric devastated by the war. "The most destructive plague of national sentiment appears in some areas to creep in to such a degree that not only does the legislation of the Constitutions and Rules against this vice seem to be minimized and little by little annulled, but also that we can fear that the hatred of kings and princes will be justly directed against us and that sometimes there will be a very great division of hearts within the Society itself."[99] The Austrian Province also sought a solution for exaggerated national sentiment, and it complained of the writings of Jesuits often critical of princes and rulers.[100] The Upper German Provincial Congregation, in which both Vervaux and Wangnereck participated, lamented the manner in which Jesuits often published pieces against each other, sometimes sharply written, to the delight of the heretics.[101] But few showed concern in the provincial congregations about the direct participation of Jesuits in political affairs.

The General Congregation opened in Rome on November 21, 1645. Urban VIII had died in late July 1644, about six months before Vitelleschi. The cardinals elected Giovanni Battista Pamphili his successor on September 15, 1644, and he took the name Innocent X. In sharp contrast with the francophile Urban VIII, Innocent tended to favor the Habsburg powers, especially Spain. He quickly became embroiled in a quarrel with Cardinal Mazarin, who then challenged the legality of his election, and the dispute intensified after Innocent began to prosecute members of the Barberini family for malversation of papal funds. His dispute with France made it impossible for him to mediate the conflict among the states. Furthermore, he was to a greater degree than Urban a canon lawyer who tended to see the negotiations then in progress even more from the juridical perspective of the rights of the church and to be less ready than Urban to recognize, unofficially at least, the need for flexibility.[102]

The new pope surprised the general congregation with an unprecedented action as it convened. Even before the congregation sent the

99 Ibid., 70, f. 89.
100 Ibid., f. 49.
101 Ibid., ff. 65, 67.
102 Konrad Repgen, "Der päpstliche Protest gegen den westfälischen Frieden und die Friedenspolitik Urbans VIII," in id., *Von der Reformation zur Gegenwart: Beiträge zu Grundfragen der neuzeitlichen Geschichte*, eds. Klaus Gotto and Hans Günter Hockerts (Paderborn, 1988), 50–2.

vicar general of the Society to seek the usual papal blessing, the pope summoned him and presented him with a list of eighteen questions that the delegates were to consider before they elected the new superior general.[103] This was a sharp break with the normal procedure, which called for the election of a new superior general before taking up any other business. Francisco Aguado, one of the Spanish delegates, persuaded the fathers to remonstrate with the pope, but Innocent refused to alter his directives.[104]

Innocent's questions required that the delegates reevaluate elements of the Constitutions themselves, such as the life term of the superior general, the interval between general congregations, and the manner of selecting provincial and local superiors. The item that interests us was the second on the list: The fathers were to consider whether Jesuits observed to the full the canons and their own Constitutions regarding involvement in secular affairs. The congregation dutifully appointed deputations or committees to take up each of the pope's questions. In any event, the pertinent committee and then the congregation itself only recommended more-complete adherence to present legislation regarding political activity, but the opinions drawn up by some delegates reveal a range of thinking on the issue.

Nearly all the surviving twenty opinions stated that there was no need for any new legislation or regulation.[105] What was required was a diligent execution of the norms laid down in the Constitutions and in decrees of former congregations and in the Instruction for Confessors of Princes. This amounted to a criticism of Vitelleschi, but it failed to take into consideration the circumstances in which he found himself. The delegates frequently distinguished, as did many of the documents, between secular affairs, which involved more properly political activity or "reason of state," and other secular matters, such as assisting family or friends in legal matters or interceding with princes on behalf of family or benefactors, which was a regular practice of Vitelleschi himself. Mingling in political affairs was considered the more serious offense, though the two types of activity often shaded into each other. The Society's

[103] Who was behind this papal action is not completely clear. One person who was clearly involved was the Jesuit Melchior Inchofer, a native of Vienna who taught for many years at the Roman College. Drafts of his letters to the pope highly critical of Vitelleschi and Sangria – he wrote of the "monarchy" of Vitelleschi – and questioning the life term of the superior general, are found in ARSJ, Cong. 20d. Inchofer was severely disciplined by Carafa in 1648, and he died that same year. See Antonio Astraín, *Historia de la Compañía de Jesús* 5 (Madrid, 1916): 266, n. 2.

[104] Ibid., 264–71.

[105] These opinions are found in ARSJ, Cong. 20c. Some are very brief, others extensive; some are individual statements, and others represent a province or even an assistancy.

documents should be shown to the pope, wrote Forer, and he should be asked to provide specific instances of their violation. If he could supply them, then violators should be punished; if he could not name individuals, then it would be clear that Jesuits were being falsely charged. Councillors often blamed Jesuits, especially confessors, for unpopular actions, he attested, in order to divert ill will from themselves. But Forer himself, perhaps understandably, cited no concrete instances.[106]

The three delegates from the Austrian Province, including the provincial Turcovich, asserted blandly in a joint opinion that it had always been the mind of the Society to remain apart from secular affairs. The new superior general should be instructed to carry out the legislation already in place.[107] Bartholomew Jacquinot, whom we have met as provincial of the Province of Paris, said nearly the same and cited the relevant Jesuit documents. Francisco Barreto from Cochin China called for better observance of current legislation but added "with proper respect, however, for princes upon whom in their realms the Society depends for its continued existence."[108] So he raised a point taken up by seven delegates from various provinces in a joint opinion: Participation in politics was often requested or imposed on Jesuits by princes and rulers who wanted to make use of their services. It sometimes was difficult to refuse them because of the Society's dependence upon them for support for its ministries, as Nuno da Cunho of Portugal implied in a separate opinion.[109] The seven recommended that the superior general be deprived of the power to grant dispensations allowing Jesuits to participate in political affairs and that the pope be asked to intervene to prevent princes from requiring their services. Yet they, too, seemed to allow for some exceptions.[110] Aguado, who had the case of Salazar in mind, was among those who wanted the congregation to prohibit the superior general from granting dispensations.[111] In fact, we have found no examples of Vitelleschi granting a formal dispensation to participate in political affairs because he did not think it necessary when religion was at issue and because he came to recognize that conscience and politics frequently overlapped as he indicated to Vervaux.[112] Occasionally, he did show uncertainty when he recommended Italian noblemen to

106 ARSJ, Cong. 20c, ff. 600–1.
107 Ibid., f. 589.
108 Ibid., ff. 553–3′; 554.
109 Ibid., f. 564.
110 Ibid., f. 559.
111 Ibid., ff. 558–8′.
112 Vitelleschi sometimes did grant dispensations to confessors of princes regarding residence in a Jesuit community or administration of funds, but this does not touch directly on the issue of involvement in politics.

the northern courts, but in these cases his desire to maintain the goodwill of benefactors and friends usually prevailed.

Most realistic in his assessment was Nicasius Widuman, provincial of Upper Germany and thus the superior of Vervaux and Wangnereck. He questioned whether it was possible to forbid Jesuits to become involved in the affairs of princes, including those related to reason of state, such as treaties of peace, especially with heretics; the imposition and relaxation of taxes; the banishment of heretics from Catholic churches and territories; princely alliances; and arrangement of marriages. Was it not permitted to court confessors and theologians to give their opinions in such matters, both privately and publicly in the prince's council, because these were all matters of conscience? Does this mean that Jesuits cannot undertake missions when princes ask them or even require them to do so in the above matters – Maximilian had sent Vervaux to Paris in the spring of 1645 with Widumann's enthusiastic support – especially when the conversion of heretics and the spiritual good of subjects are advanced thereby? Widuman realized the intimate connection of religious and political matters, all touching conscience, that many of his fellow delegates failed to acknowledge. What were we to do when we could not refuse these services without seriously offending rulers? This certainly had been Vitelleschi's view. Widuman was less tolerant of Jesuit involvement in the promotion of private interests for families or benefactors, though here, too, he seemed to allow room for advancing these with princes who were sympathetic to Jesuit goals and purposes, and Jesuits certainly did do so. All these matters, he recommended, should be brought up for discussion after the election of the superior general. "At the present time, however, it seems best that the congregation ask the Supreme Pontiff humbly, that His Holiness deign to state his complaints, if he has any against the Society in the matter at hand, and in particular to make clear what matters especially ought not to be taken up by the Society."[113]

In their formal response to Innocent X, the fathers of the congregation declared that it was their unanimous view "that the men of our Society should refrain from secular affairs foreign to the sacred canons and to our Constitutions but that whatever can be prescribed in this matter has been decreed by previous general congregations." They indicated the main features of the Jesuit legislation, and they called attention in particular to the Instruction for the Confessors of Princes, which prohibited confessors "from becoming involved in external and political matters, but [directed them] to attend only to those matters which had to do with

[113] Ibid., 596–8.

and pertained to the prince's conscience," without adverting at all to the connection between matters of conscience and political affairs that was at the root of the difficulty. They also pointed to the requirement that before a Jesuit accepted a position of confessor to a prince he was to show the Instruction to the prince and secure the prince's acceptance of its terms. As we know, this was not always the case in practice. All that was needed, the congregation maintained, was observance of the legislation in place. After the election of the superior general, the fathers affirmed, they would discuss remedies for failures to carry out the current directives. They concluded by asserting that sometimes those who complained of Jesuit involvement in political matters wished to transfer blame from themselves to the Society and that at other times Jesuits were virtually compelled to carry out the orders of princes, which they could not easily refuse.[114] Pope Innocent did not urge the matter further; he failed to mention it in his response to the Jesuits of January 1, 1646.[115]

The congregation then proceeded to the election of the superior general. On January 7 its choice fell on Vincenzo Carafa, then provincial of Naples with a reputation for preaching as well as for personal holiness of life. Subsequently, the fathers devoted most of their attention to the modifications of the Society's government urged by Innocent. But from February 21 to 26 the issue of Jesuit involvement in secular affairs returned as a topic for discussion, but the delegates seem to have realized the impossibility of promulgating a detailed decree,[116] and in fact they left the matter up to the new superior general. Shortly after his election Carafa, in a circular letter to the whole Society titled "On the Means of Conserving the Society's Primitive Spirit," emphasized the need to refrain from "the business of the world and temporal matters," citing the Gospel passage where Jesus refused to serve as a judge (Luke 12, 14), and he cautioned Jesuits from allowing themselves to be dragged into these matters by others, even by princes. But he did not mention politics or matters of state any more specifically.[117] He was going to take a harder line than Vitelleschi.

Like his predecessor, Carafa came from an aristocratic family. He belonged to the renowned Neapolitan Carafas who had produced leaders of church and state, including the formidable Pope Paul IV in the sixteenth century. His mother and his father stemmed from different branches of the family. His maternal great-grandfather had received the

114 Ibid., 497–7'.
115 Constitution of Innocent X, Jan. 1, 1646, *Institutum Societatis Jesu* (Florence, 1892) 1: 177–9.
116 ARSJ, Cong. 1c, 136–41 (nearly illegible notes).
117 *Epistolae praepositorum generalium Societatis Jesu* 1 (Ghent, 1847): 463, 465.

title prince of Stigliano back in 1522 from Charles V. In 1580 his mother Maria at age fourteen married Fabrizio Carafa, duke of Andria and head of his branch of the family. Their marriage was not a happy one, and her husband was murdered in 1590, leaving her a widow at age twenty-five. Meanwhile, she had given birth to three sons, the third of whom, Vincenzo, was born on May 9, 1585. Unusual piety had characterized the young woman, and in 1608 she entered the Dominican Convent of Santa Maria della Sapienza in Naples, where she died in 1618 with a reputation for sanctity.[118]

Vincenzo's mother gave him a careful religious upbringing, and he entered the Jesuit novitiate in Naples in 1604. After his ordination, the Society entrusted him with the direction of the Congregation of Nobles, which was associated with the professed house in Naples. In this position he worked to expand the congregation's works of charity. Gradually, he served in different positions of Jesuit government: novice master, rector of the college in Naples, three times superior of the professed house there, and then provincial of the Neapolitan Province. The general congregation elected him superior general on its first ballot in 1646.[119] In Naples the popular celebration of his election lasted for three days.[120]

118 Biagio Aldemari, *Historia genealogica della famiglia Carafa* 2 (Naples, 1691): 381–4.

119 Daniello Bartoli, *Della vita del Vincenzo Carafa, settimo generale della Compagnia di Gesu* (Rome, 1651), 3–12, 27, 40–2, 52, 57–8.

120 Nithard Biber, S.J., to Anselm Casimir, Elector of Mainz, Rome, Jan. 20, 1646, Georg Hansen, "Briefe des Jesuitenpaters Nithard Biber an den Churfürsten Anselm Casimir von Mainz, geschrieben auf seiner Romreise 1645/46," *Archivalische Zeitschrift*, new series 9 (1900), 54.

CHAPTER 8

Carafa and the Struggle over the Peace of Westphalia, 1645–1649

THE formal conclusion of the Peace of Westphalia in the town hall of Münster on October 24, 1648, ended the seemingly endless Thirty Years War. Long years of negotiations preceded the event. The Treaty of Hamburg of December 25, 1641, among the emperor, Spain, France, and Sweden transferred negotiations from Cologne and Hamburg to the two Westphalian towns, about thirty miles apart, Münster and Osnabrück. Representatives of France, Spain, and the Catholic states assembled in the former, those of Sweden and its Protestant allies in the latter. The emperor maintained a delegation in both cities. Slowing the process were the hopes of the negotiators during the winter months each year for the improvement of their military fortunes in the following summer campaigns. But gradually, the French, the Swedes, and their allies prevailed in the field. Delegations began to appear in the second half of 1643, but the Congress of Westphalia did not formally open until December 4, 1644, with a Mass and procession. Not until June 11 of the next year did the French and Swedish delegates submit their formal proposals, to which the imperials responded on the following September 25.[1] Meanwhile, on August 29, 1645, the German territorial states obtained the right to make war and peace (*jus belli ac pacis*) and with it the right to participate fully in the conference. This signaled a major victory for French policy that aimed at weakening the Habsburg emperor's position in the empire. It also gave the conference the additional character of an imperial diet. A crucial date was November 30, 1645, when the imperial plenipotentiary, Trautmannsdorf, arrived in Münster with the authority to make widespread concessions for the sake of peace. By the time he departed in June 1647, nearly all the issues regarding the religious settlement in Germany had been resolved.[2]

[1] Ronald G. Asch, *The Thirty Years War: The Holy Roman Empire and Europe, 1618–1648* (New York, 1997), 134.
[2] Geoffrey Parker, ed., *The Thirty Years War*, 2nd ed. (London, 1997), 155, 160.

The strategies of Ferdinand III and Maximilian remained roughly consistent throughout the negotiations. The emperor aimed to conciliate Sweden and the German Protestant states in order to split Sweden from France and then to unite the German states, both Catholic and Protestant, with the German and Spanish Habsburgs in order to obtain a favorable peace or to continue the war with the common Habsburg enemy, France. To this end Ferdinand and his minister Trautmannsdorf were ready to make substantial concessions on religious issues to the Protestants. The Bavarian elector, while honoring his obligations toward the emperor, looked first to an arrangement with Catholic France for himself and the Catholic ecclesiastical states, which he considered more likely to guarantee his position in the Palatinate and, generally, the Catholic position in the empire. So Maximilian was initially less ready to make religious concessions than Ferdinand but more inclined to surrender Habsburg lands in the west of the empire to France. From March to September 1647, compelled by the suffering of his people and the ravagement of his territory, he concluded an armistice with France and Sweden, which, however, did not bring the anticipated benefits. France for its part was determined to drive a wedge between the two Habsburg powers, the emperor and Spain, and it ultimately succeeded in doing so. The emperor's decision in late September 1648, under persistent pressure from Maximilian and other German princes, to make a separate peace with France removed the final obstacle to the settlement. France and Spain continued to war for another eleven years.

The Congress of Westphalia stands out as the first general European peace conference, and it resulted in the first general European peace settlement. All the major European states except England and Russia participated, as did many of the medium-sized and smaller states, including those of the empire and Italy. Altogether 176 plenipotentiaries acting for 194 European rulers, many with extensive entourages, crowded into the two Westphalian towns. The French delegation with roughly 200 men, women, and children outstripped the others. Delegates, of course, communicated regularly if slowly with their home courts or governments, letters to Paris or Vienna taking ten to twelve days, to Madrid twenty-three to thirty days.[3]

Many delegates gathered regularly at the Jesuit college in Münster for informal conferences or entertainment. This gave local Jesuits the opportunity to mingle with them. Delegates of the Catholic states frequently conferred there, and Protestant as well as Catholic envoys attended student theater productions. Early in the course of the congress a member

[3] Ibid., 159.

of the imperial entourage suggested to Vienna that Gans be encouraged to convince Jesuit superiors not to permit such frequent public performances at the college because the French attended regularly, the Spaniards stayed away, and the imperials did likewise to show their sympathy for the Spaniards.[4] In 1646 the students of rhetoric designed a booklet with anagrams for the names of all the delegates Protestant and Catholic in which they expressed their longing for peace.[5]

The contest between the militants and moderates among the Catholics and within the Society of Jesus persisted during the negotiations. The moderates prevailed at the crucial Catholic courts of Vienna and Munich, and their predominance was no longer seriously threatened. But the militants kept up a spirited rearguard action and often obtained a majority when the German Catholic states met separately because of the large number of delegates from ecclesiastical states. They were well represented at the congress, even though Augsburg's Heinrich von Knöringen had died. Among their leaders were Maximilian's cousin, Franz Wilhelm von Wartenberg, who was bishop of Osnabrück and Minden, both occupied by the Swedes at the time; Adam Adami, Benedictine prior of Murrhart, who represented a number of abbeys in Württemberg and environs that were likely to lose their lands as a result of the amnesty; and Dr. Johann Leuxelring, representative of the bishop of Augsburg, a number of Swabian imperial cities, including Dinkelsbühl and Rottweil, and the Swabian imperial counts. Often in league with them and probably influenced by them was Fabio Chigi, later Pope Alexander VII, erstwhile nuncio in Cologne and now extraordinary nuncio for the peace conference. Having arrived in, for him, dreary and depressing Münster in 1644, he remained until 1650, and he often proved to be an effective mediator between the Habsburg powers and France while holding to the juridical position of the papacy on religious issues.[6]

The rector of the Jesuit college at the start of the congress, Johann Schucking, seems to have kept his politics to himself.[7] But his successor, Gottfried Cörler, did not do so. He identified with the Catholic extremists yet was a frequent guest to dinner in the quarters of an imperial delegate Johann Maximilian von Lamberg.[8] In late February 1647 Carafa informed the provincial superior of the Lower Rhine Province

[4] Johann Weikard Auerspurg, Osnabrück, to Ferdinand Kurz von Senftenau, Vienna, July 7, 1644, APW 2, A, 1: *Die kaiserlichen Korrespondenzen 1643–1644* (Münster, 1969), no. 317: 526.

[5] Ludwig Steinberger, *Die Jesuiten und die Friedensfrage in der Zeit vom Prager Frieden bis zum Nürnberger Friedensexekutionshauptrezess, 1635–1659* (Freiburg, 1906), 54.

[6] See APW 3, C, 1, *Diarium Chigi, 1639–1651* 1: *Text*, ed. Konrad Repgen (Münster, 1984).

[7] Steinberger, 55.

[8] APW 3, C, 4: *Diarium Lamberg 1645–1649*, ed. Herta Hageneder (Münster, 1986).

that word had reached him that Cörler had publicly criticized prospective terms of the peace. If this were true, the provincial was to impose a public penance on the rector and remind all the Jesuits that the Society prohibited public discussion and even more so criticism of the actions of princes, whatever advice one might give in the private interior forum. Such public statements could stir up a storm for the Society.[9] A later Carafa letter criticized excessive socializing with the delegates. The superior general then explained to Cörler himself what improper involvement in "matters of war and peace" meant. It did not restrict consultation in confession, but it forbade public discussion of such issues or writing on them – by this time Jesuits were writing on the issues, as we shall see – and it required great circumspection in private discussions.[10] This was certainly a tighter interpretation than Vitelleschi's.

One unnamed Jesuit, probably Johannes Mulmann, helped bring together early in the negotiations the Spanish delegate, Diego Saavedra Fajardo, with José Fontanella, representative of the Catalans then in rebellion against Spain with French support. But Saavedra soon sought another middleman because, as he wrote back to Spain, religious do not keep secrets well and the Jesuits are extremely hesitant to engage in activity harmful to the interests of France because of their fear of expulsion from that kingdom.[11]

When Trautmannsdorf arrived in Münster at the end of November 1645, he carried with him a secret instruction that Ferdinand III had drawn up in his own hand.[12] Trautmannsdorf's goal according to the instruction was to unite the German estates, Protestant and Catholic, and then to make peace with the two crowns, Sweden and France, or, if necessary, continue the war with them. To secure this goal, Ferdinand allowed his minister considerable latitude for concessions, but only gradually and some only at the point of absolute necessity. Trautmannsdorf, for example, was to insist on the maintenance of the Ecclesiastical Reservation for

9 Carafa to Gottfried Otterstedt (provincial), Feb. 27, 1647, Steinberger, Document 5: 197.

10 Carafa to Otterstedt (provincial), Oct. 26, 1647, cited in Steinberger, 88; Carafa to Cörler, May 23, 1648, ibid, Document 9: 199. That same day Carafa directed the provincial Otterstedt that Jesuits were to be prohibited from engaging in planning or plotting to expel forces of either side from places then held by princes "under whom God has placed us. Our task is to treat of spiritual things and through them to lead all men according to their capacity to the love of God. So let each [Jesuit] observe carefully what Rule 43 of the Summary prescribes, to embrace in the Lord with a universal love all parties even those at odds with one another." May 23, 1647, ARSJ, Rhen. Inf. 81, f. 73.

11 Saavedra Fajardo to Philip IV, Mar. 19, 1644, *Correspondencia diplomático de los plenipotenciarios españoles en el Congeso de Münster* 1 (Madrid, 1884): 56.

12 Oct. 16, 1646, APW, 1: *Instruktionen* 1: *Frankreich, Schweden, Kaiser* (Münster, 1962): no. 29: 440–52.

the future, that is, not to surrender any ecclesiastical territories then in possession of the Catholics and to guarantee their future existence. But the minister was given broad scope to give up Catholic claims to ecclesiastical territories, mostly in the north and northwest, that the Protestants currently held, most already for many years. Trautmannsdorf was also empowered to grant French demands in the west of the empire, first Alsace, then Breisach, and in case of extreme necessity, the Breisgau. Though many delegates knew of the existence of this instruction, its contents remained hidden from most.

Early in February 1646 while the Jesuit general congregation was still in session, the newly elected Carafa beseeched both Gans in Linz, where Ferdinand III then kept court, and Vervaux in Munich to encourage their princes to stand firm and not to compromise the Ecclesiastical Reservation even in the face of such desperate conditions. "A peace which will enslave souls is worse than any war," he wrote, "and the ruin of souls is more to be avoided than that of bodies. It is evident to Your Reverence the innumerable evils that would come over the church [should concessions be made], nor are there arguments lacking for protecting piety and the Catholic religion to suggest to a most pious and religious prince."[13]

Probably some fathers in Rome or, more likely, figures in the papal curia persuaded Carafa to write this letter after rumors about Trautmannsdorf's instruction reached there. It remained vague on specifics, apart from mention of the Ecclesiastical Reservation, which Ferdinand had no intention of abandoning for the future anyway. Only in this single instance did Carafa seem to take sides between the moderates and the militants or even to deal at all with the substance of the issues at the peace conference.

Later in February Ferdinand sent two long instructions to Trautmannsdorf in which he elaborated a more detailed program of possible concessions.[14] The minister was to hold firm on the Ecclesiastical Reservation for the future, but he might accept 1627 as the normative year for the possession of ecclesiastical lands and privileges and thus the surrender of the ecclesiastical territories held by the Protestants at that time. Furthermore, they might be yielded until Catholics and Protestants reached a general agreement on religious issues, which meant indefinitely or permanently. This went beyond the Peace of Prague, where similar concessions had been made only for forty years and so remained

[13] Carafa to Gans, Feb. 3, 1646, ARSJ, Aust. 5II, f. 1019. A notation in the register indicates that a similar letter was sent to Vervaux.

[14] Ferdinand to Trautmannsdorf, Linz, Feb. 27, 1646, APW 2, A, 3: *Die kaiserlichen Korrespondenzen 1645–1646*, nos. 177 and 178: 279–311, 311–26; see also p. xxi.

at least in theory provisional. The permanence and thus the finality of the concessions remained a stumbling block for many Catholics.

Prior to these instructions Gans and Quiroga approved the position as well as the inclusion of Calvinists in the peace, a concession that had been sanctioned once already at Regensburg in 1641. The two theologians insisted on the right of reform of religion for each imperial territory as in the Peace of Augsburg; this ensured the emperor the full determination of religion in his hereditary lands.[15] Trautmannsdorf in a visit to Wartenberg in Münster explained in simple fashion the rationale for the concessions. Only in this way, given the desperate military situation, could one retain the ecclesiastical territories that the Catholics still held.[16] But at this time Bavaria was not yet ready to agree to a permanent surrender of the ecclesiastical states held by the Protestants in 1627, preferring to stick with the Peace of Prague. Papal permission was thought to be needed for a permanent renunciation. Vervaux had a hand in the formulation of this stance.[17]

The imperial theologians reiterated on April 27 their position on the permissibility of permanent concessions, which Ferdinand, they argued, could make with or without the consent of the Catholic states.[18] Mainz soon came over to the imperial position, as did Maximilian, if only fitfully and reluctantly, after learning of Ferdinand's positive response to France's territorial designs in Alsace and becoming aware of the approval of the imperial and Mainz theologians.[19] Discussion of the issue among the Catholics continued on and off until late November. On November 30, 1646, Trautmannsdorf issued a formal declaration for the Protestants to the effect that Ferdinand was now prepared to make concessions on the basis of 1624 as the normative date, thus giving the Protestants a further advantage and yielding permanently fourteen ecclesiastical territories, all of which were then in Protestant possession,

15 "Judicium Theologorum Caesareorum ratione mediorum pro compositione gravaminum," Linz, Feb. 16, summarized in APW, ibid., no. 180: 328, n. 3. A third theologian signed this memorandum, Thomas von Saxius, whom neither the editor nor I can identify. This memorandum was sent to Trautmannsdorf for his attention before the two instructions; see Trautmannsdorf to Ferdinand III, Münster, Feb. 27, 1646, pp. 326–8.

16 Mar. 26, 1646, APW 3, C, 3: *Diarium Wartenberg 1644–1648*, ed. Joachim Foerster (Münster, 1988), 1: 423.

17 Dieter Albrecht, *Maximilian I. von Bayern, 1573–1651* (Munich, 1998), 1034; Gerhard Immler, *Kurfürst Maximilian und der westfälische Friedenskongress: Die bayerische auswärtige Politik von 1644 bis zum Ulmer Waffenstillstand* (Münster, 1992), 290.

18 May 6, 1646, APW 3, C, 2: *Diarium Volmar 1643–1649*, eds. Joachim Foerster and Roswitha Philippe 2 (Münster, 1984): 619, citing the memorandum of the imperial theologians of April 27. Dr. Isaak Volmar was the chief imperial negotiator at Münster.

19 Albrecht, 1035–6, but see Bernhard Duhr, *Geschichte der Jesuiten in den Ländern deutscher Zunge* 2 (Freiburg, 1913), 1: 478–81, on Mainz's continued hesitation.

and admitting their administrators to a seat and a vote in the diet.[20] These were to be the terms of the eventual peace. The two electors, Maximilian and Anselm Casimir of Mainz, supported the imperial position, as did the important Franconian bishops of Würzburg and Bamberg, and the elector of Cologne followed a little later. But the militant party continued to oppose the concessions vigorously, eventually inciting a heated pamphlet war.

In contrast to his predecessor Lamormaini as imperial confessor, Gans carried on scarcely any correspondence regarding ecclesiastico-political matters with Carafa. But his behavior at court had long concerned superiors. Charges arrived in Rome of excessive eating and drinking, inappropriate socializing, and neglect of the vow of poverty. In September 1646, after receiving a list of Gans's defects from the provincial superior Turcovich, Carafa followed Turcovich's advice. He sent a letter to Ferdinand, which Turcovich was to deliver and explain to the emperor.[21] Many complaints had reached him, Carafa wrote Ferdinand, as they had his predecessor, about the conduct of Gans; details would be supplied by the provincial if necessary. "For the spiritual good of the father in question, the integrity of the whole order, and that Your Imperial Majesty may be served blamelessly by us, I humbly beseech [Your Imperial Majesty] that you allow him to be recalled from the court where he is endangered [spiritually] and be placed under religious discipline in our colleges, where he will be better looked after." Carafa offered the emperor any Jesuit he desired as a replacement.

Turcovich judged Carafa's letter to be unsuitable, and so the superior general directed a second one to Ferdinand in mid-November in which he did not mention the defects of Gans but explained that the confessor's involvement in so many affairs distracted him unduly; his spiritual growth required his removal from court and life under the discipline of a college.[22]

Carafa's communication must have reached Ferdinand before Turcovich took the matter up personally with the emperor. This caused a problem. Ferdinand obviously did not want to let Gans depart. The

[20] Albrecht, 1037–41. The ecclesiastical territories were the archbishoprics Magdeburg and Bremen and the bishoprics Verden, Halberstadt, Meissen, Naumburg, Merseburg, Lebus, Brandenburg, Havelberg, Lübeck, Kamin, Schwerin, and Ratzeburg. Minden was added shortly thereafter, and a deal was struck over Osnabrück whereby Catholics and Protestants would alternate as prince-bishops.

[21] Carafa to Ferdinand III, Sept. 15, 1646, ARSJ, Germ. 113a, f. 73; Carafa to Turcovich (provincial), Sept. 15, 1646, ARSJ, Aust. 5II, f. 1062.

[22] Carafa to Ferdinand III, Nov. 17, 1646, ARSJ, Germ. 113a, f. 76; Carafa to Turcovich (provincial), Nov. 17, 1646, ARSJ, Aust. 5II, f. 1068.

complaints against the confessor did not originate because of his position regarding the negotiations at Münster. But Ferdinand may have wanted to retain Gans because of his sympathetic theological evaluation of the concessions to the Protestants. In any event, Carafa now thought that the best way to proceed was to induce Gans to resign on his own.[23]

But the matter of Gans soon became known at court. He clearly was not inclined to resign. Carafa wrote directly to the confessor, admitting that he may have acted precipitously on the complaints against him, and he explained that he had always intended to keep the whole matter confidential. He even instructed Turcovich to punish any Jesuit who may have revealed Carafa's intention. After a talk with Turcovich, Gans promised improvement, and this satisfied Carafa for the time being.[24]

Carafa's contacts with the Bavarian confessor Vervaux were much more regular and dealt with many more issues than in the case of Gans in Vienna. When Vervaux heard from Carafa in February 1646 expressing alarm about rumored concessions to the Protestants in the empire, he assured the superior general that there would be no liberty of religion permitted in the emperor's hereditary lands and that the Ecclesiastical Reservation would be maintained, and so he lessened Carafa's fears. Gans had not answered Carafa in any detail.[25]

Later that year Carafa declined Vervaux's request, evidently supported by Maximilian, to be allowed to participate in council meetings. Papal pressure to reduce Jesuit activity in political affairs may have induced Carafa to adopt this strict position. Vitelleschi, it will be recalled, allowed Vervaux to be present at the meetings but not to speak or vote. According to Carafa, the Seventh General Congregation of 1615 had "laxly enough" interpreted the Fifth General Congregation's (1593/94) prohibition of involvement in political affairs. "I would judge Your Reverence to be content with this broad scope [that he already had]," he wrote, "and not to agree that a greater laxity be sought, certainly because business and other similar [matters] ... are prohibited so gravely and severely to Ours." This amounted to a criticism of Vitelleschi's practice. Carafa hoped that Vervaux would understand his

[23] Carafa to Turcovich (provincial), Jan. 19, 1647, ARSJ, Aust. 5II, f. 1078.

[24] Carafa to Gans, Feb. 9, 1647, Aust. 5II, f. 1082; Carafa to Turcovich (provincial), Feb. 9, 1647, ibid., f. 1083.

[25] Carafa to Vervaux, Apr. 24, 1646, ARSJ, Germ. Sup. 8, f. 117. Vervaux did not indicate in what sense the Ecclesiastical Reservation would be maintained, whether only for those ecclesiastical territories then in Catholic hands or for others then in Protestant hands. Precisely at this time the issue was being negotiated. Gans did respond to Carafa's letter; but judging from Carafa's further response, he did not comment on the issues at hand; see Carafa to Gans, Mar. 24 and Apr. 21, 1646, ARSJ, Aust. 5II, ff. 1027, 1033.

position and thought that Maximilian surely would if it was explained to him. To the elector he offered one thousand Masses and Rosaries for himself, for his family, and for the happy outcome of his efforts for the defense and propagation of the faith.[26]

But this by no means ended the matter. To Vervaux's response Carafa agreed that the confessor could indeed counsel Maximilian privately outside confession for the direction of his conscience but that he could not attend council meetings.[27] Carafa would soon discover that Vervaux was attending these meetings with Vitelleschi's earlier approval.

Maximilian now intervened personally, asking that Vervaux be permitted to participate in meetings of the privy council, hear the views of the councillors, and then give his own opinion, "within the limits of his religious vocation." Carafa confessed to the prince that he found himself in a difficult situation; he wanted to accede to a request from Maximilian, but he was pledged to uphold the Society's directives. He explained to the elector that to yield to his request would cause "great prejudice" to the Society, and this for three reasons. First, it would seriously violate the Society's decrees. The preservation and apostolic fruitfulness of any religious order, for the prince, his people, and the church, depended upon fidelity to its laws. The Society had prohibited, under pain of the most serious ecclesiastical penalties, "that any of Ours become involved in matters of state or participate in public councils dealing with them." Even though Maximilian's confessor spoke in council only on matters of conscience, people would not make this distinction, and so the whole Society, not just one member, would be exposed to the tongues of ill-wishers, as often did happen. Second, other princes would want to make use of Jesuits in a similar fashion, but without the restraint of Maximilian, thus dragging the Jesuits further into politics. Finally, many decisions unpopular with the people or with other princes were frequently taken in council, for which the Society would have to bear the odium. Certainly, Maximilian could consult his confessor privately as often as he wanted for the direction of his conscience. Furthermore, there were many outstanding theologians who were secular priests whom the prince might consult. Carafa seemed to be suggesting an arrangement similar to the practice in Vienna, where Gans had little influence, and he indicated that he had recently come to such an agreement with the Republic of Genoa.

But after making his argument, Carafa backed off from a confrontation with a prince of Maximilian's authority who so generously supported

[26] Carafa to Vervaux, Nov. 3, 1646, ARSJ, Germ. Sup. 8, f. 73'. This letter is extremely difficult to read because of disintegrating paper as well as the script.

[27] Carafa to Vervaux, Jan. 19, 1647, ibid., f. 80'.

the Society. If the elector still persisted in his desire that Vervaux be present at council sessions, the superior general would yield to such a great prince, but he then "most humbly beseeched" the prince that the confessor not be compelled to give his opinion in the presence of the others, but to explain it privately to the prince so that only a little of the resentment that might follow a decision fall upon the Jesuits.[28] That Carafa was not completely happy with this arrangement emerged from his letter to Johann Sigersreitter, rector of the college in Munich. He realized that he had been caught between a rock and a hard place (*scopulos*), and he asked the rector to urge Vervaux to have Maximilian consult others on questions that were dangerous and potentially harmful to the Society's standing with other princes.[29]

Maximilian then did broaden the circle of those he consulted on the negotiations then in progress with France to include more Jesuits. He also accepted the proposal of Carafa for the activity of Vervaux in the future; the confessor was to listen in on meetings of the privy council, but then to give his own moral evaluation to the prince privately. This gratified the superior general.[30]

But renewed complaints about Vervaux reached Rome after March 14, 1647, when Maximilian broke with the emperor and signed at Ulm an armistice with France and Sweden. One source of complaint was the confessor of the elector of Mainz, Nithard Biber.[31] Carafa cited verbatim for Vervaux the words of an unnamed prince, undoubtedly the elector of Mainz, transmitted by Biber: "The Most Serene Elector of Bavaria was leaning in the council and on the point of remaining with the emperor, and the councillors were comfortable with this, when the prince of demons led the prince's confessor along with the whole synagogue of Jesuits from Munich to Wasserburg, where the Most Serene [Prince] resided. There they persuaded the Most Serene Elector that he was not only permitted in conscience but obligated [to break with the emperor]." Vervaux was the culprit. This account was to be heard in all the major

[28] Carafa to Maximilian, Apr. 20, 1647, ARSJ, Germ. 113a, ff. 93–5. At nearly the same time, Carafa confronted the same issue with the Jesuit Albert Kurz, rector of the college in Neuburg an der Donau, confidant of Duke Wolfgang William, and brother of Ferdinand Kurz von Senftenau, Ferdinand III's minister, and Maximilian Kurz von Senftenau, Maximilian's councillor. There had been complaints that Kurz took part in sessions of the council where he presented his views. With reference to the same decrees of general congregations that he cited with Vervaux, he made it clear that he could in no way permit this activity, and he reminded Kurz of the problems it often brought the Society. See Carafa to Kurz, Feb. 16, 1647, and Jan. 25, 1648, ARSJ, Germ. Sup. 8, ff. 82, 128.

[29] Carafa to Sigersreitter (rector), July 27, 1647, ibid., ff. 103'–4.

[30] Carafa to Vervaux, June 15, 1647, ARSJ, Germ. Sup. 8, 100.

[31] Carafa to Biber (Frankfurt), May 4, 1647, ARSJ, Rhen. Sup. 2, f. 37.

German courts, Carafa related, and it brought down upon the Society every sort of curse and obloquy. Friends of the Society wanted to know whether it was true and how the Jesuits would defend themselves against charges of this political involvement so inconsistent with their Institute.

Other news seemed to confirm this charge. Two years before – it was right at the time when Vitelleschi died – Carafa only now learned, Vervaux had undertaken a mission to Paris to pursue a separate peace treaty for Maximilian, to the harm of the emperor and the German princes. Given Vervaux's virtue, the superior general continued sounding like Vitelleschi; he believed him to be innocent, but how was he to exculpate Vervaux and, indeed, the whole Society with others?[32]

What role did Vervaux actually have in the armistice signed at Ulm in March 1647? Maximilian's efforts at an understanding with France dated back to the 1620s, when Contzen had vigorously advocated one. French failure to rescue him at the time of Gustavus Adolphus's invasion disillusioned the elector in the 1630s, but he began to look westward again in the 1640s, seeing in an arrangement with France the best way to secure peace for a war-torn Bavaria, assert his interest in the Palatinate, and benefit the German Catholics. He hoped to incorporate the emperor in any such agreement, but if this were not possible, because of Ferdinand's unwillingness to break with Spain or any other reason, then he would proceed without him. Vervaux's mission to Paris in 1645 produced few concrete results, but Maximilian maintained contacts with France through the nuncio in Paris Niccolò Guidi di Bagno.[33] At an extraordinary meeting of the privy council on September 15, 1645, where Maximilian himself, his brother Prince Albrecht, and Vervaux were all present, the majority, including Vervaux, voted to continue the war rather than to seek an armistice, but the council was divided.[34] There was great hesitation to act without the emperor. That fall the military situation began to look up for the elector, and Trautmannsdorf was preparing to set out for Münster. In spring and summer of 1646 the imperial minister accepted territorial concessions to France in the west, and progress was made on the empire's religious issues.

Then late summer and fall saw a drastic deterioration in the field. French and Swedish troops overran large portions of western Bavaria, and the imperial army under Archduke Leopold Wilhelm performed pitifully.[35] For the second time during the war enemy troops ravaged

32 Carafa to Vervaux, May 4, 1647, ARSJ, Germ. Sup. 8, f. 90'.
33 Immler, 140.
34 Ibid., 126–7.
35 Ibid., 322, 361–2.

Bavaria. On October 9, 1646, Vervaux attended a privy council session at Wasserburg, where the elector had been compelled to move. The confessor found no fault with a separate arrangement with France if a more general agreement including the emperor could not be reached, but the council made no decision about it.[36] But on November 19 the privy council advocated negotiations for a general armistice if possible, otherwise a particular one with France. Vervaux justified the initiative on the grounds that Maximilian was not only permitted but bound in conscience to consider in the first place the welfare of his own subjects if the alternative was to expose himself and them to clear and grave danger, and he stuck to the same position at the meeting of January 12, 1647, when a majority again approved a separate armistice with France.[37] Accounts of these meetings must have leaked out and served as the basis of the charges against Vervaux. Late in January, then, negotiations began in Ulm between Bavarian delegates and those of France and Sweden. Mazarin insisted upon the inclusion of his ally.

One sticky issue arose from the demand of France and Sweden for the surrender of three imperial cities then occupied by the Bavarians: Memmingen, Heilbronn, and Überlingen. Catholic Überlingen raised a special problem because its abandonment to the Lutheran Swedes would endanger the practice of the Catholic faith there. Vervaux initially opposed giving up the cities because of the threat to the faith in Überlingen and also because Maximilian had no legal jurisdiction over the cities as imperial cities.[38] But a distinction was then worked out between the formal surrender of a city and a mere withdrawal of a garrison from it. The latter was permitted, and so the negotiations proceeded. Maximilian's general, Count Gronsfeld, who was in fact spying for Spain, in a letter to a Spanish diplomat referred to this distinction as "devilish *Cabulistik*" on the part of Vervaux, a "rascally and vile traitor." But it is not evident that the confessor was responsible for the distinction.[39]

On March 14, 1647, Maximilian's delegates signed the Treaty of Ulm for him and for his brother, the elector of Cologne, along with the representatives of France, Sweden, and Hesse-Kassel. It called for an armistice among the signatory princes to continue until the conclusion of a general peace. Maximilian and his brother also promised to provide no aid to either the emperor or Spain and to take measures to prevent their demobilized troops from entering the service of either. Another

36 Immler, 355–6; Duhr 2, 1: 480.

37 Immler, 400–1, 475–7; Steinberger, 93. Duhr 2, 1: 480, n. 6 cites comments of Vervaux from the minutes of the November 19 meeting.

38 Immler, 426–9.

39 Ibid., 425, 429–30.

provision required that the Swedes not interfere with Catholic worship in Überlingen.[40]

But there remained the matter of ratification. Maximilian still hesitated. The council was divided; it was not true, as the complaints to Carafa alleged, that all the councillors opposed the armistice. Theologians in Munich quickly produced a theological memorandum that justified the agreement with France. It set aside any reservations about the cities, and it laid the responsibility for the treaty on the emperor for his attachment to Spanish interests, which accounted for his persistent refusal to make peace. Vervaux's part in this is unclear. Fortified with this memorandum, the elector ratified the armistice, but not before he inserted in it a phrase that recognized his obligations to the emperor and the empire. This was clearly a sensitive matter to him.[41]

In a letter to Ferdinand III justifying his action, Maximilian appealed to the position of his theologians, but he did not explicitly accuse the emperor of placing Habsburg above imperial interests. The letter asserted a point made earlier by Vervaux, that the prince had to look to the welfare of his own people. Only with the armistice could he deliver them from the horrors of war. The Bavarian and imperial armies no longer measured up to the task. With regard to the imperial cities, the Bavarian garrisons could not have held out there much longer in any event.[42] The Jesuit poet Jacob Balde, the "German Horace," who stood out among the Munich Jesuits as a Francophile, celebrated the armistice in a long poem, "A Georgic Drama," which was completed by July 25.[43] Dedication was to Claude de Mesmes, count d'Avaux, one of the two French delegates at Münster. In the interest of peace Balde had honored him with a poem the previous year at the behest of a Jesuit friend in Münster. The "Georgic Drama" amounted to an apology for Bavaria. In it there came to the fore themes that we have consistently encountered: the obligation of self-preservation that required the agreement with France and the predominance of Spanish influence at the court of Vienna, which stood in the way of peace.[44]

Vervaux succeeded in clearing himself with Carafa for his part in the armistice, though he may not have been entirely forthright. The superior general obviously inclined to accept the confessor's explanation. He

[40] Ibid., 444–53.
[41] Ibid., 454; Steinberger, 94–5. Two undated and unsigned theological opinions in favor of the treaty with France are found in Munich, Bayerische Staatsbibliothek, Handschriftenabteilung, Cgm. 2613, 2, ff. 129, 129′–32.
[42] Immler, 443.
[43] "Drama Georgicum."
[44] Steinberger, 95–6.

heard gladly from Vervaux that Maximilian had not been led to withdraw his support from the emperor by his "persuasion or instigation."[45] To Biber, who had alerted Carafa to his activities, Vervaux denied the "calumny" circulating about him in Rome. The armistice was not his doing but that "of many other grave men and Doctors of Theology, to whom I had to yield."[46] Carafa for his part assured Biber that Vervaux had "remained within the limits of a director of conscience and had been far from advocating an armistice; much less did he seem to have pronounced the Most Serene Elector obligated [to seek an armistice]."[47] Vervaux was not the only Jesuit to argue in favor of the armistice, but he clearly was one of them to do so.

Maximilian had hoped that the armistice with France would develop into a defensive alliance that would protect him against Sweden and benefit the Catholics in the empire. In March and April 1647, while the armistice was in effect, the Protestant princes and then Sweden accepted Maximilian's retention of the electoral title and the Upper Palatinate and the creation of an eighth electorate for the heir of Frederick of the Palatinate and the return to him of the Lower Palatinate.[48] France had insisted that Sweden be included in the armistice – the Swedes were never enthusiastic about it – and now feared that further negotiations with Bavaria would undermine its relationship with its ally. So the mission that Maximilian sent to Paris in May returned empty handed. In other words, Sweden was much more important to Mazarin than Bavaria and its Catholic allies. By this time the electorates of Brandenburg, Saxony, and Trier had all withdrawn from the war. By July the Bavarian elector realized that the armistice would not likely lead him further in this direction, and he began to reevaluate it. The armistice obviously angered Ferdinand III. Maxmilian's abandonment of the emperor was not popular with the officers in the Bavarian army, and the armistice had not solved his problem with winter quarters for his soldiers.

So the elector began to consider a return to the emperor, who needed Bavarian military assistance as well as diplomatic support in Münster. But when he asked his theologians whether he was obliged to seek an alliance with Ferdinand once again, their first response was, on the contrary, that he was in conscience bound to stick to the Treaty of Ulm "because valid agreements must be kept." They did not change their view, even when the majority of the privy council advised the prince to

45 Carafa to Vervaux, June 15, 1647, ARSJ, Germ. Sup. 8, 100.
46 Vervaux to Biber, Nov. 13, 1647, cited in Duhr 2, 1: 480, n. 5.
47 Carafa to Biber, June 15, 1647, ARSJ, Rhen. Sup. 2, f. 41.
48 Albrecht, 1028–9.

turn back to the emperor. The theologians inclined more to France than did the privy councillors, partly because of their hope that French assistance would obviate concessions to the Protestant states in Germany. Moreover, Maximilian himself remained uneasy about the concessions that the emperor was ready to make to the Protestants and that he himself had approved; perhaps the militant attacks on them affected him. Yet the theologians also reassured him that he was not required to attempt to modify the concessions already agreed to by the emperor.[49] An agreement was reached between Ferdinand and Maximilian between September 7 and October 17. It provided that neither would make peace or an alliance without the consent of the other. Ferdinand accepted Maximilian's claim on the Palatinate, and he also agreed that Bavarian troops would be employed only against the Swedes, who were then threatening Bohemia. Maximilian renounced the armistice with Sweden on September 24. He had intended to maintain the armistice with France, but Mazarin, after some hesitation, in turn ended the armistice with Bavaria on December 29, 1647. In the last year of the war Bavaria underwent devastation from the Swedes for the third time, and Maximilian was forced once more to flee for a time to the safety of the archbishopric of Salzburg.[50]

Meanwhile, there erupted a storm in the form of a pamphlet war between Catholic militants and moderates that called for the intervention of Carafa. The militants attempted to stave off the concessions to the Protestants that were being negotiated. Toward the end of 1646, just when Trautmannsdorf laid out the final imperial declaration on the religious issues that incorporated the concessions endorsed by the major Catholic states, there appeared in Münster a pamphlet titled *A Theological Judgment on the Question, Whether the Peace that the Protestants Desire Is by Its Nature Illicit* under the pseudonym Ernestus de Eusebiis. The *Theological Judgment* was the work of a master polemicist, who later turned out to be Wangnereck; it was in the form of a position paper or memorandum for the princes. Essentially, the pamphlet represented a reworking and an elaboration of his "A Difficult Question," which had been prepared for the Diet of Regensburg. The *Theological Judgment* argued a well-reasoned theological case not only against the terms proposed by Trautmannsdorf but against the Peace of Augsburg itself, which even Laymann in *The Way to Peace* had accepted. Wangnereck objected principally to the permanence of any concessions made to the

[49] Undated, HStA, Jesuiten, 704, f. 76; see Steinberger, 98–9.
[50] Albrecht, 1066–79.

Protestants; concessions whether of church property or toleration could only be granted for a specific length of time, as in the Peace of Prague, or as long as necessity required. Furthermore, the Peace of Augsburg made Protestants and Catholics equal in law. This was unacceptable, as was the right of reformation given princes, which permitted Protestant princes, to pressure Catholics to convert and thus to endanger their salvation.

Wangnereck encouraged Catholic princes to confidence in God, and he attributed the decline in Catholic military fortunes to divine displeasure with the concessions made at Prague. But missing was any element of Lamormaini's or Contzen's belief in a divine mission to restore Catholicism, nor did Wangnereck claim that divine assistance guaranteed them victory if the Catholics acted boldly. If the Catholics went under, he declared, at least they had not sinned by facilitating the advance of Protestantism. Wangnereck wrote primarily to exhort the militants to stand firm, not to persuade the moderates of his position. If the militants could not prevail within the Catholic camp, and Wangnereck seemed to recognize that they could not, then they should enter a formal protest against the provisions of the projected settlement, but they should not attempt to prolong the war. Wangnereck's position was juridical, not political, and thus similar to the papacy's. The Protestants would never accept it. The author's claim that the church tolerated Protestants in the same way that it tolerated Jews, usurers, and prostitutes was certain to enrage them.[51]

Behind the *Theological Judgment* stood Wartenberg and his fellow militants. For an effective argument against the moderates in Vienna and Munich they had turned again to Wangnereck, now superior of the Jesuit mission in Lindau on Lake Constance. He wrote anonymously, and only in 1663 did the German Protestant savant Hermann Conring prove that he was the author.[52] Wangnereck had not intended that the pamphlet be published but that it circulate in manuscript among the Catholics, especially the militants. Nuncio Chigi generally backed its contents. For tactical reasons, however, he also did not want it to be published, principally because of the violent reaction that he anticipated from the Protestants. The main force behind the publication of the booklet seems to have been Elector Anselm Casimir of Mainz, who in his last months – he died on October 9, 1647 – became less flexible

[51] Ernestus de Eusebiis (pseud.), *Judicium theologicum super quaestione, an pax qualem desiderant Protestantes sit secundum se illicita?* (Ecclesiopoli, ad Insigne pietatis, 1648). I have used the microfilm copy in the Perkins Library of Duke University. See Steinberger, 76–7; according to him (71, n. 5), editions appeared in 1646, 1647, and 1648, with different types but the same content.

[52] Steinberger, 63.

about concessions to the Protestants. The pope welcomed the pamphlet when a copy reached him, and it appeared again in 1647 and 1648.[53]

The *Theological Judgment* did anger many Protestants, and it played into the hands of Protestant militants who could represent it as the genuinely Catholic position and so justify their own rigidity. But it was above all the Catholic moderates whom it outraged. Trautmannsdorf called it a "Bacchanalian production," or the product of an orgy, and Isaak Vollmar, the veteran imperial representative in Münster, referred to it as "sophistic cavilling and foolish dreams."[54]

But there was still more to come. Early that summer of 1647, as negotiations between Protestants and Catholics continued, another anonymous pamphlet followed up on the *Theological Judgment*; its title was *A Vehicle for the Theological Judgment*, its purpose to convey and elaborate briefly the message of its predecessor. Wangnereck does not seem to have been the author.[55] Fathers Cörler and Johannes Mülmann of the Münster college, whose sympathies lay with the militants and who may have had a hand in its composition, sent a copy to Gans in Vienna, where we can imagine how it was received.[56] Wangnereck, however, was not inactive. Just about a month later, at the instigation of the militants, his *Weighing of a Proposal for Peace* appeared in Münster pseudonymously.[57] It compared the terms of the agreement on the religious issues that Trautmannsdorf had reached with the Swedes and the German Protestants with the Catholic position as he had laid it out in the *Theological Judgment*, where the obvious conclusion was that it fell far short of what Catholics, understood as militant Catholics, could accept. These pamphlets had little impact on the policy of the emperor, Maximilian, and the major Catholic states,[58] though they may have given the elector some second thoughts. They did represent serious resistance to the terms of the peace on the part of an important Catholic party and did both represent and influence the views of many smaller Catholic states who stood to lose more by the peace.

As one might expect, the moderates responded to the challenge of the militants. Sometime between early June and early October 1647 a pamphlet from the pen of Vervaux began to circulate in Münster, "Remarks on the *Theological Judgment*." It remained in manuscript, and

53 Ibid., 67, 74–5.
54 Ibid., 76–7.
55 Ibid., 85–6; *Vehiculum judicii theologici*, s.l., s.d., in only one edition.
56 Ibid. 86–7.
57 *Instrumenti pacis a Dominis Plenipotentiariis Caesareis statibus Sacri Romani Imperii mense junio exhibiti Ponderatio*. Only one edition appeared.
58 Steinberger, 91.

was intended for the Catholic representatives but inevitably found its way into the hands of Protestants. It severely criticized the main points of the *Theological Judgment*.[59] Chigi took vigorous exception to the statement in the "Remarks" that in an emergency the elector could dispose of ecclesiastical property without the pope's approval.[60] Vervaux probably had in mind the ambivalence of the papacy under Urban VIII that we have regularly noticed. Biber, who was in Rome for the General Congregation, had written Anselm Casimir of Mainz on March 3, 1646, that he was told that Pope Innocent would protest the terms of the agreement with the Protestants but that he did not want to hinder the conclusion of peace.[61] In any event, Vervaux now counted among the militants as a "semi-heretic."[62]

Others also responded to Wangnereck. Most prominent among the theologians publicly defending the moderate position was the maverick Spaniard Johann Caramuel y Lobkowicz, abbot of Montserrat, then residing in Vienna, who was close to Quiroga. So a Jesuit was not in the forefront of the public defense of the moderate position in Vienna. Caramuel's *A Demonstration that the Peace of the Holy Roman Empire Is Licit* appeared first in early 1648, then in a second edition later that year at Frankfurt, and finally in a third edition in Vienna in 1649.[63] This volume by the "prince of laxists," as he was later called, had a significant impact. Protestants also joined the attack on Wangnereck; among them were the Saxon lawyer and official, Benedict Carpzov, who remained anonymous,[64] and the Strasbourg theologian Johann George Dorsche, who did not.[65]

A Jesuit from Mainz, Melchior Cornäus, now joined the fray; he probably had a hand in the gradual movement of Anselm Casimir, the elector of Mainz, to the militant side in his last months. In early 1648 Cornäus directed his pseudonymous volume explicitly against Dorsche but also had words for Vervaux, his fellow Jesuit in Munich, in his defense of Wangnereck.[66] But Wangnereck himself did not remain silent. Called

59 "Notae in Consilium [i.e., Judicium] Theologicum Ernesti de Eusebiis super quaestione an pax qualem desiderant Protestantes sit secundum se illicita," cited in Steinberger, 173–5.
60 Steinberger, 104.
61 Biber to Mainz, Mar. 3, 1646, Hansen, 165–6.
62 Steinberger, 105.
63 *Sacri Romani Imperii pax licita demonstrata*, Steinberger, 78–80. On Caramuel and his relationship with Chigi, see Pietro Bellazzi, *Juan Caramuel* (Vigevano, 1982), esp. 61–3.
64 *Discussio brevis Judicii theologici . . . pridem in publicum emissi nec non Vehiculi ab eodem autore Judicio illi nuper succenturati*, s.l., 1647, 2nd ed. 1648.
65 Dorsche published at least three works in this war of words; Steinberger, 108.
66 *Crisis Anticrisios et triga opisodromos sive examen et excussio judicii Joan-Georgii Dorschaei*, s.l., 1648; Steinberger, 109–10.

upon again by the militants in Münster, he produced by late 1647 his *Theological Response*, which was intended as an answer to Vervaux's "Remarks on the *Theological Judgment*," and it was published in early 1648, pseudonymously.[67] In this piece Vervaux was dubbed "Irenicus," ironically, because of his inclination to peace, and he was also accused of bad faith. As with the *Theological Judgment*, Wangnereck did not foresee publication, but he yielded again to the militants and permitted the work's publication. But it was published by a small, private publishing house, to prevent it from getting into the hands of the Protestants. Wangnereck's militant patrons also made changes in the text before the book went to press that were to have serious consequences later. Critical comments were inserted not only about the points at issue but also about Maximilian's foreign policy, especially about the Treaty of Ulm with France. Added as well was an implicit comparison between the policy of Maximilian's pious but ineffective father, Duke William V, and the present elector. What would Duke William have said about any agreement with heretics? Chigi sent a copy of the *Theological Response* to Rome, where the pope praised it.[68] Maximilian would be infuriated when he later learned of it. Carafa found himself between the two of them.

The exchange of pamphlets continued, with Protestants as well as moderate and militant Catholics getting into the action. One important contribution in support of the Catholic moderates with the title *A Catholic Consultation on a Permanent Peace with the Protestants* appeared in early 1648 under the pseudonym of "an Austrian theologian, Irenaeus Eubulus." Only much later did the Protestant Conring, a moderate, admit to its authorship.[69] Chigi encouraged the Catholic militants to further publications. The Benedictine prior Adam Adami published his *Anti-Caramuel* in 1648,[70] and Wangnereck was diligently preparing a grand work, to be called simply *Apology*, which subsequent developments prevented him from publishing.[71]

[67] *Responsum theologicum super quaestione: an pax, qualem desiderant Protestantes, quaeque nunc Monasterii et Osnaburgi tractatur, sit secundem se illicita*, s.l.; manuscript copy, Munich, HStA, Jesuitica 705.

[68] Steinberger, 112–18, 176–9.

[69] *Pro pace perpetua Protestantibus danda consultatio Catholica*, Auctore Irenaeo Eubulo Theologo Austriaco, Frideburgi, Apud Germanum Patientem, 1648. The fictional place and publisher point up the author's plea for peace; Steinberger, 123–4. Quiroga had suspected a similar tactic on the part of Protestant hardliners when Wangnereck's *Theological Judgment* first appeared.

[70] *Anti-Caramuel sive examen et refutatio disputationis theologico-politicae quam de potestate imperatoris circa bona ecclesiastica proposuit Joannes Caramuel Lobkovitz*. Humano Erdeman Oecomontano auctore. Trimonadi (Dortmund?), 1648.

[71] *Apologeticus*; Steinberger, 126–7, 130.

The polemics of neither Wangnereck nor Vervaux found their way at first to Jesuit headquarters in Rome, perhaps because people in the north knew that Carafa as well as Vitelleschi frowned on this type of pseudonymous publication. It was Maximilian himself, finally, alerted by Vervaux no doubt, who in a vigorous letter of January 3, 1648, informed the superior general of Wangnereck's pamphlets. He warned him to take prompt and serious measures to restrict the writings and criticisms of Wangnereck and others. Otherwise, the Society would suffer severe harm as a result of the offense and scandal that it was generating. Their pamphlets were undermining the search for peace, scaring many estates from supporting the peace through arguments allegedly based on conscience but in fact false. If Jesuits should be deemed responsible for the prolongation of the war, the Society would incur an enormous odium and hatred in Germany.[72]

Immediately, Carafa rushed two letters off to the provincial of the South German Province, Laurentius Keppler. The first instructed Keppler to remind the Jesuits in his province of the prohibition of and penalties for taking sides publicly in the war and in particular for writing or publishing for one side or another.[73] The second dealt with the case of Wangnereck. The provincial was to determine whether he truly was the author of the works in question. If he was, then Keppler was to remove him from office as superior in Lindau, transfer him elsewhere, and inform him that he had incurred the penalties decreed by the Fifth General Congregation for involvement in political affairs.[74] A month later another letter to Keppler bemoaned the scope of the grounds that the Society had given to Maximilian for complaint.[75]

Chigi meanwhile lauded Wangnereck's efforts in his reports to Rome, and he criticized the "Remarks on the *Theological Judgment*," which he correctly attributed to Vervaux, as well as Bavarian policy in the negotiations. Abbot Schönhainz, whose main concern was the monasteries in Württemberg, also complained of Maximilian to Rome. Vervaux, Quiroga, and Caramuel, he asserted, confirmed the Catholic princes in their readiness to make concessions disastrous for the church and the salvation of souls.[76] Wangnereck himself in February requested a renewal of the papal blessing that Chigi had obtained for him. The next month

72 Maximilian to Carafa, Jan. 3, 1648, Steinberger, Document 7, p. 198.

73 Carafa to Keppler (provincial), Jan. 25, 1648, HStA, Jesuitica 658, f. 3.

74 Carafa to Keppler (provincial), Jan. 25, 1648, ARSJ, Germ. Sup. 8, f. 128.

75 Carafa to Keppler (provincial), Feb. 22, 1648, ibid., ff. 132'–3.

76 Abbot George von Schönhainz to Pope Innocent X, Baden (Switzerland), Nov. 6, 1647, W. Friedensburg, "Regesten zur deutschen Geschichte aus der Zeit des Pontifikats Innocent X (1644–1655)," *Quellen und Forchungen aus italienischen Archiven und Bibliotheken* 6 (1904): 150–2.

Chigi urged the secretary of state, Cardinal Panciroli, to put pressure on Carafa on behalf of Wangnereck.[77]

The upshot was that Carafa was compelled to back off. He reported to Keppler on April 4 that the nuncio had intervened for Wangnereck, and he instructed the provincial not to issue any penalties against Wangnereck until he, Carafa, could consult with the pope. But he was to prevent, if he could, any further publications of Wangnereck on the peace issue and send copies of all the relevant pamphlets to Rome.[78] After his meeting with Innocent, Carafa informed Keppler that Wangnereck was not to be removed from office until his normal term of three years expired. The pope, he noted, favored Wangnereck's lucubrations.[79] The pope also desired that no Jesuit make a further attempt to respond to Wangnereck; this applied above all to Vervaux, who had never published his "Remarks on the *Theological Judgment*."[80] Carafa passed on the pope's desire to Vervaux and urged the confessor to refrain from any response and thus show himself to be an obedient son of the Holy See.

So, Maximilian's efforts to silence Wangnereck failed. The superior general now had another serious complaint against Vervaux. He had learned that the confessor once again was engaged in correspondence with the court of France in an attempt to mediate between the two princes or even to arrange another armistice, and indeed he was.[81] A certain exasperation emerged in Carafa's communication to Vervaux. Did not the confessor realize that he already had a reputation with the pope and other princes of involvement in politics well beyond what was suitable for a religious and that some held him responsible for the armistice of the previous year? What will they say if they learn that you are fostering another armistice, and this information is bound to become public? Certainly if the harm that this activity does to the Society is explained to Maximilian, he will not entrust you with it and will turn to those ministers who are competent in the matter. "I ask you most insistently, that Your Reverence excuse yourself quietly and submissively from those matters and tasks which are able to stir the anger of those others [princes] and restrict yourself exclusively to the forum of conscience according to the nature of our Institute." Carafa again exhorted Vervaux to urge Maximilian to turn to others for guidance

77 Steinberger, 118–19.
78 Carafa to Keppler (provincial), Apr. 4, 1648, ARSJ, Germ. Sup. 8, f. 136'.
79 Steinberger, 138; an effort of Chigi to exempt Wangnereck completely from the internal censorship of the Society came to nothing.
80 Carafa to Keppler (provincial), May 16, 1648, ARSJ, Germ. Sup., f. 140'.
81 Steinberger, 99.

of his conscience so that all the responsibility did not fall upon the Society.[82]

Before a response to this letter could have reached Rome, communications from both Vervaux and Maximilian arrived in the Eternal City. Carafa commended the confessor for the tactful way he was attempting to end his correspondence with Paris, and he regretted the offense that his action had caused the elector, but there was no way that he could dispense Vervaux from the prohibition of political activity by the Fifth General Congregation.[83] With Maximilian himself he stood his ground. Once again he acknowledged the many benefits that the Society had received from the elector. He had no intention of restricting Vervaux's participation in council meetings, as they had earlier agreed. But again he urgently requested the prince not to employ Vervaux in matters of state and rehearsed the arguments about the harm that this brought the Society.[84] Following Maximilian's complaint that the Holy See was so poorly informed about German affairs, the superior general suggested to Vervaux that the prince keep the pope better informed through his agent in Rome who had access to the Holy Father.[85]

The long war finally came to an end with the Peace of Westphalia of October 24, 1648. Before long the delegates began to depart for home. But many of them then found themselves reconvening in Nuremberg shortly thereafter to deal with the problems of implementing the terms of the peace and especially demobilizing the armies. They did not complete the Nuremberg Agreement on Demobilization with Sweden until June 26, 1650, and with France until July 2. Before then it seemed at times that hostilities might resume.

The delegates anticipated a protest from the pope against the religious provisions of the peace and especially against the surrender of ecclesiastical territories, most of them in Protestant hands anyway, as well as of the church lands in Württemberg that the Catholics were required to evacuate. So they wrote into the peace an article invalidating any such protest. In 1647 and 1648 Chigi had protested, in one case secretly, against various provisions of the treaty. His goal was to show that neither he nor the papacy recognized these terms, so it could not be argued subsequently that the papacy had accepted them by its silence. But the papal brief formally and publicly protesting the peace, *Zelo Domus Dei*, was held back until August 20, 1650, so after the conclusion of the

82 Carafa to Vervaux, June 27, 1648, ibid., Document 10, pp. 199–200.
83 Carafa to Vervaux, July 25, 1648, ARSJ, Germ. Sup. 8, ff. 144–5'.
84 Carafa to Maximilian, July 29, 1648, ARSJ, Germ. 113a, f. 140.
85 Carafa to Vervaux, Aug. 29, 1648, ARSJ, Germ. Sup. 8, f. 148.

Nuremberg Agreement on Demobilization, and it was then backdated to November 26, 1648. The reason for this long delay was that the brief was not intended to have a political but a juridical effect. The papacy did not want to afford any pretext for prolonging the war, to which it too desperately desired an end, and certainly it did not want to bear the odium should the conflict resume. The purpose of the protest was to preserve the juridical claims of the church, which in an unknown future might sometime be advanced once again.[86]

The contest between the Catholic militants and moderates continued after the conclusion of the peace and in the circumstances might have been used to justify a return to the battlefield. Only in November 1648 did a copy of the *Theological Response* arrive in Munich and Maximilian learn that Wangnereck was its author too. The pamphlet landed like a bombshell; with its abusive criticism it wounded the aging elector profoundly where he was most sensitive, in his honor. First, on November 18 he expressed to Johann Philip von Schönborn, the newly elected, moderate archbishop-elector of Mainz, his fear that the incendiary pamphlet might undermine the fragile trust that had been built up between Catholics and Protestants and led to the peace. The Protestant states should be assured that the Catholics were ready to prosecute the author, whom he refrained from naming, as a violator of the peace, as was foreseen in the treaty itself for those who challenged its terms.[87]

The very next day the embittered elector addressed an unusually sharp and threatening letter to Carafa. He was astonished, the prince wrote, to find an ecclesiastic and especially a Jesuit who could so irresponsibly and vitriolically scold princes. Wangnereck's book brimmed over with insults and calumnies against the emperor and the princes who had painstakingly worked out the settlement that at last had brought peace to Germany. He called them "enemies of the divine honor and corrupters of religion." In reality, the peace fostered divine worship and the conservation of the Catholic religion and the Society of Jesus. The alternative to it was the ruin of the empire and with it all religion. In the long negotiations toward peace, Maximilian had looked to the good of the commonwealth and of the Catholic religion to the best of his ability.

The whole Christian world knew how he had championed the faith, Maximilian went on. "We would have hoped to merit a reward other

[86] See Konrad Repgen, "Die Proteste Chigis und der päpstliche Protest gegen den westfälischen Frieden (1648/1650)," in *Staat, Kirche, Wissenschaft in einer pluralistischen Gesellschaft: Festschrift zum 65. Geburtstag Paul Mikat* (Berlin, 1989), 623–47; M.F. Feldkamp, "Das Breve '*Zelo Domus Dei*' vom 26 November 1648. Edition," *Archivum historiae pontificiae* 31 (1993): 293–305.

[87] Steinberger, 138–9, 142–3.

than the cuts and stings of this most impudent man, and what exacerbates the offense is that in light of the benefits we have bestowed on your Society, it can scarcely escape the charge of extreme ingratitude." Wangnereck had reviled the reputation not only of Maximilian but of other Catholic princes and the emperor himself. "We demand . . . that you punish him in a suitable fashion, and since he has defamed us in his writings no less calumniously than publicly, that you make a public example of him to satisfy Us." Otherwise, he threatened, he would be compelled to resort to his own measures suitable for the defense of his honor. "For we want Your Paternity to know that in the future we will show ourselves towards Your Society as its merits require and especially according to the way it eliminates this notorious affront. And while we confidently anticipate the effect [of this letter] without any delay or excuse, we embrace Your Paternity with our gracious favor."[88]

Maximilian's resentful and ominous words elicited a rapid yet thoughtful response from Jesuit headquarters in Rome. Carafa was greatly pained by the offense to a long-standing, generous patron of the Society and worried about what might result from it.[89] Four letters dealing with the case were dispatched to Germany on December 19. In all of them Carafa emphasized that he ventured no judgment between the positions of the militants and the moderates. His objections were to the insulting style and acerbic pen of Wangnereck, his attack on Maximilian and other princes, and his ill treatment of a fellow Jesuit, the author of the "Remarks on the *Theological Judgment*," whom he dubbed "Irenicus" and who in fact was Vervaux.

To Keppler, the provincial superior in Munich, Carafa indicated that it was necessary to impose an exemplary punishment on Wangnereck as Maximilian demanded. "If he were not a professed father," Carafa wrote, "he would have to be dismissed from the Society," but it was not permissible to expel a professed father.[90] Carafa determined a three-fold punishment for the delinquent Wangnereck. First, for the time being he was to be kept in "prison," or the equivalent of house arrest. Second, he was to be deprived of active and passive voice, which presupposed his removal as superior. Third, he was to undergo a public penance in the refectory, where he would also be openly reproved for his offenses. If it were possible for him to secure access to the prince, Keppler was to explain to him the measures that the superior general had ordered

88 Maximilian to Carafa, Nov. 19, 1648, Steinberger, Document 11, pp. 200–1.

89 Carafa to Vervaux, Dec. 19, 1648, ARSJ, Germ. Sup. 8, ff. 167–7'.

90 The complicated procedures required to expel a professed father from the Jesuits made dismissal at the initiative of superiors extremely rare.

and to inquire whether Maximilian required more from the Society.[91] To Wangnereck himself Carafa explained the charges against him and the threats of the elector. Both called for a penance to be imposed upon him, the nature of which the provincial would communicate to him. Carafa then dealt pastorally with the delinquent Wangnereck, exhorting him "to undergo it [the penance] in a ready and courageous spirit. You know the words of St. Ambrose," he continued, " 'to have incurred guilt is the part of nature, to have washed it away, the part of virtue.' Wash away, then, with your humility, obedience, and patience what you have committed through thoughtlessness. It will be to the good of Your Reverence and of the whole Society."[92] The use of the word "thoughtlessness" diminished the guilt of Wangnereck; he had not acted out of malice or ill will, but probably out of zeal, misguided though it was.

To Vervaux, Carafa claimed that he would have punished Wangnereck earlier had it been possible, but there had been good reasons not to do so, as the confessor would recall, namely the intervention of the pope, which the superior general did not mention explicitly. However, now that the elector had complained and insisted upon an exemplary punishment, action was necessary to satisfy him. Carafa repeated what he wrote Keppler about the impossibility of expelling Wangnereck from the Society and about the punishments that he had determined for the Jesuit offender. Vervaux could be expected to pass on the contents of the letter to Maximilian. A second letter to Vervaux, while acknowledging that the confessor had a legitimate grievance, turned down his request to publish an answer to Wangnereck's *Theological Response* and alluded to the pope's desire that this not be undertaken.[93] Carafa encouraged Vervaux to leave the punishment of Wangnereck and the vindication of the confessor's reputation up to him, and he exhorted him to accept this prohibition as a way of imitating the suffering Christ.[94]

Nor did Carafa overlook the nuncio Chigi, still in Münster. He asked Cörler, the rector in Münster, to explain to Chigi why he had imposed a penance on Wangnereck. He recounted for him the vigorous complaints and threats of Maximilian, mentioning in particular the possibility that Wangnereck be prosecuted as an example to those who publicly challenged the peace and that his book be burned publicly. Others had then read the book at Carafa's request, and he himself had looked at passages in it. All agreed that Wangnereck had offended grievously with his sharp

91 Carafa to Keppler (provincial), Dec. 19, 1648, ARSJ, Germ. Sup. 8, f. 157.
92 Carafa to Wangnereck, Dec. 19, 1648, ibid., 8, f. 158.
93 An apparent draft of Vervaux's planned response is found in HStA, KSch, 8165.
94 Carafa to Vervaux, Dec. 19, 1648, Steinberger, Document 12, p. 202.

tone and his berating of princes. To prevent worse from happening to him and to the Society, the superior general had then decided on appropriate punishment for Wangnereck, "not because of the substance of the doctrine," he emphasized, "but because of the way in which he proceeded." The rector was to wait for a favorable time to communicate this to the nuncio in a suitable fashion.[95]

Maximilian seemed to be appeased with the measures to be taken against Wangnereck. This pleased Carafa, as did the pope's apparent readiness to let the matter die.[96] Later Maximilian did declare to Carafa that he was satisfied with the disciplining of Wangnereck and with the apology that he had received from the Jesuit. Wangnereck had claimed, questionably, that the passages that had most offended the prince did not stem from him but were inserted by those in Münster who had overseen the book's publication.[97] Carafa commended Vervaux for putting aside his intent to publish his further response to Wangnereck.[98]

But the affair was not to be laid to rest so quickly. Even before the provincial Keppler met with him at the College of Constance to inform him of his punishment, Wangnereck had appealed to Pope Innocent X to permit him to publish his apology, which would be directed chiefly against Caramuel and would summarize anew his arguments against the peace.[99] Immediately after his meeting with Keppler on February 6, Wangnereck had sought the assistance of both Chigi and the pope. But even before Chigi heard from him, on the basis of other information, the nuncio had interceded for Wangnereck in Rome. Members of the militant party in Münster added in an attached communication that others were responsible for passages at which Maximilian took offense. So Chigi pressed his efforts for Wangnereck in Rome.[100]

Carafa was forced to retreat again. On February 13 he informed Vervaux that he had been ordered to revoke Wangnereck's penances. "Your Reverence can easily conjecture where this came from," he added, and he instructed Vervaux to explain to the elector that he was not able fully to translate into deeds his desire to serve and accommodate the prince.[101] The provincial Keppler received notice to lift Wangnereck's punishment. Carafa informed him also of complaints to Rome from

95 Carafa to Cörler, Dec. 26, 1648, ARSJ, Rhen. Inf. 8I, f. 144.

96 Carafa to Vervaux, Feb. 6, 1649, ARSJ, Germ. Sup. 8, f. 162.

97 Maximilian to Carafa, Feb. 26, 1649, cited in Steinberger, 151; see ibid., 152–3.

98 Carafa to Vervaux, Feb. 6, 1649, ARSJ, Germ. Sup. 8, f. 162.

99 Wangnereck to Pope Innocent X, Saint Gallen, Feb. 5, 1649, Steinberger, Document 14, pp. 203–4.

100 Chigi to Cardinal Panciroli (secretary of state), Jan. 22, 1649, Steinberger, Document 13, pp. 202–3; ibid., 151–4.

101 Carafa to Vervaux, Feb. 13, 1649, ARSJ, Germ. Sup. 8, f. 164'.

several German provinces about Vervaux's activity in political matters and especially his participation in council meetings. The Society was reaping ill will from this, they alleged.[102] The superior general explained the arrangement that he had worked out with Maximilian and Vervaux about the latter's attendance at council meetings. Keppler was to determine whether it was being observed. If not, he was to admonish Vervaux paternally in Carafa's name.

Carafa announced the lifting of his penance to Wangnereck on March 6; at the same time, he notified him of Maximilian's satisfaction with the situation and especially with the Jesuit's apology. But he urged Wangnereck to set aside his work in progress against Caramuel, lest once again the Society run afoul with princes. There were others on whom the nuncio could call to write against the peace. Such "imprudent" writings – not only from Wangnereck but from other unnamed Jesuits – worried Carafa.[103]

Wangnereck, meanwhile, raised two serious grievances with Carafa. He picked up on the point that the case against him had been based not on the content of his writings but on their tone and language. He claimed that he had only imitated the prophets and early Fathers of the Church like Basil and Chrysostom in speaking the truth to unjust princes; in doing so he appeared to take responsibility for the language of his polemic. Carafa in turn disclaimed any wish to present a brief for princes, but he denied the parallel between rulers of earlier times and the princes currently ruling in Germany.

Carafa's response to the second grievance of Wangnereck is instructive, in that it revealed the necessity he felt to appease princes. Wangnereck resented deeply the statement of the superior general, related to him by Keppler, that had he not been a professed father, he would have been dismissed from the Society. Carafa explained, in reply, "that in order to appease human Princes, we are compelled occasionally to resort to remedies . . . which we are unwilling [to use]. Just as in the case of a . . . body, in order to preserve its life, we are permitted also sometimes, at the cost of great pain, to cut off a member, so also the Society is at times required to dismiss one of its sons from its body in order to mitigate the anger of princes or if this is not possible because of his status as a professed, with great sorrow to punish him." Carafa then illustrated this with two examples. In 1630 Vitelleschi had dismissed a priest from the English Province who had bitterly criticized Cardinal Richelieu in private correspondence that fell into the

[102] Carafa to Keppler (provincial), Feb. 13, 1649, ibid., f. 164.
[103] Carafa to Wangnereck, Mar. 6, 1649, Steinberger, Document 16, pp. 165–6; see also Carafa to Keppler (provincial), Mar. 20, 1649, ARSJ, Germ. Sup. 8, ff. 167'–8.

hands of the cardinal. Only the year before, Carafa himself had publicly punished Jean-Baptiste de Cortas, a well-known preacher of the Gallo-Belgian Province, because of unseemly remarks in a private letter about the prince of Condé that then became public.[104]

Two weeks later Carafa expressed to Wangnereck his regret for the pain he caused him by imposing a penance on him "in order to placate great princes who were extremely angry" and to avoid harm to the Society. Now as a consolation he offered Wangnereck assignment to any house that he desired, and he reminded him that he had never opposed the substance of his teaching but only the style and tone.[105] But the superior general was determined not to permit any Jesuit, including Wangnereck, to publish anything against the recently concluded peace. So he reassured Maximilian, who had written him again after learning of Wangnereck's plan to respond to Caramuel.[106] In any event, Wangnereck completed his apology but, apparently heeding Carafa, did not publish it.[107]

Vincent Carafa died on June 6, 1649, after only three-and-one-half years as Jesuit superior general. That spring of 1649 famine and accompanying disease visited Rome, and Carafa took a leading part in organizing the provision of food and care of the sick. He died as a result of sickness contracted in their service.[108]

By the time of his death Carafa had become, in effect, a moderate, even though his principal intent was to avoid taking a position between militants and moderates and, in accord with his understanding of Jesuit legislation and at papal behest, to keep the Jesuits out of politics. At its provincial congregation of 1649 the Lower Rhine Province requested that the new superior general loosen the restrictions imposed by Carafa on those zealous Jesuits who wanted to write in support of the rights of the church against those "politicians" who were indifferent to the advance of heresy.[109] Carafa prohibited the militants from writing because he feared offending princes, especially Maximilian, and obstructing a lasting peace settlement in Germany. In this latter regard Carafa's policy was similar to that of the papacy itself, which while issuing a protest

104 Carafa to Wangnereck, Apr. 10, 1649, ibid., f. 170. On de Cortas, see Alfred Poncelet, *Histoire de la Compagnie de Jésus dans les anciens Pays-Bas* 2 (Brussels, 1927): 377. The name of the English priest has been crossed out and become illegible.

105 Carafa to Wangnereck, Apr. 24, 1649, ibid., f. 171'.

106 Carafa to Maximilian, Mar. 20, 1649, ARSJ, Germ. 113a, f. 156.

107 Duhr 2, 1: 488.

108 Daniello Bartoli, *Della vita del Vincenzo Carafa, settimo generale della Compagnia di Gesu* (Rome, 1651), 98, 102.

109 Duhr 2, 1: 489, n. 2.

against the Peace of Westphalia in order to preserve the juridical position of the church, held off this protest for two years so that it could not be used as an excuse to renew hostilities. In practice, for both Jesuit headquarters and the papacy at this point, the highest priority was peace.

While the general congregation was in session in Rome to elect the new superior general, letters of Father Reinhard Faust, a Jesuit in Nuremberg, became public in which he decried Maximilian's alleged compromise of the church's interests. For this the archbishop-elector of Mainz, Schönborn, called the local superior on the carpet and demanded that Faust be punished. The vicar-general of the Society, Florence de Montmorency, then notified the acting provincial – the provincial was in Rome – that Faust was to be transferred and disciplined for his offense.[110]

After the dismissal of Olivares in 1643 little correspondence of a political nature passed between the superior general in Rome and the court or the Jesuits in Madrid. These were Vitelleschi's last years, when his correspondence fell off noticeably, and the brief period of Carafa's generalate. In 1643 Vitelleschi requested the assistance of Aguado, Olivares's confessor, in a case before the court of the free county of Burgundy involving the Jesuit college in Besançon. Aguado excused himself on the grounds that the count-duke had been dismissed, implying that he could do little.[111] The next year, Vitelleschi acceded to the wishes of the viceroy of Naples to send the Jesuit Francisco Benavides on a mission to Madrid; it was necessary, as he wrote Benavides, to obey the viceroy "in everything." But he also warned him to avoid any involvement in matters of "reason of state," which the Society's legislation prohibited.[112]

Two contrasting tendencies of Vitelleschi appeared here again. First was his deference to princes and persons of high estate. Second was his greater strictness toward Jesuit political activity in Spain, where the Society did not supply the king's confessor and so was not directly involved with the royal conscience, where the contest with heresy was more remote, and where Catholic enemies did not threaten the Society as they did in France. Carafa, in an early letter to Philip IV, acknowledged in the name of the general congregation the many ways in which the Society was obligated to the king, expressed the Jesuits' desire to serve him, and requested royal protection for the Society. He also designated

110 Montmorency to Vice-Provincial (unnamed), Würzburg, Nov. 6, 1649, ARSJ, Rhen. Sup. 2, f. 108.

111 Vitelleschi to Aguado (provincial), Sept. 13, 1642, ARSJ, Hisp. 71I, f. 30'; Vitelleschi to Pedro Gonzalez de Mendoza (provincial), July 14, 1643, ibid., f. 46.

112 Vitelleschi to Benavides, June 16, 1644, ibid., ff. 62–2'; Vitelleschi to the viceroy of Naples, June 16, 1644, ibid., ff. 61'–2.

10,000 Masses to be offered for the king and his intentions during the coming year.[113] Compared to Vitelleschi, the new superior general was sparing in his requests to the court of Spain – and other courts, too, for that matter – on behalf of Italian noblemen or ecclesiastics.

With the deaths of Richelieu and Louis XIII in 1642 and 1643, the position of the Jesuits at the court of Paris diminished as their enemies mounted an offensive, but they won a major victory with the appointment of a Jesuit as confessor to the young Louis XIV in 1649. In France the Society was vulnerable following the death of its two consistent protectors, Richelieu and Louis XIII, who had paid tribute to the Jesuits on his deathbed. The Jansenist controversy began to heat up in the 1640s; in 1640 the *Augustine* of Jansen appeared posthumously, and three years later Antoine Arnauld published his *On Frequent Communion*. Factions at the University of Paris and among the diocesan clergy took aim at the Jesuits.[114]

Vitelleschi hastened to shore up support for the Society. Upon the death of the king, he addressed letters of condolence to Gaston of Orléans, the king's brother, and the prince of Condé, his cousin, both members of the regency council.[115] Vitelleschi was confident, he wrote Condé, that as new political arrangements were made in France "Your Highness would nevertheless not be unmindful of us, following the example of the great God (whose place on earth princes take), and would be an aid to the orphans and the poor," that is, the Jesuits. His communication to Gaston took up the theme of the Jesuits as orphaned by the two recent deaths and asked that the prince show the same tender care for the Society that his brother had. The archives contain no letter for either the regent, Queen Anne, or Mazarin, who gradually slid into the shoes of Richelieu. Sublet de Noyers, the great Jesuit friend at court, was outmaneuvered by Mazarin and mildly disgraced shortly before Louis's death because of his efforts to obtain for Queen Anne a prominent place on the council of regency.[116] Vitelleschi, aware of his fall from power, consoled him, stressed the Society's gratitude to him for his assistance, and promised the Jesuits' continual loyalty to him.[117] Sublet de Noyers did return to court in October 1643, but not to his former positions, and he died in 1645.

113 Carafa to Philip IV of Spain, Apr. 30, 1646, ARSJ, Hisp. 71I, f. 97'.

114 See, for example, Godefroi Hermant, *Mémoires de Godefroi Hermant sur l'histoire ecclésiastique du xviie siècle (1630–1663)*, ed. A. Gazier, 1: *1630–52* (Paris, 1905).

115 Vitelleschi to Condé, June 25, 1643, ARSJ, Gallia 46I, ff. 254'–5; Vitelleschi to Gaston de Orléans, June 25, 1643, ibid, f. 254'.

116 Pierre Chevalier, *Louis XIII, roi cornélien* (Paris, 1979), 636; Henri Griffet, *Histoire du règne de Louis XIII* (Paris, 1758) 3: 598–601.

117 Vitelleschi to Sublet de Noyers, Oct. 1, 1643, ARSJ, Gallia 46I, ff. 257'–8.

In 1644 Vitelleschi gratefully acknowledged the assistance of Gaston, Condé, and Pierre Seguier, chancellor of the realm, in maintaining immunity from various taxes for Jesuit houses.[118] These were the same three figures in France who received notice of the death of Vitelleschi from the vicar general of the Society as well as letters from Carafa announcing his election as the new superior general.[119] Obviously, they were the ones to whom the Society in Rome initially looked for help in France after the death of Richelieu and Louis XIII and the disgrace of Sublet de Noyers. Neither Queen Anne nor Mazarin was on the list. Mazarin, who had been educated by the Jesuits in Rome and whose uncle had been a well-known Jesuit preacher, was not known as a friend of the Society. In late 1643 the Jesuit preacher Jacques Nouet had been compelled to apologize before the cardinal for sermons that he had preached against Arnauld's *Frequent Communio*.[120]

Yet both the queen and the cardinal turned to the Jesuits when in early 1647 they began to think about a permanent confessor for the nine-year-old king. Shortly after the death of her husband, Anne had promised the Jesuits, as she wrote later to the vicar general of the Society, that when the time came she would choose the child's confessor from among them.[121] The Jesuits clearly hoped for this, and they were awaiting an announcement already in 1646. Louis Mairat, the provincial superior, suggested to Carafa in early 1647 that he raise the issue with Anne and Mazarin, but the superior general forcefully rejected any idea of an attempt to intervene in the selection of a confessor.[122]

So Anne and Mazarin took the initiative. Why did Mazarin confirm Anne in her inclination toward a Jesuit confessor for Louis? Apart from conviction that a Jesuit would be best for the post and awareness that Anne was determined on this, one can speculate that he had come to see the Society as an ally against the Jansenists and the obstreperous *parlementaires*, who to a degree overlapped. The rebellion that would be known as the Fronde was approaching. Shortly after his election in 1646 Carafa wrote the superior of the professed house in Paris of the debt of gratitude that the Society owed not only to the princes, that is Gaston and Condé, but also now to Queen Anne and Mazarin, "who

118 Vitelleschi to Gaston d'Orléans, Condé, and Seguier, Mar. 3, 1644, ibid., 261′–2′.

119 Carlo Sangrio, Vicar General, to Gaston d'Orléans, Feb. 9, and to Condé and Seguier, Feb. 20, 1645, ibid., f. 270; Carafa to the same, Jan. 7, 1646, ibid., ff. 276′–7′.

120 Hermant, 222–4.

121 Queen Anne to Florence de Montmorency, vicar general of the Society of Jesus, Oct. 28, 1649, cited in P.H. Cherot, *La première jeunesse de Louis XIV, 1643–1653* (Paris, 1892), 41.

122 Mairat (provincial) to Carafa, Jan. 3, 1647, Vanves, Collection Prat 37, ff. 88–8′; Carafa to Mairat, Feb. 15, 1647, cited in Cherot, 23.

after God serve as a shield for us against the insults and petitions of our enemies even the domestic ones."[123] This probably referred to efforts of the Assembly of the Clergy then meeting in Paris to restrict privileges of the religious orders, including the Jesuits, and in general to assert themselves against the royal power, that is, Anne and Mazarin, now that Richelieu and Louis XIII were dead.[124] Mazarin came to recognize that it was to his and the king's advantage to have the Jesuits as allies. Early in 1647 he reassured Carafa that he would see to the protection of the Jesuits at Dillingen, which was close to the center of fighting at the time, and he added that both he and the regent shared a particular fondness for the Society.[125]

That fall of 1647 the new superior of the professed house in Paris, Charles Paulin, informed Carafa with satisfaction that Mazarin had decided to entrust his nephew to the Society for his education, and Mazarin declared later to Carafa that he did this as a deliberate sign of his support for the Jesuits.[126] Relations between the court and the parlement were now deteriorating rapidly and as a result of the outbreak of hostilities, Louis, Anne, and Mazarin fled Paris on January 6, 1649. The Peace of Reuil ended the first phase of the Fronde the following April 1, but only in August did the court return to Paris. There they were welcomed back by the Jesuits, who greeted them at their church of St. Louis on the feast of St. Louis on August 25. Normally, the king came to the Jesuit church for this feast, but in 1649 the celebration took on the character of a reconciliation of the king with the people of Paris.[127]

Two months later the king's preceptor, Hardouin de Péréfixe, arrived at the residence of the Jesuit provincial superior to inform him that the king had chosen Charles Paulin as his confessor and would confess to him for the first time on the approaching feast of All Saints, November 1.[128] The Queen and Mazarin both informed Florence de Montmorency, vicar general of the Society after the death of Carafa, of the selection of Paulin. Mazarin stated that this was the Queen's choice but that he had done his part "to continue in the Society this great

123 Carafa to de la Haye (superior of the professed house), May 15, 1646, ARSJ, Francia 6I, f. 263'.

124 Pierre Blet, *Le clergé de France et la monarchie: Étude sur les Assemblées Générales du Clergé de 1615 à 1666* (Rome, 1959) 2: 3, 34–5; id., "Le chancelier Seguier protecteur de Jésuites, et l'Assemblée du Clergé de 1645," AHSJ 26 (1957): 177–98.

125 Mazarin to Carafa, Jan. 23, 1647, ARSJ, Epp. Ext. 4, f. 308.

126 Paulin to Carafa, Oct. 11, 1647, ARSJ, Francia 47, f. 156; Mazarin to Carafa, Dec. 24, 1647, ARSJ, Epp. Ext. 4, f. 323. In this letter Mazarin also thanked Carafa for an unnamed favor.

127 Cherot, 37–40.

128 Ibid., 24–5.

prerogative by representing to His Majesty its merits with the Crown, the satisfaction that the deceased king of happy memory had always had with his confessors, and the virtues and particular qualities of Father Paulin, which make him worthy of his most important task."[129] The Jesuits, of course, were delighted with this development.

Paulin had been born at Orleans in 1593 and entered the Jesuits in Paris in 1610. His work had been as a teacher of rhetoric and as a preacher in a number of colleges, including Clermont and La Flèche. In 1645 the Society designated him superior of the professed house in Paris. It was he who had made the arrangements for Mazarin's nephew to study with the Jesuits, and during the first Fronde he had helped mediate between Mazarin and his rival Paul de Gondi, the future Cardinal de Retz, then auxiliary bishop of Paris, whom Paulin had once taught as a student at Clermont. A reputation for moderation and conciliation attached to Paulin, qualities in short supply during this time of strife.[130] Two early tasks for Paulin were to prepare Louis for the sacrament of Confirmation, which he received on December 8, and then for his First Holy Communion on Christmas. Paulin remained loyal to Mazarin during the uprising of the nobles known as the second Fronde and always encouraged Louis to heed the cardinal's advice.[131] Paulin died on April 12, 1653, but all his successors as Louis's confessors would be drawn from the Society of Jesus. Thus was forged a firm bond between the Jesuits and the Sun King that would endure throughout his reign.

129 Mazarin to Montmorency, Oct. 29, 1649, ARSJ, Epp. Ext. 4, ff. 341–1'. Queen Anne's letter to the vicar general of October 28 is cited in Cherot, 41.
130 Cherot, 27–30, 38.
131 Ibid., 150–1, 155.

CHAPTER 9

Conclusion

At the start of this narrative three basic questions were proposed as governing it. First, what influence on policy in the war did the Jesuits exercise at the four courts of Vienna, Munich, Paris, and Madrid? Second, was there a "Jesuit" policy toward the war or a uniform position on the desirable relationship between religion and politics? Third, what were the principles and policies of the superior general as he guided the Society through the extended conflict? Now is the time to return to these questions and look at the responses that have emerged along with some of their implications.

One point is clear: The Jesuits were not a monolithic organization. Confessors differed from one another both in the conception of their office and in the policies that they advocated: Gans from Lamormaini, Vervaux from Contzen, Suffren from Arnoux, Aguado from Salazar. Vitelleschi as superior general had to deal with all of them, generally attempting to provide norms while at the same time respecting their individual situations. One enters in Paris a world different from Vienna or Munich.

First, during the Thirty Years War Jesuit court confessors exercised the greatest influence at the courts of Vienna and Munich. Here they had an evident impact on war policy. Apart perhaps from Arnoux's period as confessor of Louis XIII, this was not the case in Paris or Madrid. This state of affairs corresponds to the Jesuits' relatively greater influence in Catholic Germany than in either France or Spain. As we have noted, the greater prominence of the Jesuits in Germany resulted at least in part from the losses of the other religious orders during the Reformation and the relative weakness of ecclesiastical institutions in the empire. Jesuits served as confessors for other German Catholic princes besides the emperor and the elector of Bavaria, including the archbishop-electors of Mainz and Cologne.

Lamormaini and Contzen stand out as staunch advocates of the political and military measures associated with the militant Counter Reformation. They believed in and promoted a providential mission for Ferdinand II and Maximilian to restore Catholicism in Germany at least to its status in 1555 at the time of the Peace of Augsburg. They successfully championed the Edict of Restitution, where the religious nature of the long conflict appeared most clearly, and they supported its maintenance up to the Peace of Prague in 1635. They bore a responsibility for the war as both a religious conflict and a holy war. Gans, the confessor of Ferdinand III, said as much of Lamormaini. To the extent that he encouraged them in their grand project, Vitelleschi shared in this responsibility. But the initiative for this policy came from Germany not from Rome. Lamormaini and even more so Contzen expected eventual help from France for the Catholic cause in Germany, and they both were wary of Spain and its intentions. In this respect, too, they influenced Ferdinand II and Maximilian during the crucial period of the war.

After the Peace of Prague and following the appointment of the two moderates Gans and Vervaux as confessors to Ferdinand III and Maximilian, respectively, the influence of the confessors pointed to a much less militant policy. The Peace of Prague in 1635, not the Peace of Westphalia thirteen years later, marked the end of the aggressive Counter Reformation in the empire. At both courts the program of holy war and the brand of providentialism that characterized it were abandoned. This did not mean that the importance of religion diminished but that the benefit of religion was to be pursued by less militant means, which included a degree of toleration. Vitelleschi now joined the moderate camp in Germany, and so he, too, took a step, if a reluctant one, in the direction of toleration. He was moved to this by the two confessors, Gans and Vervaux, and by their princes, Ferdinand III and Maximilian. Urban VIII with his intensified search for peace also contributed to his change. The open entrance of France into the conflict in 1635 further lessened its religious character.

As a group, the German Jesuits themselves remained divided between moderates and militants. In Vienna under Ferdinand III and after the appointment of Gans, who had a much more modest conception of the role of the confessor than Lamormaini, the influence of the Jesuits at court declined substantially, as did the ecclesiastical role in general. In Munich Jesuit influence at court did not lessen with the appointment of Vervaux as Maximilian's confessor; instead, it increased. But it was now exercised in a new, moderate direction. Vervaux was even more deeply involved in politics than Contzen had been, and he seems to have enjoyed a closer personal relationship than his predecessor with

Maximilian, who entrusted him with the education of his heir, Ferdinand Maria, and the composition of his most prominent political testament. Even more than Contzen, Vervaux looked to France for help for Bavaria and the German Catholics.

Caution generally characterized the attitude of the Jesuits in France, where they had an extensive investment in schools and institutions that needed protection. Counter Reformation militance was muted. Here they faced many Catholic enemies, and their exile from most of the kingdom from 1594 to 1603 remained fixed in their collective memory. They relied on Louis and Richelieu, and this need for royal support explains Vitelleschi's extreme deference to the king and his minister as well as the Society's desire to hold on to the position of court confessor. In the early years of Louis's reign Jesuits with Vitelleschi's regular backing aided in the attempts to reconcile Louis and his mother. Some tilted toward Marie. Arnoux was attached to the *dévots;* he favored a pro-Habsburg foreign policy, as had Coton before him, and vigorous action against the Huguenots at home, against whom he called for holy war.

But after Arnoux's sudden dismissal in 1621, the court confessors in France were *bons français,* even before the advent of Richelieu to power. Suffren in his sermon after the defeat of La Rochelle called the Huguenots rebels against royal authority not heretics. The cardinal then oversaw carefully the selection and activity of the confessor, seeking to remove him as far as possible from politics. In this he generally succeeded. But in 1637 he unwisely designated Caussin Louis's confessor. Caussin alone among the Jesuit confessors in France attempted to challenge the cardinal, in a bold effort to end the war and restore peace to France and Europe. But the confessor and his accomplice lost the battle for Louis's soul. Vitelleschi's abandonment of Caussin stained his record, even if it concurred with the view of the leading French Jesuits and was understandable as necessary to preserve the Society's interests in France.

The Jesuits were least influential at the court of Spain, where they did not supply the confessor of the king himself. Other religious orders remained more vigorous here than in Germany or France. The Spaniards, to be sure, considered themselves defenders of the faith, but at least in the seventeenth century neither they nor the Spanish Jesuits saw themselves as fighting a holy or even a religious war against heretics. Counter Reformation militance was least evident here. This was a principal source of the differences between Vitelleschi and the Spaniards. The Spaniards considered Vitelleschi's support for Lamormaini's campaign for the restoration of Catholicism in the empire to be wrong-headed and inimical to their hope for imperial assistance in Italy and

The Netherlands. Vitelleschi also inclined, with Urban VIII, to oppose Spanish policy in Italy. He resisted manfully the attempt of Olivares to secure the dismissal of Lamormaini despite the threats of the count-duke, and he also worked to remove Salazar from his government positions. Vitelleschi once complained that the Spaniards felt that he was French and the French that he was Spanish. The Spaniards could make a legitimate case for their position.

Obviously, then, the response to the first part of our second question is no, there existed no grand Jesuit policy in the war. Furthermore, Jesuits varied considerably in their support of Counter Reformation measures. But was there a consistent policy among the Jesuits regarding the proper relationship between religion and politics? Here, too, the answer is no. One need only recall the exchange between Lamormaini and Suffren in 1629/30.

Ignatius Loyola himself back in 1552 had made the fundamental decision that the advantages to be gained from service as confessor to a prince outweighed the disadvantages. The Society stuck with this ministry despite the ill will and suspicion it garnered. The type of political activity to be permitted Jesuits and especially court confessors long antedated Vitelleschi as a controversial issue within the order. Several general congregations dealt with it, and in 1602 Acquaviva released his normative Instruction with its ambiguities, which general congregations in 1608 and 1615 vainly attempted to clarify. It fell then to Vitelleschi as superior general to adapt the Society's directives for confessors to the changing situations of the Thirty Years War. Gradually, he developed a flexible policy that afforded princely confessors considerable latitude. Often enough he encountered opposition from within the Society itself for his support of the confessors. As we look at his policy, we also move on to our third question: What principles and policies guided Vitelleschi during the war?

From early on Vitelleschi judged that political activity in service of the interests of the church was not only to be allowed but to be encouraged. He stated this principle clearly when in 1621 he instructed the Spanish royal preacher, Jerónimo de Florencia, to intervene at court in order to secure religious freedom for the Catholics of the Valtelline. Although involvement with matters of reason of state was normally foreign to the religious vocation, when it was a question of preserving the faith or advancing the neighbors' spiritual good or the glory of God, then the Jesuit in a position to do so not only could but was obliged to intervene in political matters. Activity against heretics justified involvement in politics by the Jesuit court confessors. This was more so the case if the pope also exhorted to action. Both Gregory XV and Vitelleschi urged

Becan to promote the transfer of the electoral title to Maximilian despite the fear of some Catholics that this would only hinder a peace settlement. Arnoux also received encouragement from Vitelleschi for Louis's campaigns against the Huguenots in 1621/22, when Gregory XV was summoning the French king to a militant policy. Certainly, Vitelleschi supported Lamormaini and Contzen in their offensive against heresy. He subsequently made the switch to a moderate policy along with Gans and Vervaux. But this change indicated less a new conception of the role of the confessor than a different policy to be advocated by him.

Even regarding issues where the interests of the church were not directly in play, Vitelleschi recognized the wide overlap in practice of matters of politics and matters of conscience, and he permitted and even advocated action by court confessors where this was the case. In the early years of his generalate, especially in the instance of Jean Arnoux, he seemed somewhat unclear and ambiguous as to where to draw the line. But his views were more definite when in 1631 he wrote to the new confessor of Louis XIII, Charles Maillan, "with regard to matters of state, the Society does not prohibit [your dealing with] those that pertain to the direction of the king's conscience, which are included in the office of confessor," but he did not provide any examples. In an apparent response to a suggestion by Vervaux in 1642 that the rule prohibiting Jesuits from political affairs be changed, he declared that there was no need for this. When a proper moral judgment or the formation of conscience required it, a Jesuit confessor could concern himself with matters of state and even be present at council meetings provided that he remain silent and not vote in the council. This Vervaux could take as "a rule of conduct."

But there were limits. Vitelleschi forcefully opposed for Jesuits the holding of government office or the appearance of holding it. He refused Arnoux's request that he be permitted to take the title of "councillor." The objection to government office came out most evidently in the long effort to end the various governmental activities of Hernando Salazar. Contzen and other Munich Jesuits served periodically on government committees; Contzen, as well as Salazar, was called upon for advice on economic policy, and both seem to have advocated unpopular taxes. But Contzen never formally held a government office, as did Salazar. Nor did Contzen attend council meetings. Vitelleschi never learned of Vervaux's mission to France for Maximilian.

Vitelleschi regularly objected to and sought to rein in the composition of political pamphlets by Jesuits, usually anonymously or pseudonymously, in the service of a prince. He constantly returned to this theme, and he addressed the whole Society in circular letters on it. Jesuits were to resist the pressures to engage in this work even if it meant offending a prince. But the superior general's efforts met with limited success. One thinks especially of the two pamphets of 1624/25, the *Political Mysteries* and the *Admonition to Louis XIII*, attacks on Richelieu written by Contzen for Maximilian. Vitelleschi never did discover the identity of the author. Keller and Fitzsimons both received punishments for their rival accounts of the Bohemian campaign glorifying their respective patrons. Vitelleschi's attempt in his early years to prevent the publication of politically controversial theological works like those on the indirect power of the pope in temporal affairs also enjoyed only modest success. Carafa faced a similar problem at the time of the Peace of Westphalia. Even with a reasonably effective procedure of censorship, it was difficult to control the polemical writings of Jesuits.

Pope Innocent X made Jesuit involvement in politics an issue for the general congregation that elected Vincent Carafa in 1646. Discussions in the congregation revealed a variety of views and criticisms of Vitelleschi; all Jesuits were certainly not of one mind on the topic. In the end, the assembly merely reaffirmed the legislation on the issue and called for effective enforcement. Carafa intended to implement the Society's directives more strictly. More than Vitelleschi, he avoided taking positions himself on political issues. In response to Vervaux's request at the behest of Maximilian to be allowed a greater role in government, he stated that the Seventh General Congregation of 1615 had laxly interpreted the Fifth General Congregation (1593/94) by allowing Jesuits to deal with political matters in the direction of a ruler's conscience, a position that implicitly questioned Acquaviva's Instruction itself. Subsequently, he agreed that Vervaux could advise Maximilian on political matters outside confession, but he could not attend council meetings as Vitelleschi had permitted.

But Carafa was not able to maintain such a strict line. His attempt to remove Gans from office, to be sure not for political reasons, failed because of the opposition of the emperor. Maximilian also eventually secured from Carafa permission for Vervaux to attend council meetings without voicing an opinion. But Carafa put his foot down and prevented Vervaux from carrying on a political correspondence with contacts in France. In the contest between the moderates, Maximilian and Vervaux on one side and the militants Wangnereck and Chigi on the other, Carafa found himself caught in the middle between two rocks, as he put it. While attempting to escape taking a position on the issue itself, he took measures against Wangnereck because of the insulting tone of his *Theological Response*. But at the insistence of Maximilian, Carafa prohibited Jesuits from writing against the peace, and in doing this he followed the lead of the papacy, which held off its protest until late 1650, thus not allowing it to be used to incite further fighting. This was a victory for the moderates.

A second principle of Vitelleschi was to foster papal policy. His background helped him to move easily in the Roman ecclesiastical world. He seems to have spoken frequently with Paul V and the particularly pro-Jesuit Gregory XV, but during the papacy of Urban VIII most of his contacts with the pope were through the papal nephew Francesco Barberini. Vitelleschi does not seem to have understood the subtleties, or inconsistencies, of Urban's policy toward the empire, especially on the Edict of Restitution. One of his consistent goals was to foster harmony between the pope and the emperor, to which he constantly exhorted Lamormaini. Overall, he shared the papal goal of unity among the Catholic princes, so as to combat Protestantism effectively and then to turn on the Turks. He supported the papal diplomatic initiative of 1632 to foster peace among the Catholic states and then in 1635 and thereafter the papal efforts at a peace conference to end the long conflict. But his fear of Richelieu made him careful not to advocate any action that might conflict with the cardinal's agenda, and his realization of his lack of influence in Madrid prevented him from advancing the papal initiative directly there. Rather, at one point he hoped to get Lamormaini to persuade the emperor to draw Madrid in this direction. Consistently, Vitelleschi served as a middleman between Rome and Maximilian, advising the elector of complaints against him circulating in Rome and supporting his requests for funds while at the same time explaining to Maximilian the papacy's reluctance to supply them.

But throughout his long tenure as superior general, Muzio Vitelleschi recognized that the Society of Jesus depended on the support of princes for the success of its apostolic ministries. This realization characterized his government of the Society, and it sometimes led to tension with the papacy, as at the time of the Santarelli affair in France, where his political skills enabled him to navigate between the demands of Urban VIII and the claims of Louis and Richelieu. "Without their [that is, the princes'] support our labor can accomplish very little or even nothing in many places," he wrote to Lamormaini in 1625, and in this context he also stressed the need to develop contacts with those around the prince. In support of this view he cited both the Constitutions of the Society and the practice of Ignatius Loyola. The Society saw in its exercise of the office of princely confessor an important means of exercising influence on rulers and maintaining support from them.

His perception of the need for princely support for the Society's work explains Vitelleschi's almost obsessive concern to avoid offending princes. The intent not to offend princes posed challenges when they were at odds with one another, as they often were. Vitelleschi found it necessary to confront "the national spirit" from the start of his generalate, and he consistently lamented the activity of Jesuits who published works in support of one ruler, often to the annoyance of another. His approach to controversial publications by Jesuits on religio-political issues was often dictated not so much by their content as by the potential they had for alienating a prince. The same held for Carafa.

The foundation and development of the Society of Jesus has generally, and correctly, been interpreted as bolstering the role of the papacy. But one can argue, on the other hand, that Jesuit support of princes in the seventeenth century also contributed to the advance of princely absolutism vis-à-vis the church. It has been noted that the Santarelli affair of 1626 marked the last time that the traditional position of Bellarmine, Suarez, and others on the indirect power of the papacy in temporal affairs became a serious issue in France and that even then significant Jesuits in France revealed clear Gallican sympathies.[1] Ferdinand II has been called the founder of Josephinism in the Habsburg Monarchy, and the Jesuits were allied with him. Lamormaini referred to those in Rome as "little dogs" who opposed the Jesuit control of the University of Prague, which the emperor desired, against the archbishop, other religious orders, and even Pope Urban. For him as well it was the Jesuits along with the Habsburgs who rescued the church in Germany after the disaster of the Reformation. Nuncio Mattei at Regensburg remarked in 1640 that the Jesuits were solid religious but that they tended to favor the interests of princes over the Holy See.

Responsibility for the image and reputation of the Society lay heavily on Vitelleschi. This is understandable. Reputation, or the opinion that others had of you, determined your credibility and your support from them, whether you were a religious order or a ruler. Credibility and support were essential for effective ministry, whether pastoral or educational. Vitelleschi feared that through the court confessor the Jesuits would be identified with unpopular policies of the prince, especially taxation and war, both of which bore heavily upon populations, and that this in turn would undermine their ministries. Lamormaini, Contzen, and even Vervaux in Germany and Salazar in Spain came in for bitter criticism, even from fellow Jesuits, for their apparent complicity in unpopular policies. It was difficult to avoid odium for these if at the same time a confessor was known to enjoy influence at court. This counted

[1] Pierre Blet, "Jésuites gallicanes au xviie siècle? À propos de l'ouvrage du P. Guitton sur le P. de la Chaize," AHSJ 29 (1960): 64–71.

as a disadvantage that attached to the position of princely confessor. Vitelleschi sought to lessen it by suggesting ways that the confessor might stay out of public view. Maximilian turned this situation to the advantage of the moderates when he warned Carafa of the resentment that the Jesuits would incur throughout Germany if they were held responsible for the prolongation of the war.

We have become familiar with Vitelleschi's mode of questioning or correcting the court confessors. Usually he would describe a charge made against them and then assert that he himself did not believe it. But, he would continue, how should we respond to those who made and repeated the charge? So he brought the matter to the attention of the Jesuit involved without accusing him. Vitelleschi also usually defended the confessors against complaints of Jesuits from the ranks. This was the case with Arnoux, Lamormaini, Contzen, and Vervaux. Caussin did not merit similar treatment. Except in his case, Vitelleschi showed that he realized the difficulty and delicacy of the confessors' task and tried to shield them from some of the criticism it inevitably evoked.

Vitelleschi has been criticized as lax in his government of the Society of Jesus, especially when compared with his predecessor Acquaviva. This seems unfair. Vitelleschi faced a more difficult situation during the Thirty Years War than had Acquaviva prior to it. Ferdinand II and Ferdinand III, Maximilian, and Louis XIII along with Richelieu were more imposing rulers than their sixteenth-century predecessors. Even if this were not the case in Spain, Philip IV supported by Olivares was a formidable king. By the seventeenth century more progress had been made in the direction of absolutism, that is, the growing centralization and consolidation of princely government. The Thirty Years War represented a high point of the influence of the Jesuit court confessors. With his tact and political sense Vitelleschi was able to keep the international Society united in a time of intense princely rivalries. That was his achievement, and despite his shortcomings we must recognize his prudence and political astuteness, as did the French ambassador back in 1626. Carafa, who once referred to lax interpretation of the Society's decrees under his predecessor, could do no better. The Jesuits were long to struggle with their relationship to politics, both in Europe and across the seas. Indeed, they do so up to the present day. But that is a further story.

Bibliography and Sources

MANUSCRIPT SOURCES

For a complete list of all manuscript sources consulted, see also, for Munich and Rome, Robert Bireley, *Maximilian von Bayern, Adam Contzen, S.J., und die Gegenreformation in Deutschland, 1624–1635* (Göttingen, 1975); and for Vienna and Rome, *Religion and Politics in the Age of the Counterreformation: Emperor Ferdinand II, William Lamormaini, S.J., and the Formation of Imperial Policy* (Chapel Hill, NC, 1981).

Louviers (France), *Médiathèque*
  Bound volume of copies of correspondence of Nicholas Caussin, S.J., 1637–43
Madrid, *Biblioteca Nacional*
  Manuscriti 2311, 2352, 2375, 2712, 2939, 4015, 4539, 7371, 7968
 Real Academia de la Historia
  Legajo 9/7259
  Tomo 159, #39
Munich, *Bayerisches Hauptstaatsarchiv*
  Jesuitica, 651, 656, 658, 659, 700, 704, 705, 706
  Kasten Schwarz 8165, 8613
 Bayerische Staatsbibliothek
  Handschriftenabteilung, Cgm, 2618, 2
Paris, *Archives Diplomatiques*
  Correspondance Rome, 1635–42, 1656–61
 Bibliothèque de l'Institut de France
  Manuscrits Godefroy, 15
 Bibliothèque National
  Collection Dupuy, 92
  Manuscrits français, 3796, 3823, 18016, 25054
Rome, *Archivum Romanum Societatis Jesu*
  Austriae Provincia 2I–II, 3I–II, 4I–II, 5I–II, 6, 21, 23, 26, 135, 136
  Bohemiae Provincia 1I–II, 11, 12, 93–5, 192, 201
  Congregationes 20a, c, d; 53–6, 66–72

Epistolae Externorum 4, 17, 31–3
Epistolae Generalium 2, 3
Franciae Provincia 3–4, 5I–II, 6I–II, 32I–II, 33I–II, 41I–II, 47
Galliae Assistentia 38, 46I–II
Germaniae Assistentia 113I–II, 113a
Germaniae Superioris Provincia 4–8
Hispaniae Assistentia 70, 71I, 82
Opera Nostrorum 246
Toletana Provincia 7I–II, 8II, 9, 10
Rheni Inferioris Provincia 5–6, 7I–II, 8
Rheni Superioris Provincia 1–2
Vitae 62, 127, 139, 158, 161

Vanves (France), *Archives Jésuites* (Archives of the French Provinces of the Jesuits)
Collection Prat, 11, 13, 18, 24, 33, 35, 37, 44, 78
(This collection is made up of copies of documents from Jesuit archives in Rome and elsewhere assembled by Jean-Marie Prat, S.J. in the nineteenth century.)

PRINTED SOURCES AND LITERATURE[1]

Published Originally before 1700

Adlzreiter, Johannes [Johannes Vervaux]. *Annales boicae gentis*. 3 vols. Munich, 1662.

Aguado, Francisco. *El cristiano sabio*. Madrid, 1638.

______. *Exhortationes varias, dotrinales*. Madrid, 1641.

Aldimari, Biagio. *Historia genealogica della famiglia Carafa*. Naples, 1691.

Andrade, Alonso de. *Vida del Venerable P. Francisco Aguado*. Madrid, 1658.

Bartoli, Daniello. *Dalla vita del Vincenzo Carafa, settimo generale della Compagnia di Gesú*. Rome, 1651.

Becan, Martin. *Manuale controversiarum hujus temporis*. Würzburg, 1623.

Bellarmine, Robert. *De officio principis christiani* (1619), in *Opera omnia* (Paris, 1873; rpt. 1965), vol. 8: 87–235.

Caramuel y Lobkowicz, Johann. *Sacri Romani Imperii pax licita demonstrata*. 3rd ed. Frankfurt, 1648.

Caussin, Nicholas. *La cour sainte*. 2nd ed. Paris, 1625.

______. *Angelus pacis: Ad principes christianos*. Paris, 1650.

______. *Apologie pour les religieude la Compagnie de Jésus*. 2nd ed. Lyons, 1644.

______. *Regnum Dei seu dissertationes in libros regum*. Paris, 1650.

Clemente, Claudio. *El machiavelismo degollado por la christiana sabiduria de España y de Austria*. Trans. from 2nd Latin ed. Alcalá, 1637.

Contzen, Adam. *Politicorum libri decem*. Mainz, 1621.

[1] Works that have been cited only once are not usually included here.

[______]. *Ad Ludovicum Decimum Tertium Galliae et Navarrae Regem Christianissimum admonitio.* 1625, n.p.

[______]. *Mysteria politica.* Naples, 1624.

[Ernestus de Eusebiis]. *Judicium theologicum supra quaestione, an pax qualem desiderant Protestantes sit secundum se illicita?* Ecclesiopoli, 1648.

Florencia, Jerónimo de. *Marial para las fiestas de Nuestra Señora.* 2 vols. Madrid, 1625.

Lamormaini, William. *Ferdinandi II Romanorum Imperatoris virtutes.* Vienna, 1638.

Laymann, Paul. *Pacis compositio inter principes et ordines Catholicos atque Augustanae Confessionis adhaerentes in Comitiis Augustae a. 1555 edita.* Dillingen, 1629.

Mercure français. Vols. 7–25. Paris, 1620–48.

Orléans, Pierre Joseph d'. *La vie de Pierre Coton de la Compagnie de Jésus: Confesseur des roys Henry IV et Louis XIII.* Paris, 1688.

Suffren, Jean. *L'année chrestienne.* 2 vols. 2nd ed. Paris, 1641.

Vitelleschi, Muzio. *Epistolae quatuor Adm. R.P.N. Mutii Vitelleschi, S.J.* n.p., n.d.

Wangnereck, Heinrich. See Ernestus de Eusebiis.

PRINTED AFTER 1700

Acta Pacis Westphalicae, ed. Konrad Repgen.
Series 1: *Instruktionen.*
Vol. 1: *Frankreich, Schweden, Kaiser.* Münster, 1962.
Series 2: *Korrespondenzen.*
Section A: *Die kaiserlichen Korrespondenzen.*
Vols. 1, 3, 5: *1643–1647.* Münster, 1969–98.
Section B: *Die französischen Korrespondenzen.*
Vols. 1, 2, 4: *1644–1645.* Münster, 1979–99.
Series 3: *Protokolle, Verhandlungsakten, Diarien, Vari.*
Section C: *Diarien.*
Vols. 1, 1 (Chigi); 2, 1–3 (Vollmar); 3, 1–2 (Wartenberg); 4 (Lamberg). Münster, 1984–93.

Adamson, John, ed. *The Princely Courts of Europe: Ritual, Politics, and Culture under the Ancien Régime, 1500–1750.* London, 1999.

Albrecht, Dieter. *Die auswärtige Politik Maximilians von Bayern 1618–1635.* Schriftenreihe der Historischen Kommission bei der Bayerischen Akademie der Wissenschaften, 6. Göttingen, 1962.

______. *Die deutsche Politik Papst Gregors XV: Die Einwirkung der päpstlichen Diplomatie auf der Politik der Häuser Habsburg und Wittelsbach 1621–1623.* Schriftenreihe zur bayerischen Landesgeschichte, 53. Munich, 1956.

______. *Maximilian I. von Bayern 1573–1651.* Munich, 1998.

______. "Zur Finanzierung des Dreissigjährigen Krieges: Die Subsidien der Kurie für Kaiser und Liga 1618–1635." *Zeitschrift für bayerische Landesgeschichte* 19 (1956): 534–67, rpt. in Hans Ulrich Rudolf, ed., *Der*

Dreissigjährige Krieg: Perspektiven und Strukturen. Wege der Forschung, 451 (Darmstadt, 1977): 368–412.

Aldea Vaquero, Quintin. "España, el papado y el imperio durante la guerra de los Treinte Años."
Part 1: "Instrucciones a los embajadores de España en Roma (1631–1643)."
Part 2: "Instrucciones a los nuncios apostólicos en España (1624–1632)." *Miscelanea Comillas* 29 (1958): 293–437; 30 (1959): 251–330.

———. "La neutralidad de Urbano VIII en los años decisivos de la Guerra de Treinta Años (1628–1632)." *Hispania Sacra* 21 (1968): 155–78.

Andretta, Stefano. "La diplomazia veneziana e la pace de Vestfalia (1643–1648)." *Annuario dell'Istituto Storico per l'età moderna e contemporanea* 27–8 (1975–6): 5–128.

Asch, Ronald G. *The Thirty Years War: The Holy Roman Empire and Europe, 1618–1648*. New York, 1997.

———. and Adolf M. Burke, eds. *Princes, Patronage and the Nobility: the Court at the Beginning of the Modern Age, c. 1450–1650*. Oxford, 1991.

Astráin, Antonio. *Historia de la Compañia de Jesús en la Asistencia de España*. Vol. 5, *Vitelleschi, Carafa, Piccolomini, 1615–1652*. Madrid, 1916.

Barozzi, N. and G. Berchet, eds. *Relazioni degli stati europei*. Series 1: *Spagna*. 2 vols. Venice, 1856/1860.

Bassompierre, François de. *Journal de ma vie*. 4 vols. Ed. A. de La Cropte de Chantérac. Paris, 1870–7.

Beguin, Katia. *Les Princes de Condé: Rebelles, courtisans, et Mécènes dans la France du Grand Siècle*. Seyssel, 1999.

Bellazzi, Pietro. *Juan Caramuel*. Vigevano, 1982.

Belvederi, Raffaele. *Guido Bentivoglio e la politica europea del suo tempo 1607–1621*. Padua, 1962.

Bentivoglio, Guido. *La nunziatura di Francia del Cardinale Guido Bentivoglio. Lettere a Scipione Borghese*. Ed. Luigi di Steffani. 4 vols. Florence, 1863–70.

Bergin, Joseph. *Cardinal de la Rochefoucauld: Leadership and Reform in the French Church*. New Haven, 1987.

———. and Lawrence Brockliss, eds. *Richelieu and his Age*. Oxford, 1992.

Bierther, Kathrin. *Der Regensburger Reichstag von 1640/1641*. Regensburger Historische Forschungen, Kallmunz, 1971.

Bireley, Robert. *Maximilian von Bayern, Adam Contzen, S.J., und die Gegenreformation in Deutschland, 1624–1635*. Schriftenreihe der Historischen Kommission bei der bayerischen Akademie der Wissenschaften, 13. Göttingen, 1975.

———. "The Origins of the *Pacis Compositio* (1629): a text of Paul Laymann S.J." *AHSJ* 42 (1973): 106–27.

———. *Religion and Politics in the Age of the Counterreformation: Emperor Ferdinand II, William Lamormaini, S.J., and the Formation of Imperial Policy*. Chapel Hill, 1981.

Blet, Pierre. "Bernardino Spada nonce auprès de Louis XIII et de Richelieu." *Studi Romangoli* 28 (1977): 281–98.

———. "Le chancelier Séguier, protecteur des Jésuites, et l'Assemblée du Clergé de 1645." *AHSJ* 26 (1957): 177–98.
———. *Le clergé de France et la monarchie: Étude sur les Assemblées Générales du Clergé de 1615 à 1666.* 2 vols. Analecta Gregoriana, 106–7. Rome, 1959.
———. *Le clergé du Grand Siècle en ses Assemblées* (1615–1715). Histoire religieuse de la France. Paris, 1995.
———. "La Congregation des Affaires de France de 1640." In *Mélanges E. Tisserant.* Vol. 4. Studi e testi 234 (Vatican City, 1964): 59–105.
———. "Jésuites gallicans au xviie siècle? À propos de l'ouvrage du P. Guitton sur le P. de la Chaize." *AHSJ* 29 (1960): 55–84.
———. "Jésuites et libertés gallicanes en 1611." *AHSJ* 24 (1955): 165–88.
———, ed. *Correspondance du nonce en France Ranuccio Scotti (1639–1641).* Paris, 1965.
Blond, Louis. "Paris, 2. La maison professe Saint-Louis de la rue Saint-Antoine (1580–1763)." In *Les établissements des Jésuites en France depuis quatre siècles.* Ed. Pierre Delattre. Vol. 3 (Enghien, 1955): 1259–1307.
Briefe und Akten zur Geschichte des Dreissigjährigen Krieges. Neue Folge: Die Politik Maximilians I. von Bayern und seiner Verbündeten 1618–1635.
Part 1
Vol. 1: *Januar 1618–Dezember 1620.* Ed. Georg Franz. Munich, 1966.
Vol. 2: *Januar 1621–Dezember 1622.* Ed. Arno Duch. Munich, 1970.
Part 2
Vol. 1: *Januar 1623–Dezember 1624.* Ed. Walter Goetz. Munich, 1907.
Vol. 2: *Januar–Dezember 1625.* Ed. Walter Goetz. Munich, 1918.
Vol. 3: *Januar 1626–Dezember 1627.* Ed. Walter Goetz. Munich, 1942.
Vol. 4: *Januar 1628–Juni 1629.* Ed. Walter Goetz, Munich, 1948.
Vol. 5: *Juli 1629–Dezember 1630.* Ed. Dieter Albrecht. Munich, 1964.
Vol. 8: *Januar 1633–Mai 1634.* Ed. Kathrin Bierther. Munich, 1982.
Vol. 9: *Juni 1634–Mai 1635.* Ed. Kathrin Bierther. Munich, 1986.
Vol 10: *Der Prager Frieden 1635.* Ed. Kathrin Bierther. 4 vols. Munich, 1997.
Burckhardt, Johannes. *Der Dreissigjährige Krieg.* Frankfurt, 1992.
Bussmann, Klaus, and Heinz Schilling, eds. *1648 War and Peace in Europe.* 3 vols. Münster, 1998.
Carayon, Auguste, ed. *Documents inédits concernant la compagnie de Jésus.* Vols. 1–3, 23. Poitiers, 1863–86.
Cartas de algunos PP. de la Compañía de Jesús sobre los sucesos de la monarquía entre los años de 1634 y 1648. Memorial Histórico Español, 13–19. Madrid, 1861–5.
Cherot, P.H. *La première jeunesse de Louis XIV, 1643–53.* Paris, 1892.
Cheruel, Adolphe. *Histoire de France pendant la minorité de Louis XIV.* 4 vols. Paris, 1879–80.
Chevallier, Pierre. *Louis XIII, roi cornélien.* Paris, 1979.
Church, William F. *Richelieu and Reason of State.* Princeton, 1972.

Constant, Jean-Marie. *Les conjurateurs: Le premier libéralisme politique sous Richelieu*. Paris, 1987.

Cordara, Givlio Cesare. *Historiae Societatis Jesu Pars Sexta, 1616–1633*. 2 vols. Rome, 1750–1859.

Correspondencia diplomática de los plenipotenciarios Españoles en el Congreso de Münster 1643–1648. 3 vols. Colección de documentos inéditos para la historia de España, vols. 82–4. Madrid, 1884–5.

Cousin, Victor. *Madame de Hautefort: Nouvelles études sur les femmes illustres et la société du xviie siècle*. 4th ed. Paris, 1874.

Croxton, Derek. *Peacemaking in Early Modern Europe: Cardinal Mazarin and the Congress of Westphalia, 1643–1648*. London, 1999.

Cueto, R. "Crisis, consciencia y confesores en la guerra de Treinta Años." *Quadernos de investigación historica* 16 (1995): 249–65.

De Carrocera, Buonaventura. "El Padre Diego de Quiroga, diplomático y confesor de reyes, 1574–1649." *Estudios Franciscanos* 50 (1949): 71–100.

Dévèze, Michel. "1635: Le heurt idéologique franco-espagnol." In *Actes du 94e Congrès National des Sociétés Savantes* (Pau, 1969) 1: 23–38.

Diaz, José Simon. *Historia del colegio imperial de Madrid*. 2 vols. Madrid, 1952–9.

Dickmann, Fritz. *Der westfälische Friede*, 7th ed. Ed. Konrad Repgen. Münster, 1998.

Didier, Hugues. "Un franc-comtois au service de L'Espagne: Claude Clement S.J. (1592–1642)." *AHSJ* 44 (1975): 254–64.

Dollinger, Heinz. "Kurfürst Maximilian von Bayern und Justus Lipsius." *Archiv für Kulturgeschichte* 46 (1964): 227–308.

Dudik, Beda. "Korrespondenz Kaiser Ferdinands und seiner Familie mit P. Martinus Becanus und Pater Wilhelm Lamormaini, Kaiserl. Beichtväter S.J." *Archiv für österreichische Geschichte* 54 (1876): 219–350.

Duhr, Bernhard. *Geschichte der Jesuiten in den Ländern deutscher Zunge*. Vol. 2, parts 1 and 2. Freiburg, 1913.

Eckhardt, Carl C. *The Papacy and World Affairs, as Reflected in the Secularization of Politics*. Chicago, 1937.

Elliott, J.H. *The Count-Duke of Olivares: The Statesman in an Age of Decline*. New Haven, CT, 1986.

Epistolae praepositorum generalium Societatis Jesu. Vol. 1. Ghent, 1847.

Ernst, Hildegard. *Madrid und Wien 1632–1637: Politik und Finanzen in den Beziehungen zwischen Philip IV. und Ferdinand II*. Münster, 1991.

Estrées, François Annibal d'. *Mémoires du maréchal d'Estrée*. Ed. P. Bonnefon. Paris, 1910.

Evans, R.J.W. *The Making of the Habsburg Monarchy, 1550–1700: An Interpretation*, 3rd ed. Oxford, 1991.

Feldkamp, M.F. "Das Breve 'Zelo Domus Dei' vom 16 November 1648. Edition." *Archivum historiae pontificiae* 31 (1993): 293–305.

Feros, Antonio. *Kingship and Favoritism in the Spain of Philip III, 1592–1621*. Cambridge, 2000.

Firpo, Luigi, ed. *Relazioni di ambasciatori veneti al Senato, tratte dalle migliori edizioni disponibili e ordinate cronologicamente*. Vols. 3, 6, 9, 10. Turin, 1965–79.

Fitzsimon, Henry. "Diary of the Bohemian War of 1620." In *Words of Comfort to Persecuted Catholics*, ed. Edmund Hogan (Dublin, 1881): 83–108.

Fois, M. "Generales: 6, Vitelleschi," in *Diccionario historico de la Compañía de Jesús*, eds. Charles E. O'Neill, S.J., and Joaquin M. Dominguez, S.J. (Rome/Madrid, 2001) 2: 1621–7.

Forschungen und Studien zur Geschichte des westfälischen Friedens: Vorträge bei dem Colloquium französischer und deutscher Historiker vom 28 April–30 April 1963 in Münster. Schriftenreihe der Vereinigung zur Erforschung der neueren Geschichte. Münster, 1965

Fouqueray, Henri. *Histoire de la Compagnie de Jésus en France*. Vols. 3–5. Paris, 1922–5.

______. "Le Père Jean Suffren à la cour de Marie de Médicis et Louis XIII, d'après les mémoires du temps et des documents inédits." *Revue des questions historiques* 68 (1900): 74–131, 445–71. Also published separately, Paris, 1900.

Friedensburg, W. "Regesten zur deutschen Geschichte aus der Zeit des Pontifikats Innocenz X (1644–1655)." *Quellen und Forschungen aus italienischen Archiven und Bibliotheken* 4 (1902): 236–85; 6 (1904): 146–73.

Garasse, François. "Récit au vrai des persécutions soulevées contre les pères de la Compagnie de Jésus dans la ville de Paris l'an 1624, 1625 et 1626." In *Documents inédits concernant la Compagnie de Jésus* 3 (Poitiers, 1864): 1–234.

Gigli, G. *Diario romano*. Ed. G. Ricciotti. Rome, 1958.

González Palencia, Angel. *Noticias de Madrid, 1621–1627*. Madrid, 1942.

Griffet, Henri. *Histoire du règne de Louis XIII, roi de France et de Navarre*. New ed. 3 vols. Paris, 1758.

Griselle, Eugène. *Louis XIII et Richelieu: Lettres et pièces diplomatiques*. Paris, 1911 (rpt. Geneva, 1974).

______. *Profils de Jésuites du xviie siècle*. Lille/Paris, 1911.

______, ed. *État de la maison du Roi Louis XIII*. Paris, 1912.

Gui, Francesco. *I Gesuiti e la rivoluzione boema: Alle origini della Guerra dei Trent'Anni*. Milan, 1989.

Günter, Heinrich. *Die Habsburgerliga, 1625–1635: Briefe und Akten aus dem General-Archiv zu Simancas*. Berlin, 1908.

______. *Das Restitutionsedikt von 1629 und die katholische Restauration Altwirtembergs*. Stuttgart, 1901.

Haan, Hainer. *Der Regensburger Kurfürstentag von 1636/1637*. Münster, 1967.

Hanotaux, Gabriel. "La crise européenne de 1621." *Revue des deux mondes* V, 7 (1902): 5–44, 481–507.

______, and La Force, duc de. *Histoire du Cardinal de Richelieu* 5: *La lutte contre la maison d'autriche*. Paris, 1944.

Hansen, Georg. "Briefe des Jesuitenpaters Nithard Biber an den Churfürsten Anselm Casimir von Mainz, geschrieben auf seiner Romreise 1645/46." *Archivalische Zeitschrift*, new series, 9 (1900): 132–75.

Hartmann, Anja Victorine. *Von Regensburg nach Hamburg: Die diplomatischen Beziehungen zwischen dem französischen König und dem Kaiser vom Regensburger Vertrag (13. Oktober 1630) bis zum Hamburger Präliminarfrieden*

(25. Dezember 1641). Schriftenreihe der Vereinigung zur Erforschung der Neueren Geschichte. Münster, 1998.

Hermant, Godefroi. *Mémoires de Godefroi Hermant sur l'histoire ecclésiastique du xviie siècle.* Ed. A. Gazier. Vol. 1: *1630–1652.* Paris, 1905.

Immler, Gerhard. *Kurfürst Maximilian I. und der westfälische Friedenskongress: Die bayerische auswärtige Politik vom 1644 bis zum Ulmer Waffenstillstand.* Schriftenreihe der Vereinigung zur Erforschung der neueren Geschichte, 20. Münster, 1992.

———. "Kurfürst Maximilian und die Kirche: Aspekte seiner Finanzpolitik während des Dreissigjährigen Krieges." *Zeitschrift für bayerische Landesgeschichte* 51 (1988): 387–409.

Institutum Societatis Jesu. 3 vols. Florence, 1892–3.

Jaitner, Klaus, ed. *Die Hauptinstruktionen Gregors XV für die Nuntien und Legaten an den europäischen Fürstenhöfen 1621–1623.* 2 vols. Tübingen, 1997.

Johnson, James Turner. *The Holy War Idea in Western and Islamic Traditions.* University Park, PA, 1997.

Jover, José Maria. *1635. Historia de una polémica y semblanza de una generación.* Madrid, 1949.

Kiewning, Hans, ed. *Nuntiaturberichte aus Deutschland nebst ergänzenden Aktenstücken*: Section 4, *Siebzehntes Jahrhundert, Nuntiatur des Pallotto 1628–1630.* 2 vols. Berlin, 1895–97.

Kleinman, Ruth. *Anne of Austria, Queen of France.* Columbus, OH, 1985.

Kroess, Alois. *Geschichte der böhmischen Provinz der Gesellschaft Jesu.* Vols. 1 and 2, section 1. Quellen und Forschungen zur Geschichte Österreichs und den angrenzenden Gebiete, 11, 13. Vienna, 1910–1927.

Lecler, Joseph. *Toleration and the Reformation.* 2 vols. Trans. from the French. New York, 1960.

Leman, Auguste. "La nomination du Maréchal d'Estrée à l'Ambassade de Rome in 1636." *Revue d'histoire ecclésiastique* 32 (1936): 598–620.

———. *Recueil des instructions générales aux nonces ordinaires de France de 1624 à 1634.* Lille, 1920.

———. *Richelieu et Olivares: Leurs négociations secrètes de 1636 à 1642 pour le rétablissement de la paix.* Lille, 1938.

———. "Le Saint-Siège et l'élection imperiale du 22 Decembre 1636." *Revue d'histoire ecclésiastique* 34 (1938): 542–55.

———. *Urbain VIII et la rivalité de la France et de la maison d'Autriche de 1631 à 1635.* Lille/Paris, 1920.

———. "Urbain VIII et les origines du Congrès de Cologne." *Revue d'histoire ecclésiastique* 19 (1923): 370–83.

Lutz, Georg. *Kardinal Giovanni Francesco Guidi di Bagno: Politik und Religion im Zeitalter Richelieus und Urbans VIII.* Bibliothek des Deutschen Historischen Instituts zu Rom, 34. Tübingen, 1971.

———. "Roma e il mondo Germanico nel periodo della Guerra dei Trent'Anni." *La corte di Roma tra cinque e seicento: "Teatro" della politica europea.* Ed. Gianvittorio Signorotto and Maria Antonietta Visceglia (Rome, 1998): 425–60.

Mazarin, Jules. *Lettres de cardinal Mazarin pendant son ministère*. Ed. Adolphe Cheruel. Vols. 1–4. Paris, 1872–1906.

Meiern, Johann Gottfried von. *Acta pacis Westphalicae publica oder westphälische Friedens-Handlungen und Geschichte*. 6 vols. Hannover, 1734–6 (rpt. Osnabrück, 1969).

Minois, Georges. *Le confesseur du roi: Les directeurs de conscience sous la monarchie française*. Paris, 1988.

Moote, A. Lloyd. *Louis XIII, the Just*. Berkeley, 1989.

Motteville, Françoise Bertaut de. *Mémoires sur Anne d'Autriche et sa cour*. New ed. Vol. 1. Ed. M.F. Riaux. Paris, 1886.

Mousnier, Roland. *The Assassination of Henry IV: The Tyrannicide Problem and the Consolidation of the French Absolute Monarchy in the Early Seventeenth Century*. Trans. from the French. New York, 1973.

______, ed. *Lettres et mémoires adressés au Chancelier Séguier, c1633–1649*. 2 vols. Textes et Documents, 6. Paris, 1964.

Novoa, Matías de. *Historia de Felipe IV, rey de España*. Colección de documentos inéditos para la Historia de España, 69, 77, 80, 86. Madrid, 1876–86.

O'Neill, Robert Keating. "Politics and the New Orders in France, 1584–1629: A Study of Jesuit and Capuchin Influence on French Foreign Policy towards the Habsburgs." Diss., University of Chicago, 1975.

Parker, Geoffrey, ed. *The Thirty Years War*, 2nd ed. New York, 1997.

Partner, Peter. *God of Battles: Holy Wars of Christianity and Islam*. Princeton, 1997.

Pastor, Ludwig von. *The History of the Popes from the Close of the Middle Ages*. Trans. from the German. Vols. 26–29. London, 1937–8.

Poncelet, Alfred. *Histoire de la Compagnie de Jésus dans les anciens Pays-Bas*. 2 vols. Brussels, 1927.

Prat, J.M. *Recherches historiques et critiques sur la Compagnie de Jésus en France du temps du P. Coton, 1564–1626*. Vols. 3–5. Lyons, 1876–8.

______. "Philippe IV, roi de Espagne, et la Compagnie de Jésus, episode historique, 1631." *Précis historique* 3 (1894): 205–17.

Ranum, Orest. *Richelieu and the Councillors of Louis XIII*. Oxford, 1963.

Repgen, Konrad. "Negotiating the Peace of Westphalia: A Survey with an Examination of the Major Problems." In *1648 War and Peace in Europe*. Eds. Klaus Bussmann and Heinz Schilling. Vol. 1 (Münster, 1998): 355–72.

______. "Der päpstliche Protest gegen den westfälischen Frieden und die Friedenspolitik Urbans VIII." In K. Repgen, *Von der Reformation zur Gegenwart: Beiträge zur Grundfragen der neuzeitlichen Geschichte*, ed. Klaus Gotto and Hans Günter Hockerts (Paderborn, 1988): 30–52.

______. "Die Proteste Chigis und der päpstliche Protest gegen den westfälischen Frieden (1645/50): Vier Kapitel über das Breve 'Zelo Domus Dei.'" In *Staat, Kirche und Wissenschaft in einer pluralistischen Gesellschaft: Festschrift zum 65, Geburtstag von Paul Mikat* (Berlin, 1989): 625–47.

______. *Die römische Kurie und der westfälische Friede: Idee und Wirklichkeit des Papsttums im 16. Und 17. Jahrhundert*. Vol. 1: *Papst, Kaiser und Reich,*

1521–1644, part 1: *Darstellung*, part 2: *Analekten und Register*. Bibliothek des Deutschen Historischen Instituts zu Rom, 24, 25. Tübingen, 1962–5.

———. "Was ist ein Religionskrieg." In K. Repgen, *Von der Reformation zur Gegenwart: Beiträge zur Grundfragen der neuzeitlichen Geschichte*, ed. Klaus Gotto and Hans Günter Hockerts (Paderborn, 1988): 84–97.

———, ed. See *Acta Pacis Westphalicae*.

———, ed. *Krieg und Politik 1618–1648*. Munich, 1988.

Richelieu, Armand-Jean du Plessis, Cardinal de. *Lettres, instructions et papier d'état*. Ed. Denis-Louis-Martial Avenel. 8 vols. Paris, 1853–77.

———. *Mémoires de cardinal de richelieu sur le regne de Louis XIII depuis 1610 jusqúà 1638*. Nouvelle collection de mémoires rélatifs à L'histoire de France, eds. Michaud and Poujoulat. Vols. 21–3. Paris. 1857.

———. *Les papiers de Richelieu: Correspondence et papiers d'état: Section politique intérieur*. Ed. Pierre Grillon. 6 vols. Paris, 1975–85.

———. *Les papiers de Richelieu: Correspondence et papiers d'état: Section politique extérieur*, empire Allemand. 3 Vols. Eds. Adolf Wild and Anja Victorine Hartmann. Paris, 1982–99.

———. *Testament politique*. Ed. Françoise Hildesheimer. Paris, 1995.

Riezler, Sigmund, ed. "Kriegstagebücher aus dem ligistischen Hauptquartier." *Abhandlungen der Phil.-Hist Klasse der Bayer. Akademie der Wissenschaften* 23, 1 (1906): 77–210.

Rochementeix, Camille de. *Nicolas Caussin, confesseur de Louis XIII, et le Cardinal de Richelieu: Documents inédits*. Paris, 1911.

Rodriguez, José Espinosa. *Fray Antonio de Sotomayor y su correspondencia con Felipe IV*. Vigo, 1944.

Ruppert, Karstens. *Die kaiserliche Politik auf dem westfälischen Friedenskongress (1643–1648)*. Schriftenreihe der Vereinigung zur Erforschung der neueren Geschichte, 10. Münster, 1979.

Rurale, Flavio, ed. *I Religiosi a Corte. Teologia, politica et diplomazia in Antico Regime*. Rome, 1998.

Sanchez, Magdalena S. *The Empress, the Queen, and the Nun: Women and Power at the Court of Philip III of Spain*. Baltimore, 1998.

Schmidt, Peer. *Spanische Universalmonarchie oder "Teutsche Libertet": Das spanische Imperium in der Propaganda des Dreissigjährigen Krieges*. Stuttgart, 2001.

Signorotto, Gianvittorio, and Maria Antonietta Visceglia, eds. *La corte de Roma tra cinque et seicento: "Teatro" della politica europea*. Rome, 1998.

Smith, Hilary Dansey. *Preaching in the Spanish Golden Age: A Study of Some Preachers in the Reign of Philip III*. Oxford, 1978.

Solnon, Jean-François. *La cour de France*. Paris, 1987.

Sorin, Adolphe. *Louise-Angelique de La Fayette: La cour-le cloître*. Nantes, 1892.

Steinberger, Ludwig. *Die Jesuiten und die Friedensfrage in der Zeit vom Prager Frieden bis zum Nürnberger Friedensexekutionshauptrezess 1635–1650*. Freiburg, 1906.

Stiegele, Rudolf. "Beiträge zu einer Biographie des Jesuiten Wilhelm Lamormaini." *Historisches Jahrbuch* 28 (1907): 551–69, 849–70.

Stradling, R.A. *Philip IV and the Government of Spain 1621–1665*. Cambridge, 1988.
Sturmberger, Hans. *Aufstand in Böhmen: Der Beginn des Dreissigjährigen Krieges*. Munich, 1959.
Tallemant de Réaux. *Historiettes*. 2 vols. Ed. Antoine Adam. Paris, 1960–1.
Tapié, Victor-L. *La politique étrangère de la France et le début de la Guerre de Trente Ans (1616– 1621)*. Paris, 1934.
Tischer, Anuschka. *Französische Diplomatie und Diplomaten auf dem Westfalischen Friedens-Kongress*. Münster, 1999.
Tongas, G. *Les relations de la France avec l'Empire Ottoman durant la première moitié des xviie siècle*. Toulouse, 1942.
Treasure, Geoffrey. *Mazarin: The Crisis of Absolutism in France*. London, 1995.
Valle, Domenico. *Le padre Pietro Monod della Compagnia di Gesú*. Turin, 1910.
Vlastimal, Kybal, and G. Incisa della Rochetta, eds. *La nunziatura di Fabio Chigi (1640–1651)*, Vol. 1, parts 1 and 2. Rome, 1943–6.
Wolf, John B. *Louis XIV*. New York, 1968.

Index